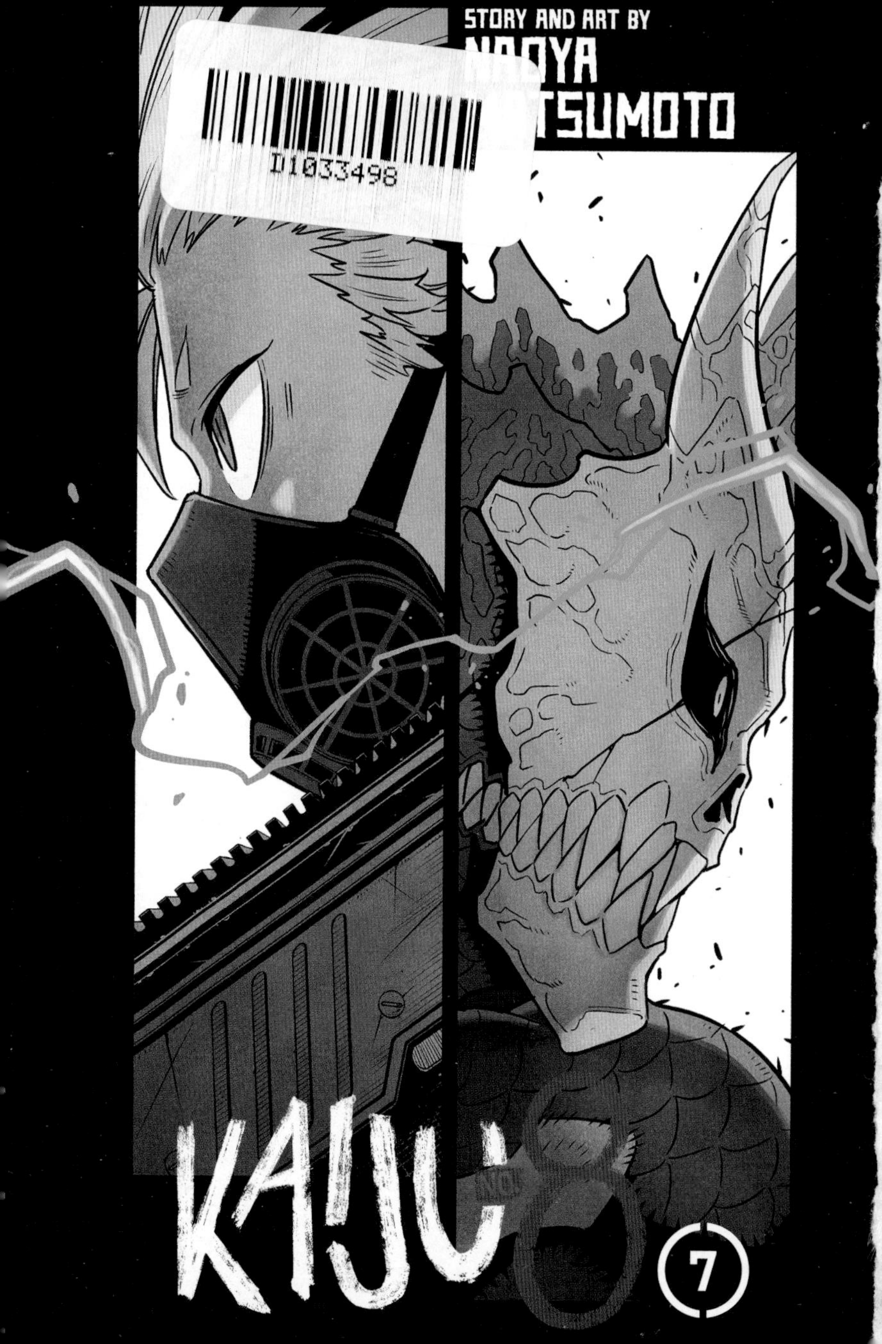
STORY AND ART BY
NAOYA
TSUMOTO
KAIJU No. 8
7

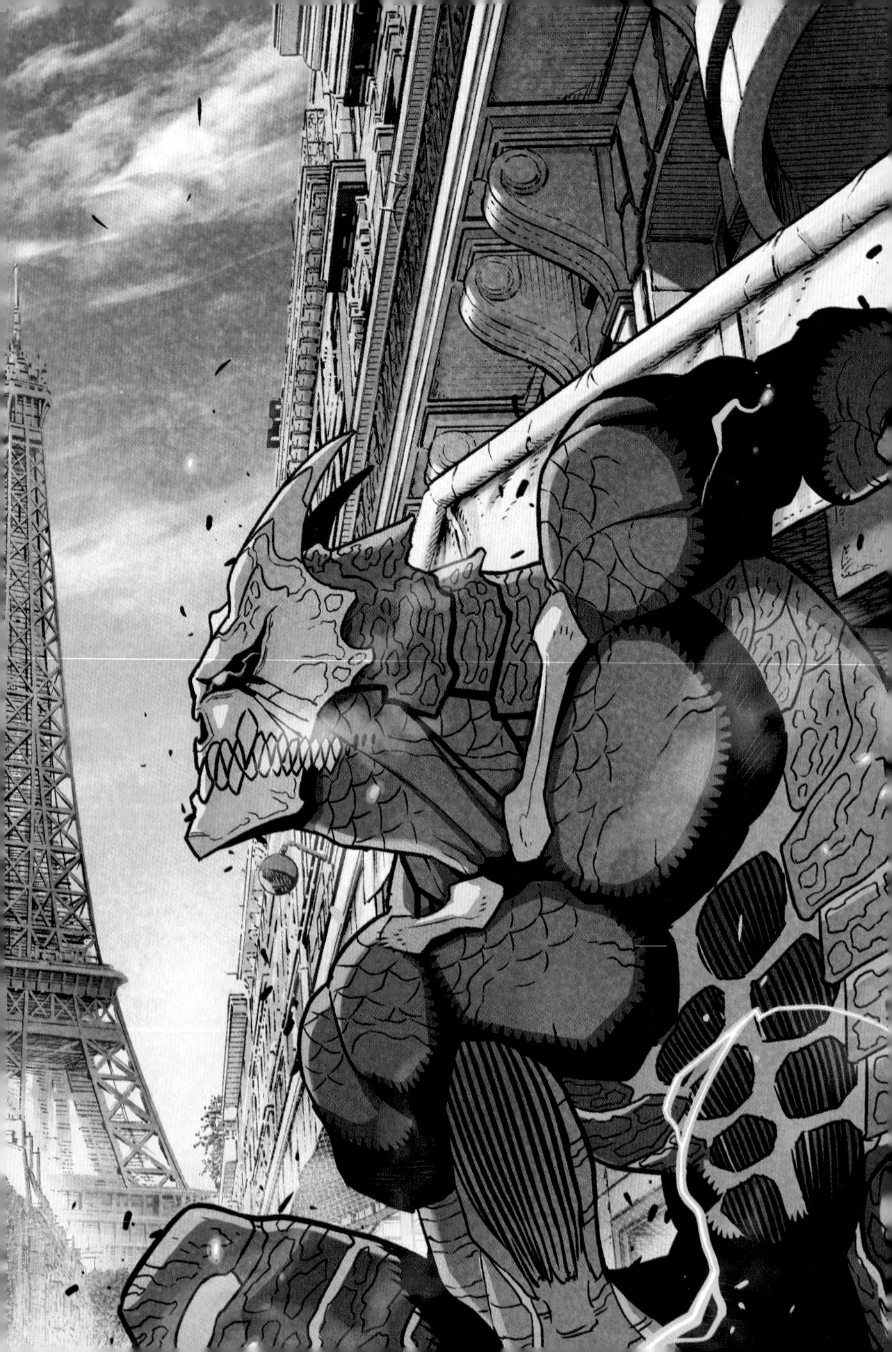

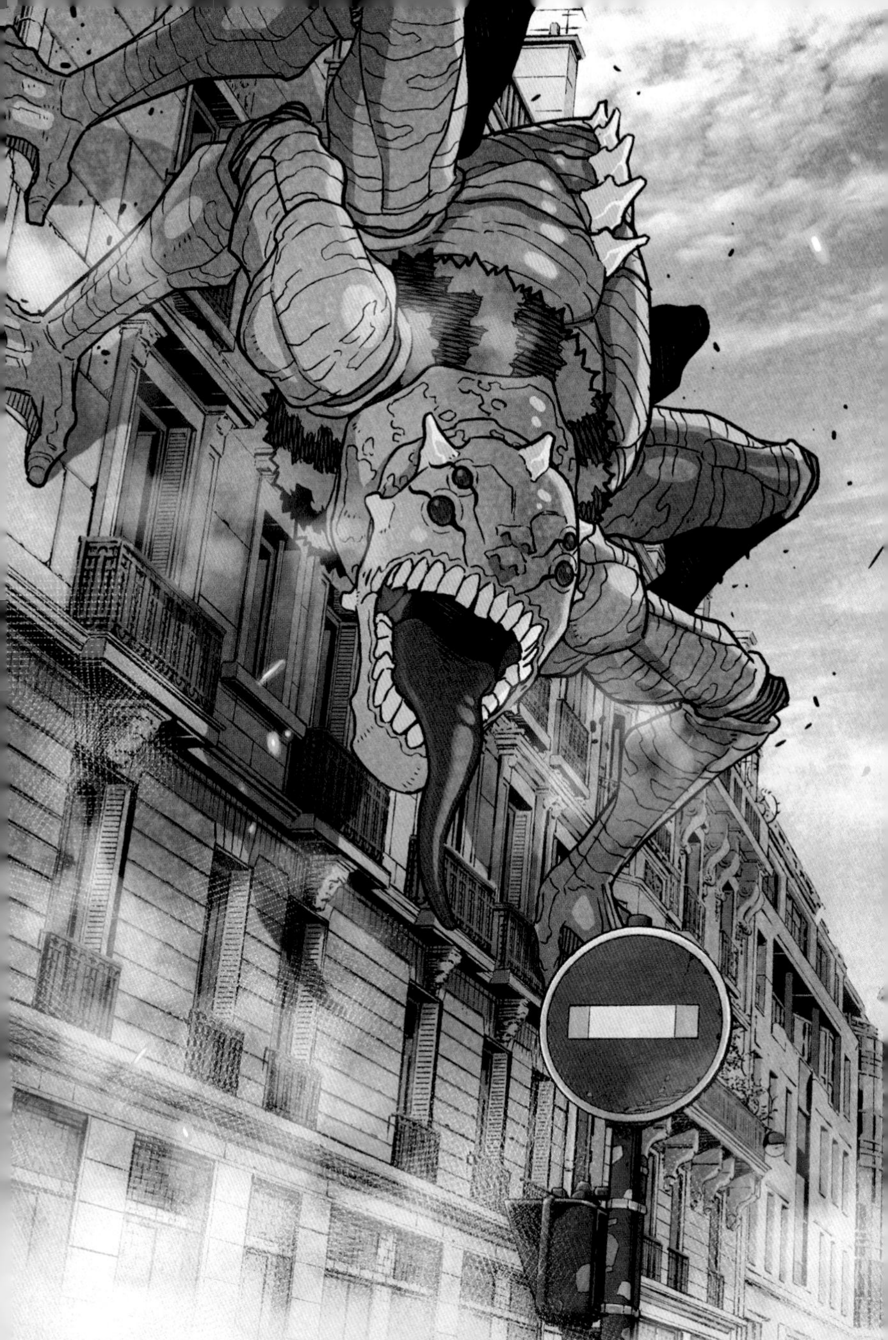

CONTENTS

KAIJU NO. 8

7

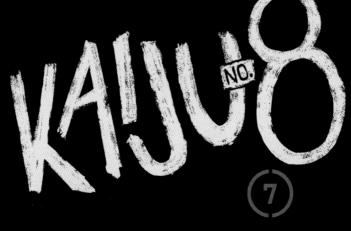

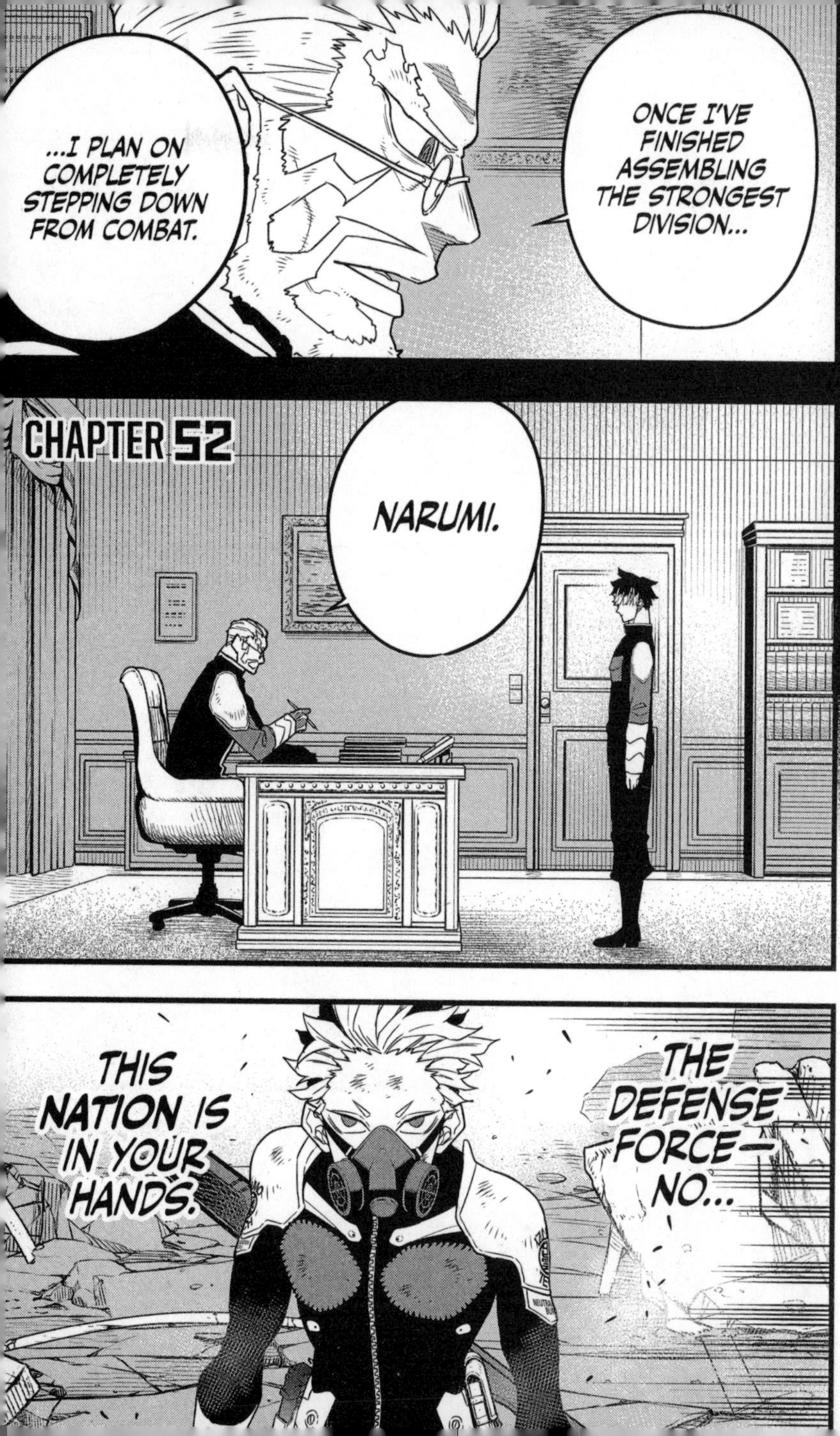
ONCE I'VE FINISHED ASSEMBLING THE STRONGEST DIVISION...
...I PLAN ON COMPLETELY STEPPING DOWN FROM COMBAT.
NARUMI.
CHAPTER 52
THE DEFENSE FORCE— NO...
THIS NATION IS IN YOUR HANDS.

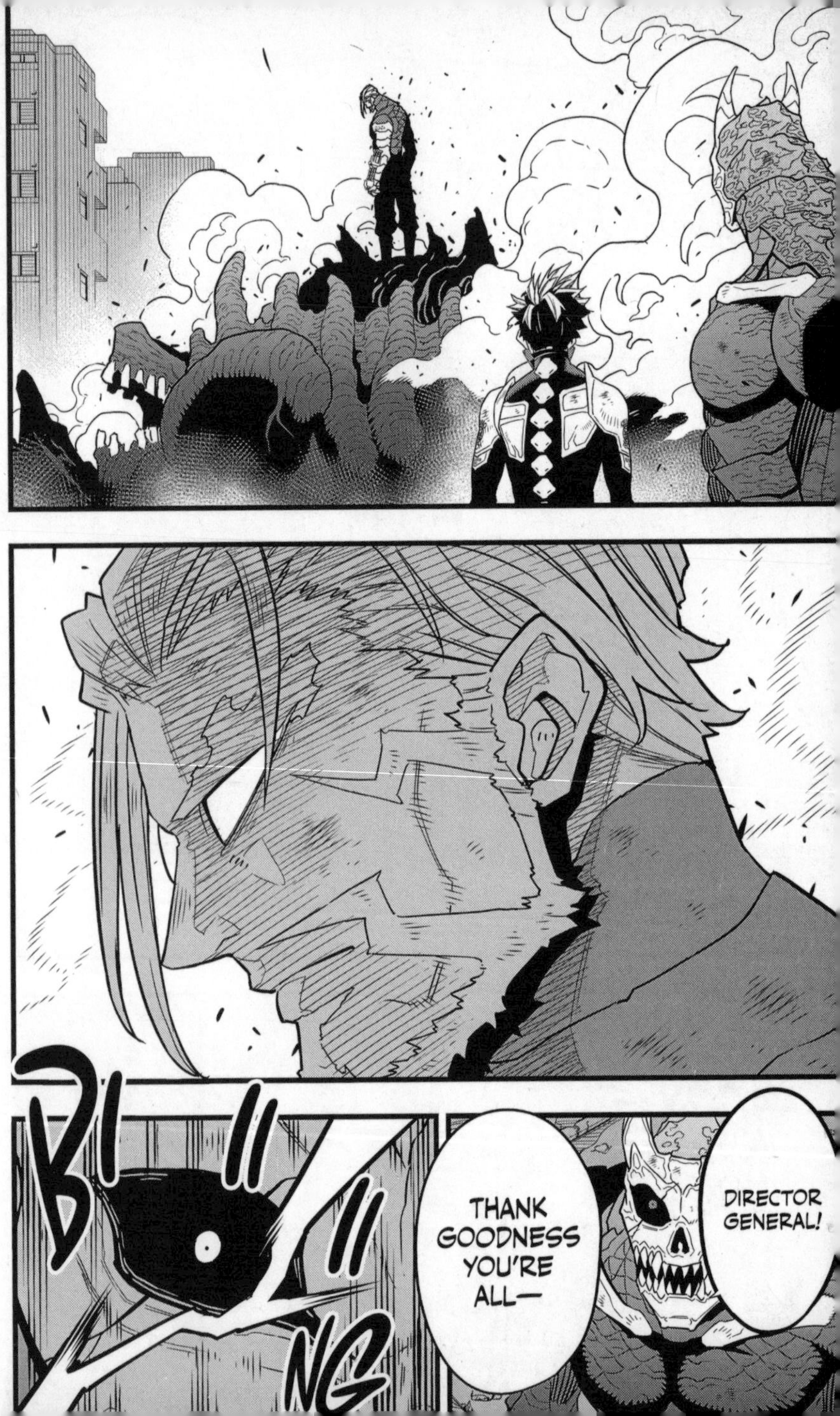
DIRECTOR GENERAL!
THANK GOODNESS YOU'RE ALL—
BIIIING

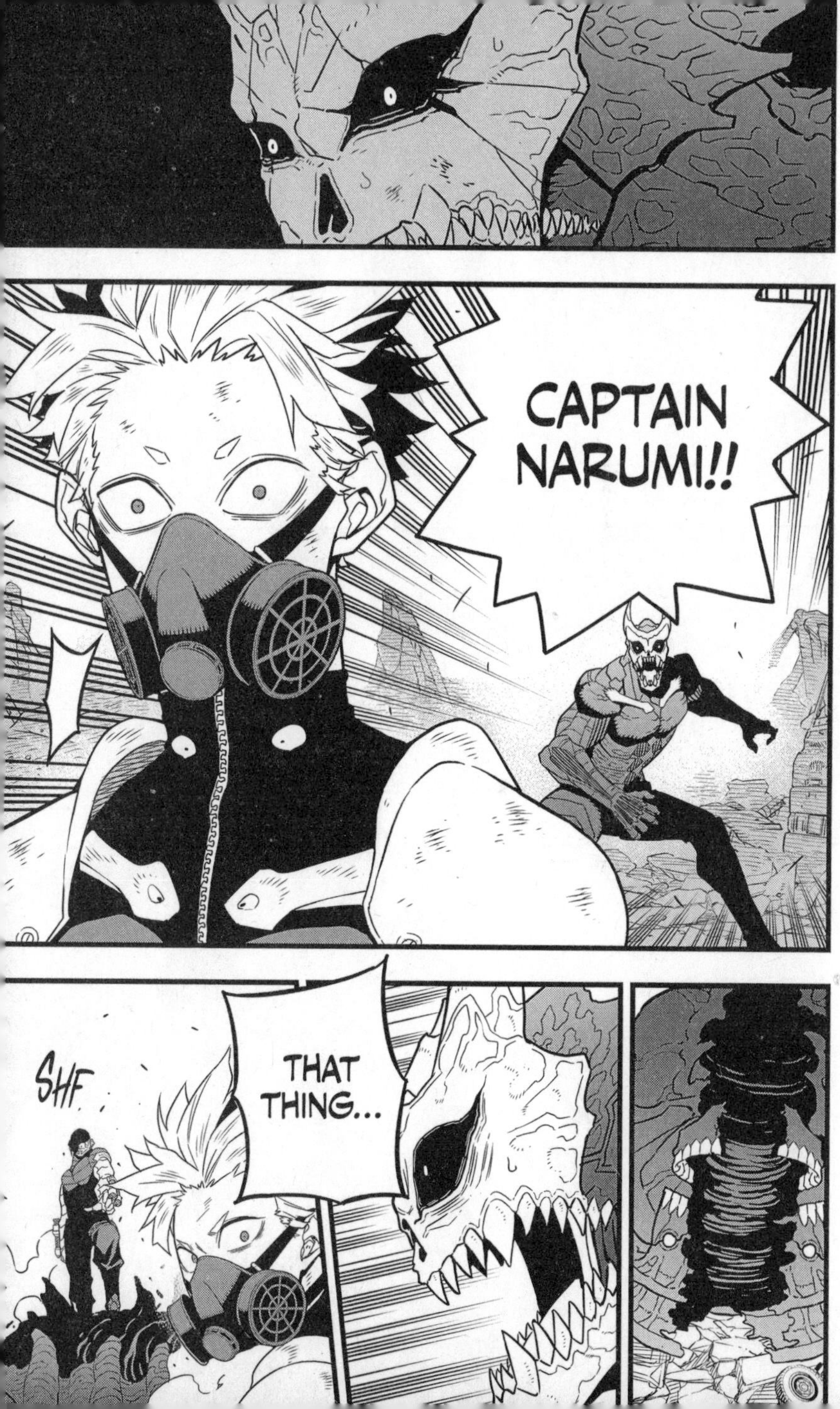
CAPTAIN NARUMI!!
THAT THING...
SHF

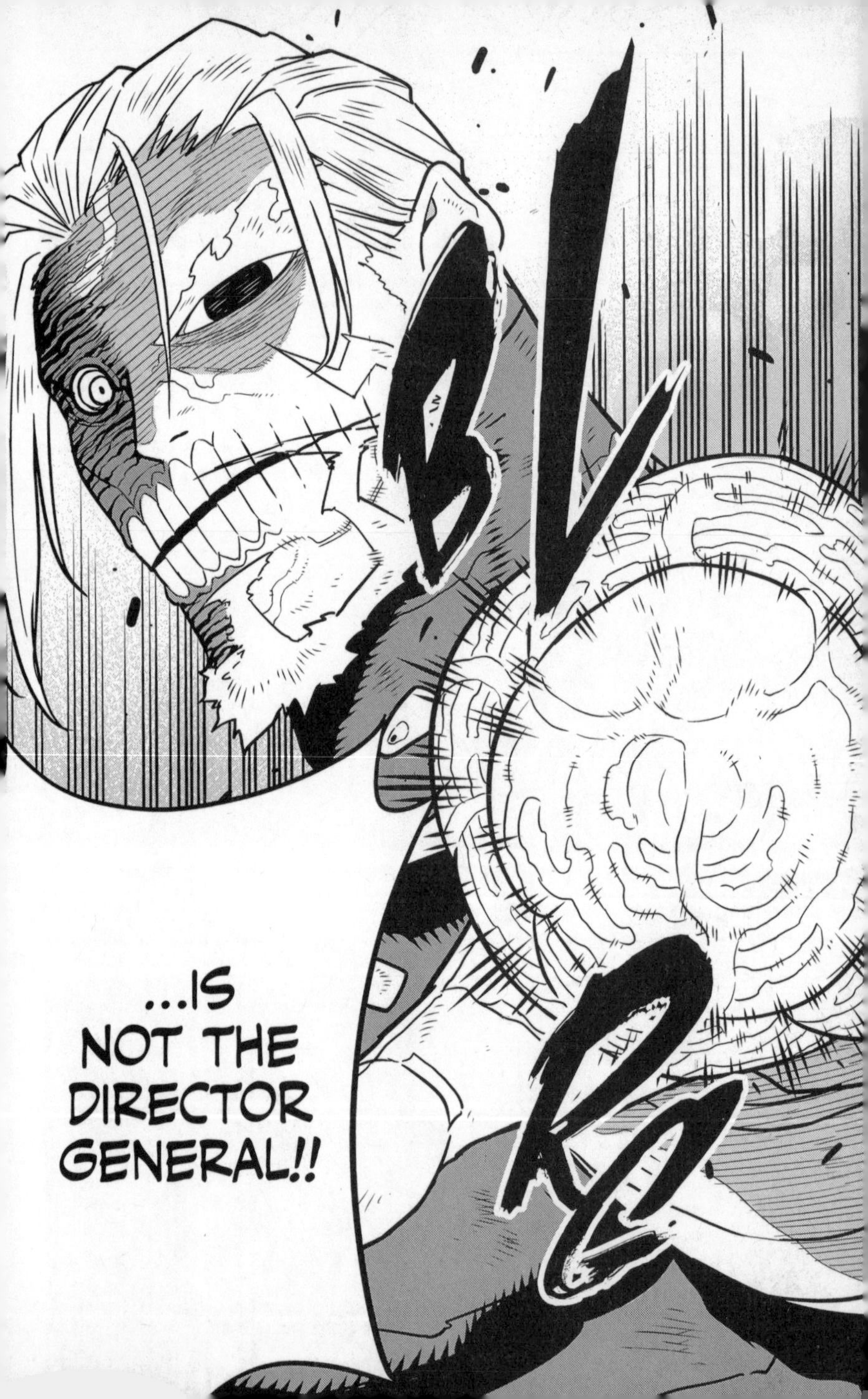
...IS NOT THE DIRECTOR GENERAL!!

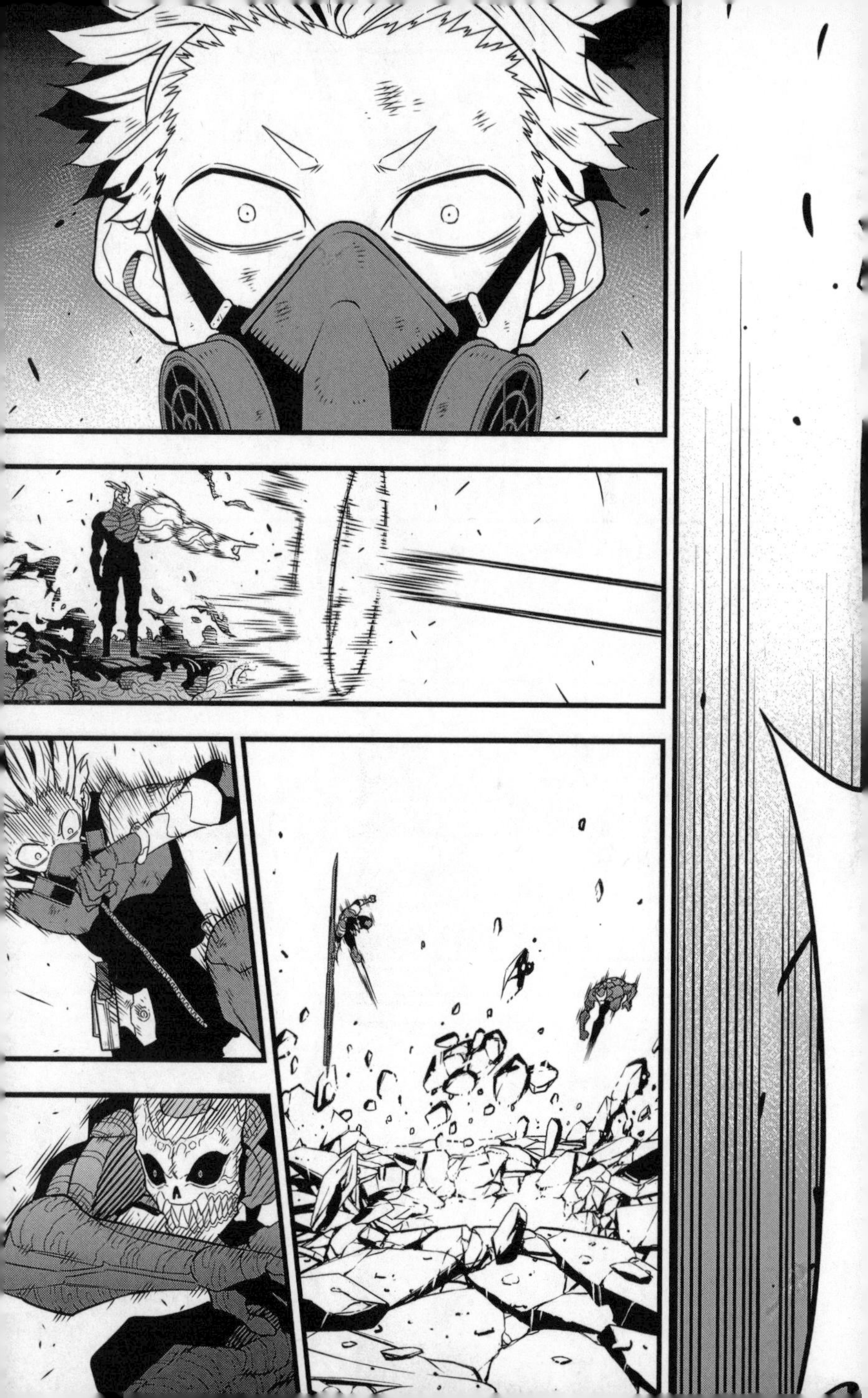

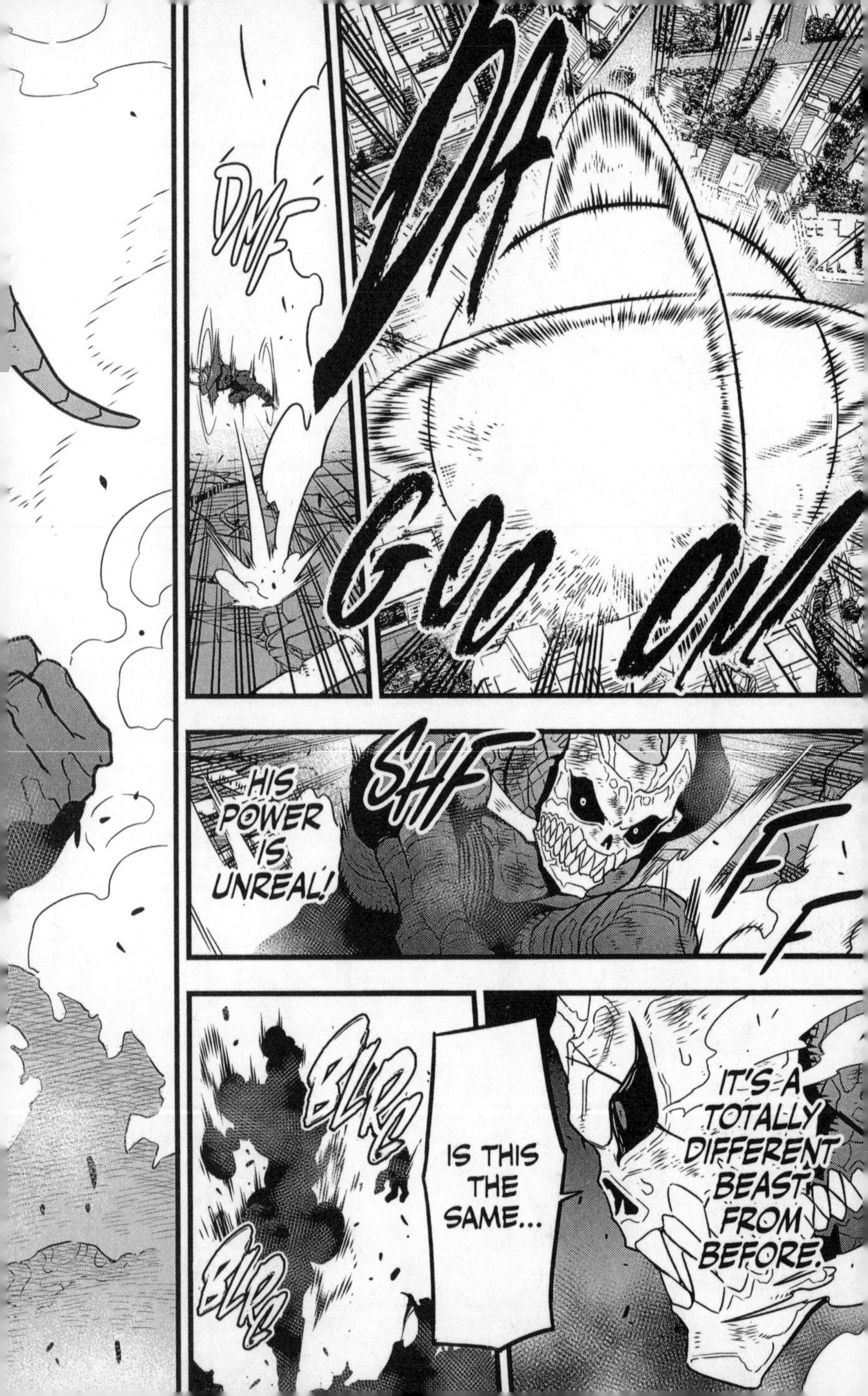
DMF
SHF
HIS POWER IS UNREAL!
IT'S A TOTALLY DIFFERENT BEAST FROM BEFORE.
IS THIS THE SAME...

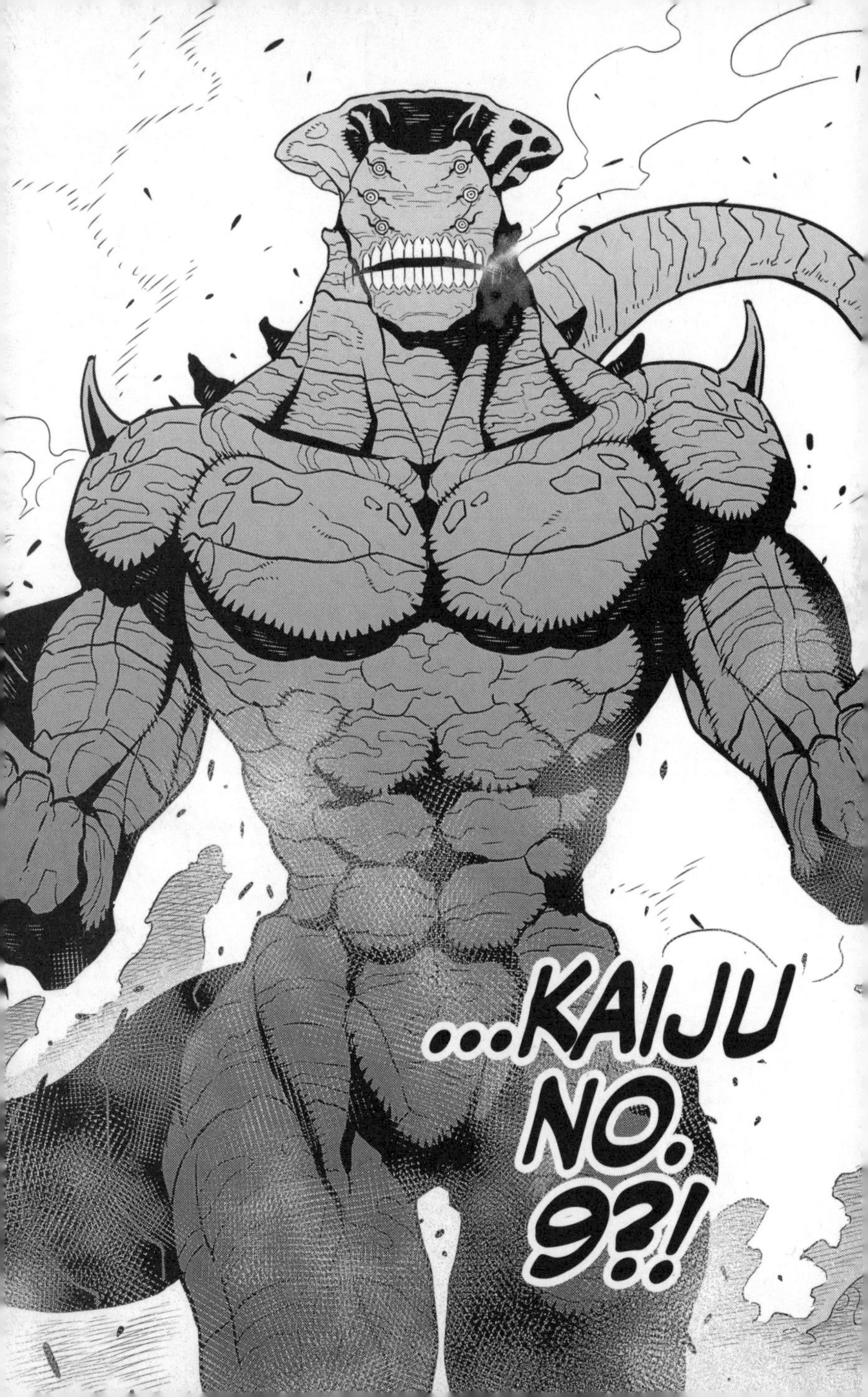
...KAIJU NO. 9?!

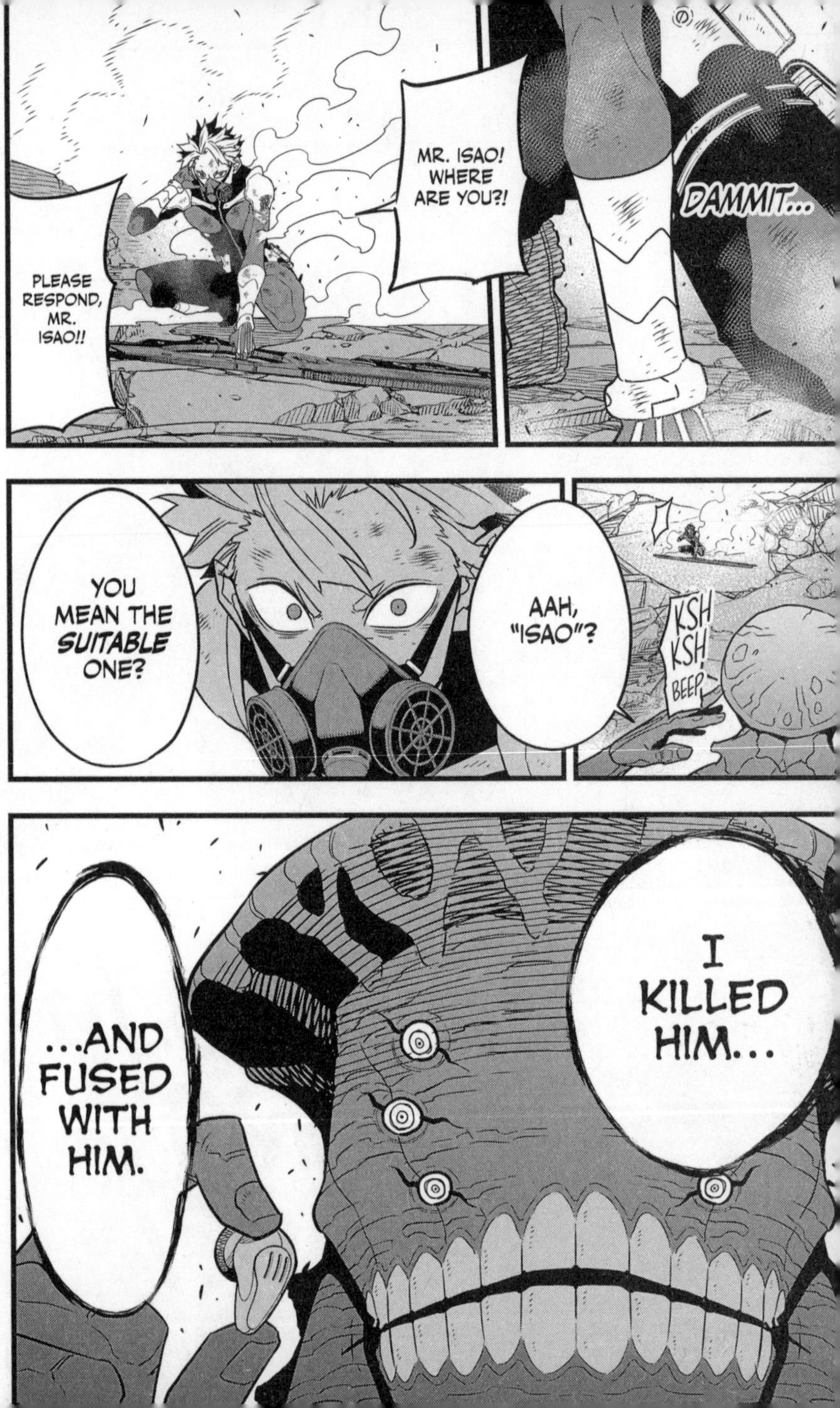
DAMMIT...
MR. ISAO! WHERE ARE YOU?!
PLEASE RESPOND, MR. ISAO!!
KSH KSH BEEP
AAH, "ISAO"?
YOU MEAN THE *SUITABLE* ONE?
I KILLED HIM...
...AND FUSED WITH HIM.

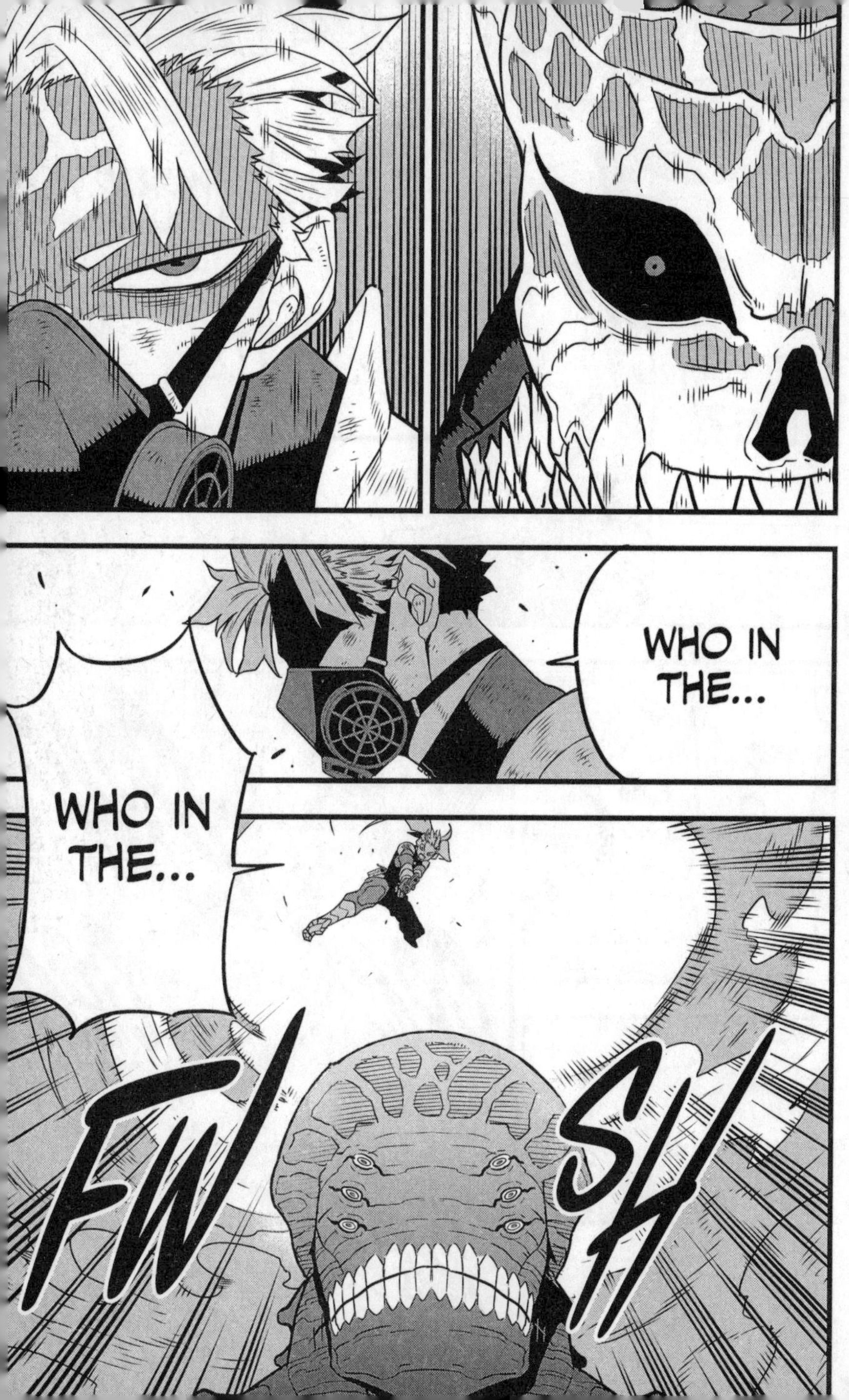
WHO IN THE...
WHO IN THE...
FWSH

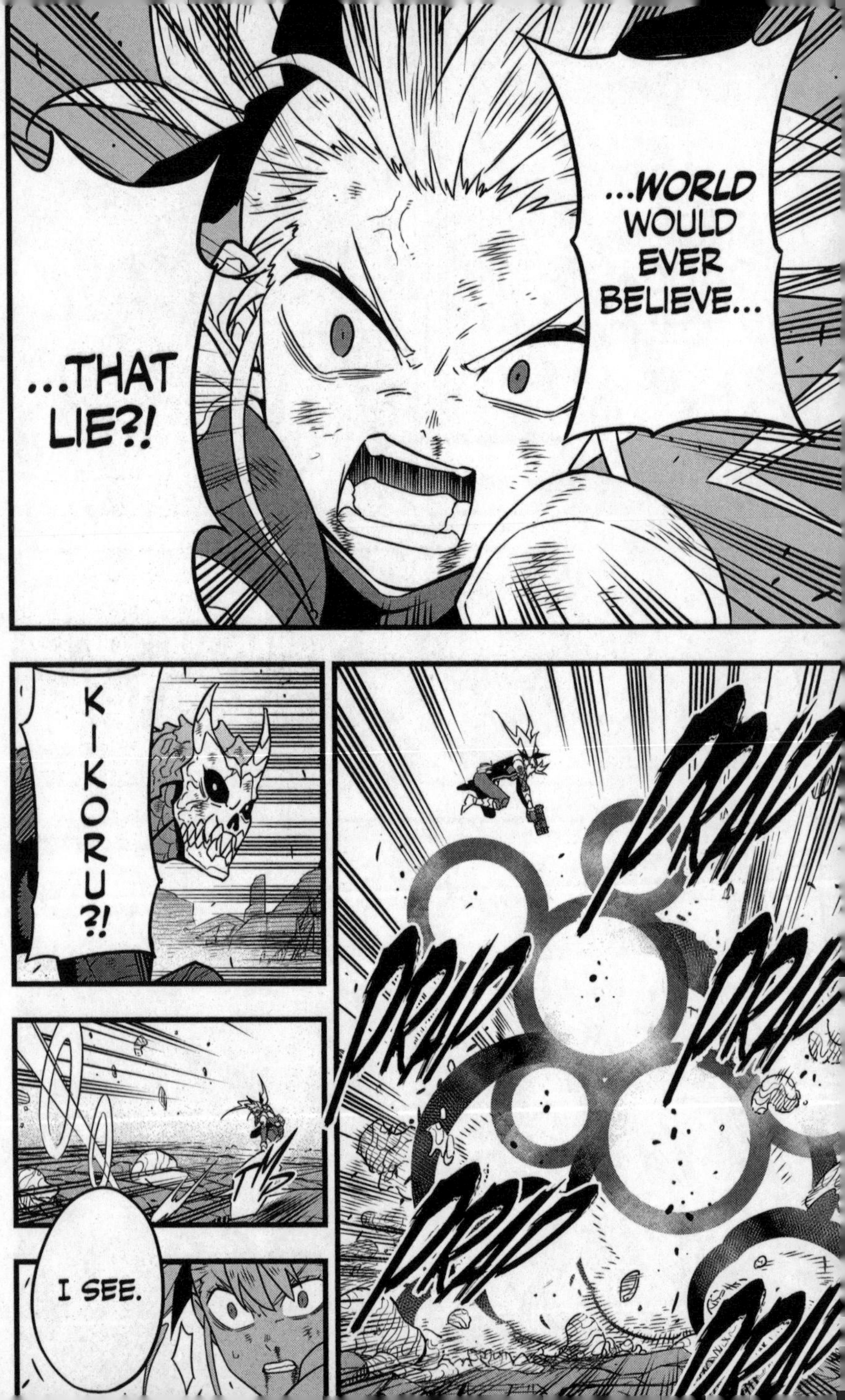
...WORLD WOULD EVER BELIEVE...
...THAT LIE?!
KIKORU?!
I SEE.

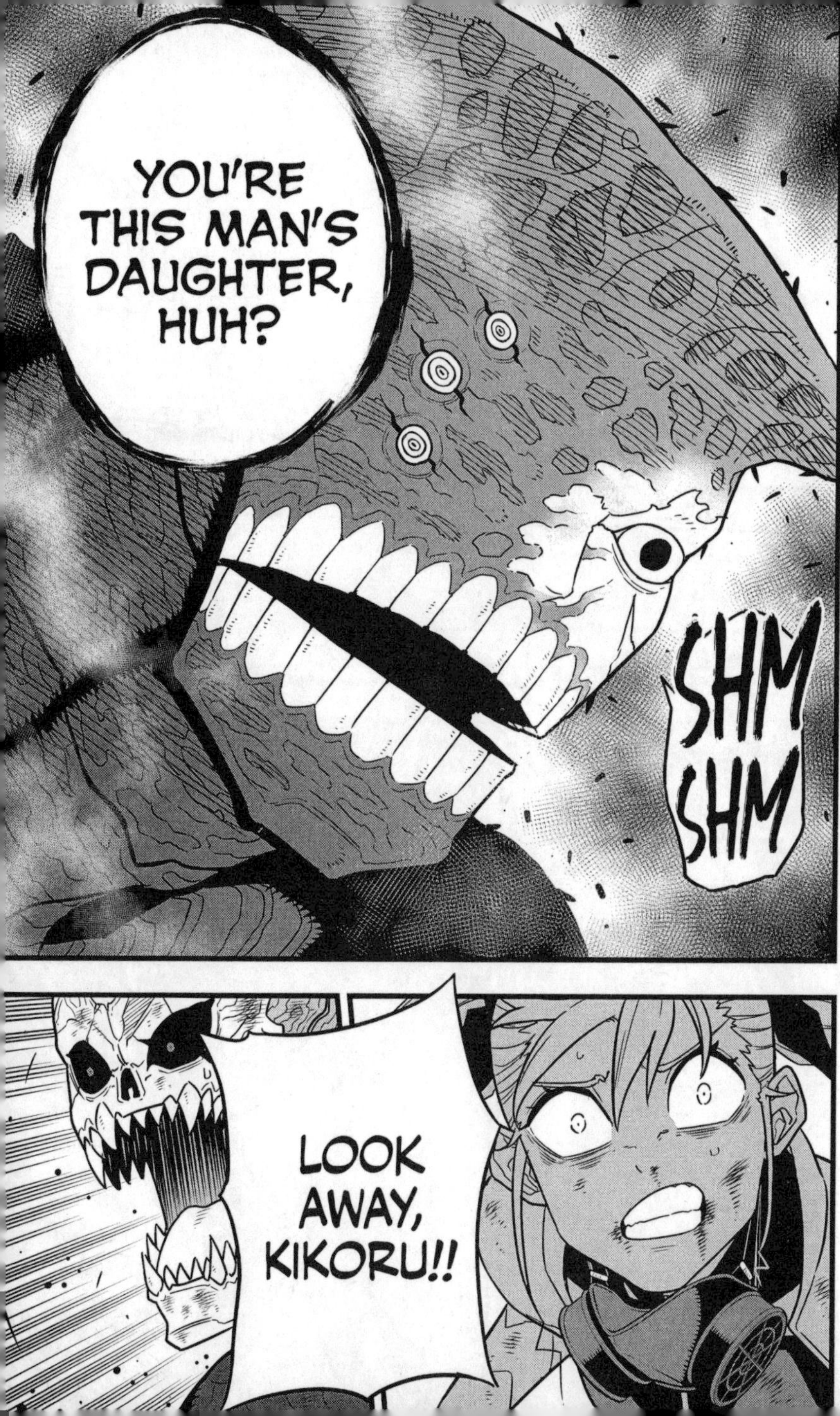
YOU'RE THIS MAN'S DAUGHTER, HUH?
SHM SHM
LOOK AWAY, KIKORU!!

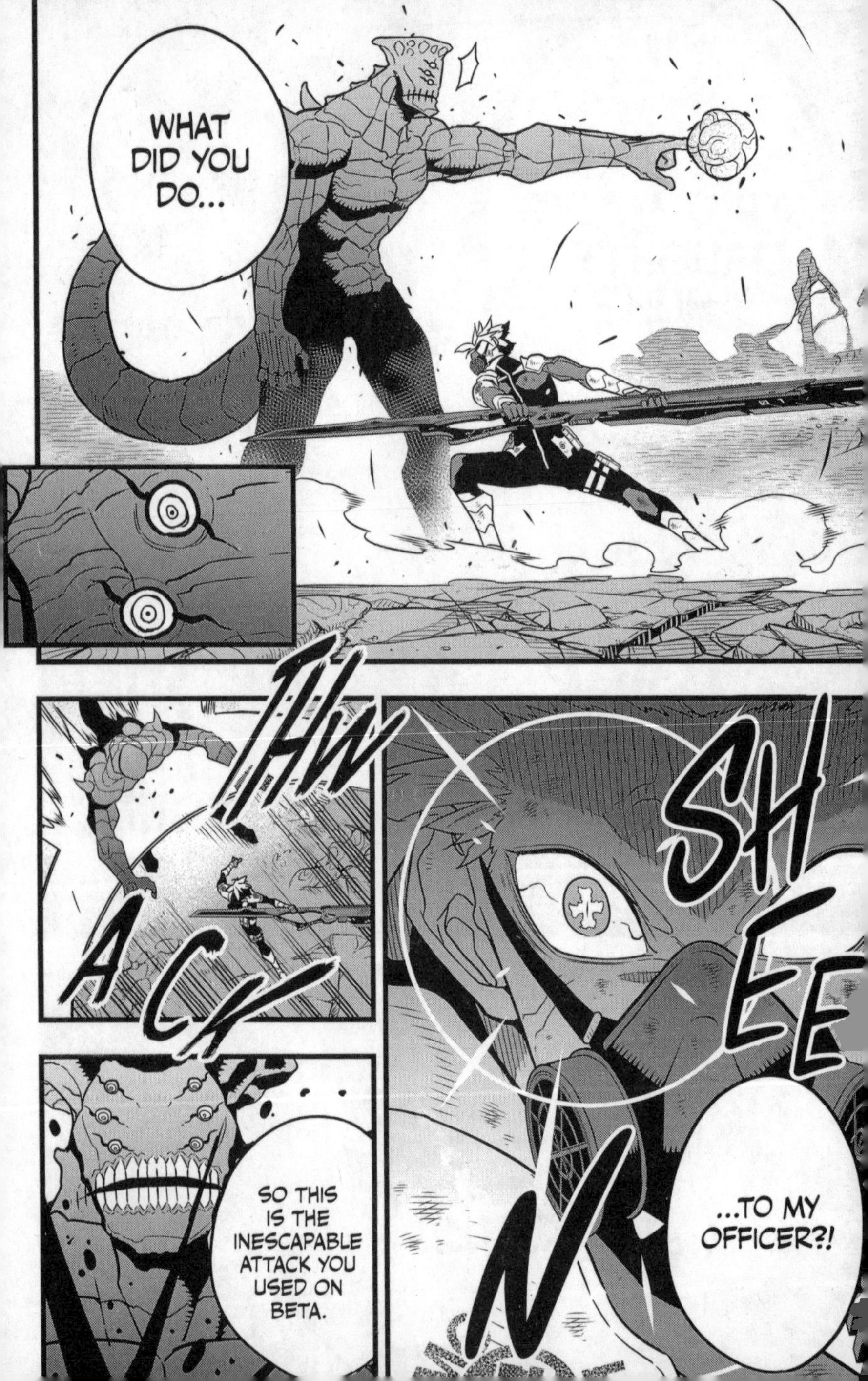
WHAT DID YOU DO...
SHEEN
...TO MY OFFICER?!
THWACK
SO THIS IS THE INESCAPABLE ATTACK YOU USED ON BETA.

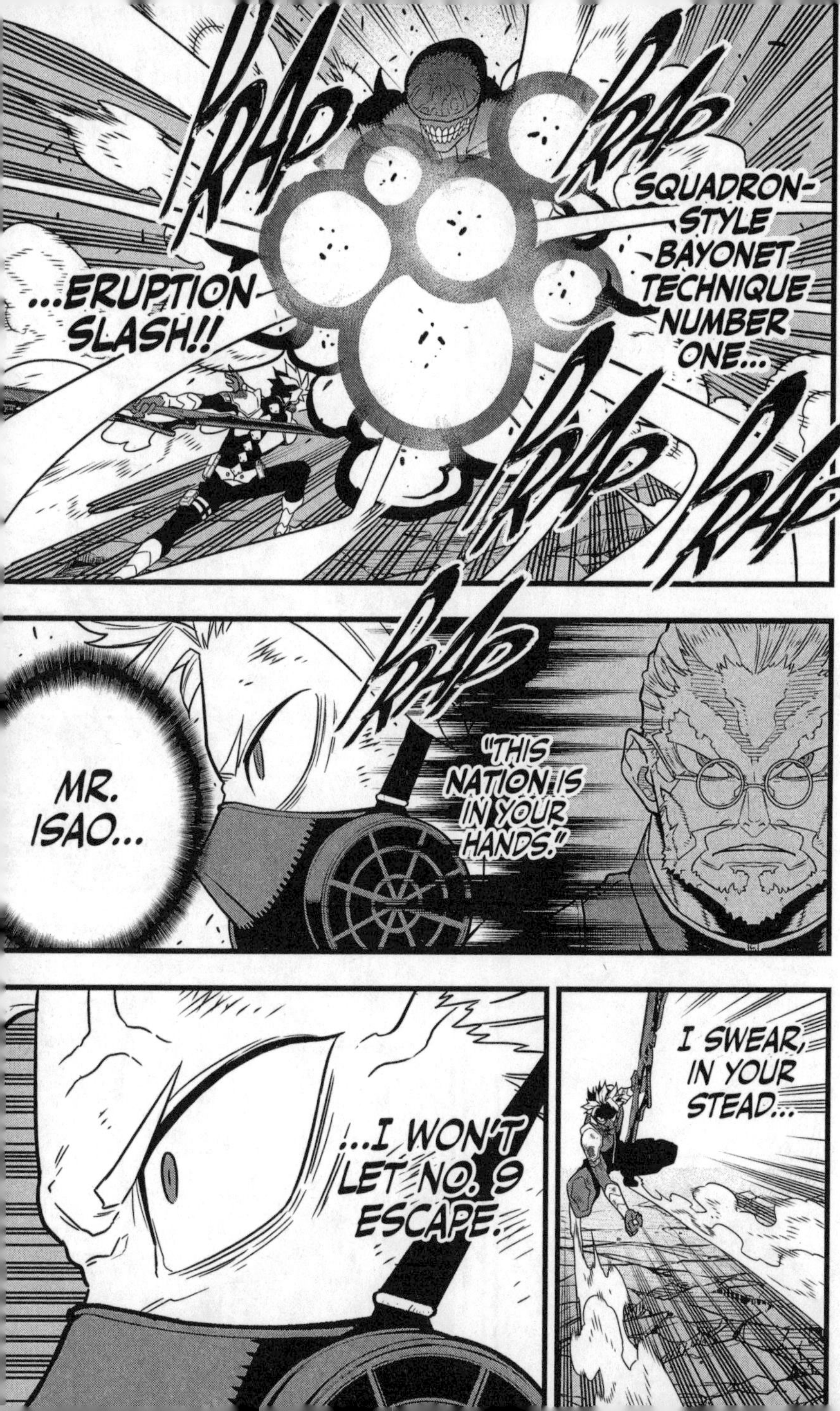
SQUADRON-STYLE BAYONET TECHNIQUE NUMBER ONE...
...ERUPTION SLASH!!
"THIS NATION IS IN YOUR HANDS."
MR. ISAO...
I SWEAR, IN YOUR STEAD...
...I WON'T LET NO. 9 ESCAPE.

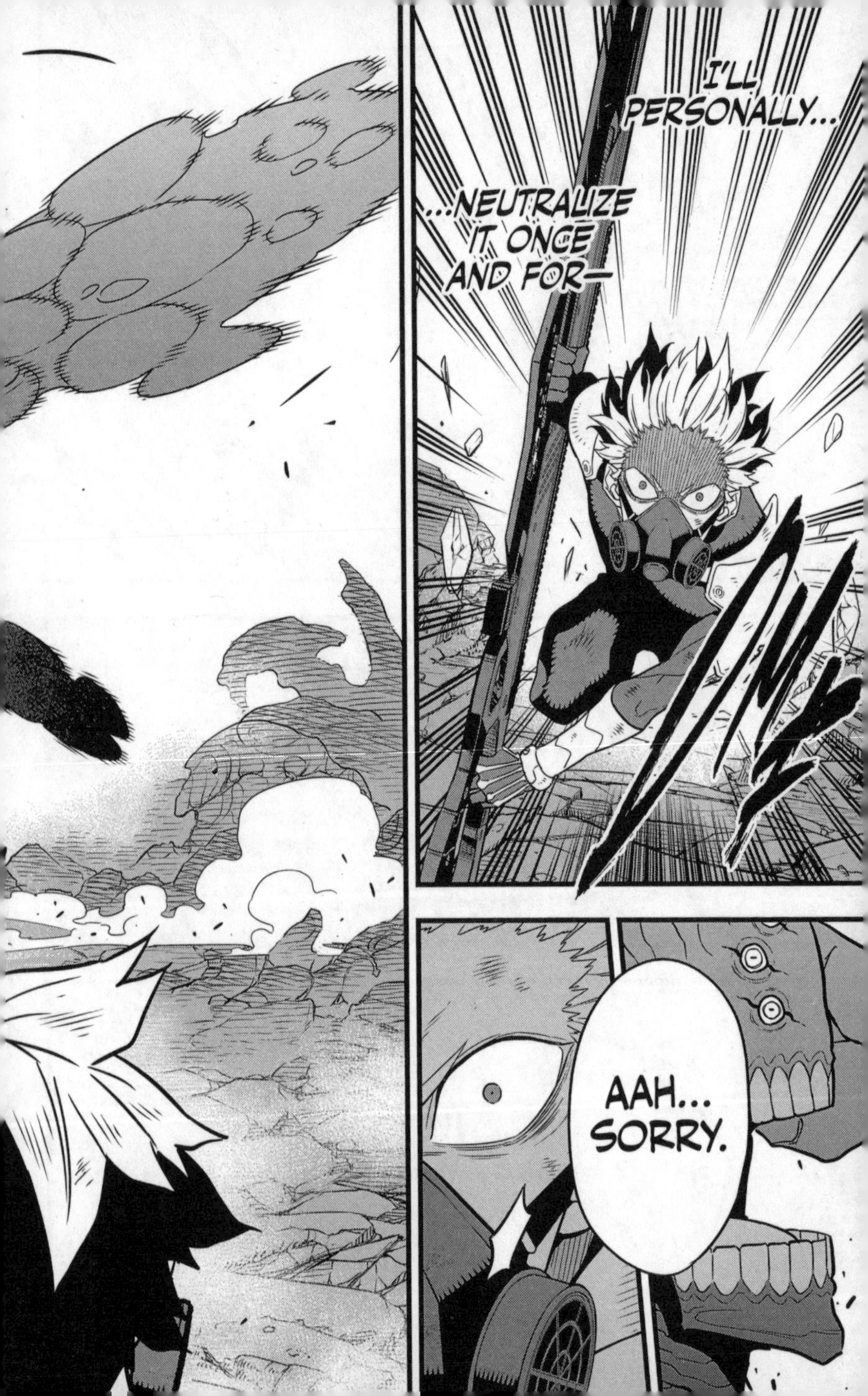
I'LL PERSONALLY...
...NEUTRALIZE IT ONCE AND FOR—
AAH... SORRY.

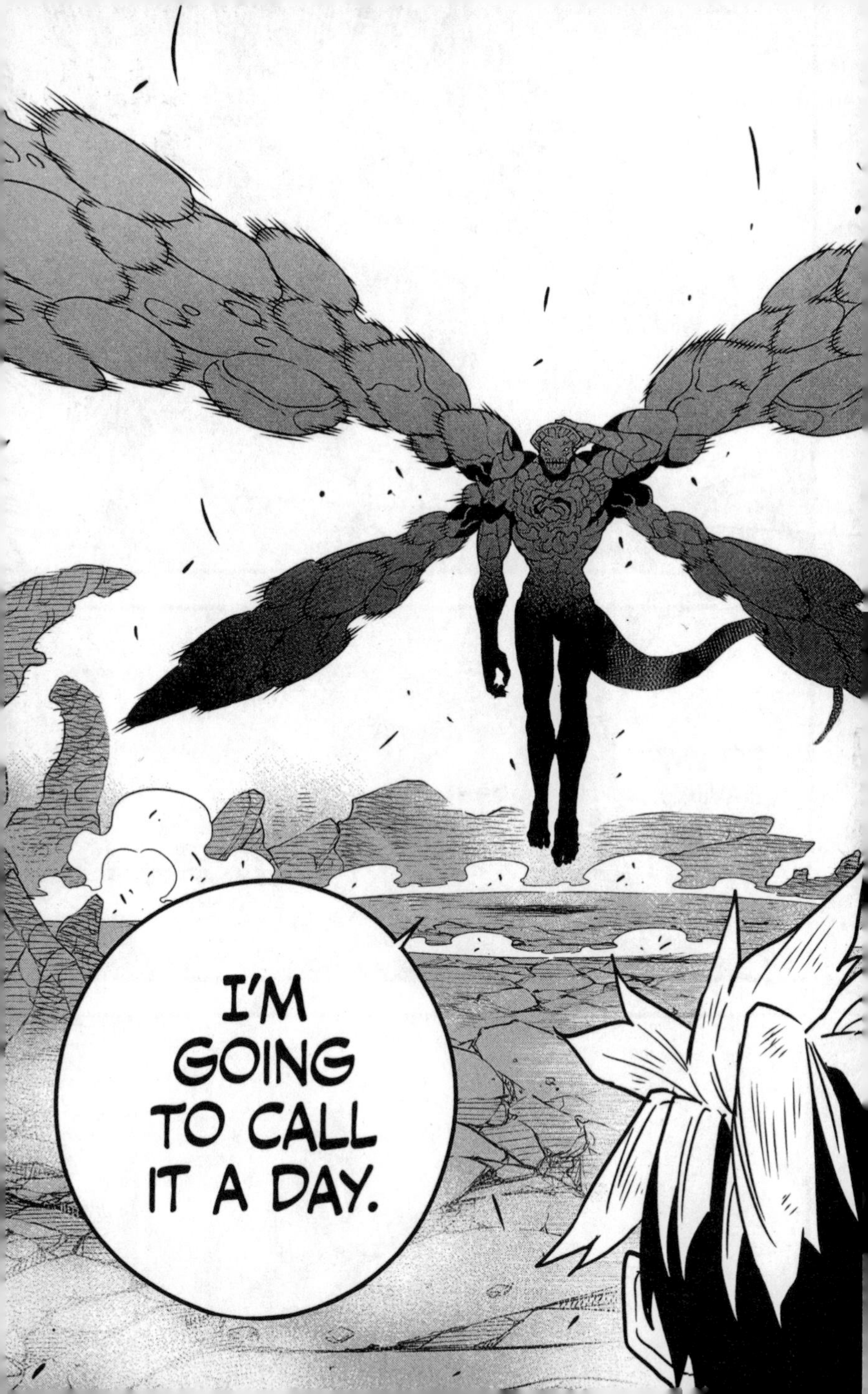
I'M GOING TO CALL IT A DAY.

YOU'RE WHAT?

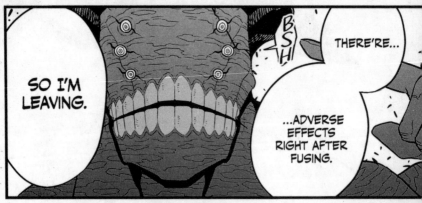

SO I'M LEAVING.

BSH

THERE'RE...

...ADVERSE EFFECTS RIGHT AFTER FUSING.

QUIT PLAYING GAMES.

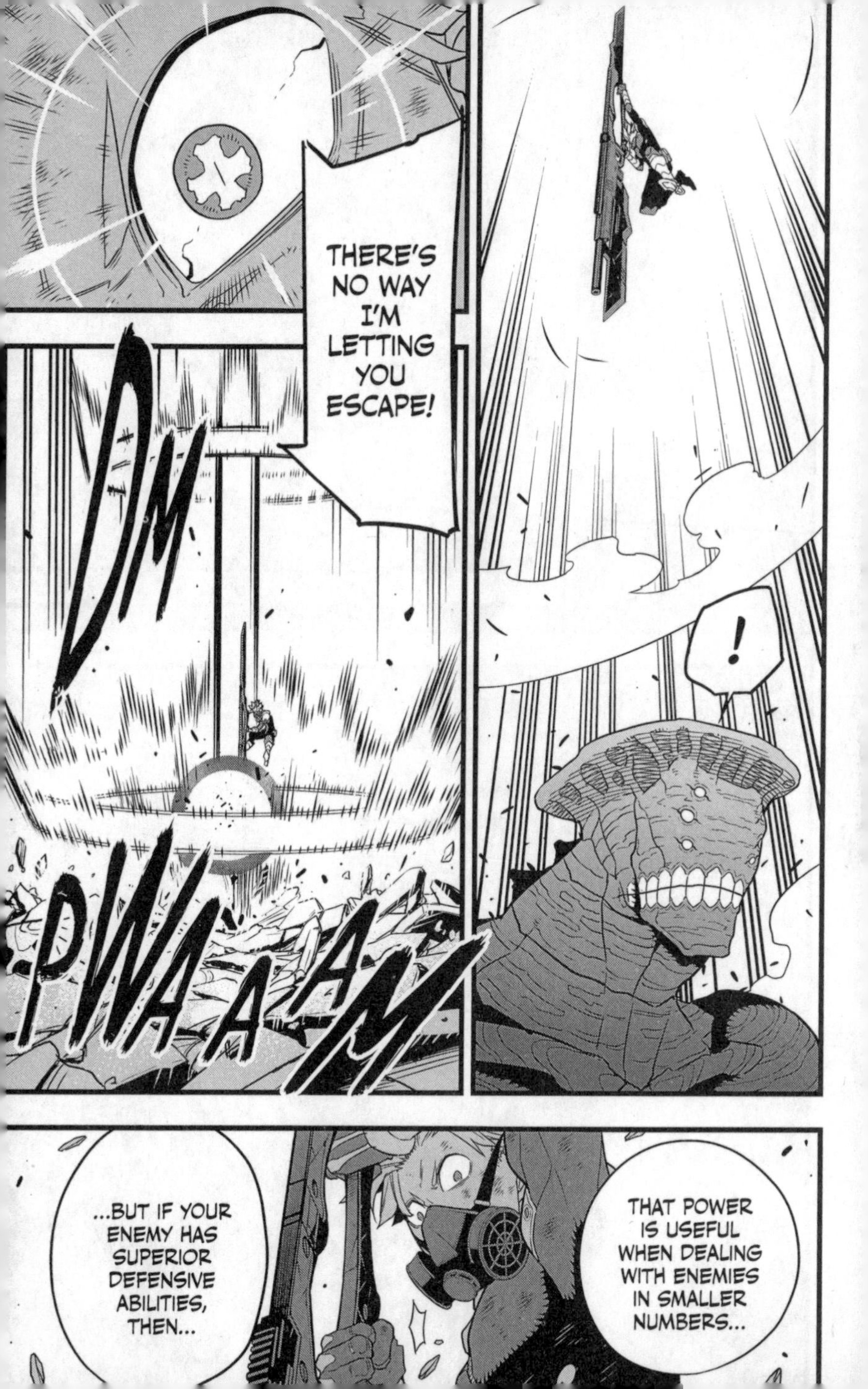
!
THERE'S NO WAY I'M LETTING YOU ESCAPE!
DM
PWAAAM
THAT POWER IS USEFUL WHEN DEALING WITH ENEMIES IN SMALLER NUMBERS...
...BUT IF YOUR ENEMY HAS SUPERIOR DEFENSIVE ABILITIES, THEN...

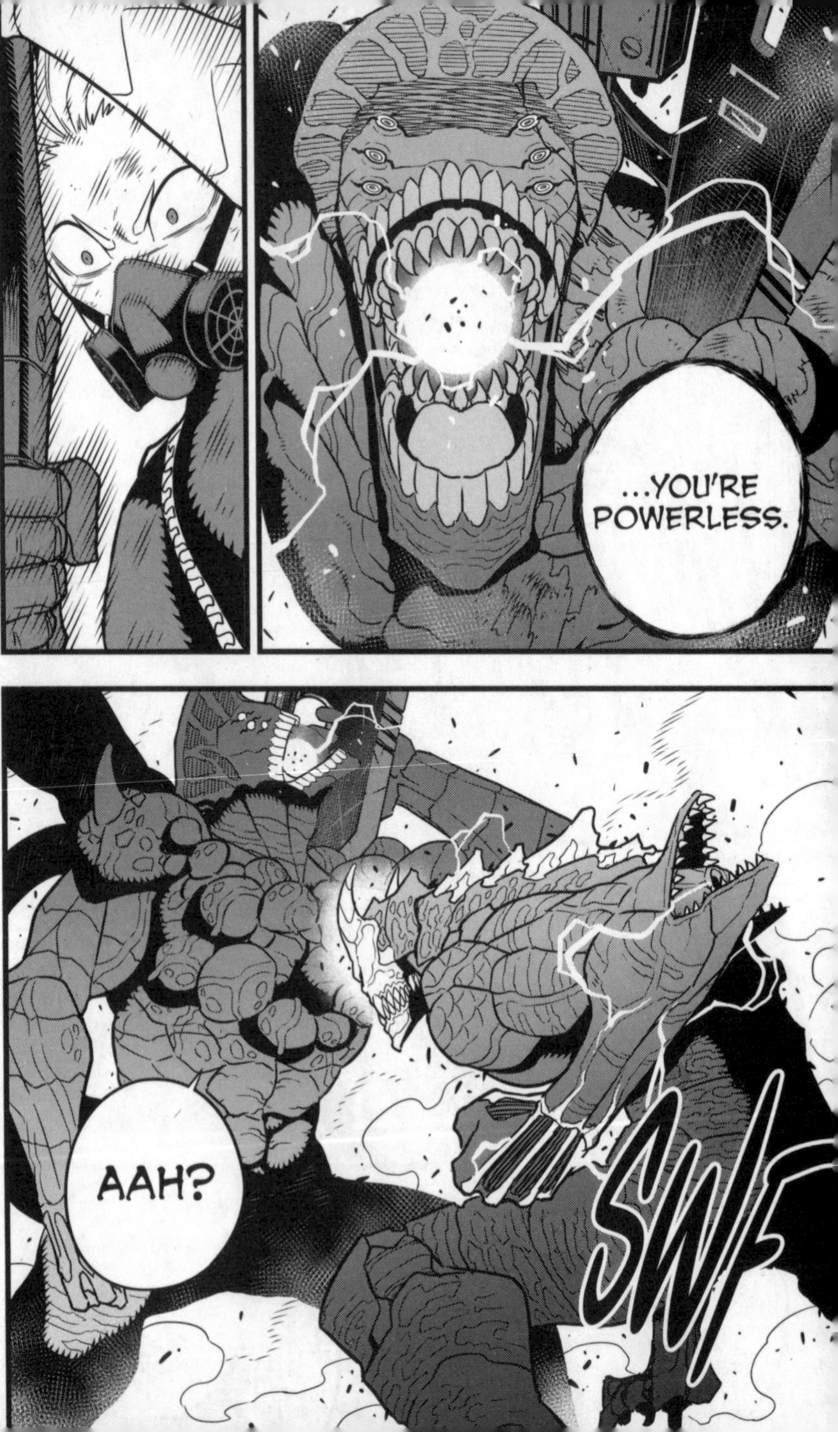
...YOU'RE POWERLESS.
SWF
AAH?

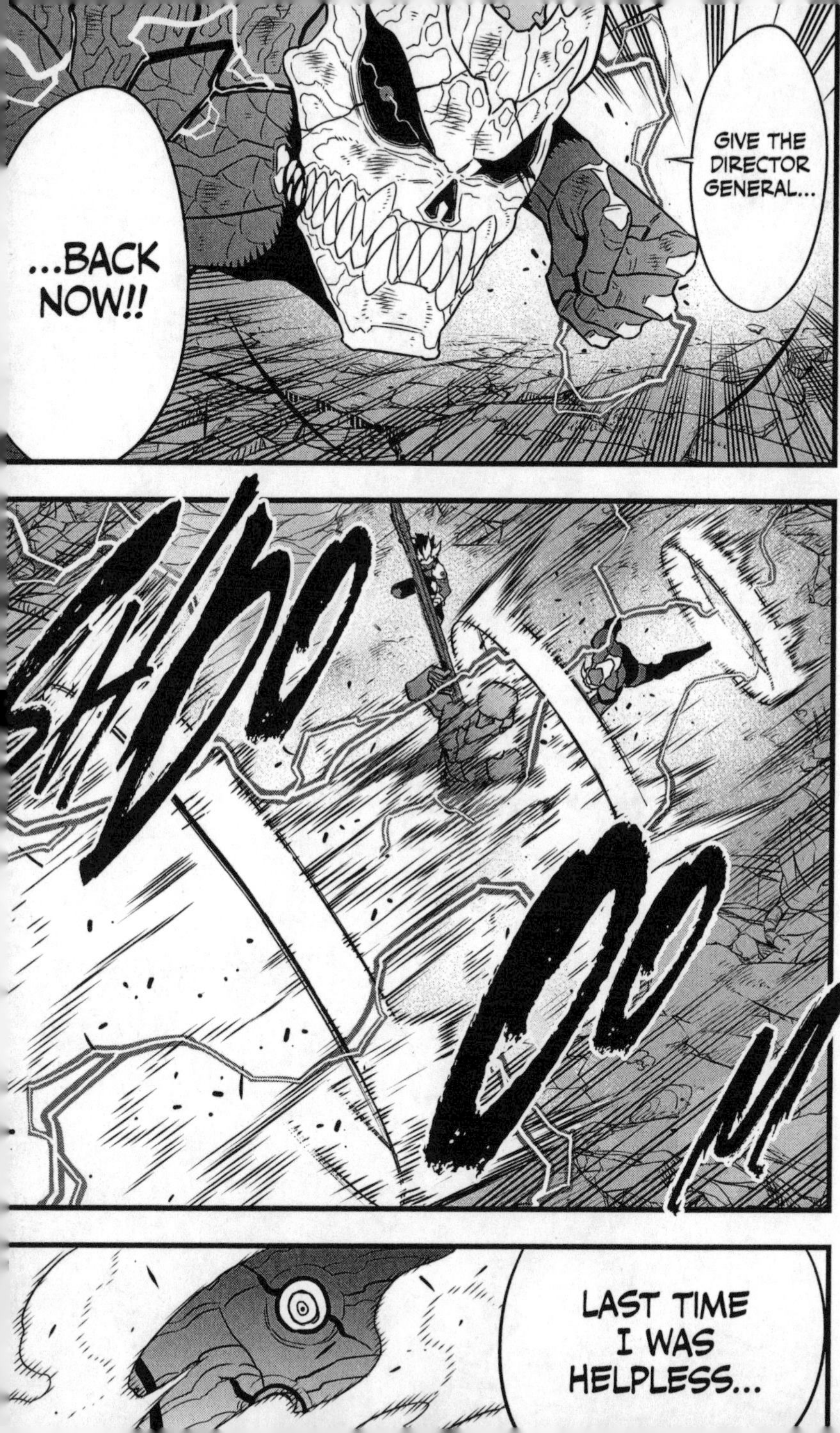
GIVE THE DIRECTOR GENERAL...
...BACK NOW!!
SHOOM
LAST TIME I WAS HELPLESS...

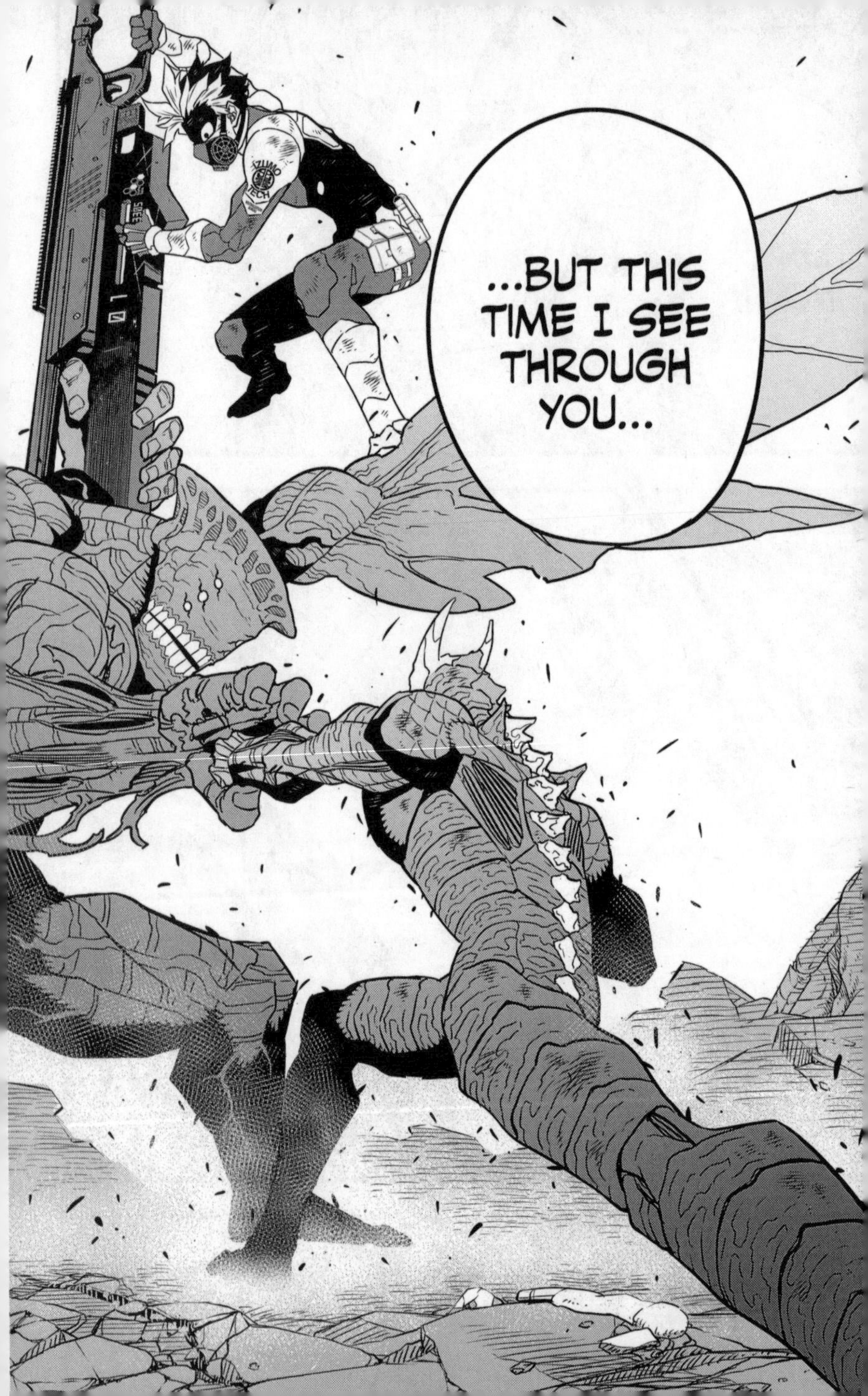
...BUT THIS TIME I SEE THROUGH YOU...

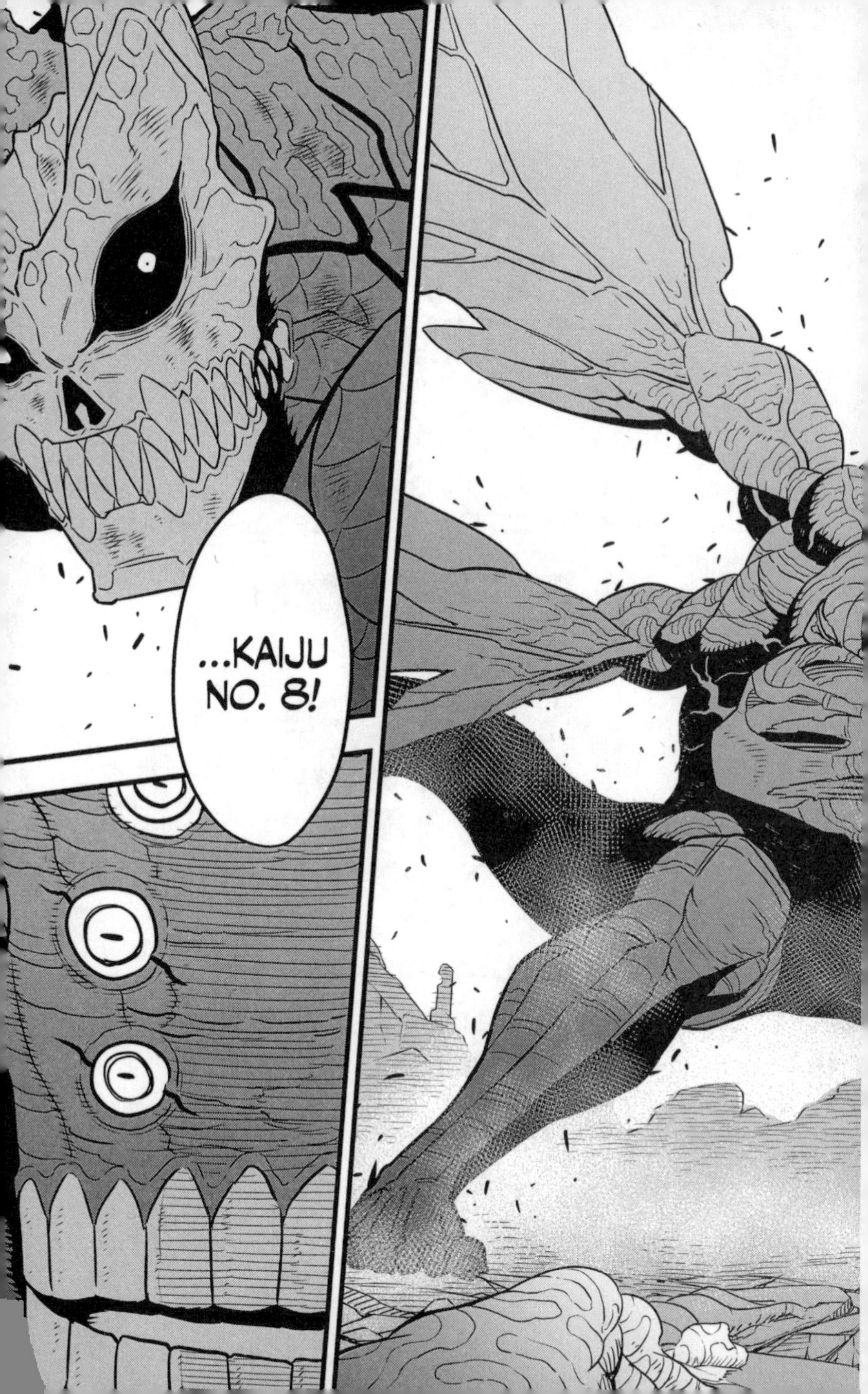
...KAIJU NO. 8!

KAIJU NO. 8
BACKGROUND
INFORMATION

First Division Insignia

This design was inspired by the First Division's designation
as "the strongest sword" of the Defense Forces.

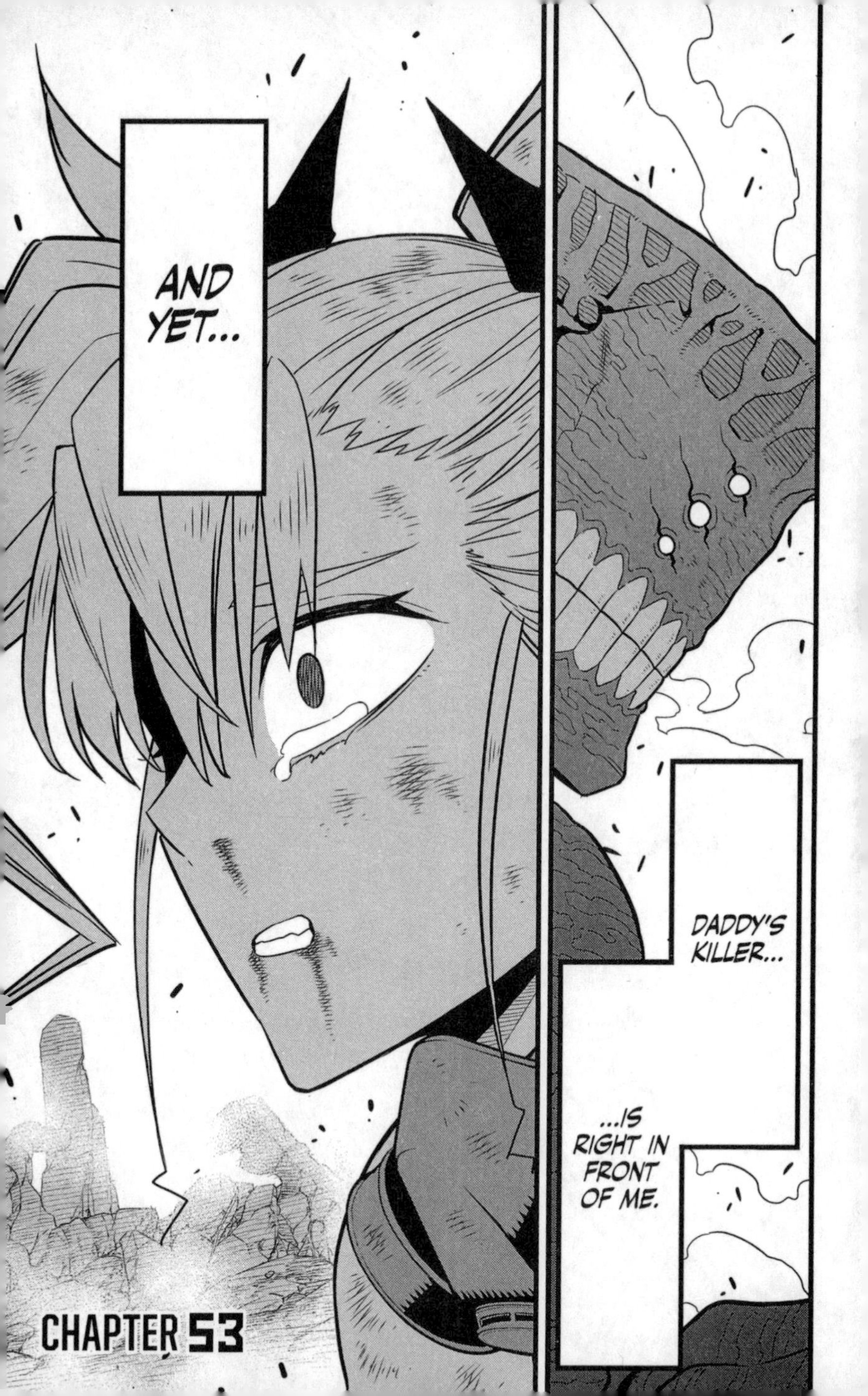
DADDY'S KILLER...
...IS RIGHT IN FRONT OF ME.
AND YET...
CHAPTER 53

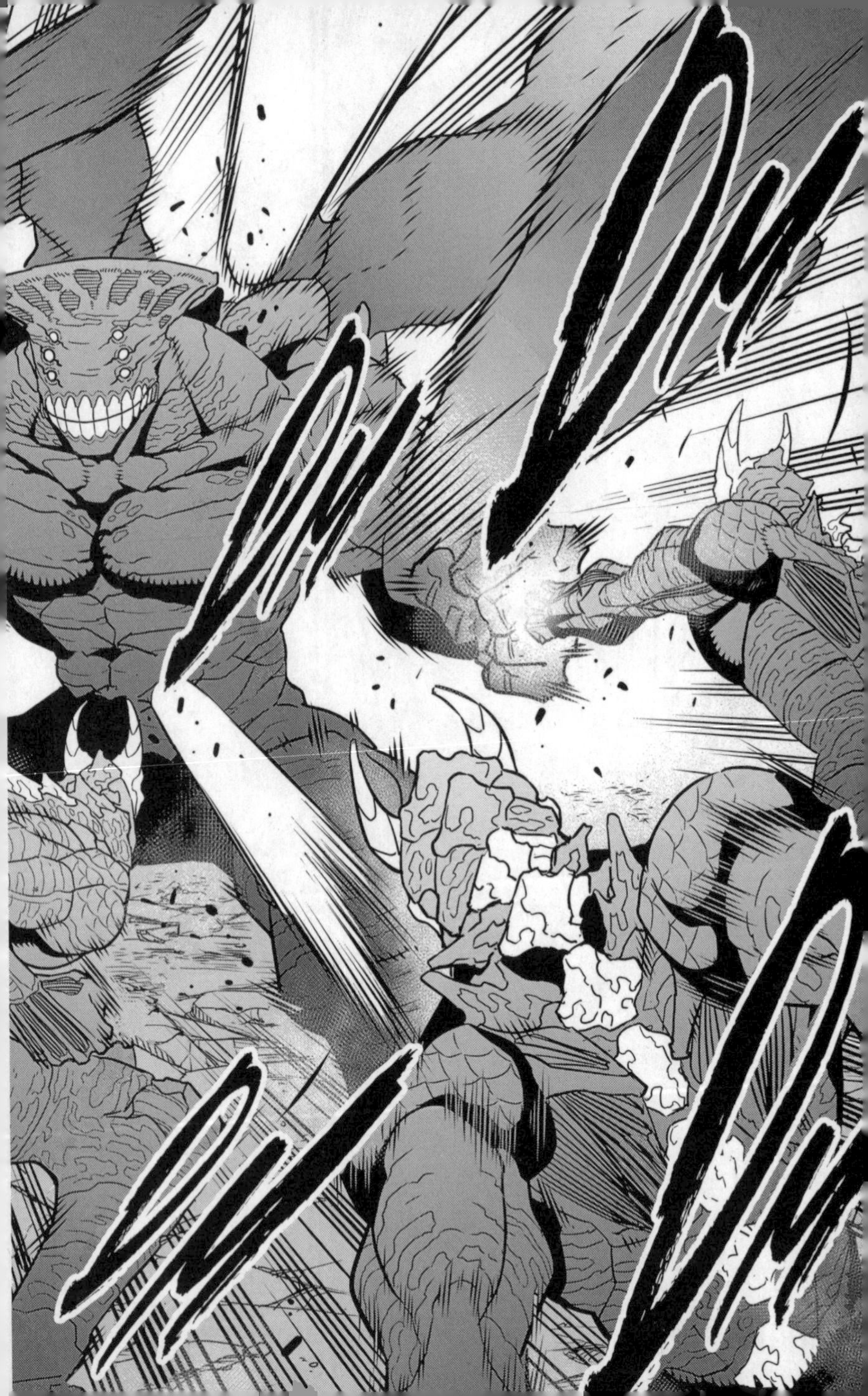

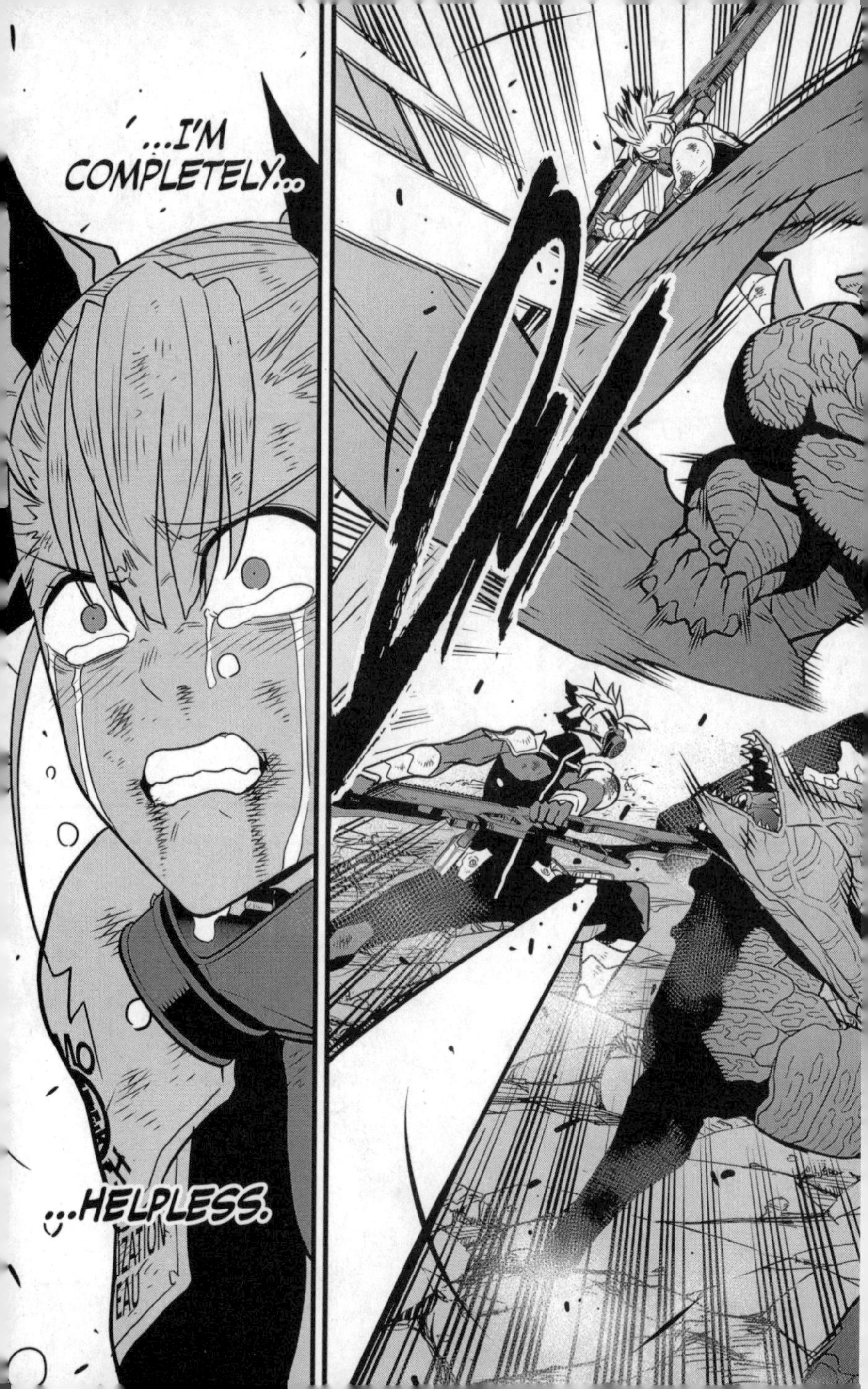
...I'M COMPLETELY...
...HELPLESS.

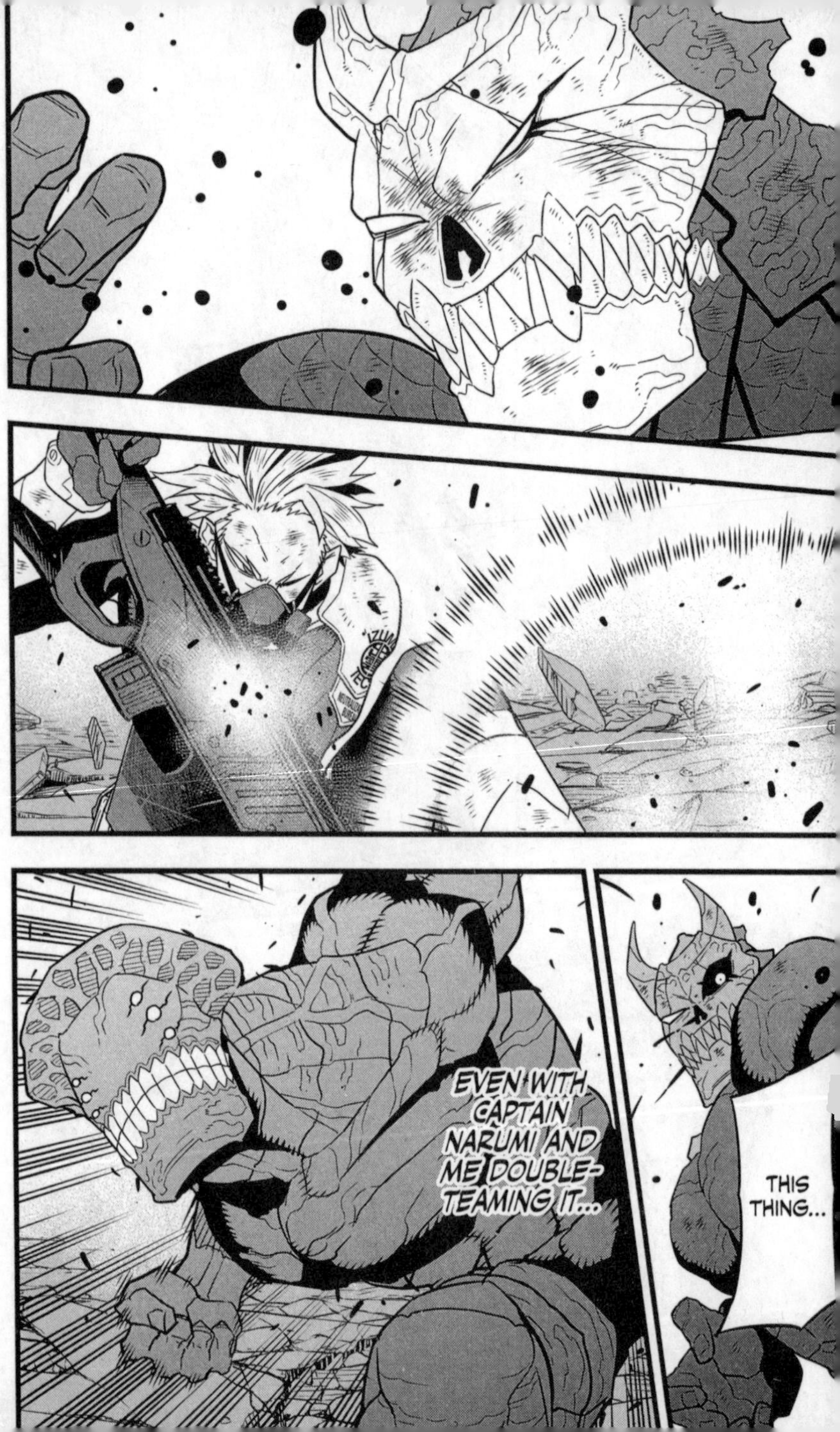
THIS THING...
EVEN WITH CAPTAIN NARUMI AND ME DOUBLE-TEAMING IT...

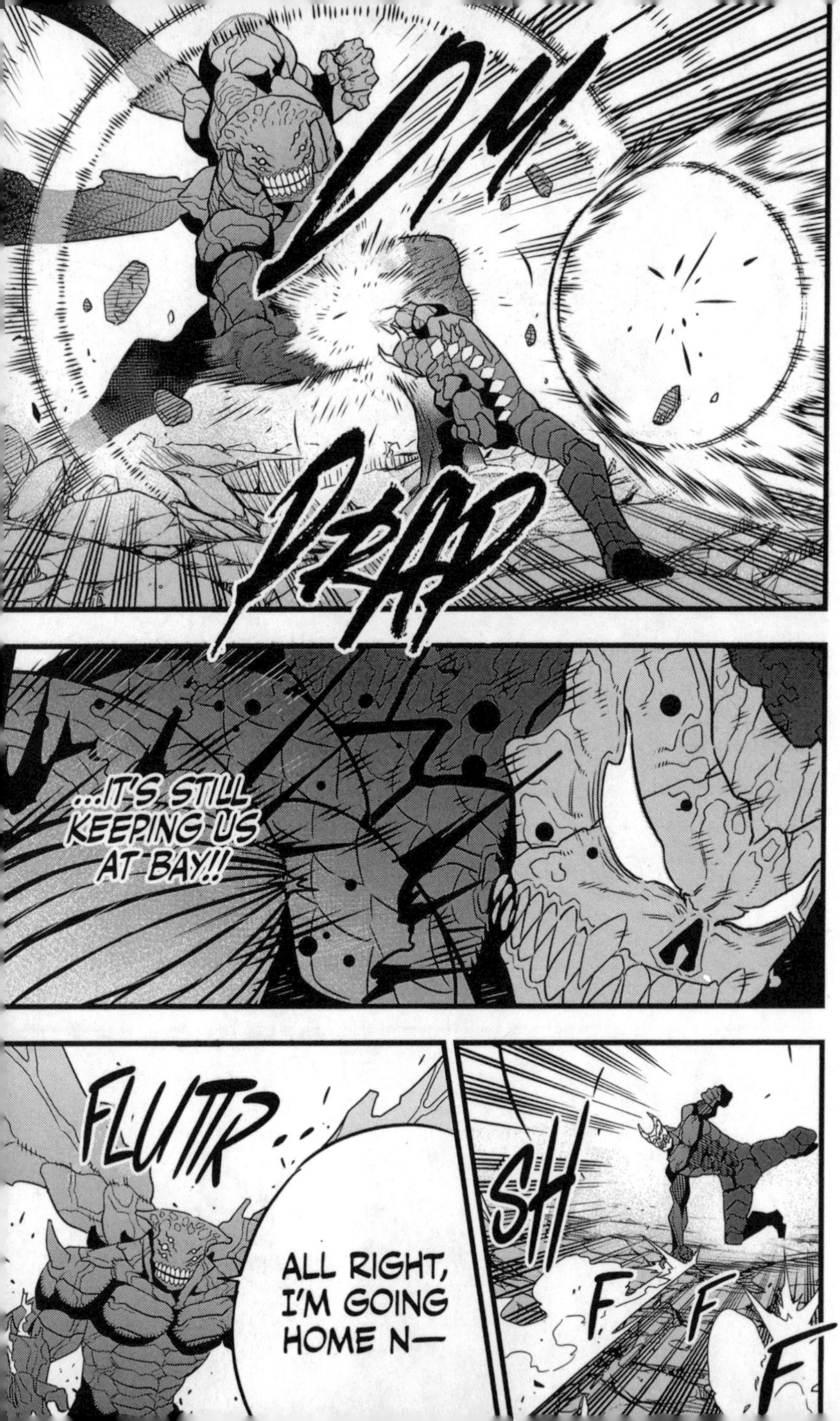
...IT'S STILL KEEPING US AT BAY!!
SH
F F F
FLUTTR
ALL RIGHT, I'M GOING HOME N—

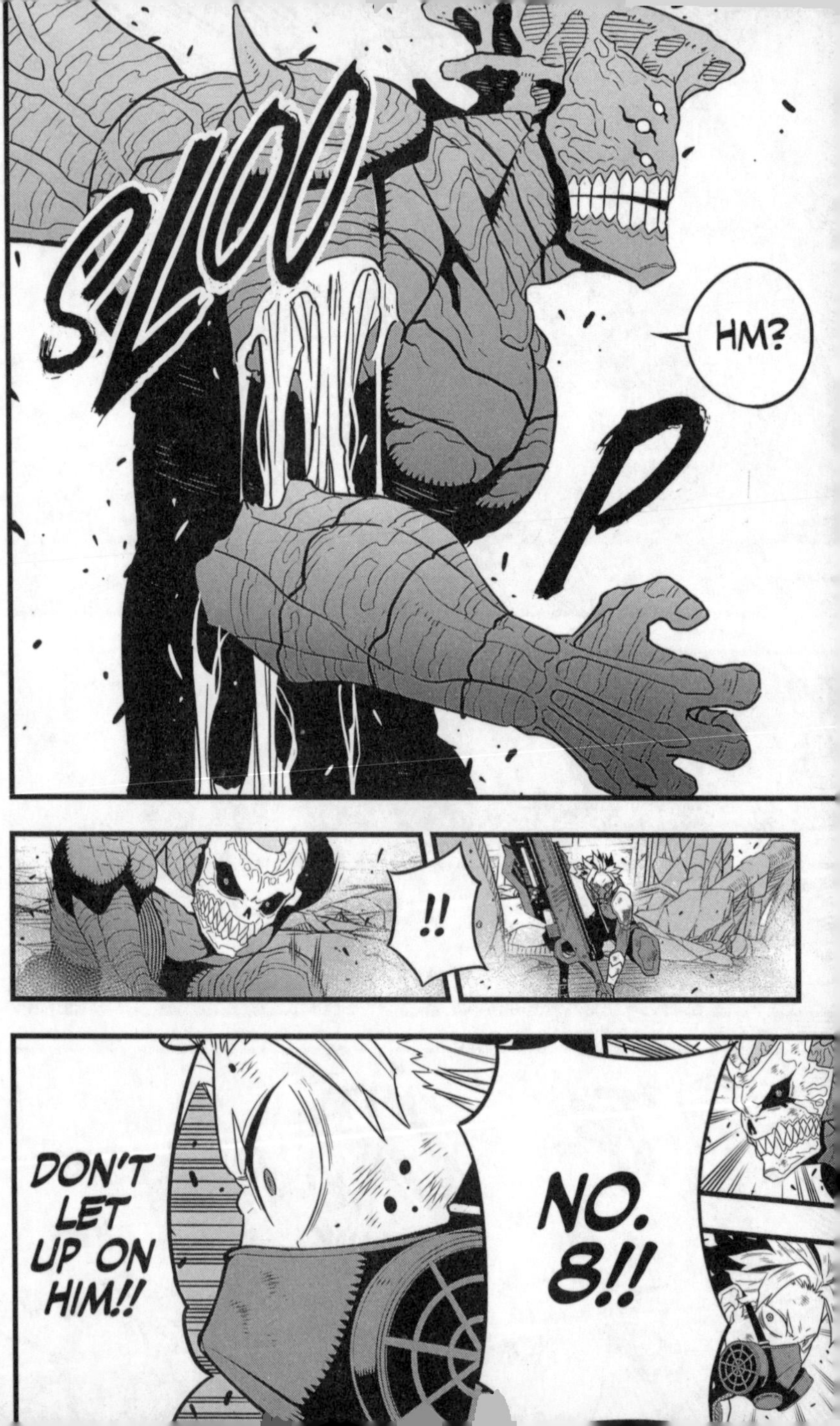
SZLOOP
HM?
!!
NO. 8!!
DON'T LET UP ON HIM!!

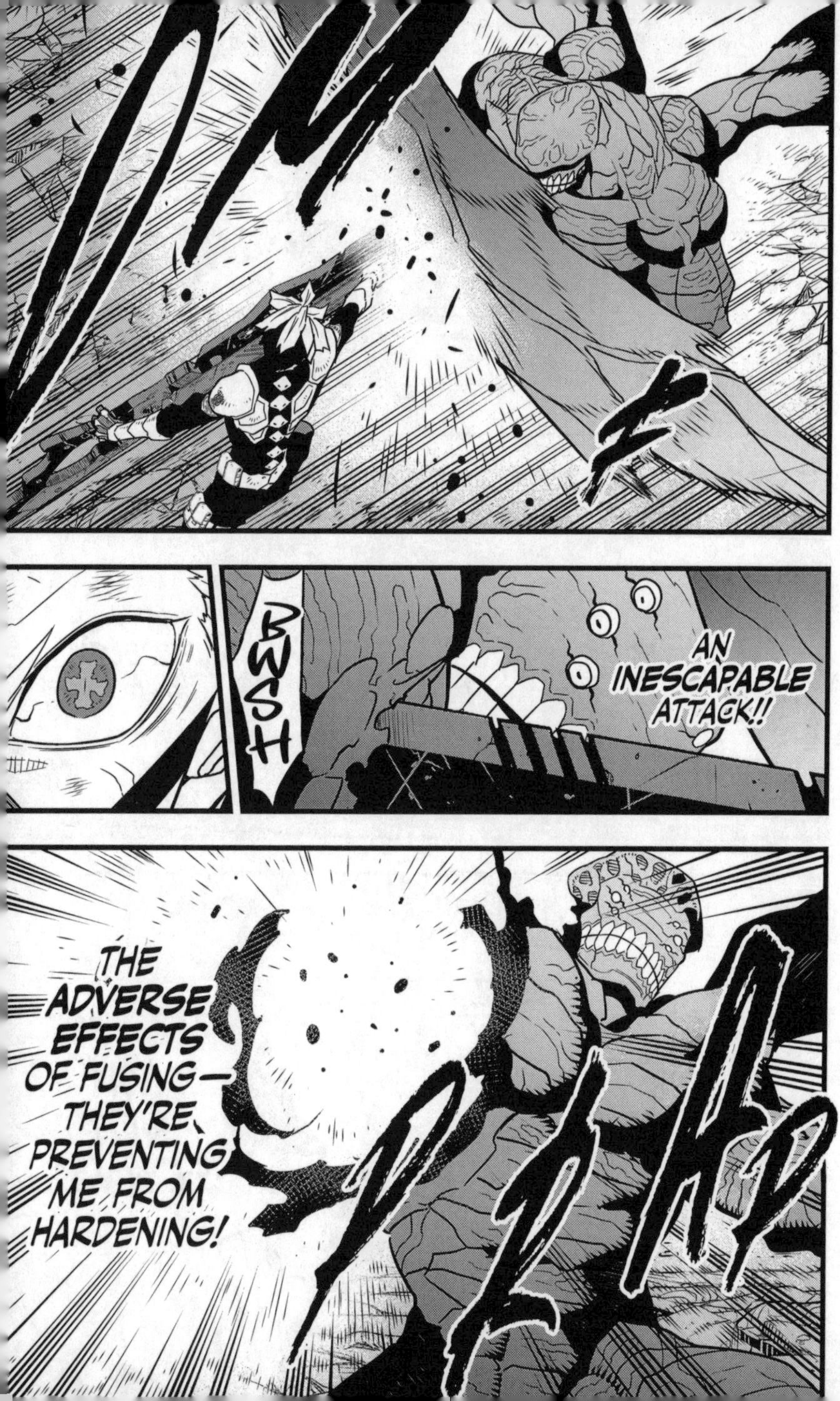
AN INESCAPABLE ATTACK!!
BWSH
THE ADVERSE EFFECTS OF FUSING— THEY'RE PREVENTING ME FROM HARDENING!

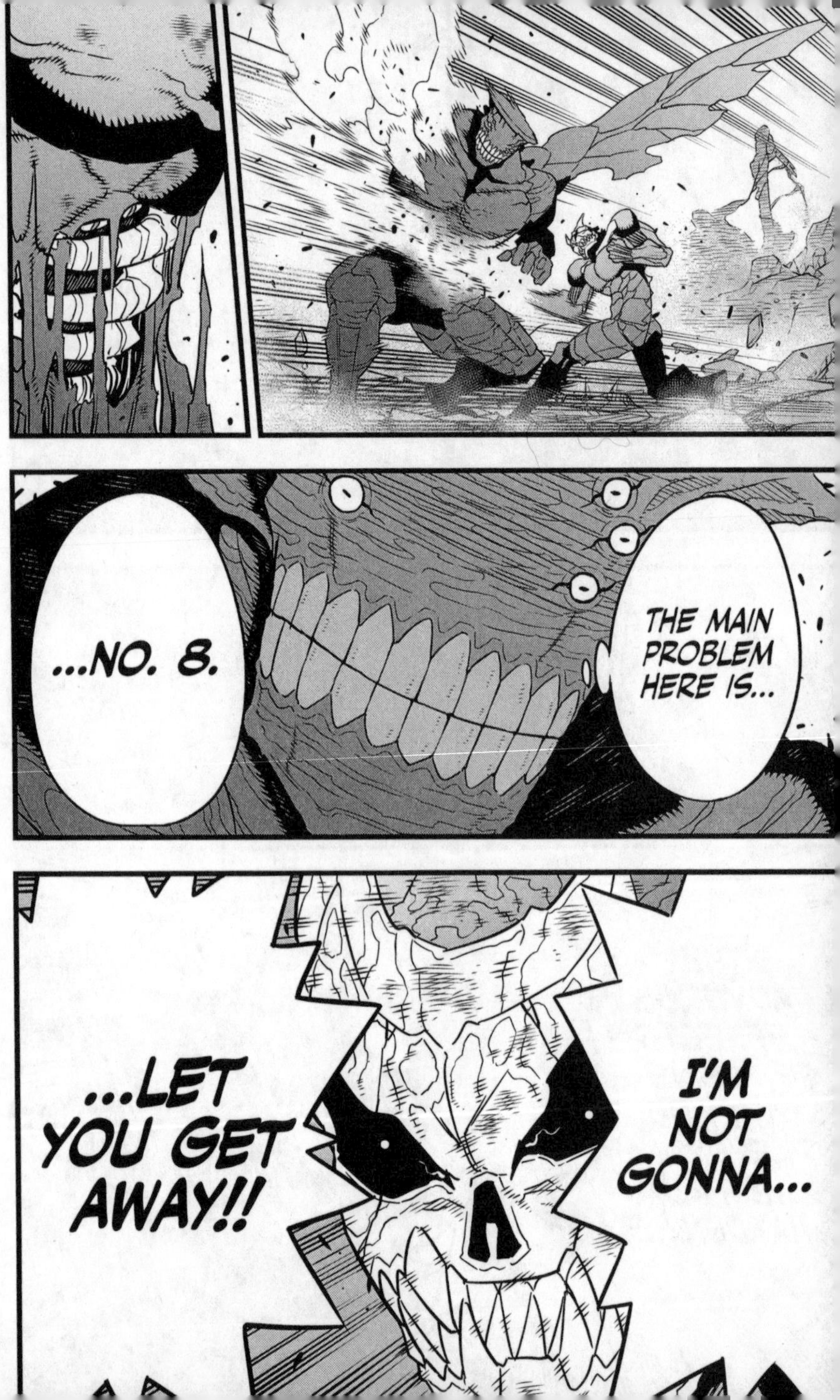
THE MAIN PROBLEM HERE IS...
...NO. 8.
I'M NOT GONNA...
...LET YOU GET AWAY!!

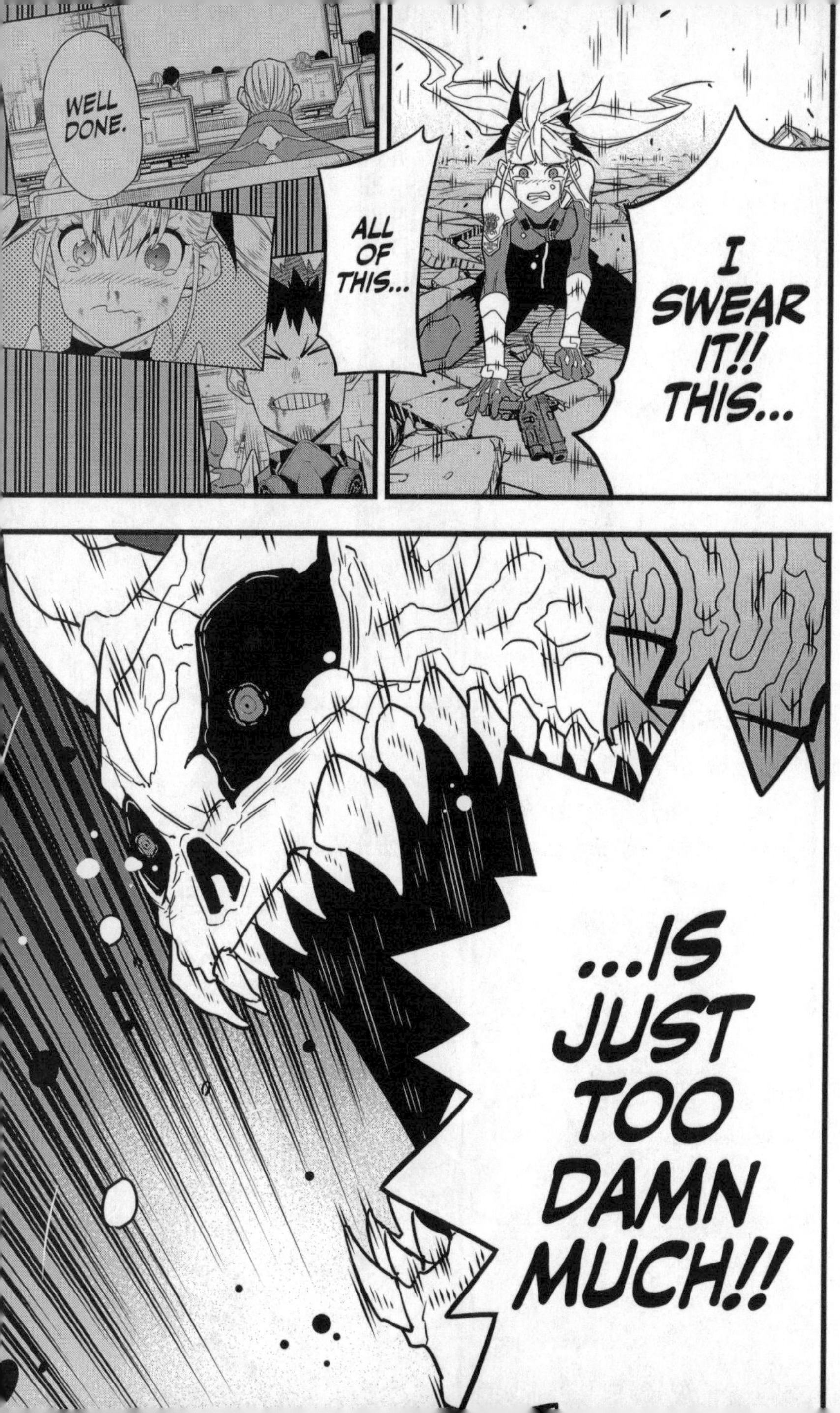
I SWEAR IT!! THIS...
WELL DONE.
ALL OF THIS...
...IS JUST TOO DAMN MUCH!!

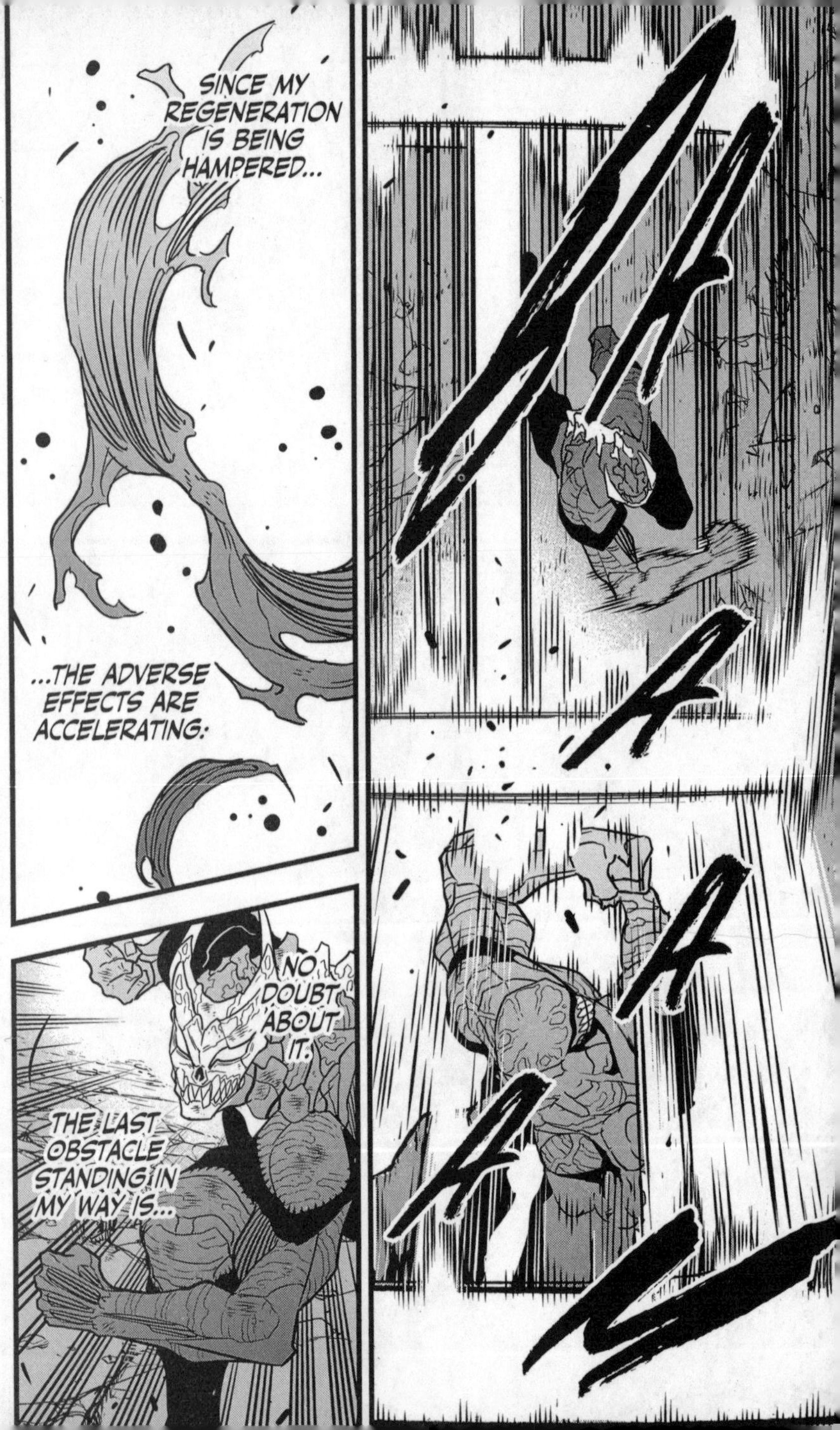
SINCE MY REGENERATION IS BEING HAMPERED...
...THE ADVERSE EFFECTS ARE ACCELERATING.
NO DOUBT ABOUT IT.
THE LAST OBSTACLE STANDING IN MY WAY IS...

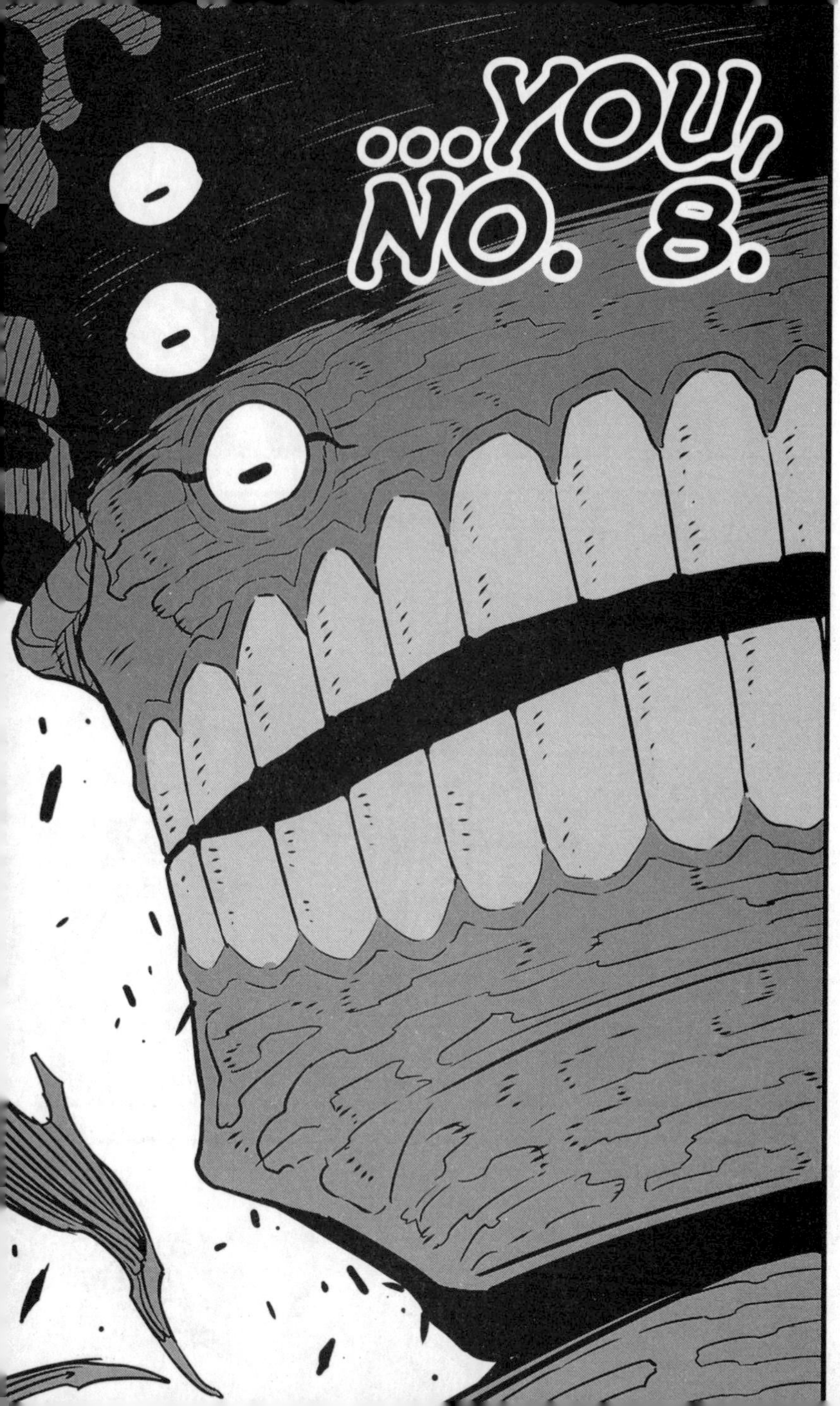
...YOU, NO. 8.

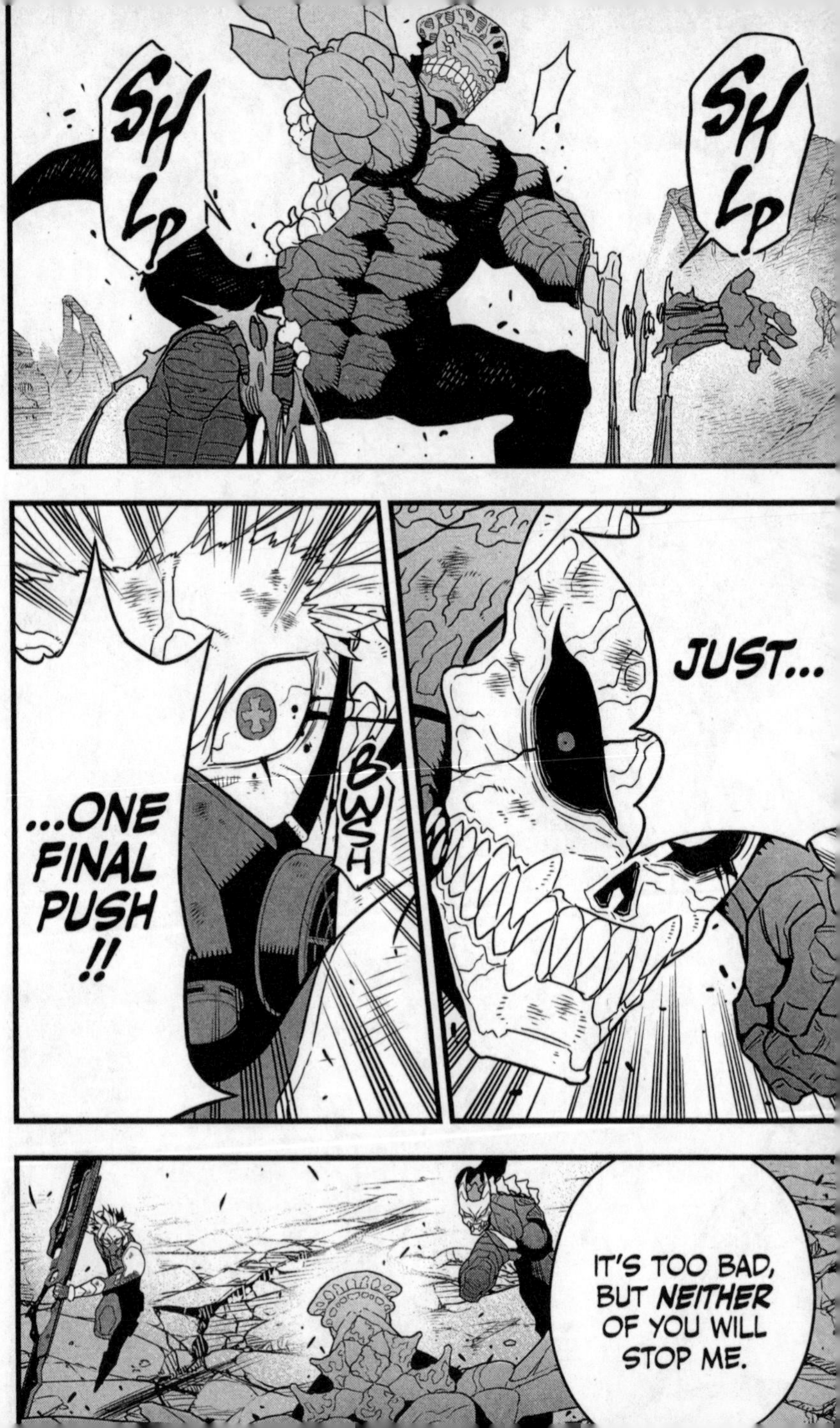
SHLP
SHLP
JUST...
BWSH
...ONE FINAL PUSH!!
IT'S TOO BAD, BUT NEITHER OF YOU WILL STOP ME.

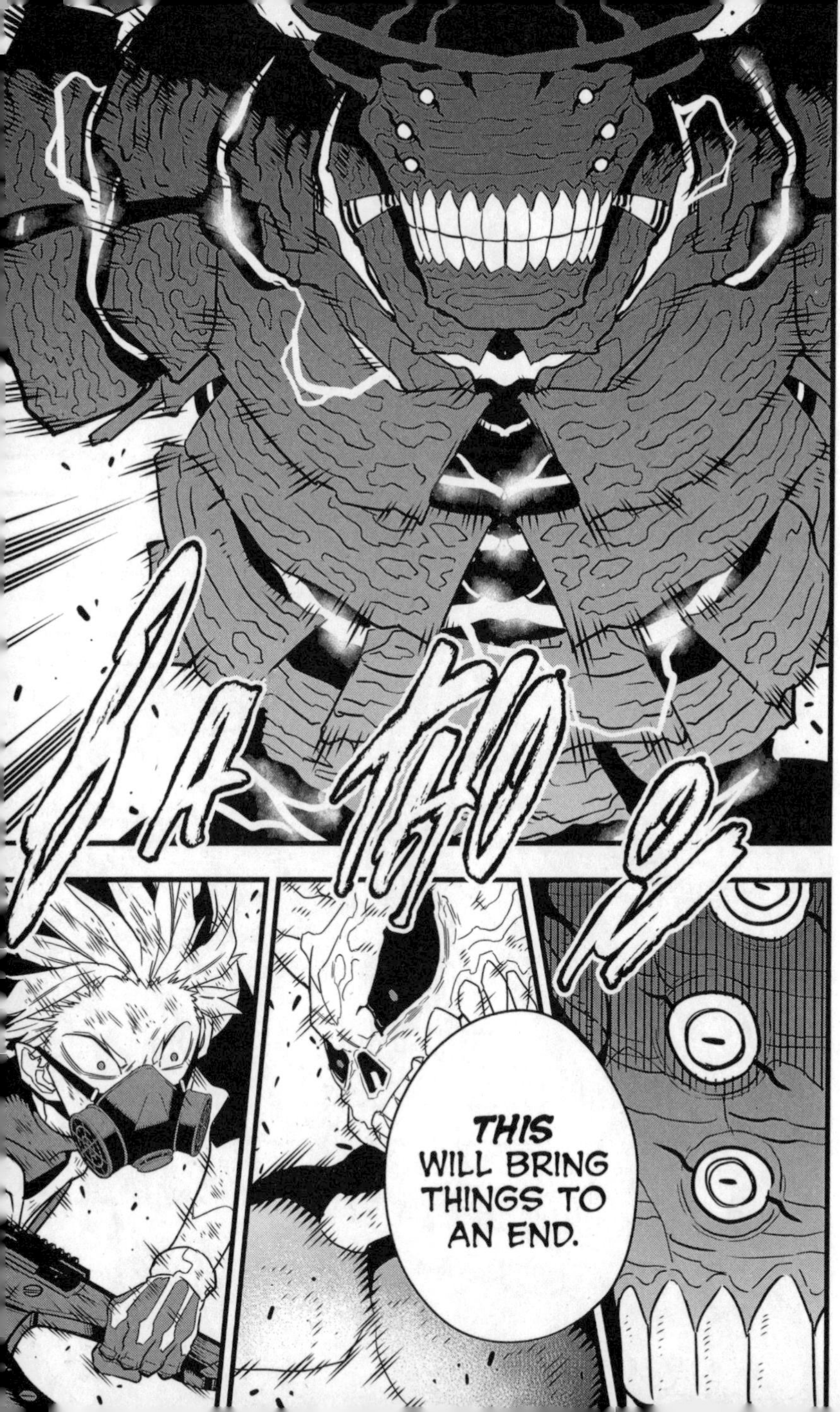
THIS WILL BRING THINGS TO AN END.

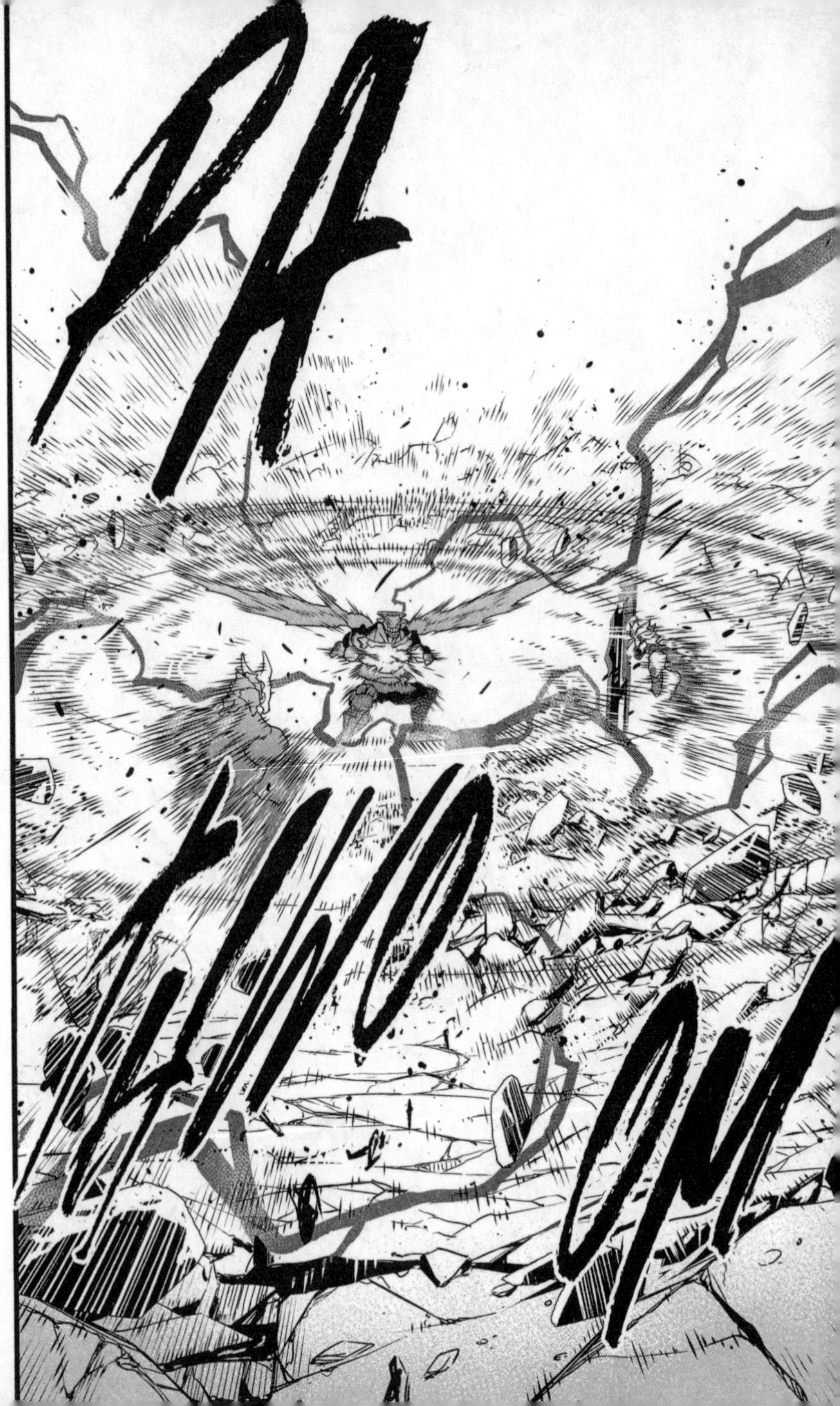

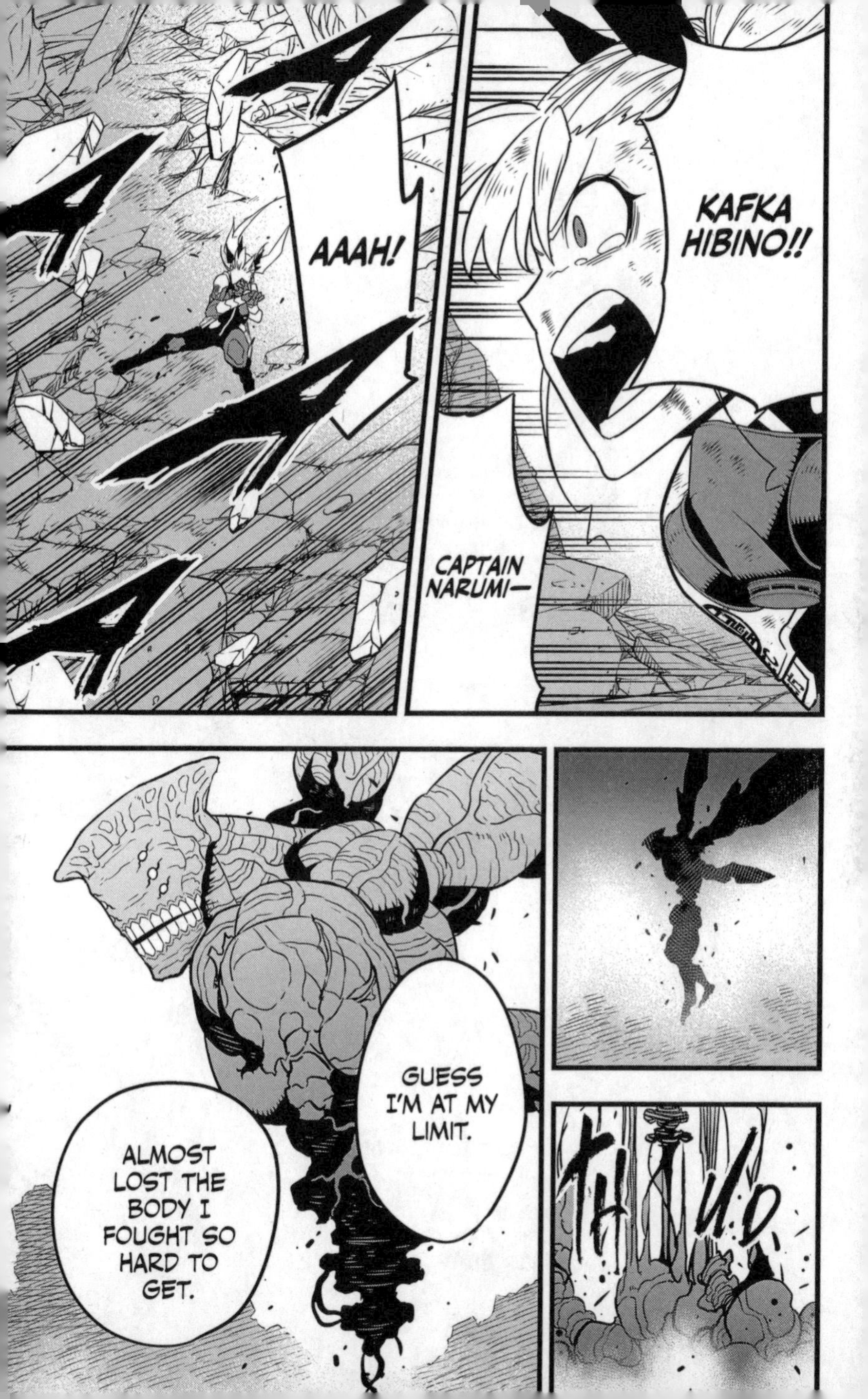
KAFKA HIBINO!!
CAPTAIN NARUMI—
AAAH!
THUD
GUESS I'M AT MY LIMIT.
ALMOST LOST THE BODY I FOUGHT SO HARD TO GET.

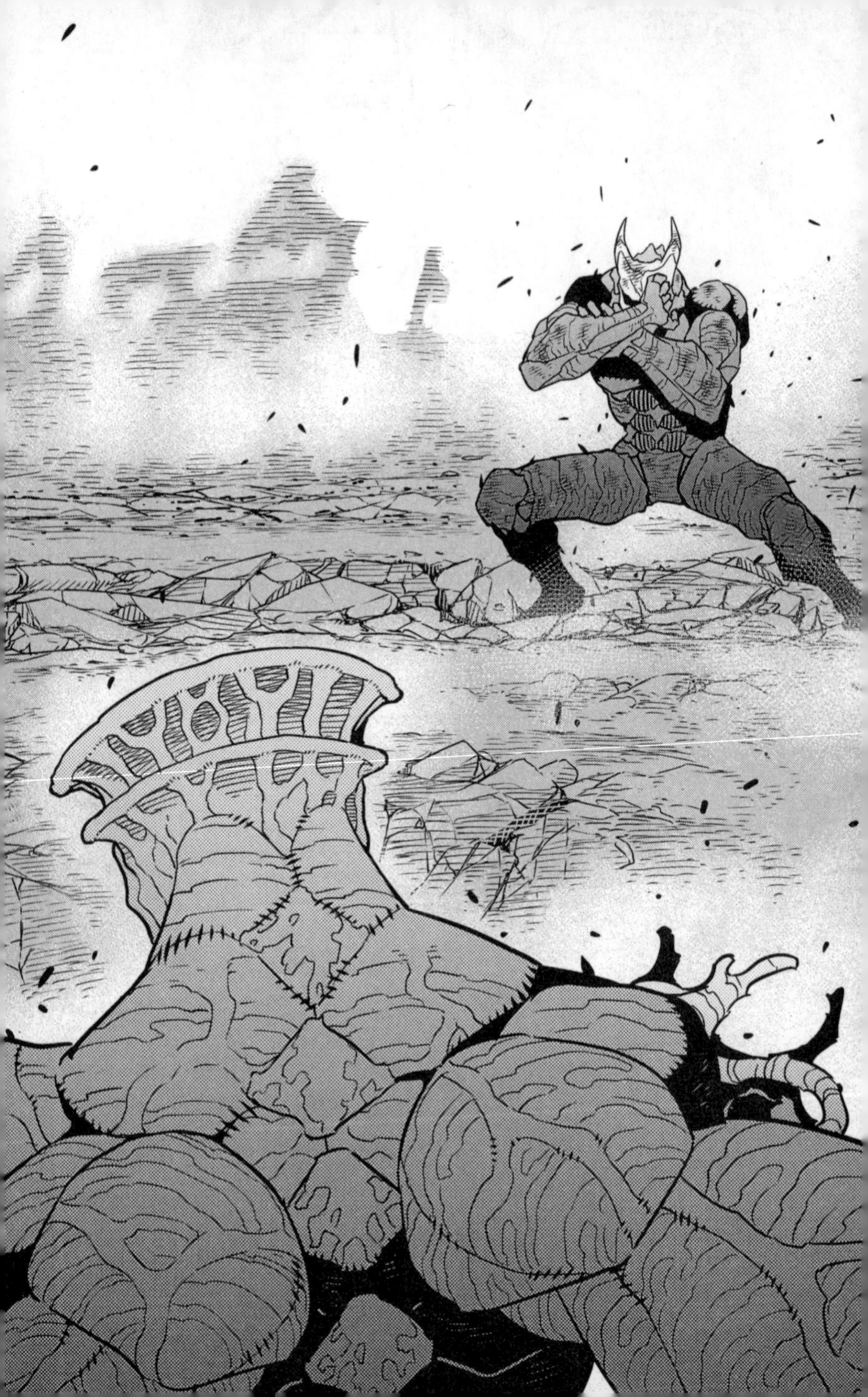

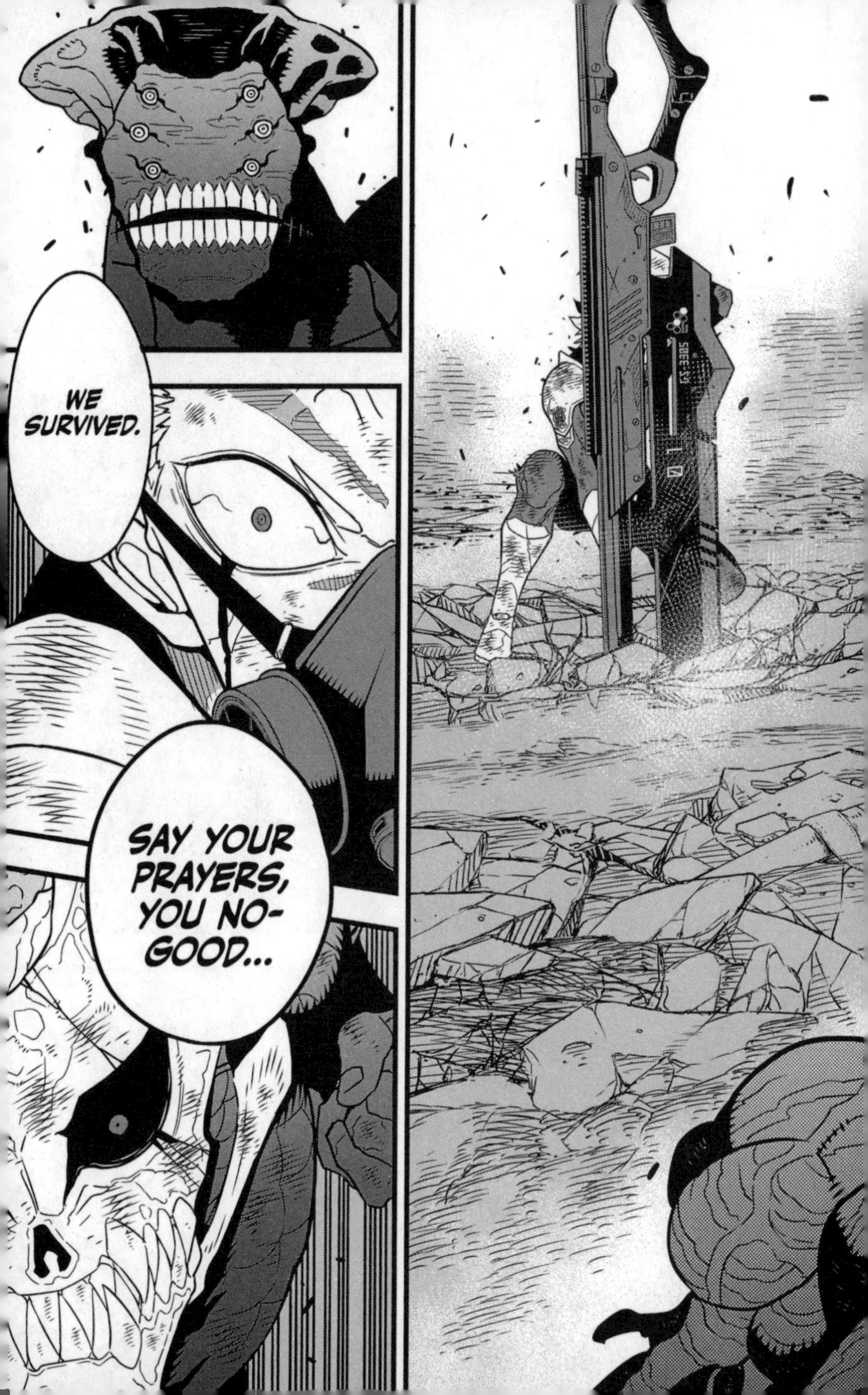
WE SURVIVED.
SAY YOUR PRAYERS, YOU NO-GOOD...

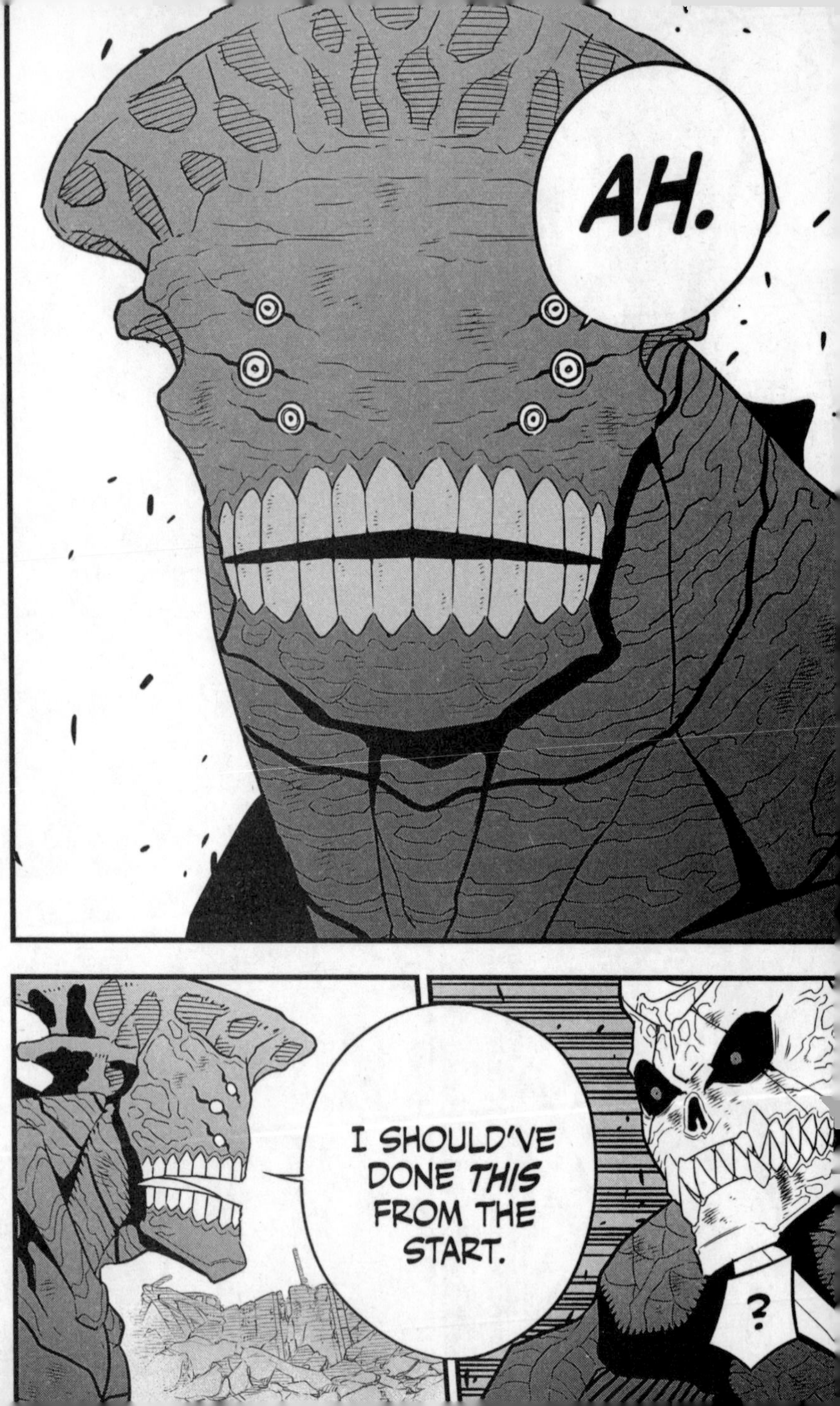
AH.
I SHOULD'VE DONE *THIS* FROM THE START.
?

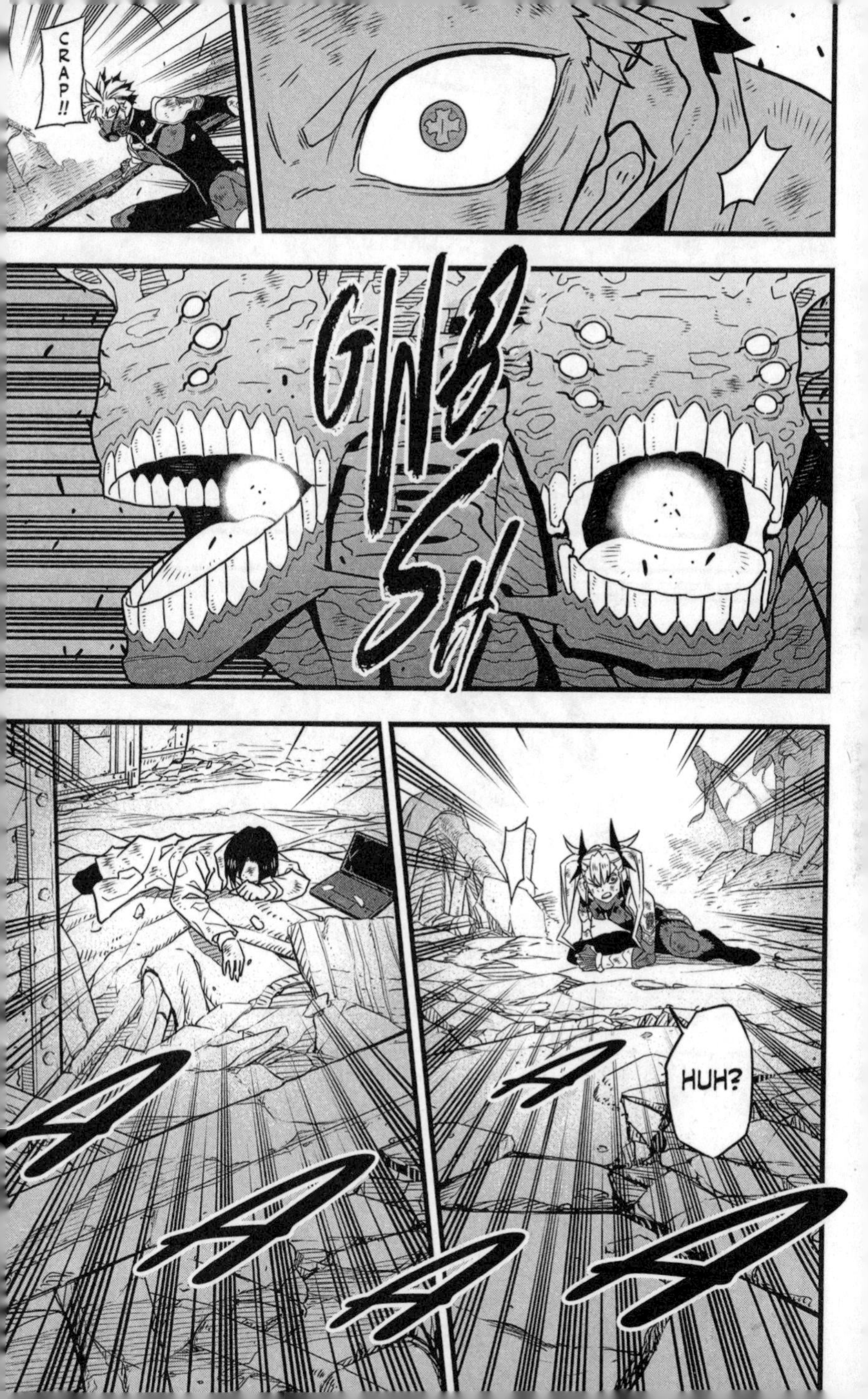
CRAP!!
GWB
SH
HUH?

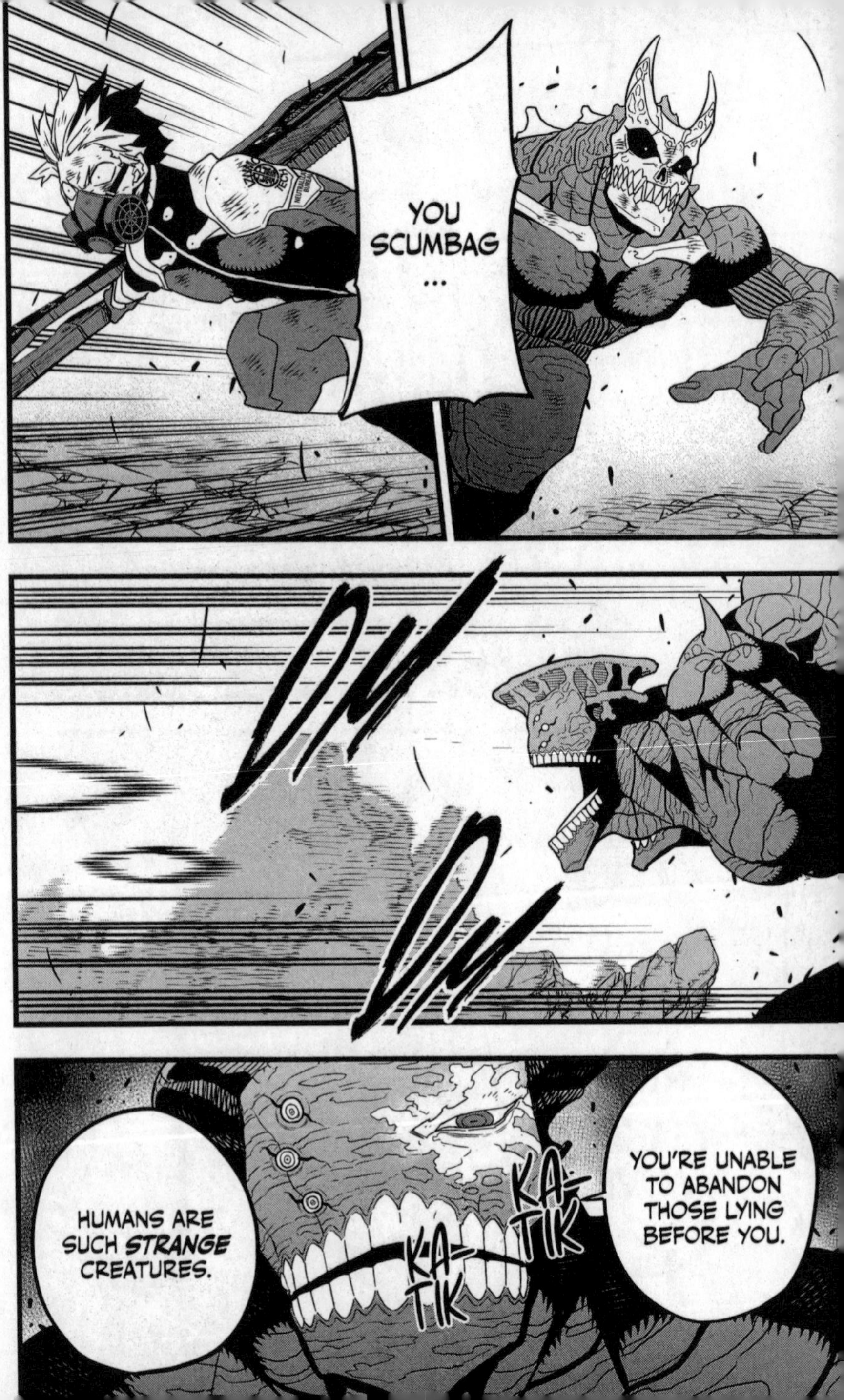
YOU SCUMBAG ...
YOU'RE UNABLE TO ABANDON THOSE LYING BEFORE YOU.
KA-TIK
KA-TIK
HUMANS ARE SUCH STRANGE CREATURES.

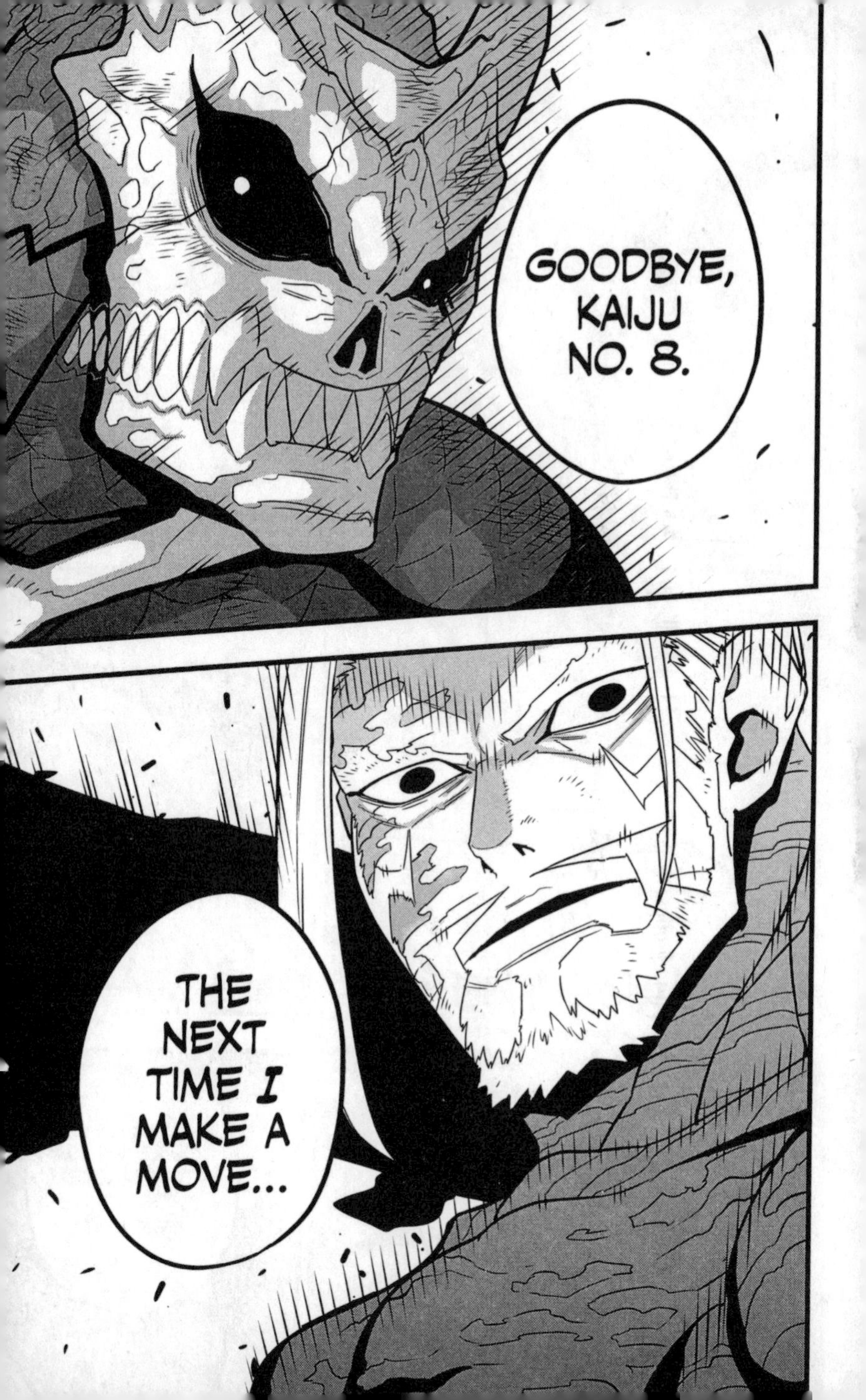
GOODBYE, KAIJU NO. 8.
THE NEXT TIME I MAKE A MOVE...

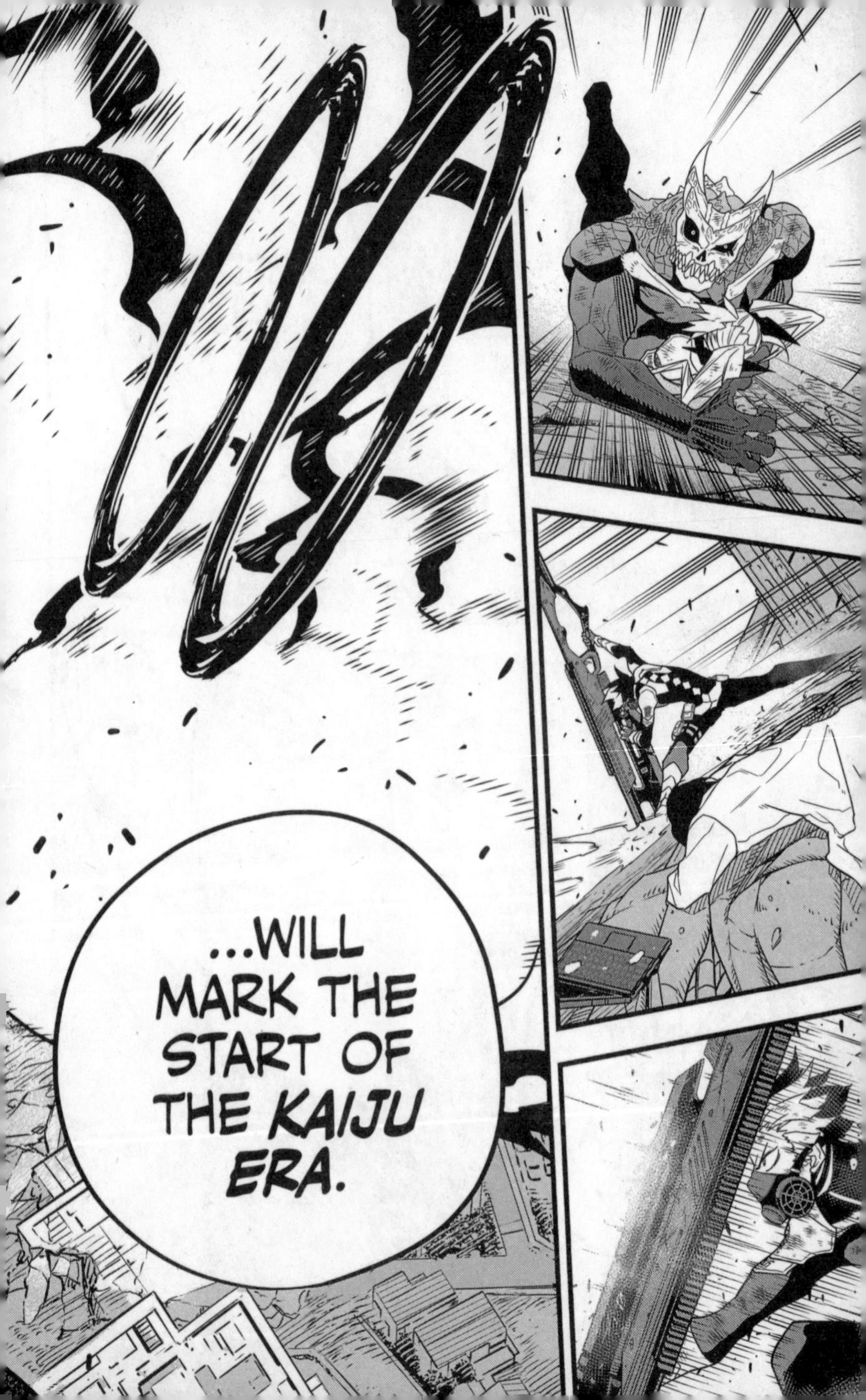
...WILL MARK THE START OF THE *KAIJU* ERA.

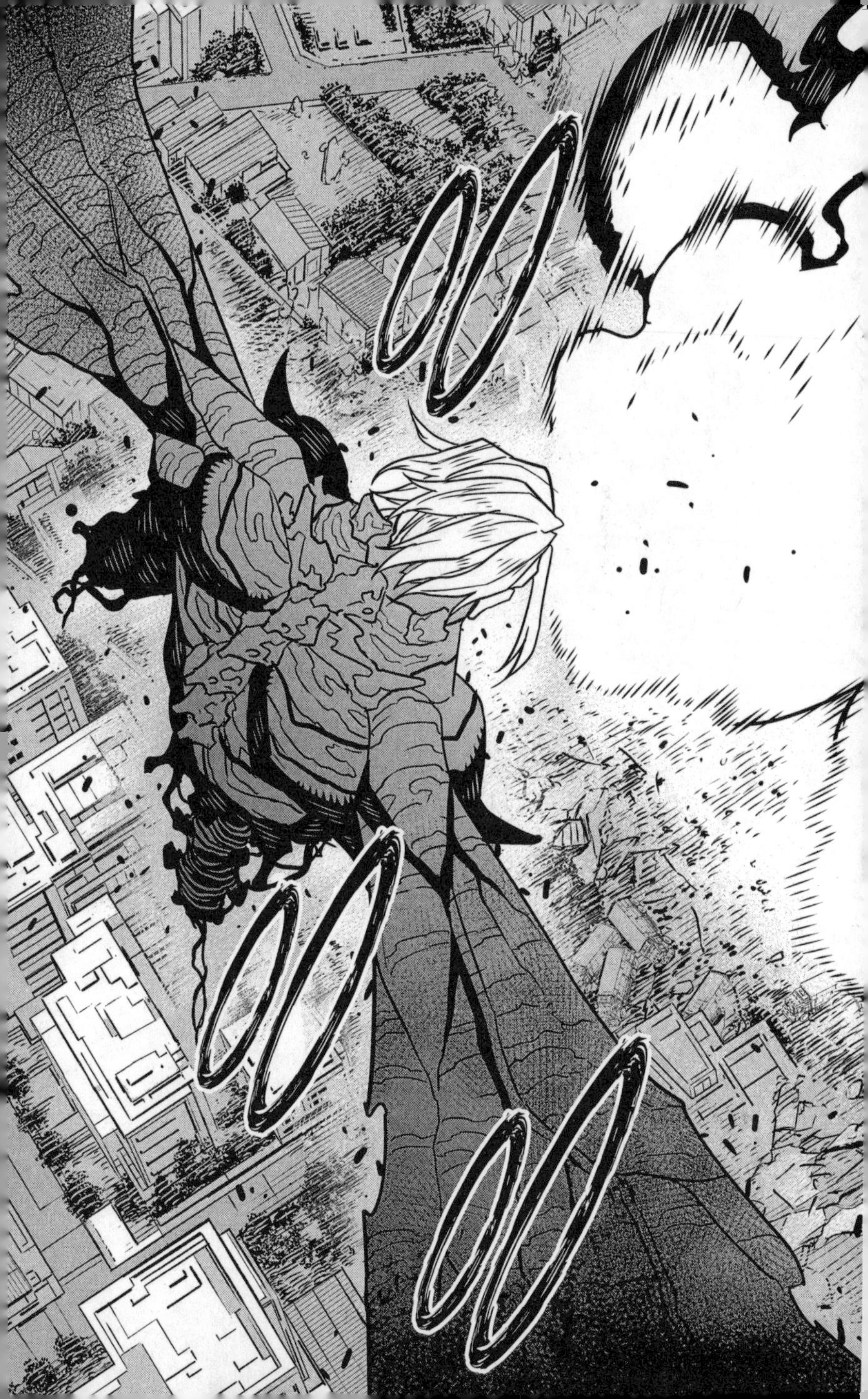

The color illustration in this volume has the Eiffel Tower in the background. I was initially inspired to draw this when the publisher who has been promoting *Kaiju No. 8* in France, KAZE, said that they would love it if I drew an illustration featuring a French locale someday. To show my gratitude for the energy they've put into promotion over there, I put in serious effort along with background artist Kowai-san to draw this as thanks. As I was drawing it, my mind started to run with ideas like, "What would the French defense force be like?"

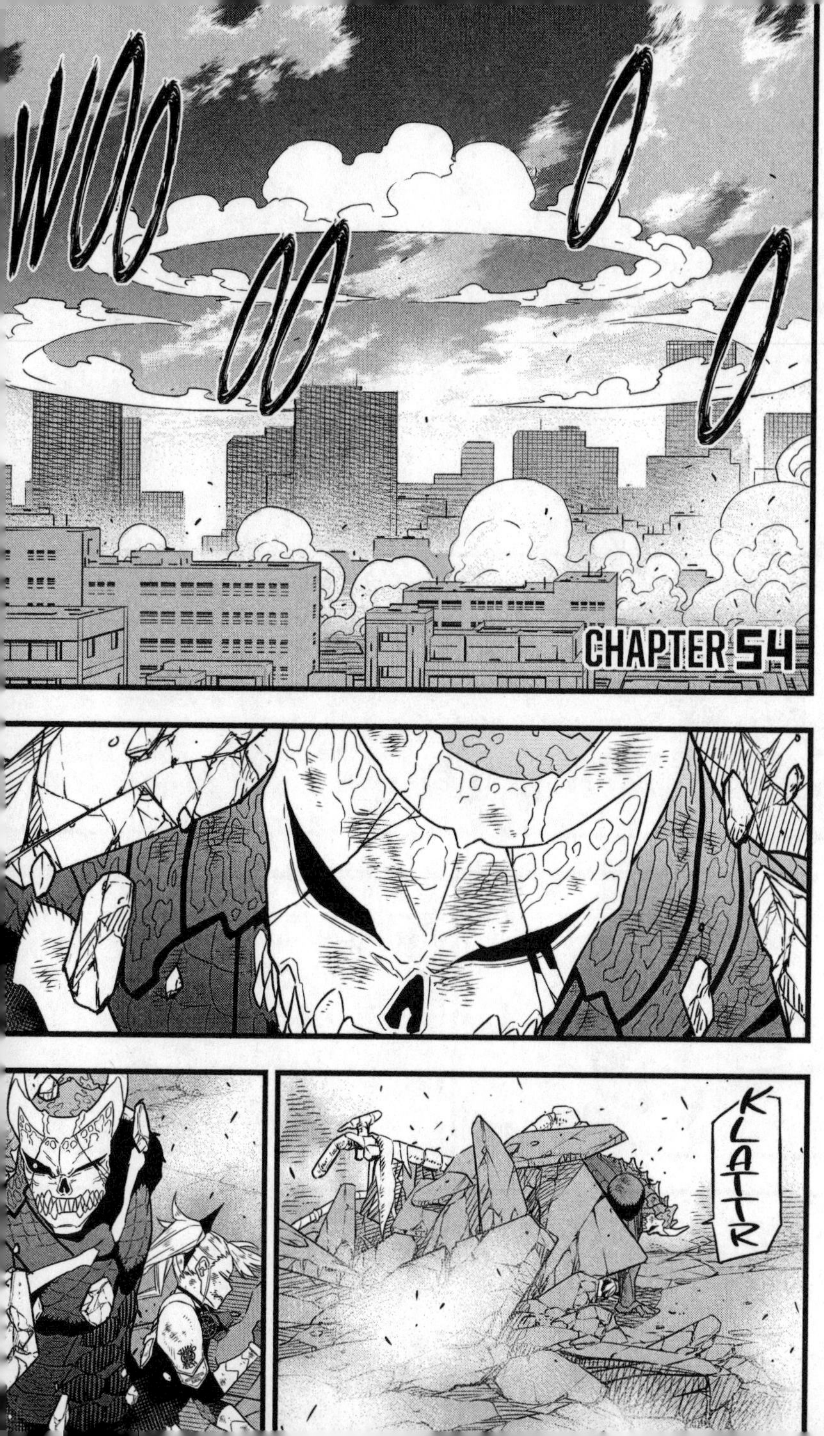
WOOOOOO
CHAPTER 54
KLATTR

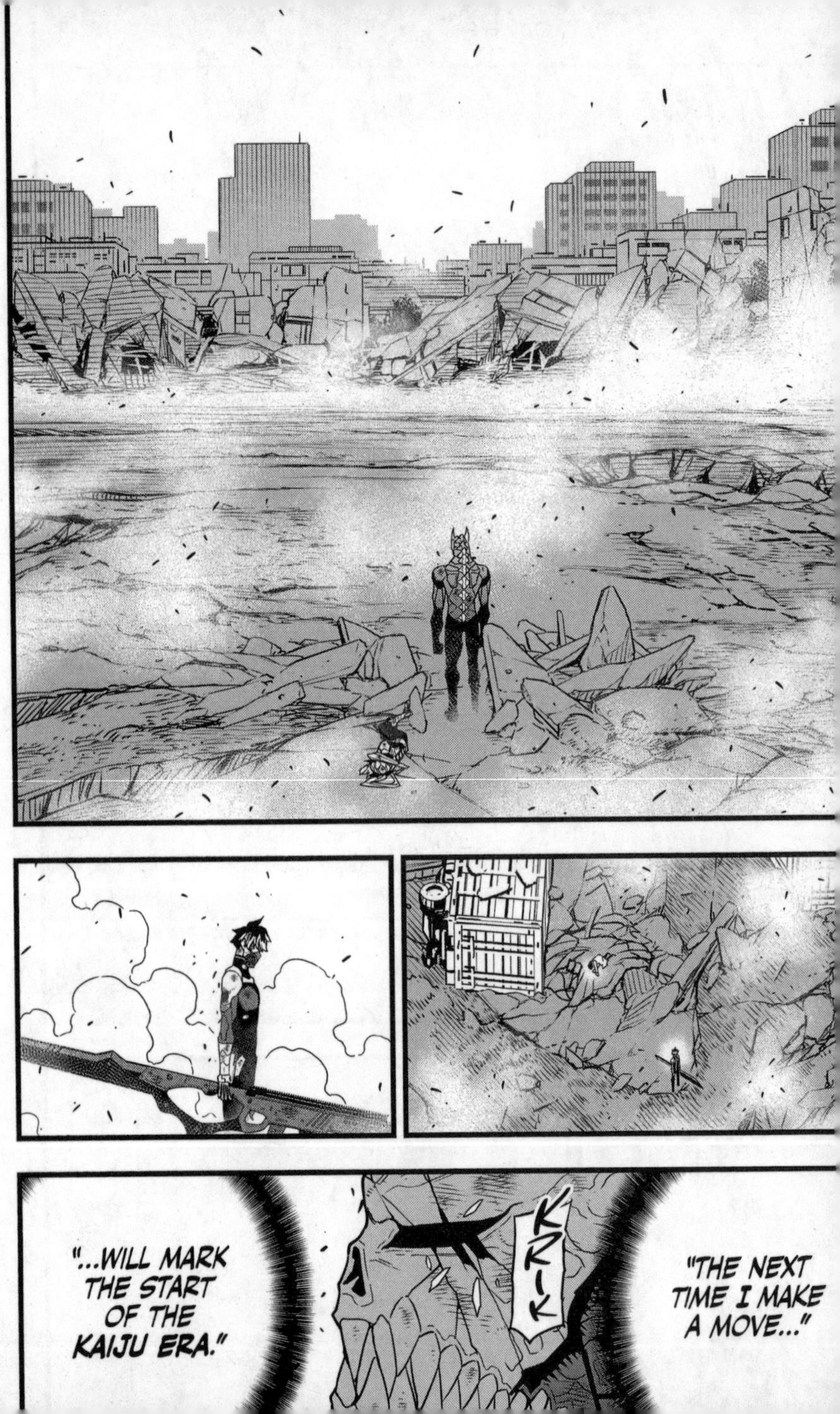
"THE NEXT TIME I MAKE A MOVE..."
KRIK
"...WILL MARK THE START OF THE KAIJU ERA."

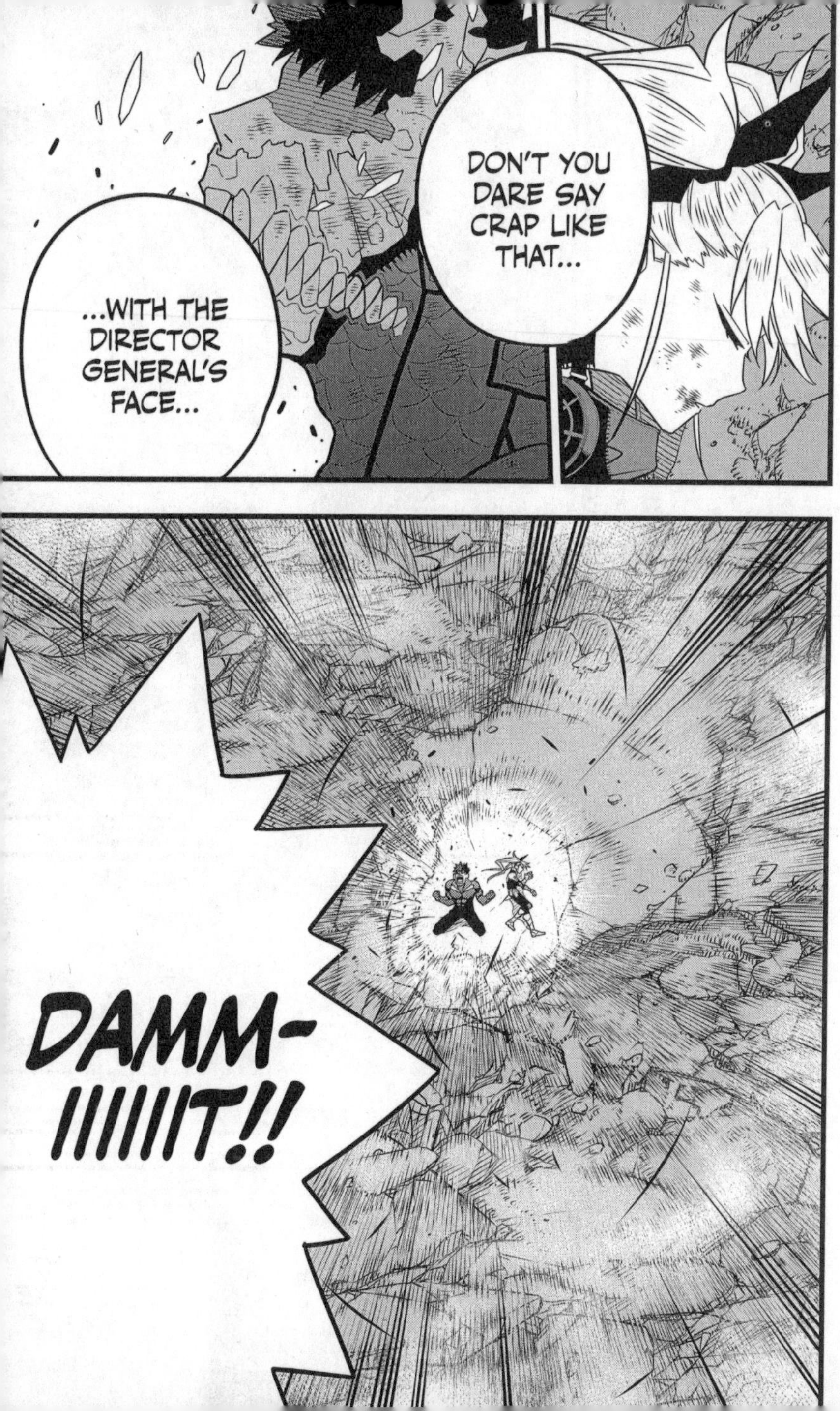
DON'T YOU DARE SAY CRAP LIKE THAT...
...WITH THE DIRECTOR GENERAL'S FACE...
DAMM-IIIIIIT!!

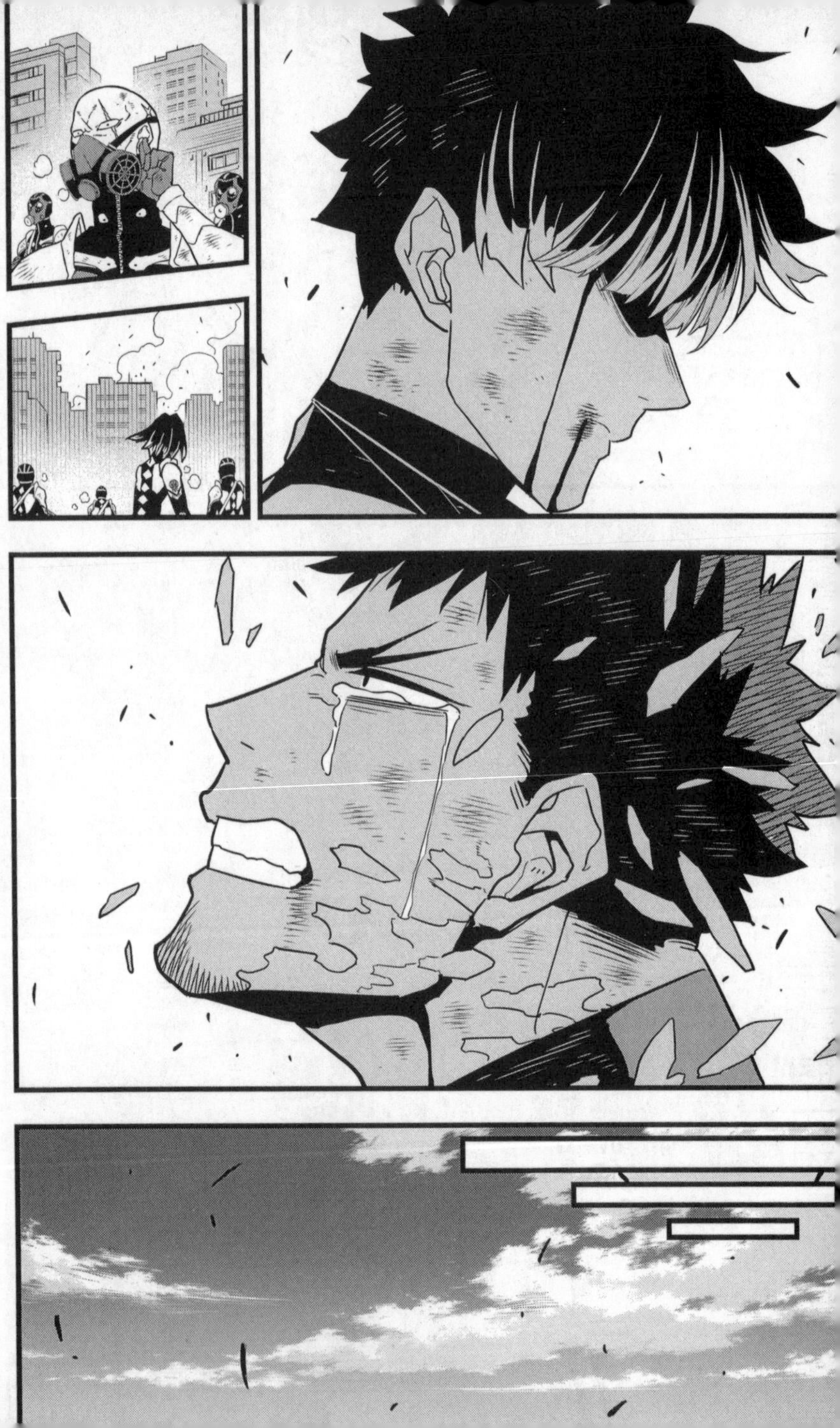

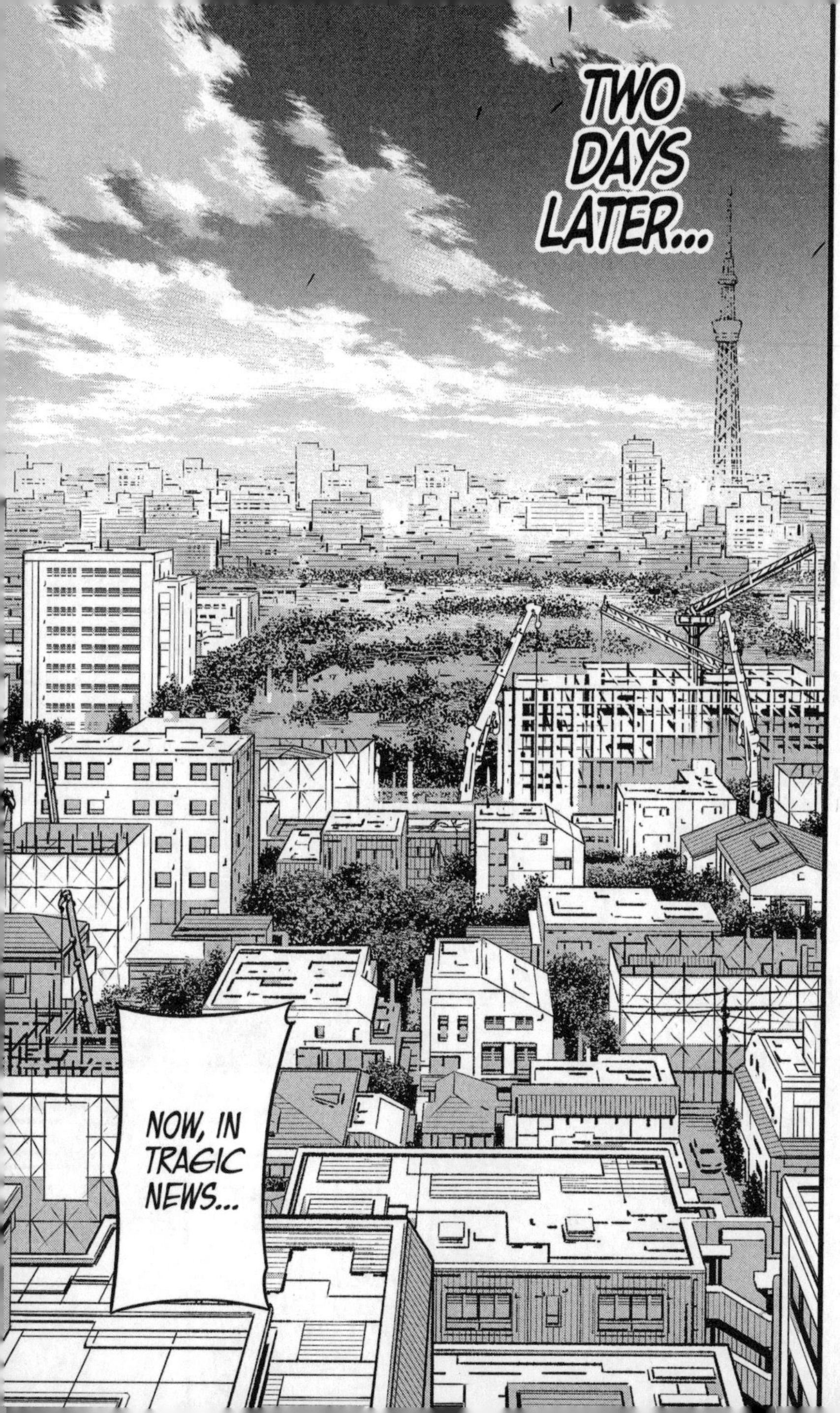
TWO DAYS LATER...
NOW, IN TRAGIC NEWS...

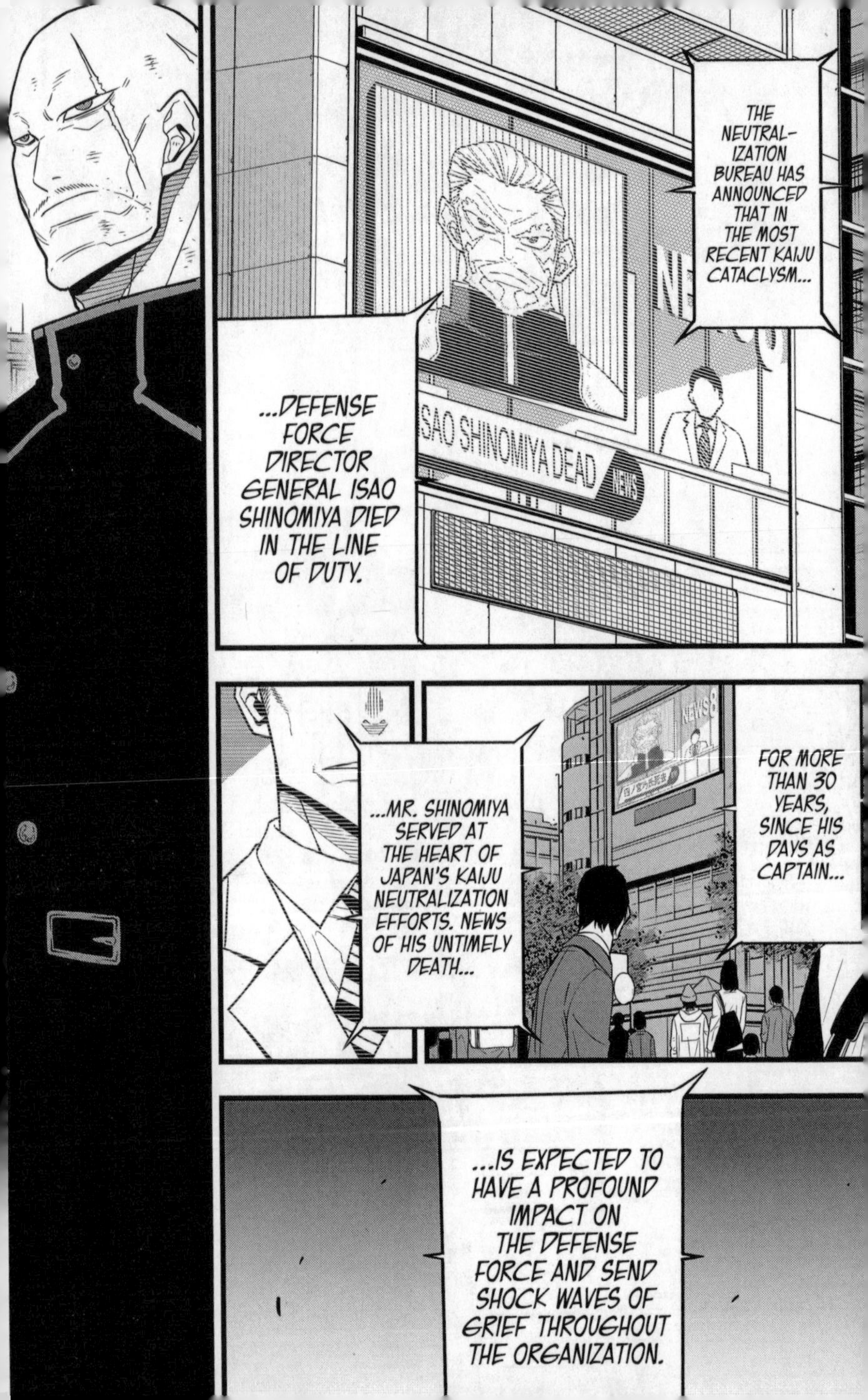
THE NEUTRAL-IZATION BUREAU HAS ANNOUNCED THAT IN THE MOST RECENT KAIJU CATACLYSM...
...DEFENSE FORCE DIRECTOR GENERAL ISAO SHINOMIYA DIED IN THE LINE OF DUTY.
SAO SHINOMIYA DEAD
NEWS
FOR MORE THAN 30 YEARS, SINCE HIS DAYS AS CAPTAIN...
...MR. SHINOMIYA SERVED AT THE HEART OF JAPAN'S KAIJU NEUTRALIZATION EFFORTS. NEWS OF HIS UNTIMELY DEATH...
...IS EXPECTED TO HAVE A PROFOUND IMPACT ON THE DEFENSE FORCE AND SEND SHOCK WAVES OF GRIEF THROUGHOUT THE ORGANIZATION.

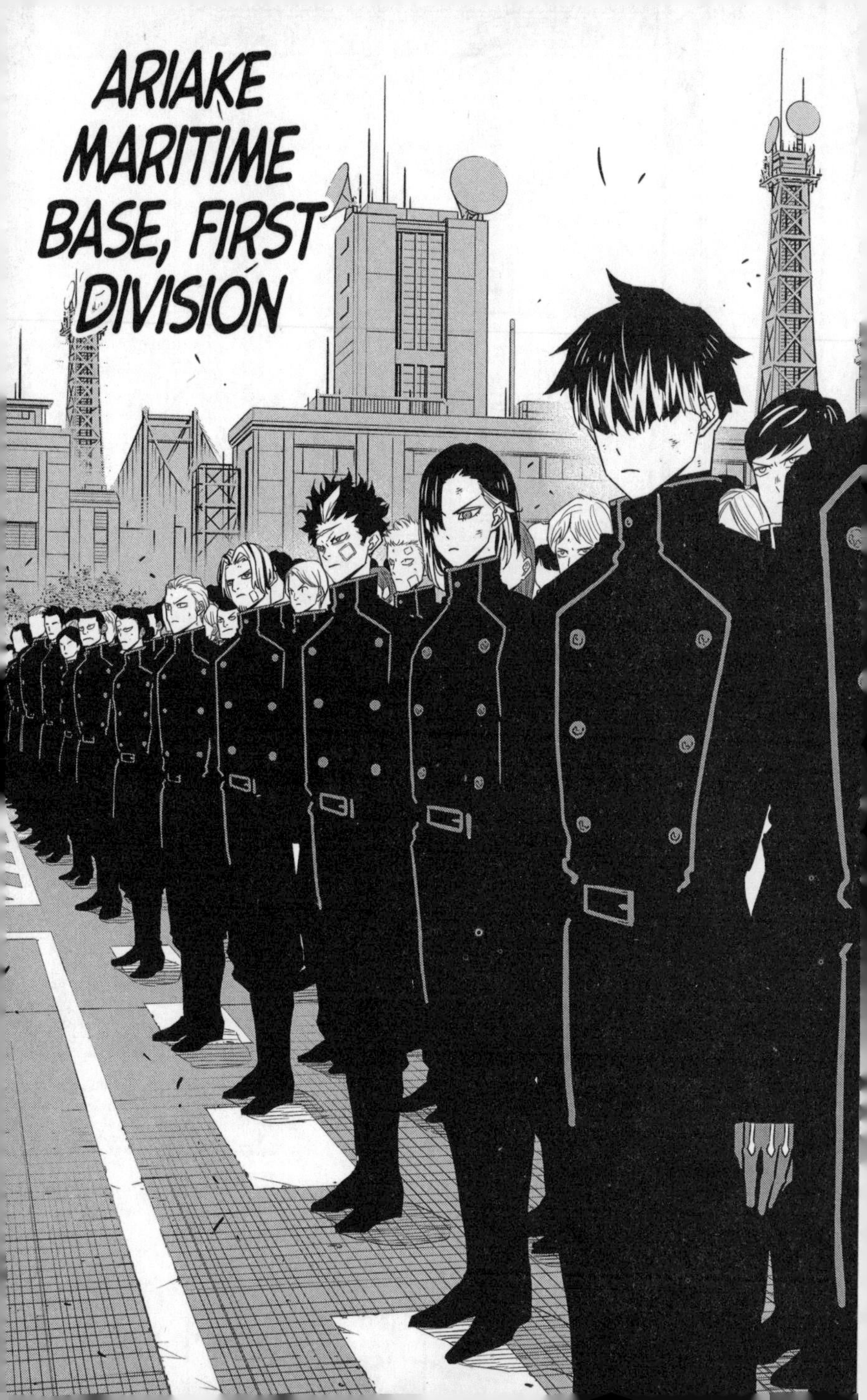
ARIAKE MARITIME BASE, FIRST DIVISION

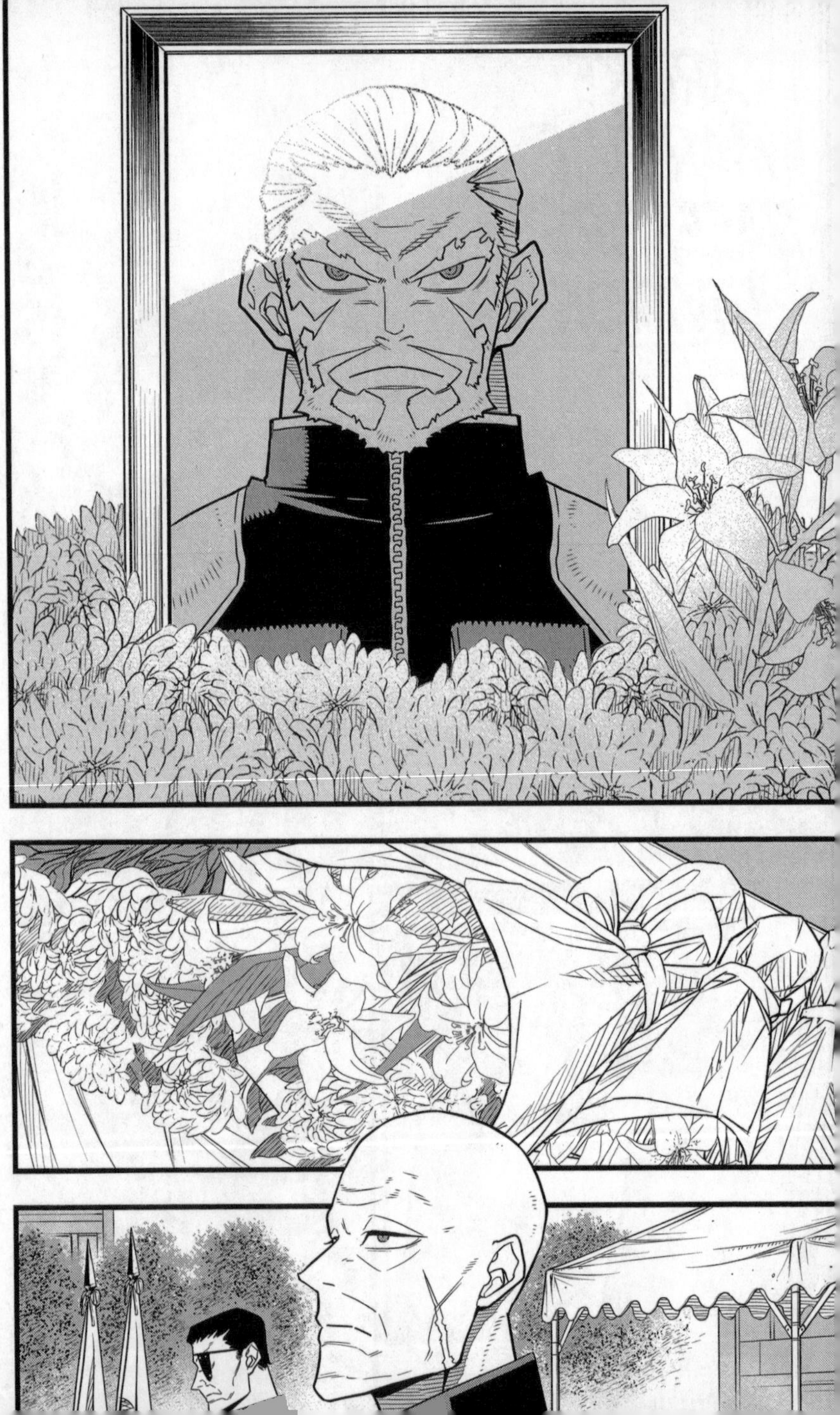

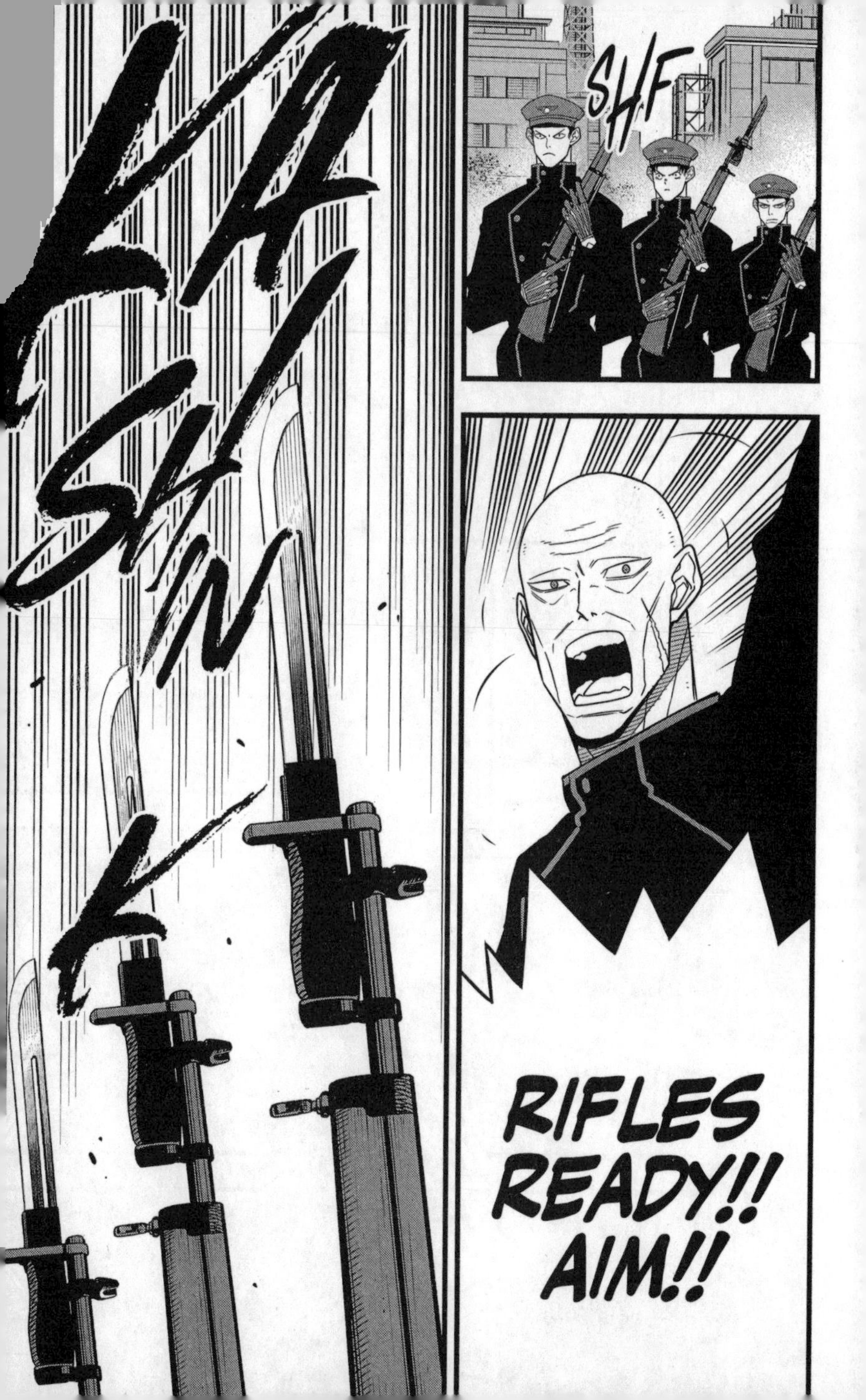
SHF
RIFLES READY!! AIM!!
KA SHNK

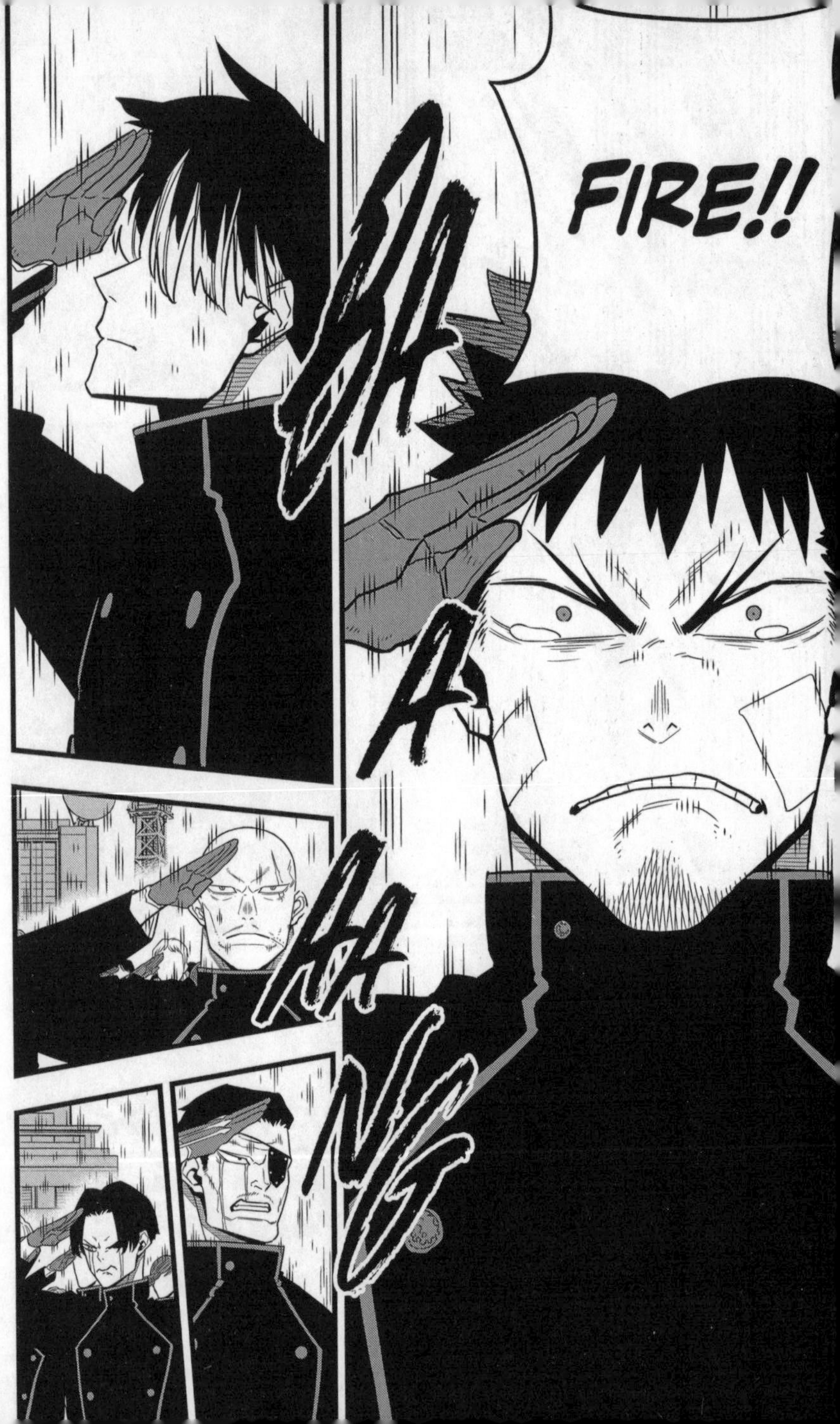
FIRE!!
BAAAANG

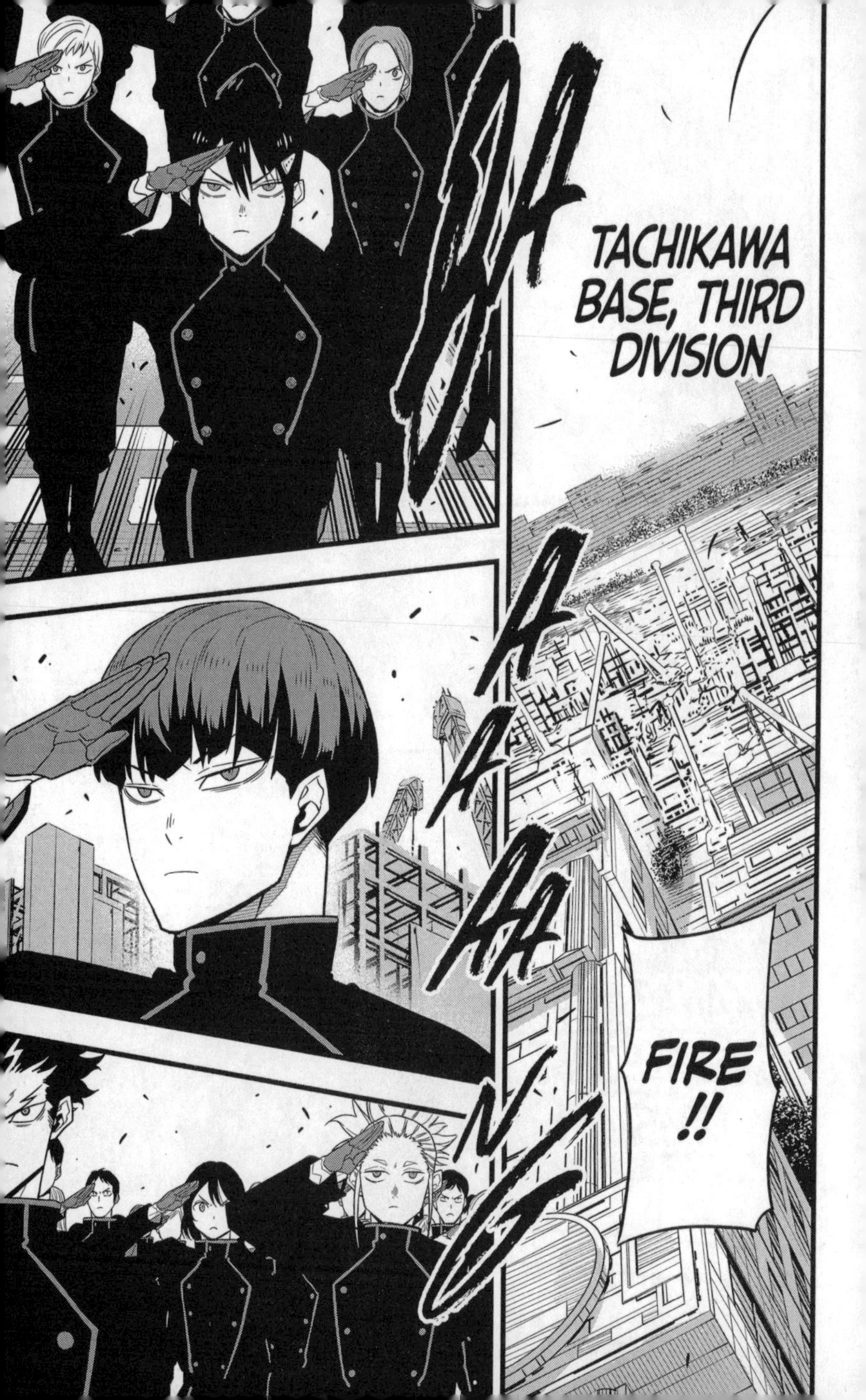
TACHIKAWA BASE, THIRD DIVISION
FIRE !!

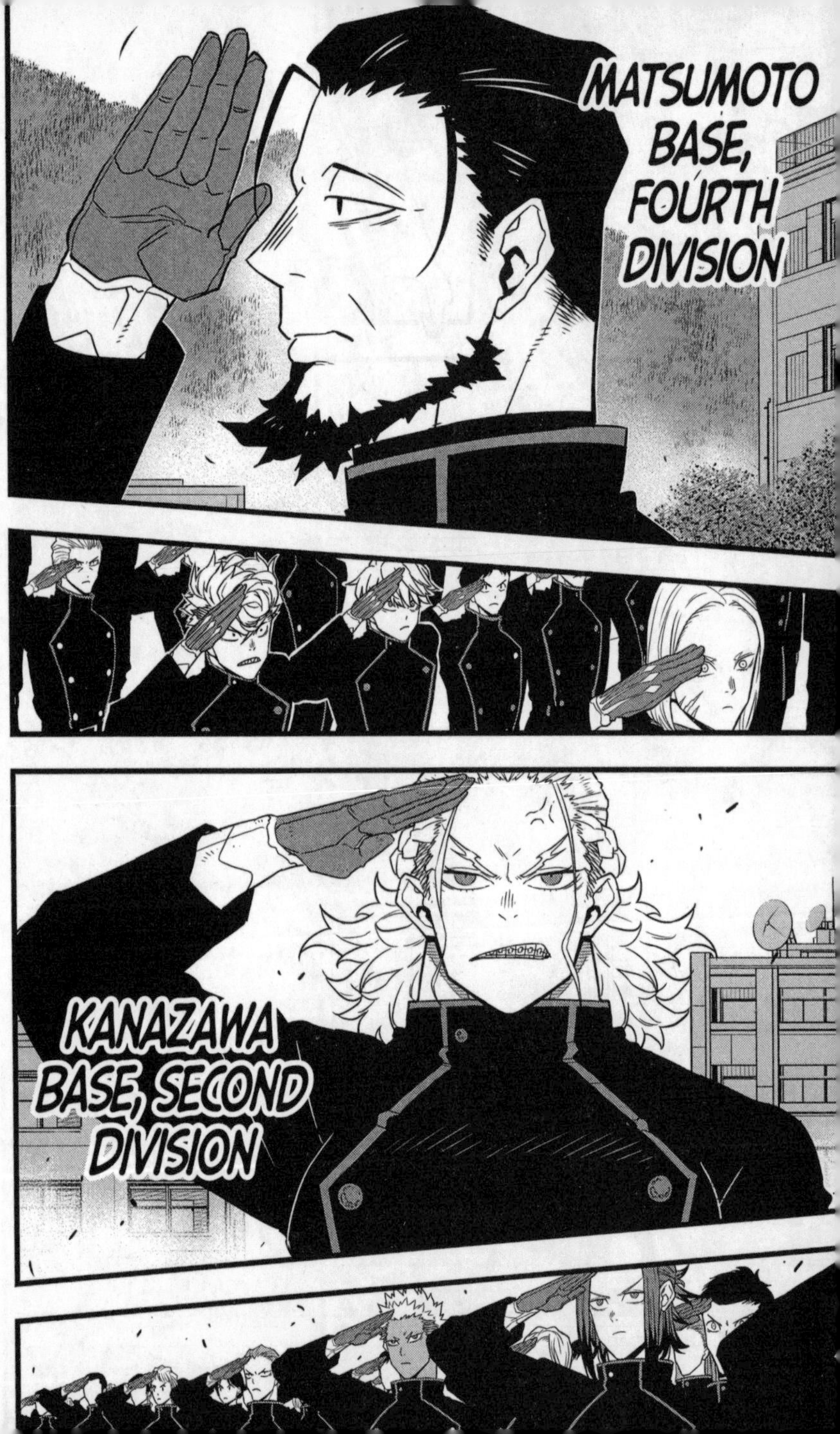
MATSUMOTO BASE, FOURTH DIVISION
KANAZAWA BASE, SECOND DIVISION

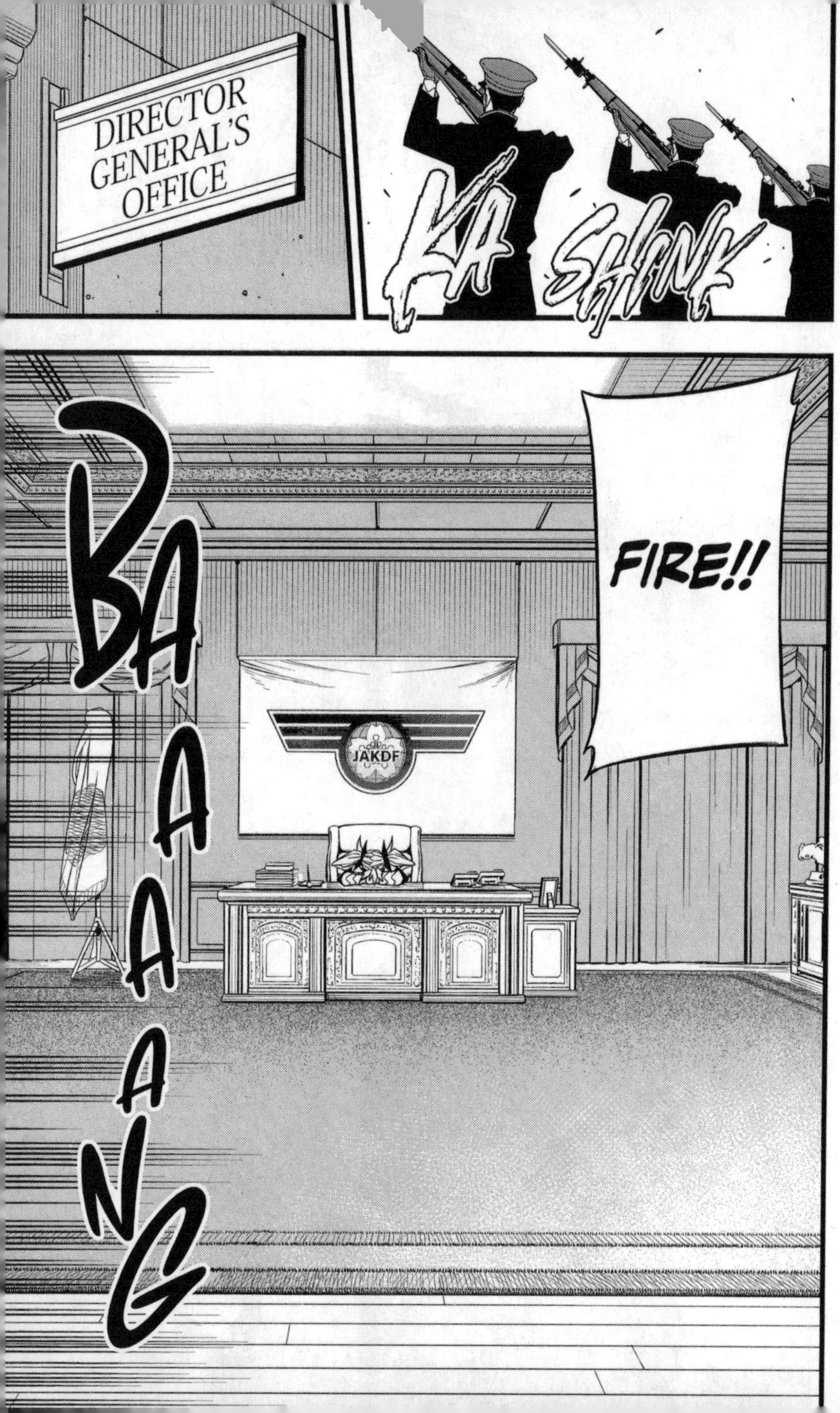
KA SHINK
DIRECTOR GENERAL'S OFFICE
FIRE!!
JAKDF
BAAAANG

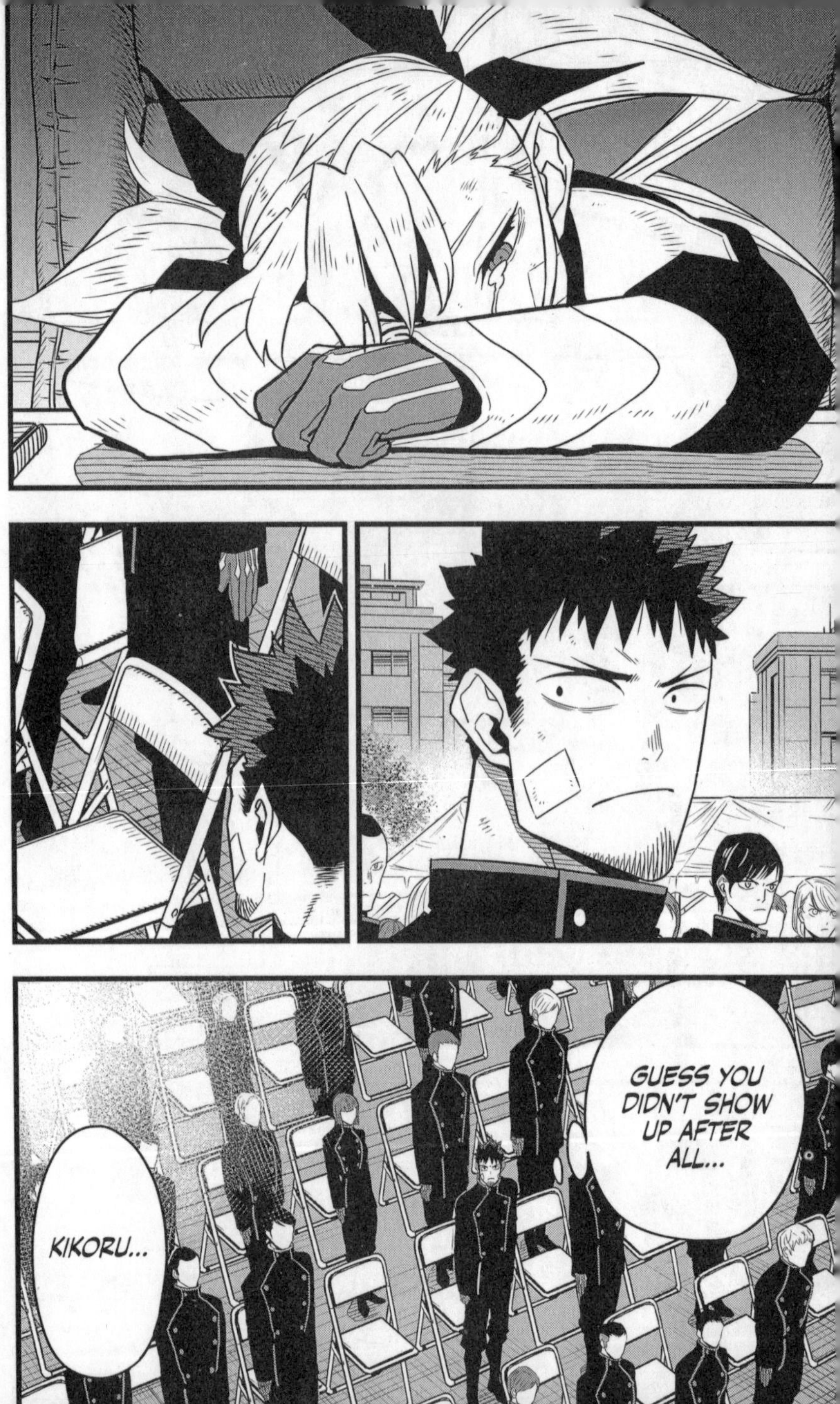
GUESS YOU DIDN'T SHOW UP AFTER ALL...
KIKORU...

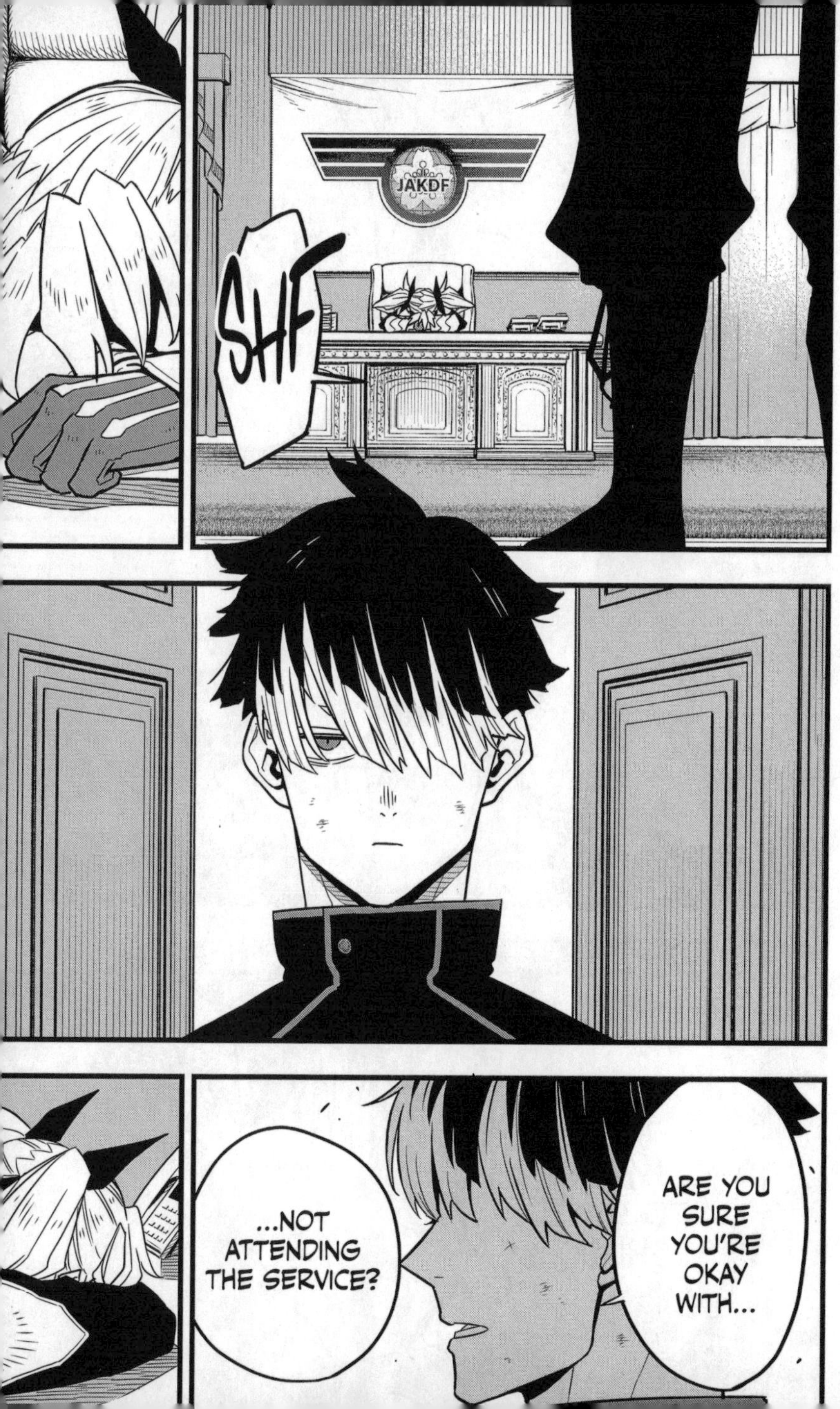
JAKDF
SHF
ARE YOU SURE YOU'RE OKAY WITH...
...NOT ATTENDING THE SERVICE?

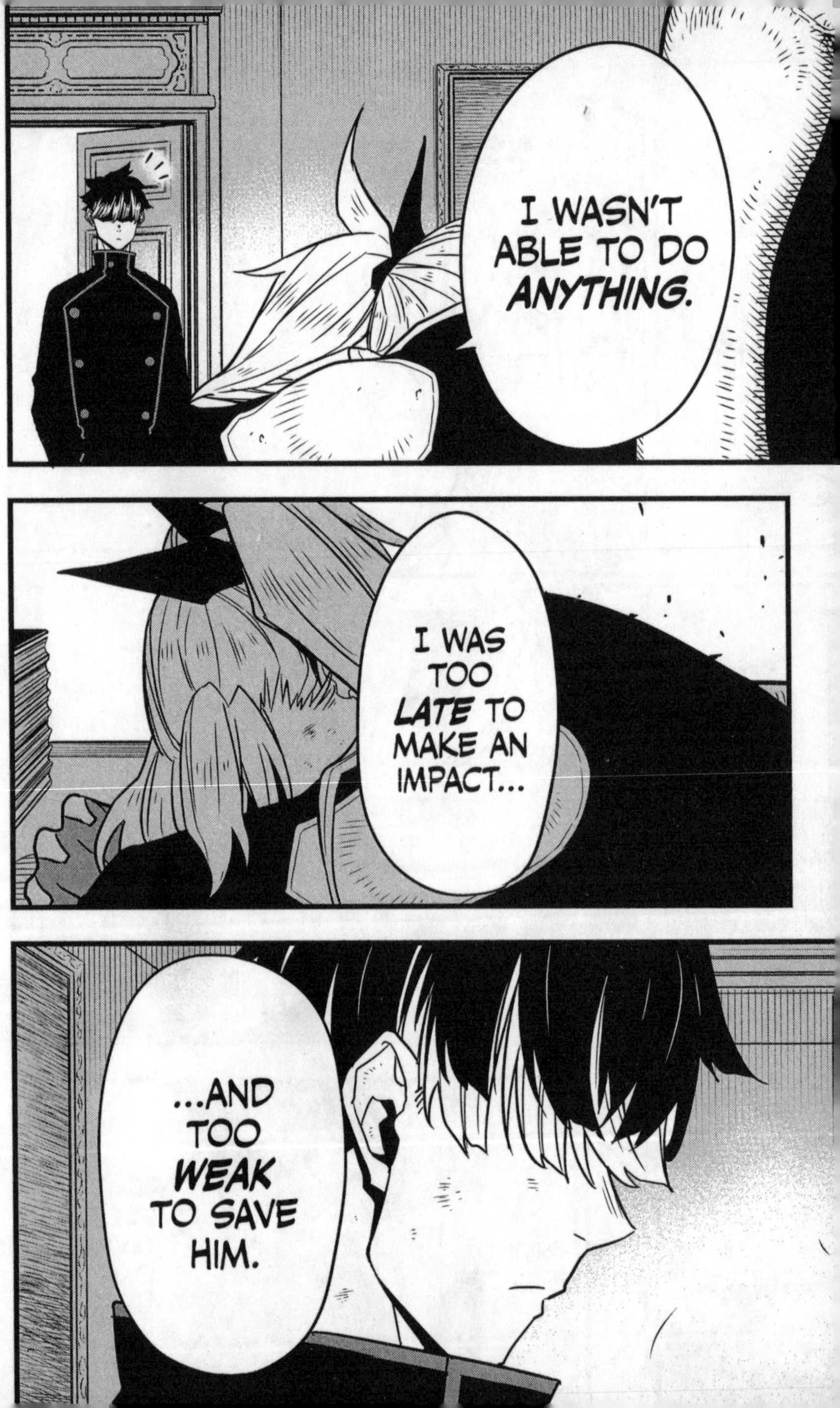
I WASN'T ABLE TO DO ANYTHING.
I WAS TOO LATE TO MAKE AN IMPACT...
...AND TOO WEAK TO SAVE HIM.

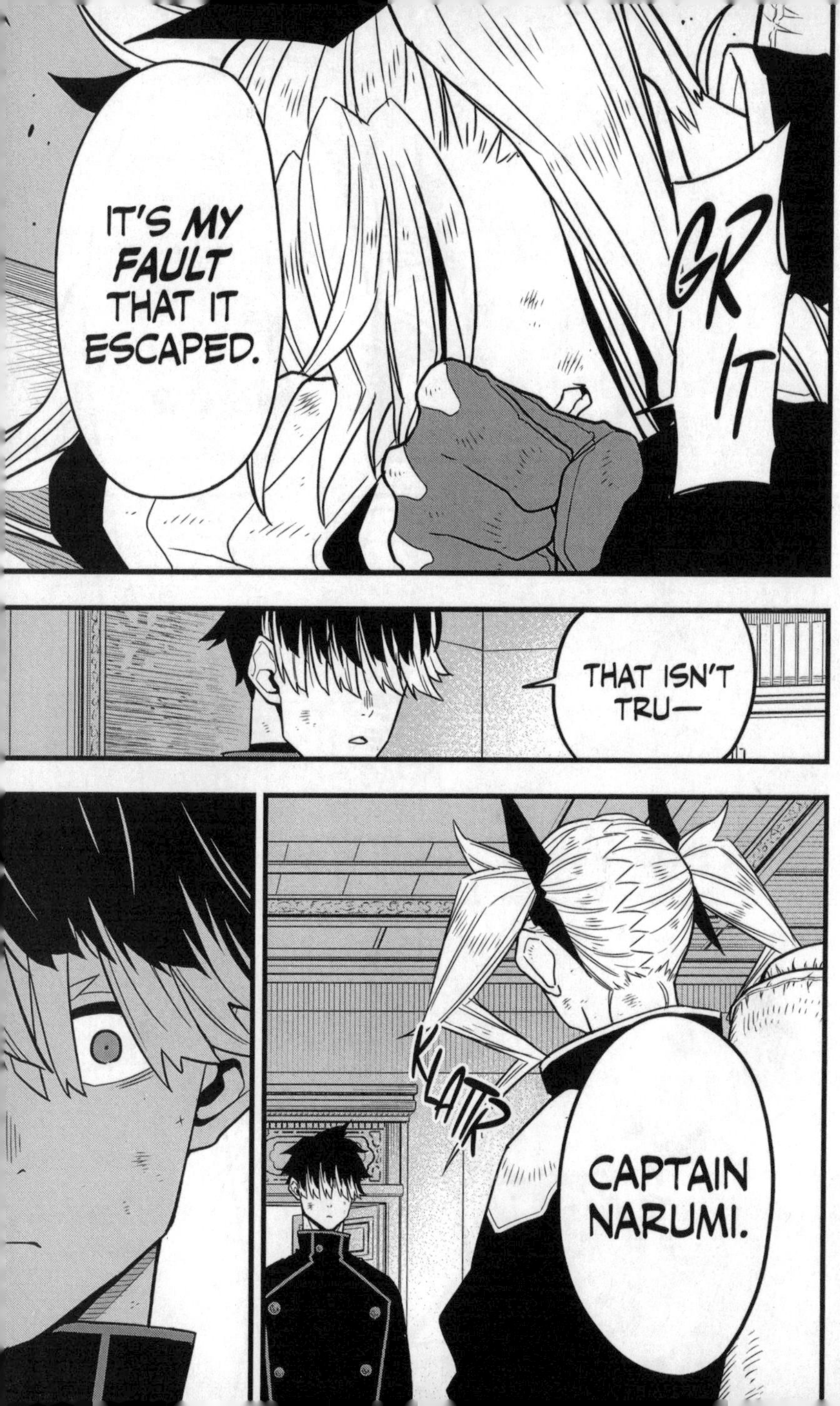
GRIT
IT'S MY FAULT THAT IT ESCAPED.
THAT ISN'T TRU—
CAPTAIN NARUMI.
KLATR

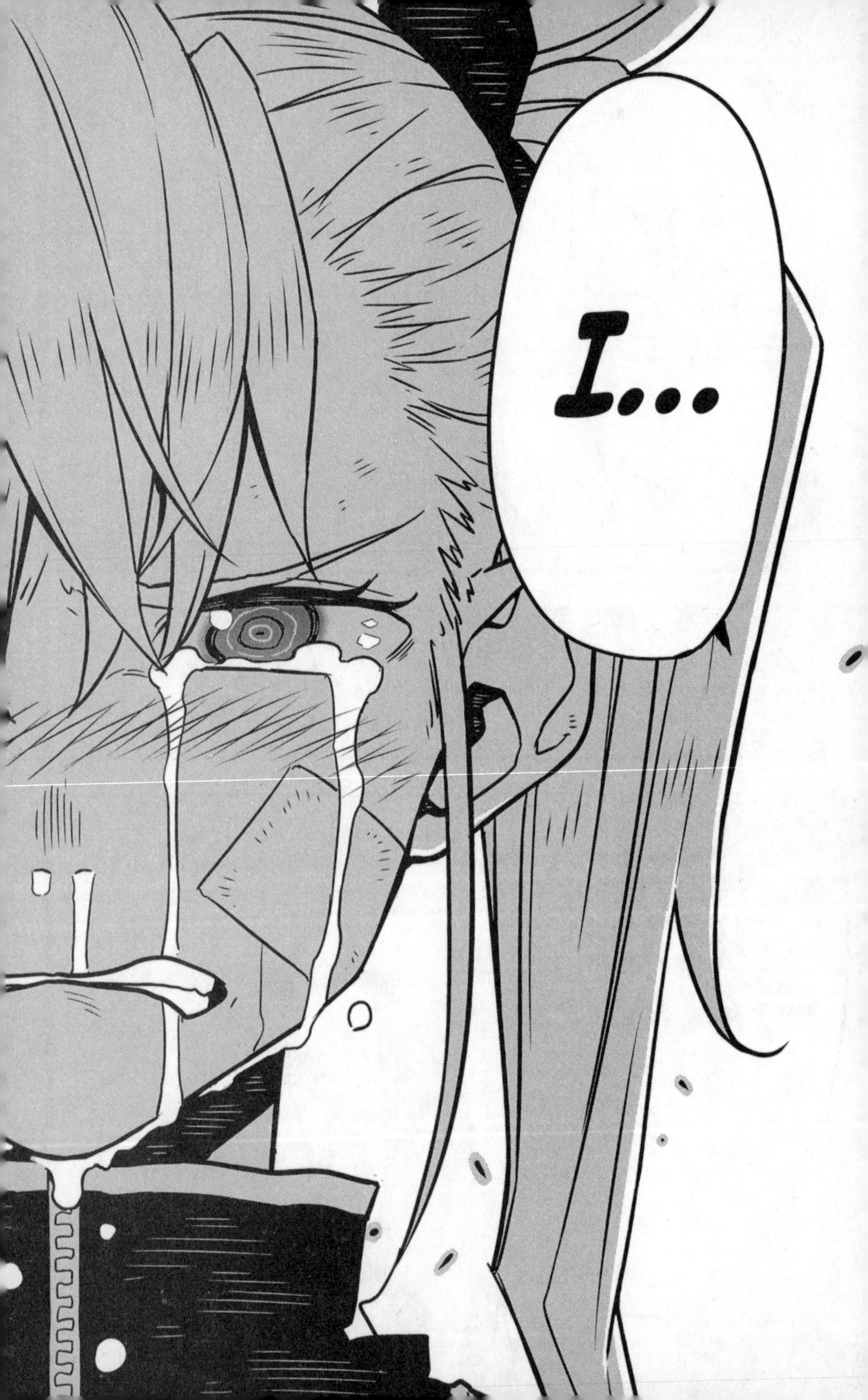
I...

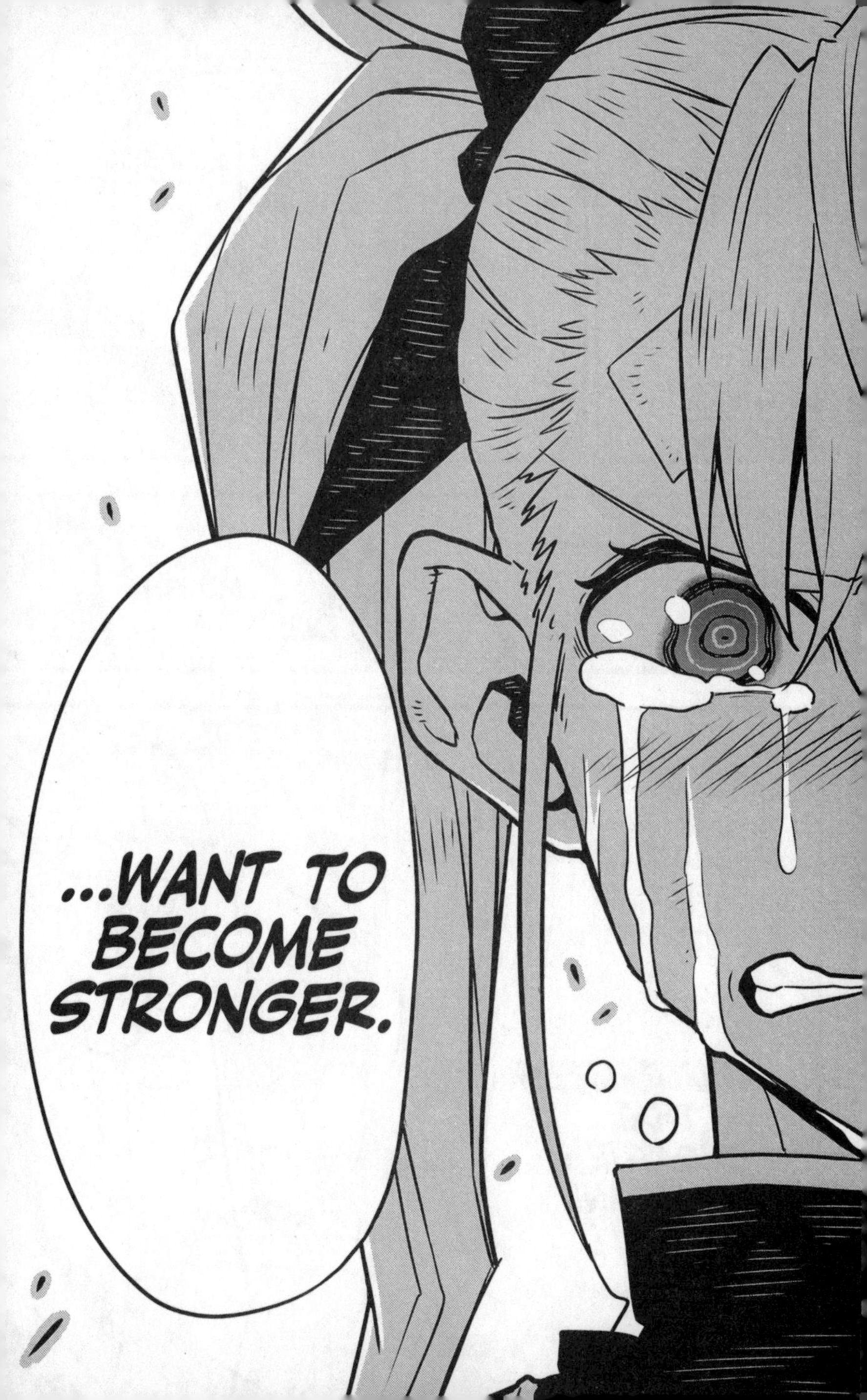
...WANT TO BECOME STRONGER.

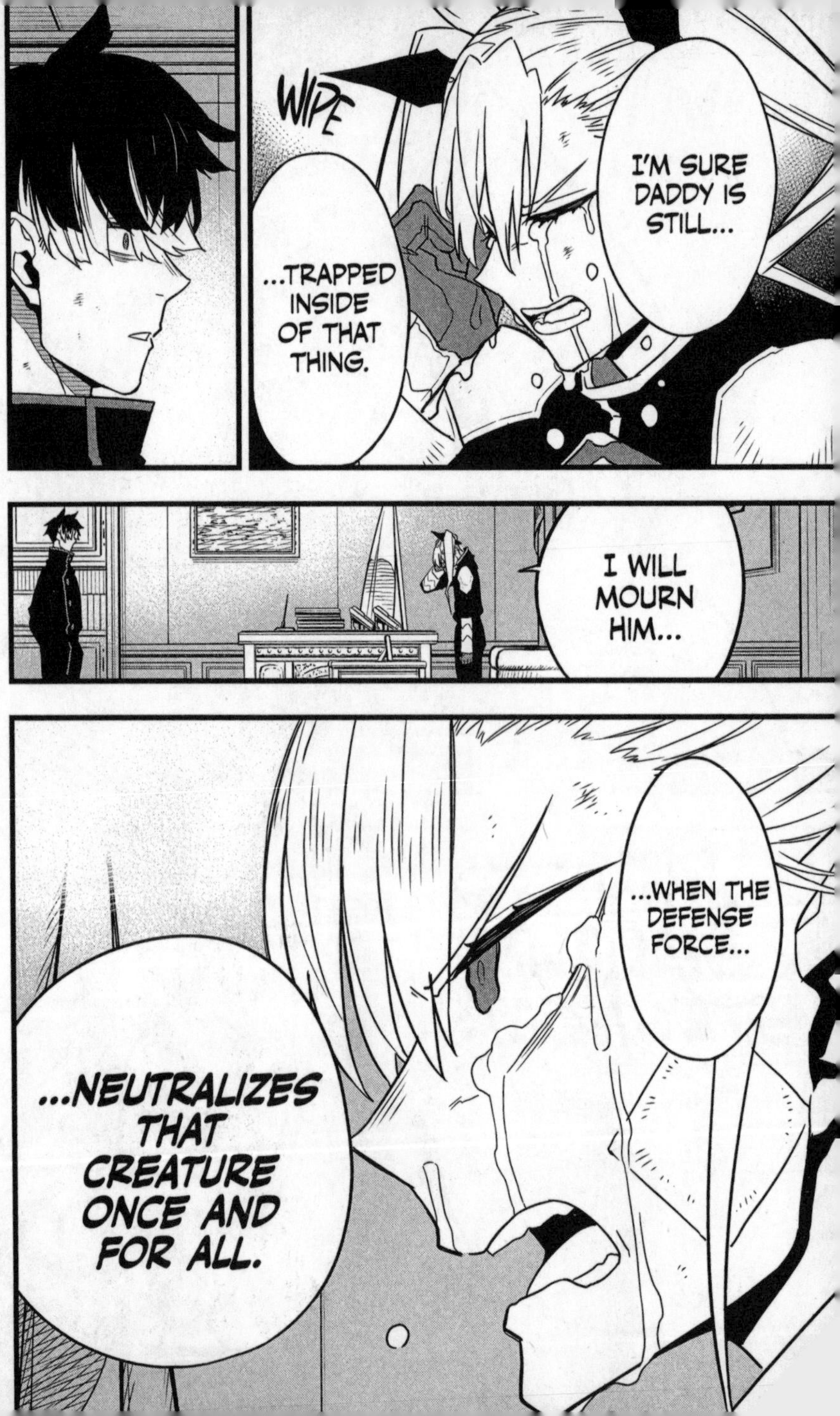

I'M SURE DADDY IS STILL...
WIPE
...TRAPPED INSIDE OF THAT THING.
I WILL MOURN HIM...
...WHEN THE DEFENSE FORCE...
...NEUTRALIZES THAT CREATURE ONCE AND FOR ALL.

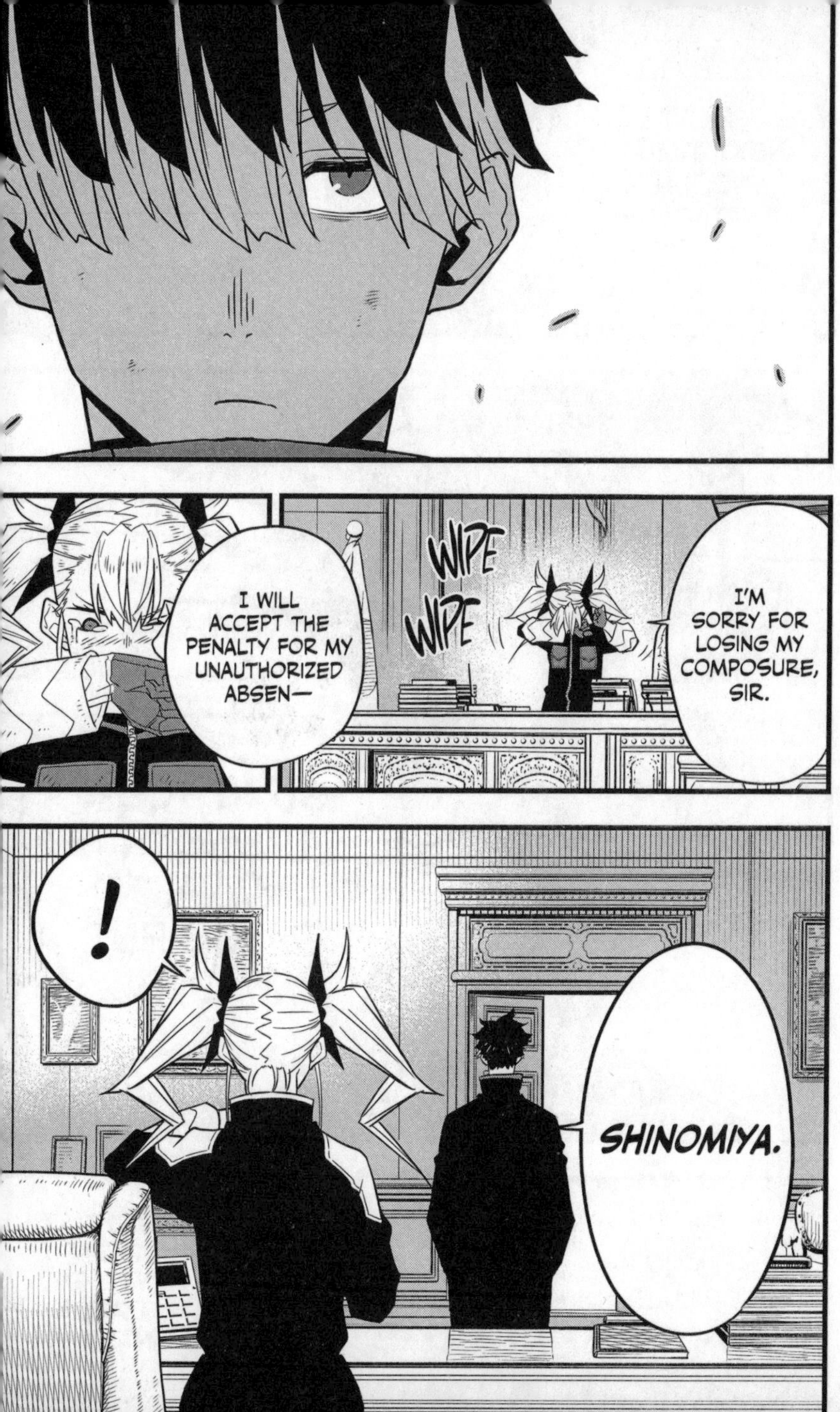

I'M SORRY FOR LOSING MY COMPOSURE, SIR.
WIPE WIPE
I WILL ACCEPT THE PENALTY FOR MY UNAUTHORIZED ABSEN—
SHINOMIYA.
!

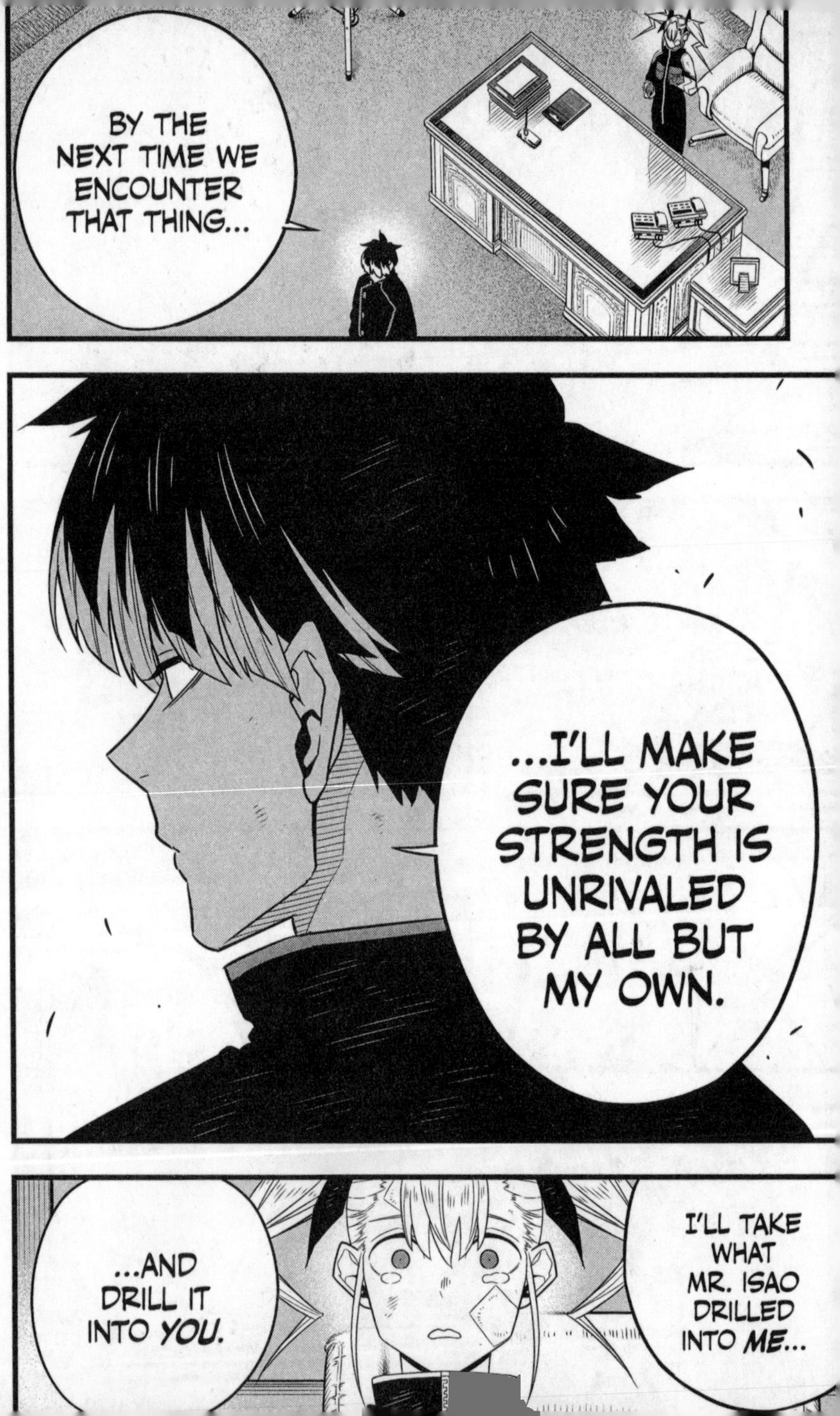
BY THE NEXT TIME WE ENCOUNTER THAT THING...
...I'LL MAKE SURE YOUR STRENGTH IS UNRIVALED BY ALL BUT MY OWN.
I'LL TAKE WHAT MR. ISAO DRILLED INTO *ME*...
...AND DRILL IT INTO *YOU*.

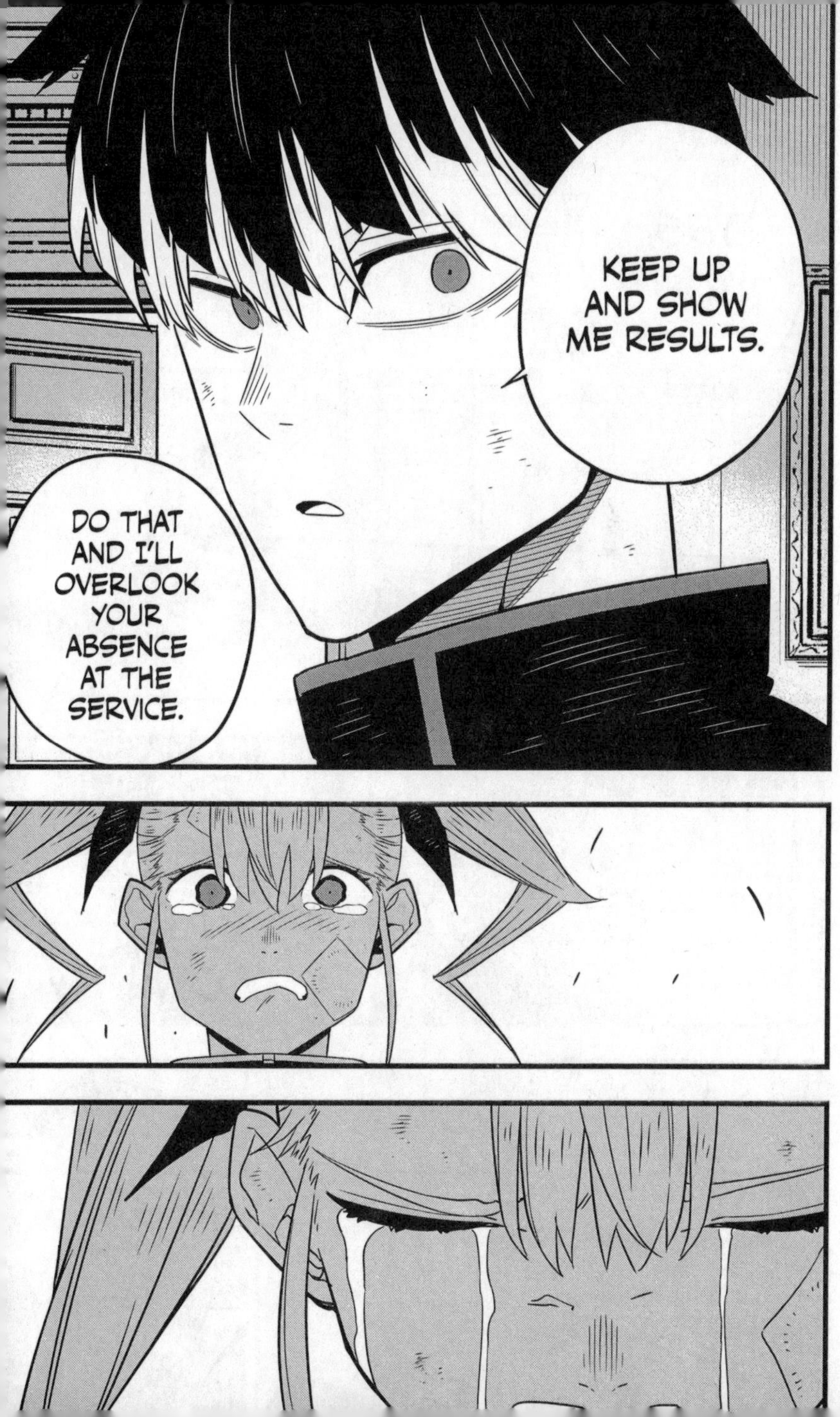
KEEP UP AND SHOW ME RESULTS.
DO THAT AND I'LL OVERLOOK YOUR ABSENCE AT THE SERVICE.

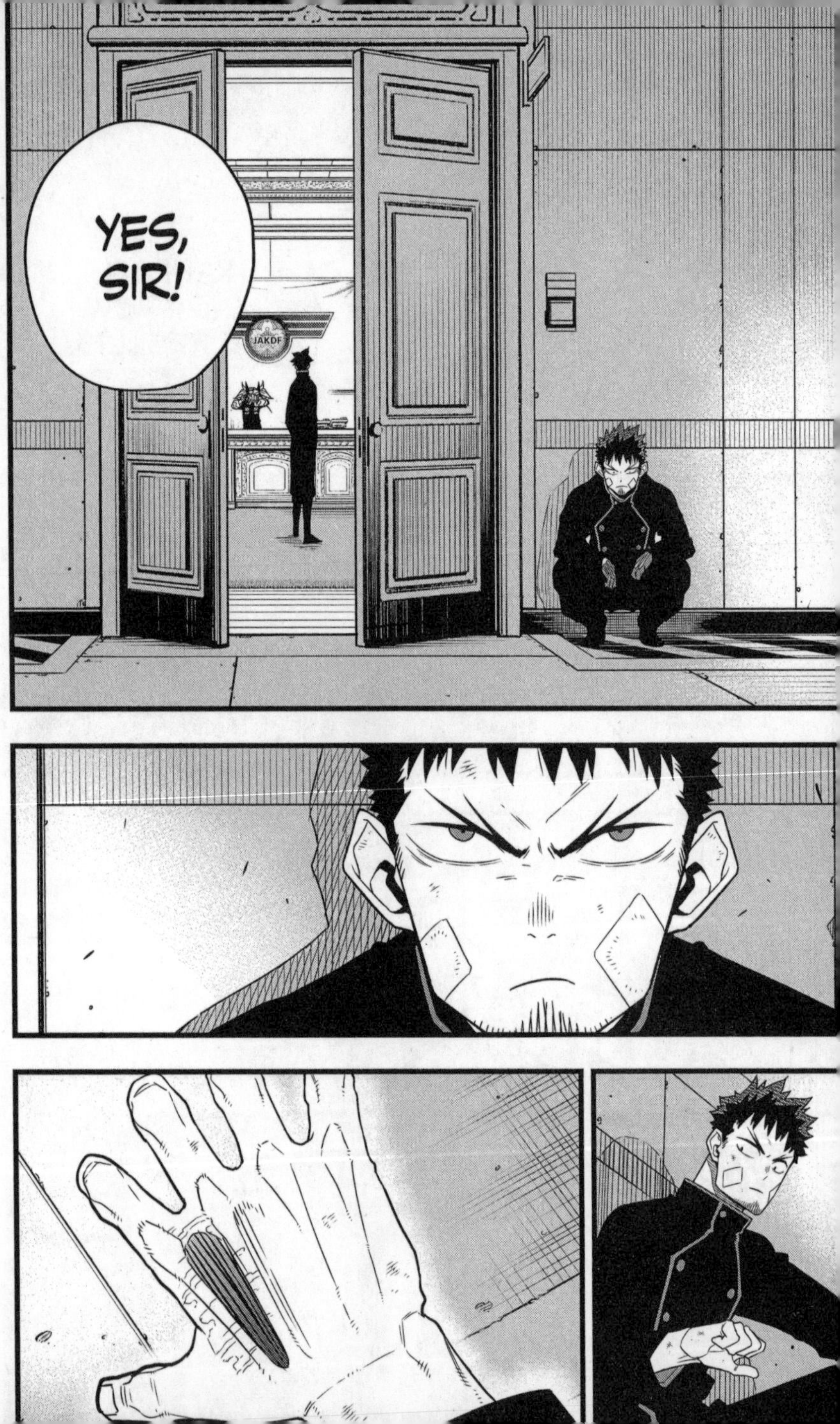
YES, SIR!
JAKDF

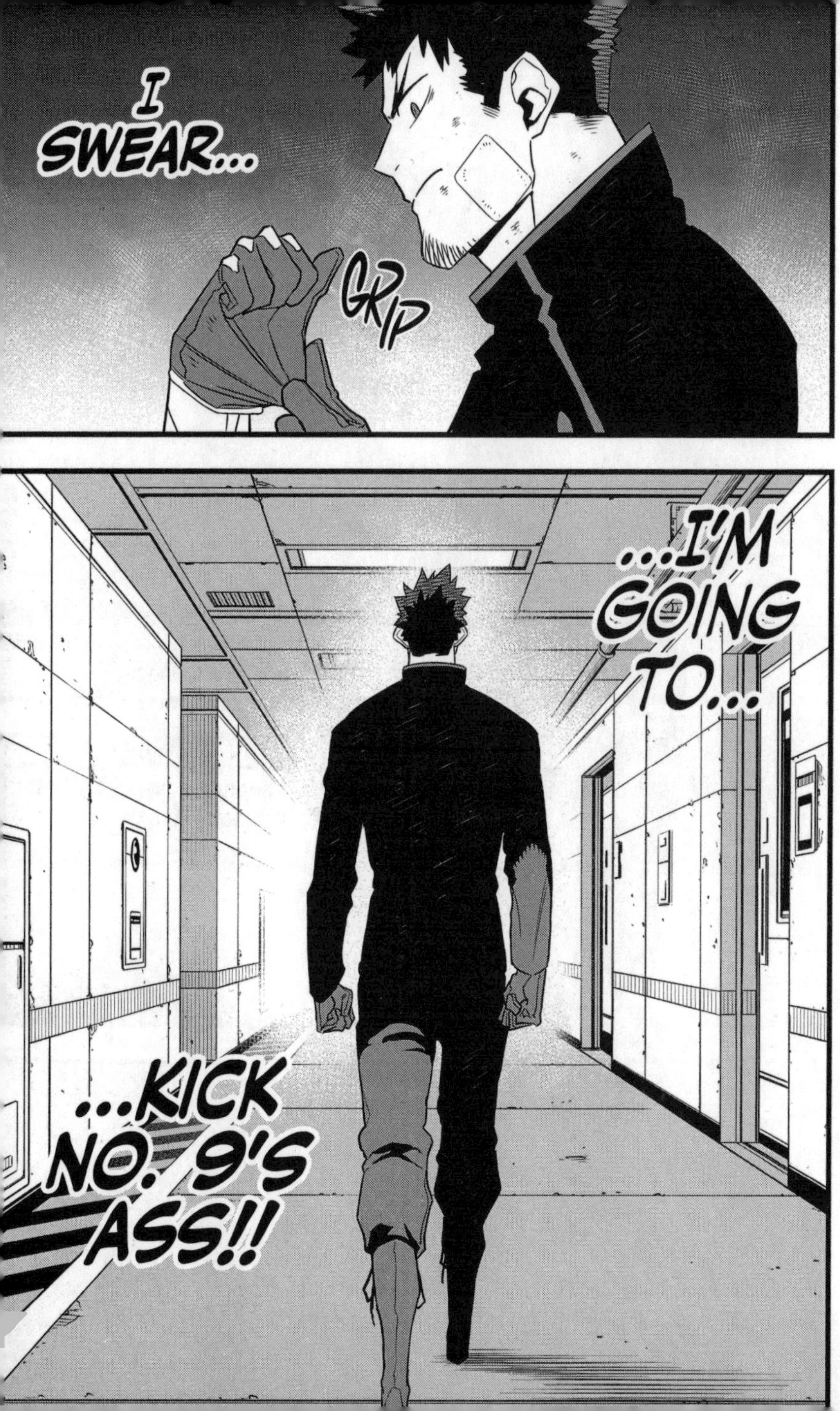
I SWEAR...
GRIP
...I'M GOING TO...
...KICK NO. 9'S ASS!!

RIN SHINONOME

Birthday:
January 26

Height:
165 cm

Likes:
Shopping, super-spicy food,
adversity

Author Comment:
The powerful platoon leader of
the elite gathering ground—
the First Division. Never losing her
composure, she prefers to view the
world through an objective lens.
However, people tend to be afraid
of her. She likes Kikoru's strong-
willed, never-back-down attitude.

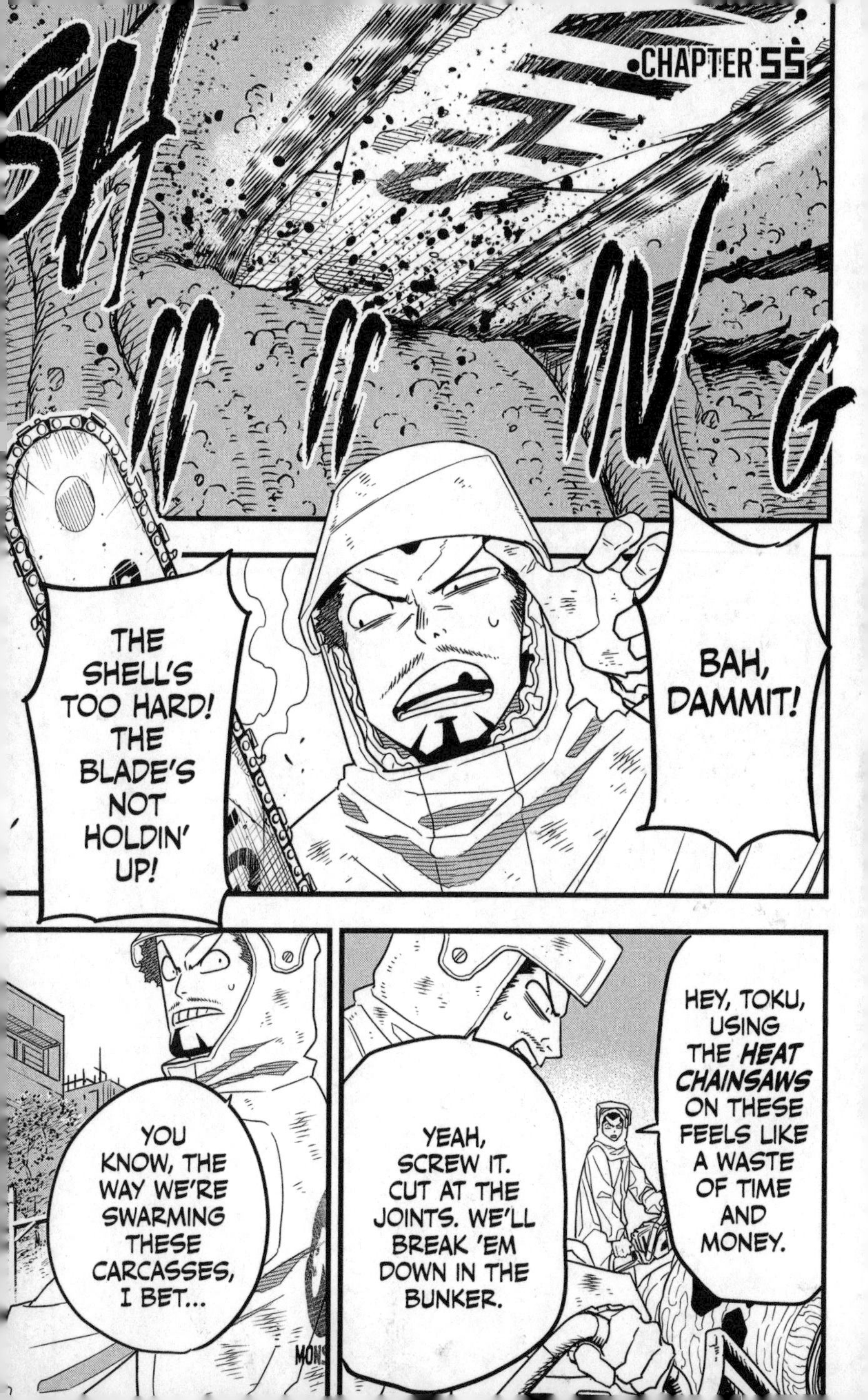
CHAPTER 55
SHIING
BAH, DAMMIT!
THE SHELL'S TOO HARD! THE BLADE'S NOT HOLDIN' UP!
HEY, TOKU, USING THE *HEAT CHAINSAWS* ON THESE FEELS LIKE A WASTE OF TIME AND MONEY.
YEAH, SCREW IT. CUT AT THE JOINTS. WE'LL BREAK 'EM DOWN IN THE BUNKER.
YOU KNOW, THE WAY WE'RE SWARMING THESE CARCASSES, I BET...

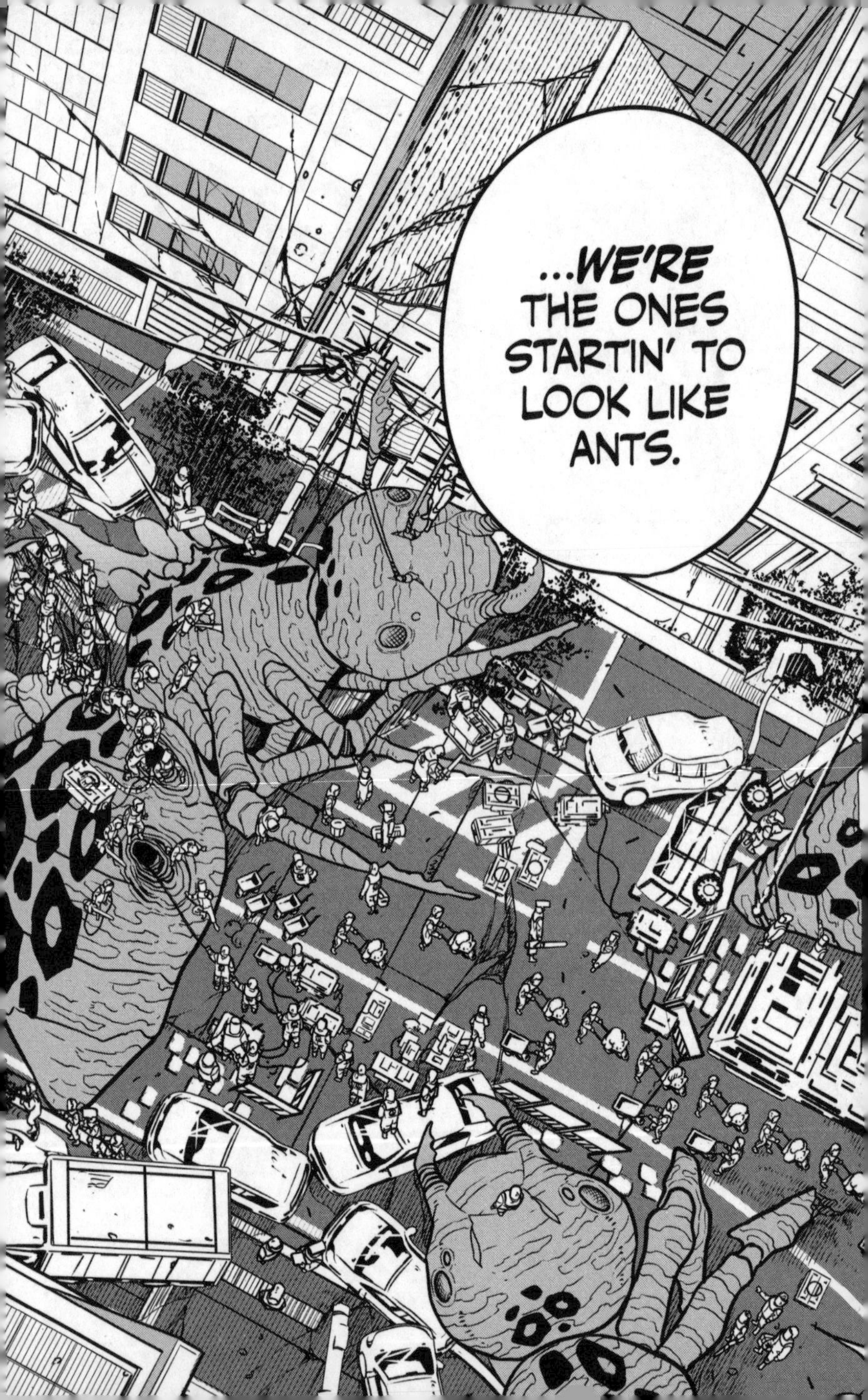
...WE'RE THE ONES STARTIN' TO LOOK LIKE ANTS.

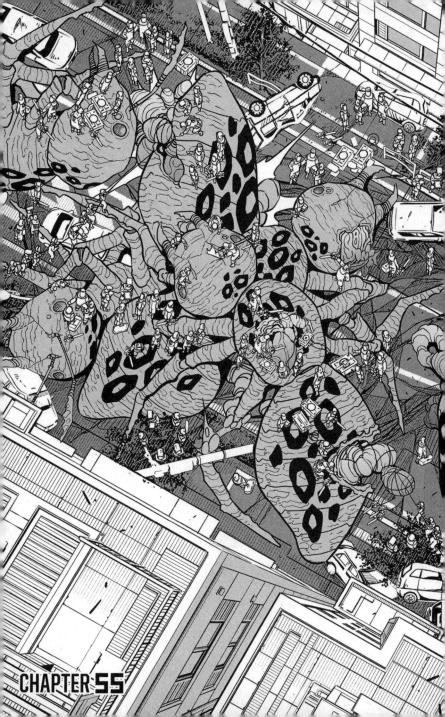

CHAPTER 55

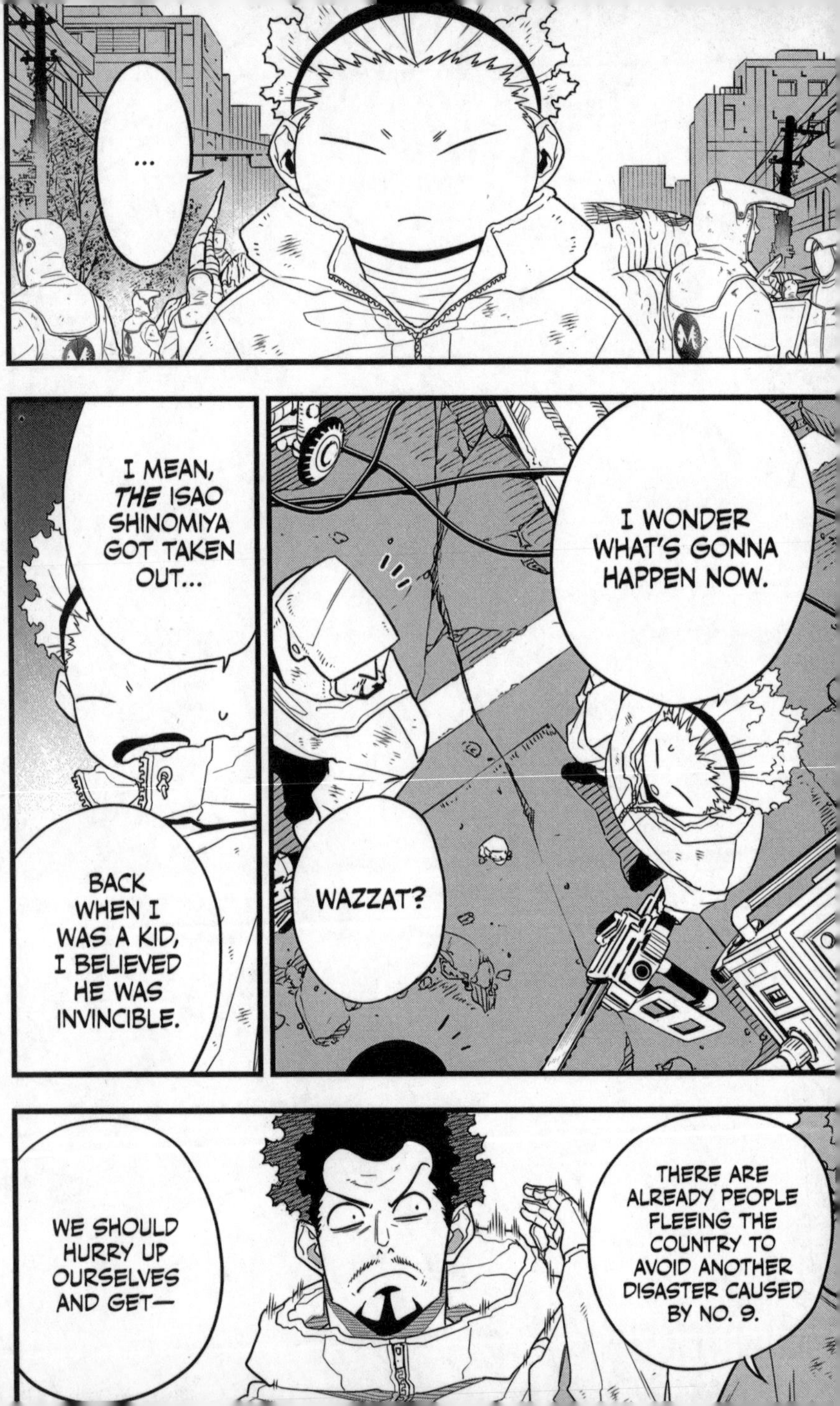
...
I WONDER WHAT'S GONNA HAPPEN NOW.
WAZZAT?
I MEAN, *THE* ISAO SHINOMIYA GOT TAKEN OUT...
BACK WHEN I WAS A KID, I BELIEVED HE WAS INVINCIBLE.
THERE ARE ALREADY PEOPLE FLEEING THE COUNTRY TO AVOID ANOTHER DISASTER CAUSED BY NO. 9.
WE SHOULD HURRY UP OURSELVES AND GET—

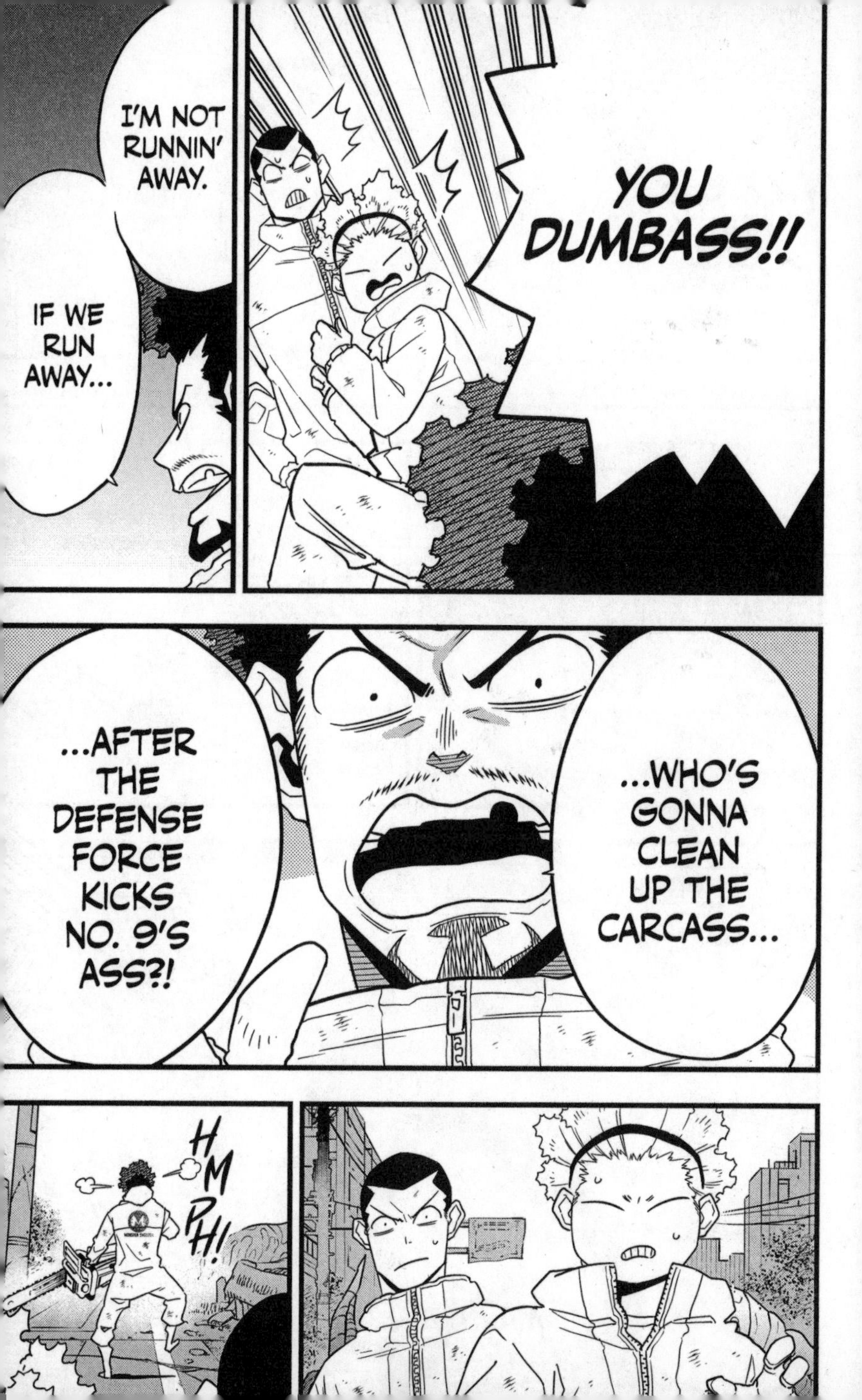
YOU DUMBASS!!
I'M NOT RUNNIN' AWAY.
IF WE RUN AWAY...
...WHO'S GONNA CLEAN UP THE CARCASS...
...AFTER THE DEFENSE FORCE KICKS NO. 9'S ASS?!
HMPH!

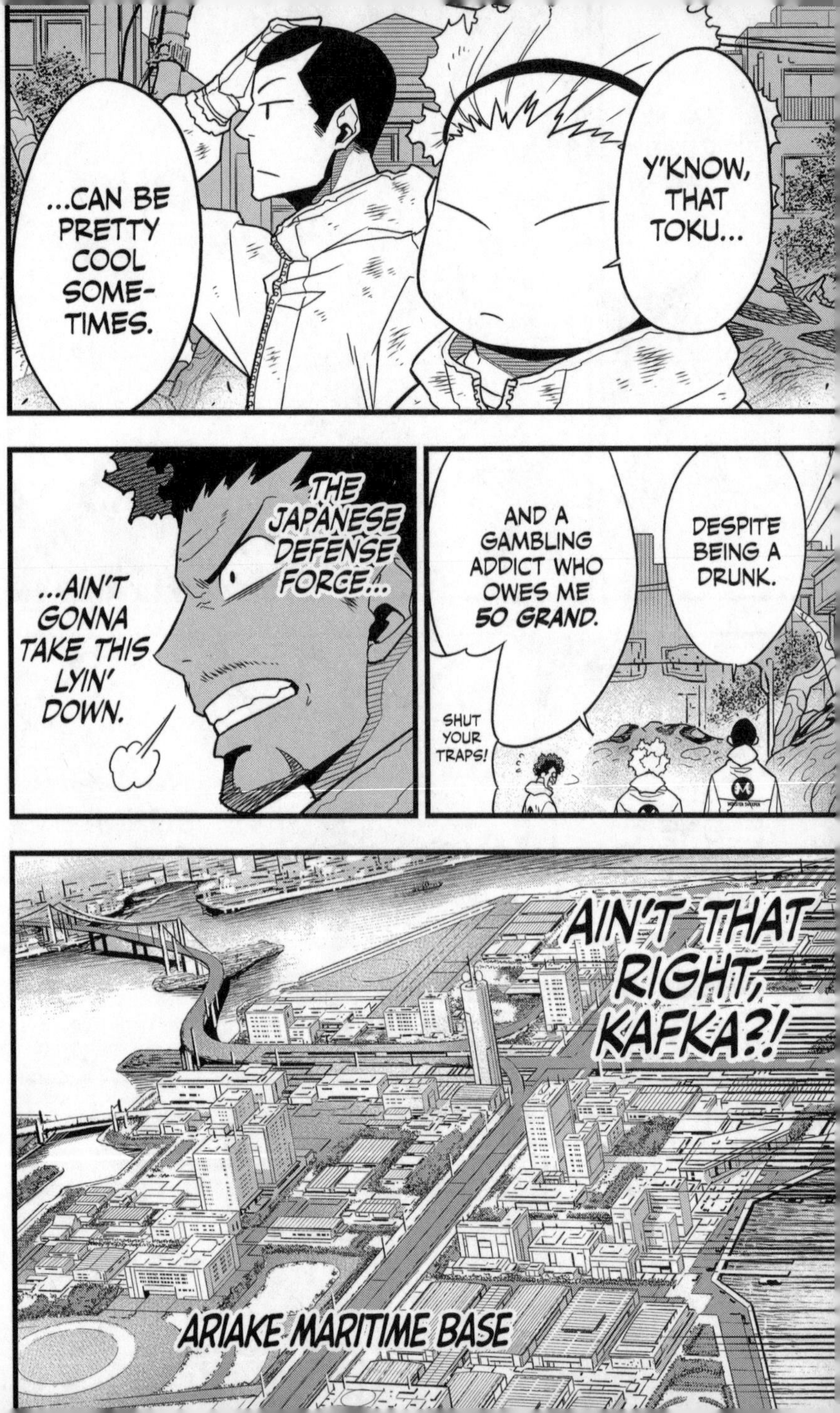
Y'KNOW, THAT TOKU...
...CAN BE PRETTY COOL SOME-TIMES.
DESPITE BEING A DRUNK.
AND A GAMBLING ADDICT WHO OWES ME 50 GRAND.
SHUT YOUR TRAPS!
THE JAPANESE DEFENSE FORCE...
...AIN'T GONNA TAKE THIS LYIN' DOWN.
AIN'T THAT RIGHT, KAFKA?!
ARIAKE MARITIME BASE

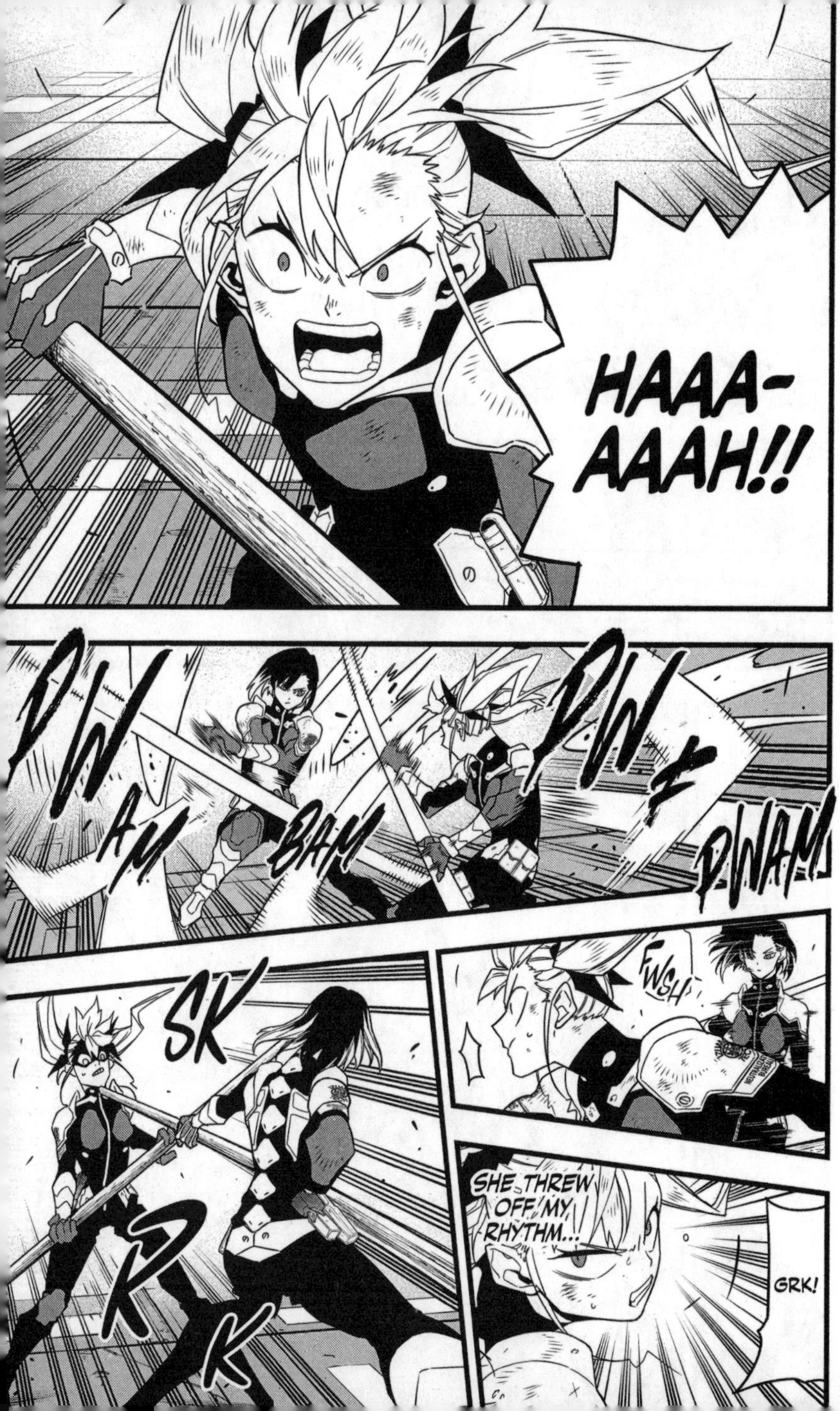
HAAAA-AAAH!!
DWAM
BAM
DWAM
FWSH
SHE THREW OFF MY RHYTHM...
GRK!
SK
SKRK

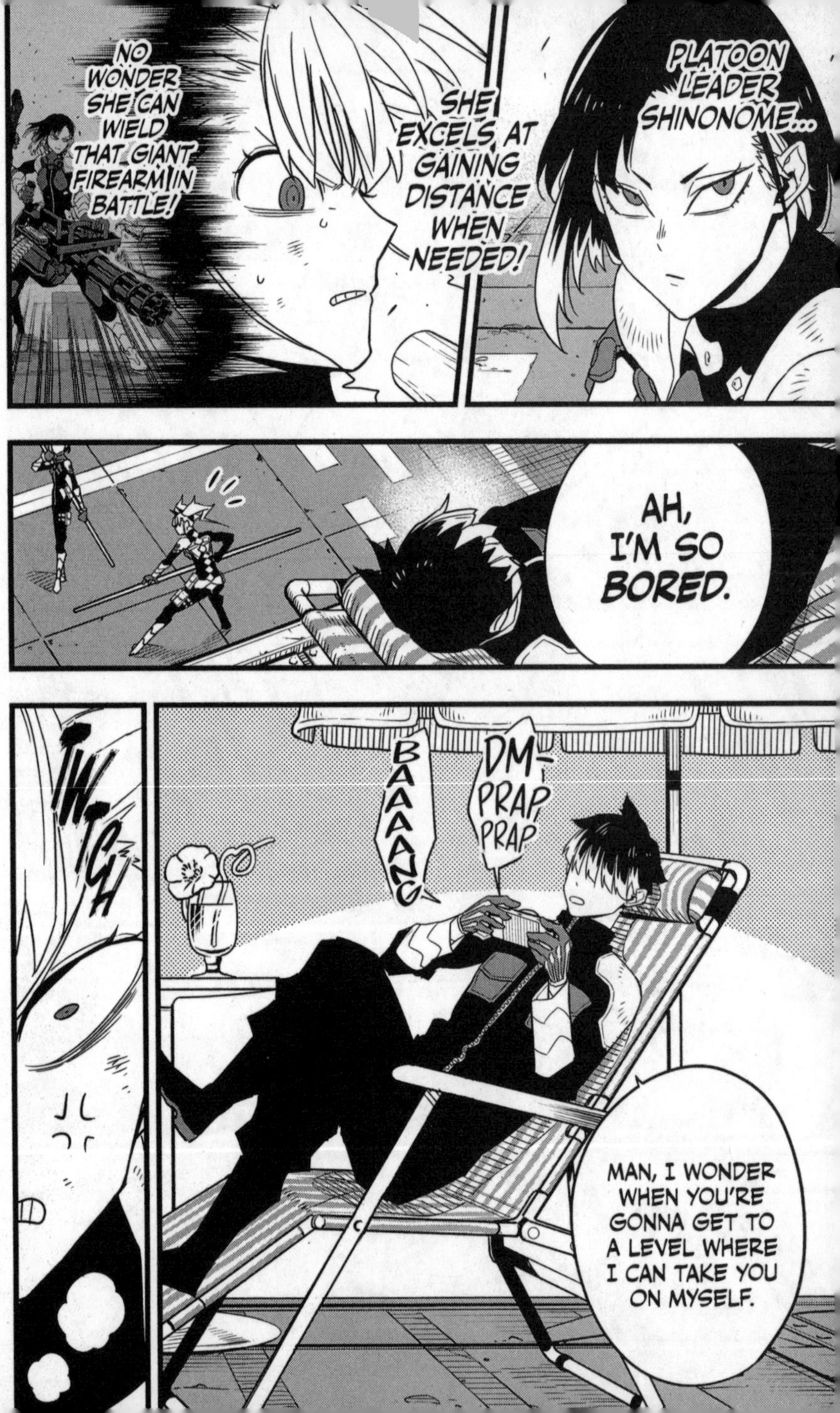
PLATOON LEADER SHINONOME...
SHE EXCELS AT GAINING DISTANCE WHEN NEEDED!
NO WONDER SHE CAN WIELD THAT GIANT FIREARM IN BATTLE!
AH, I'M SO BORED.
DM- PRAP PRAP
BAAAANG
MAN, I WONDER WHEN YOU'RE GONNA GET TO A LEVEL WHERE I CAN TAKE YOU ON MYSELF.
TWITCH

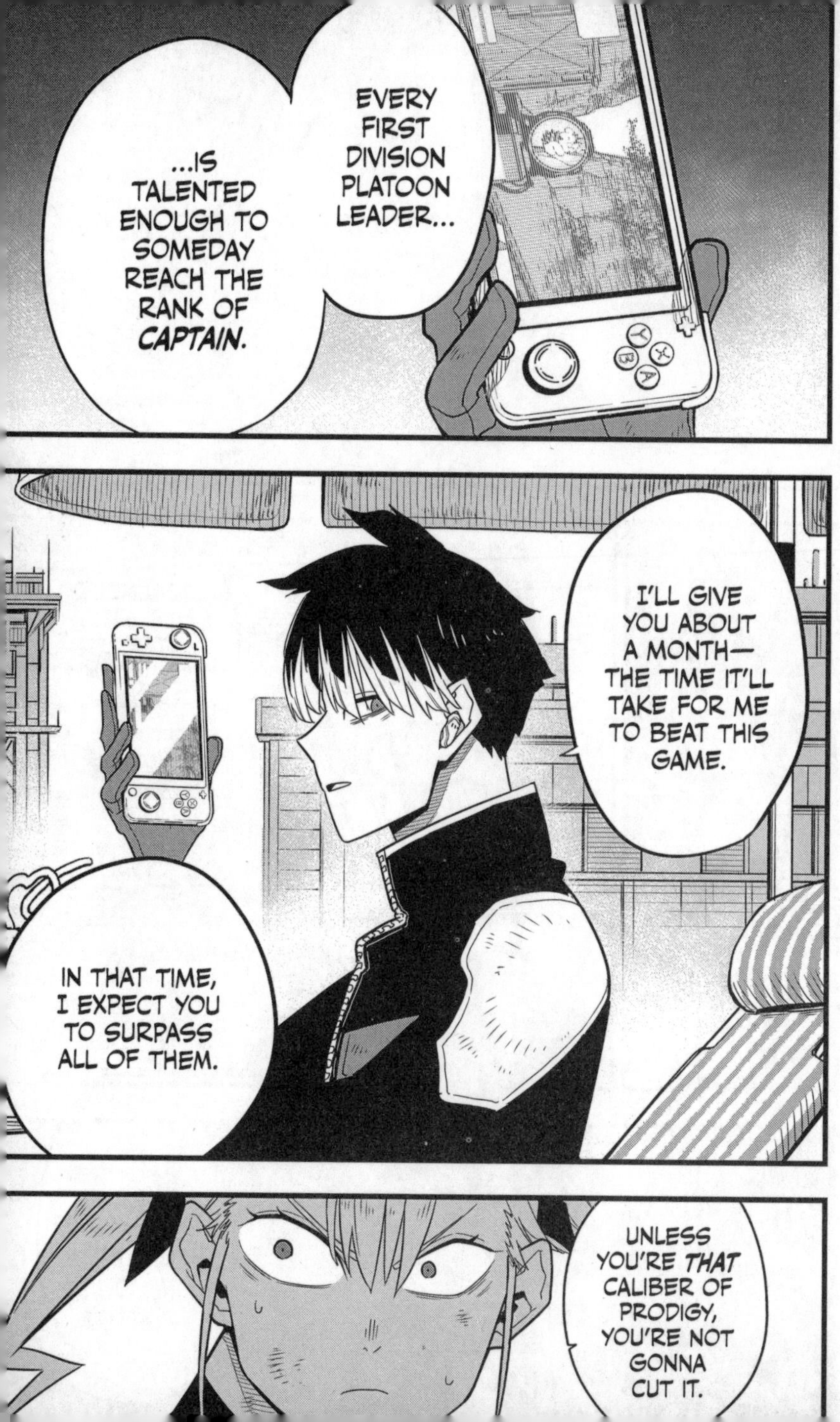
EVERY FIRST DIVISION PLATOON LEADER...
...IS TALENTED ENOUGH TO SOMEDAY REACH THE RANK OF *CAPTAIN*.
I'LL GIVE YOU ABOUT A MONTH—THE TIME IT'LL TAKE FOR ME TO BEAT THIS GAME.
IN THAT TIME, I EXPECT YOU TO SURPASS ALL OF THEM.
UNLESS YOU'RE *THAT* CALIBER OF PRODIGY, YOU'RE NOT GONNA CUT IT.

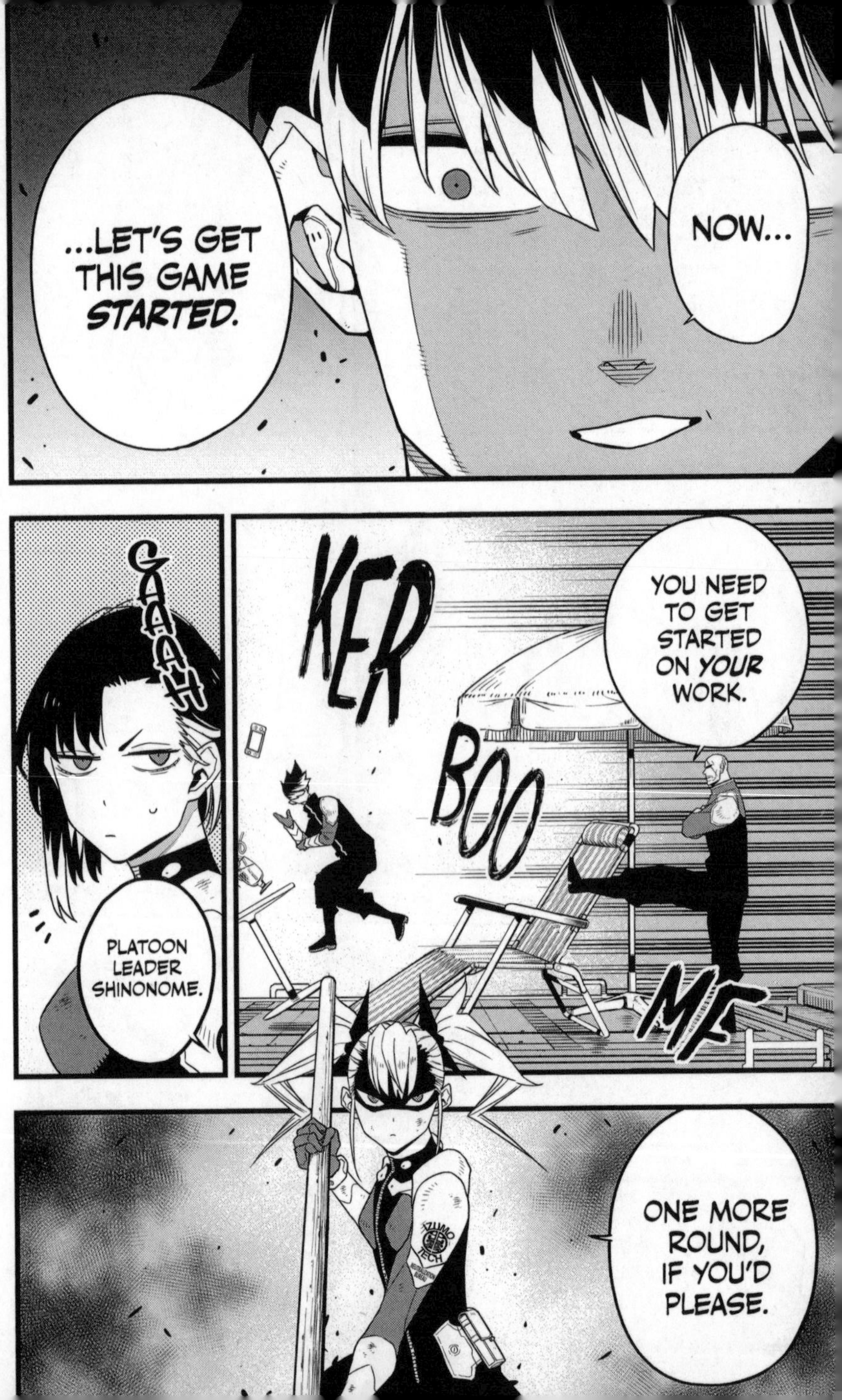
NOW...
...LET'S GET THIS GAME STARTED.
YOU NEED TO GET STARTED ON YOUR WORK.
KERBOOM
MF
GAAAAH
PLATOON LEADER SHINONOME.
ONE MORE ROUND, IF YOU'D PLEASE.

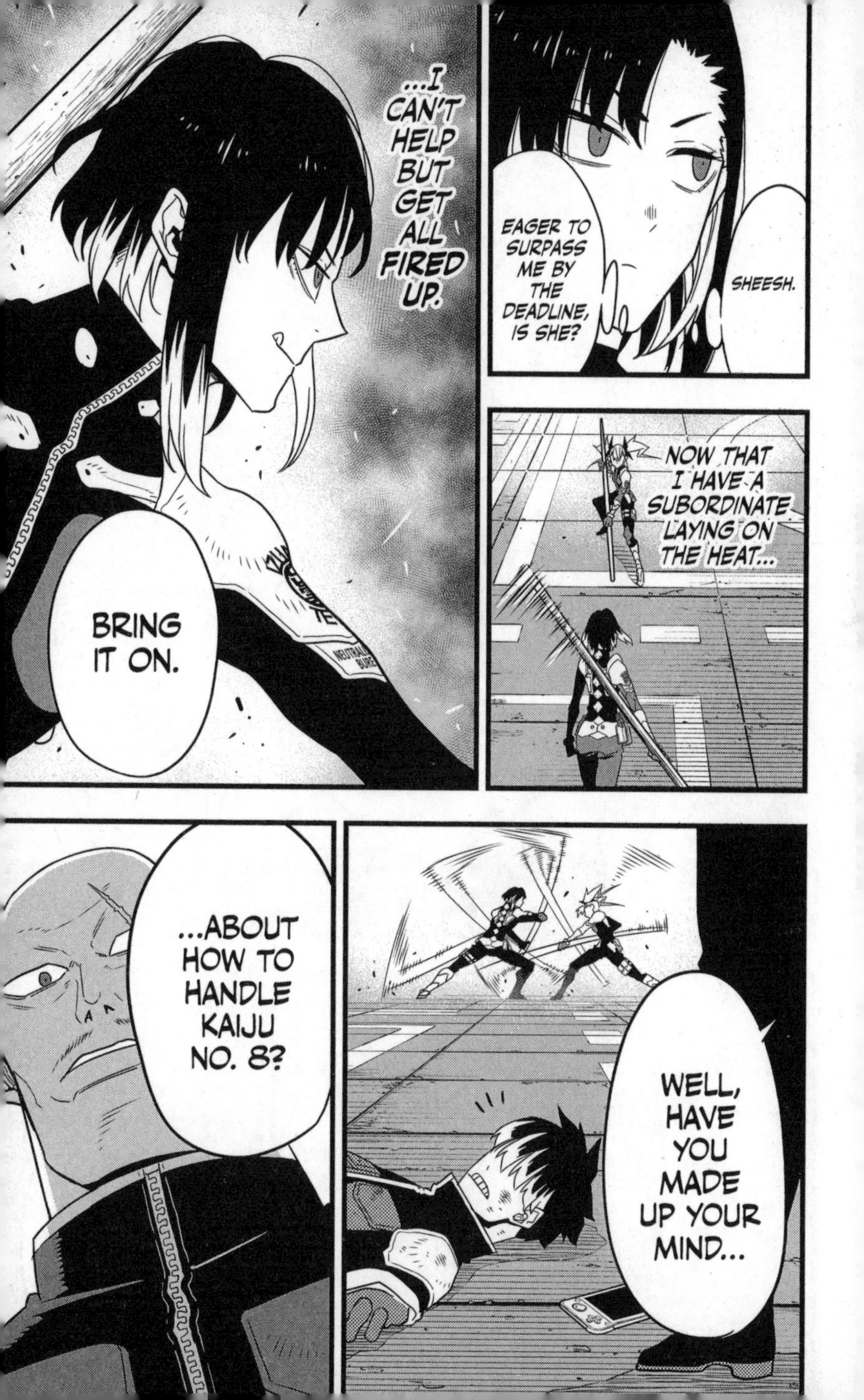
SHEESH.
EAGER TO SURPASS ME BY THE DEADLINE, IS SHE?
NOW THAT I HAVE A SUBORDINATE LAYING ON THE HEAT...
...I CAN'T HELP BUT GET ALL FIRED UP.
BRING IT ON.
WELL, HAVE YOU MADE UP YOUR MIND...
...ABOUT HOW TO HANDLE KAIJU NO. 8?

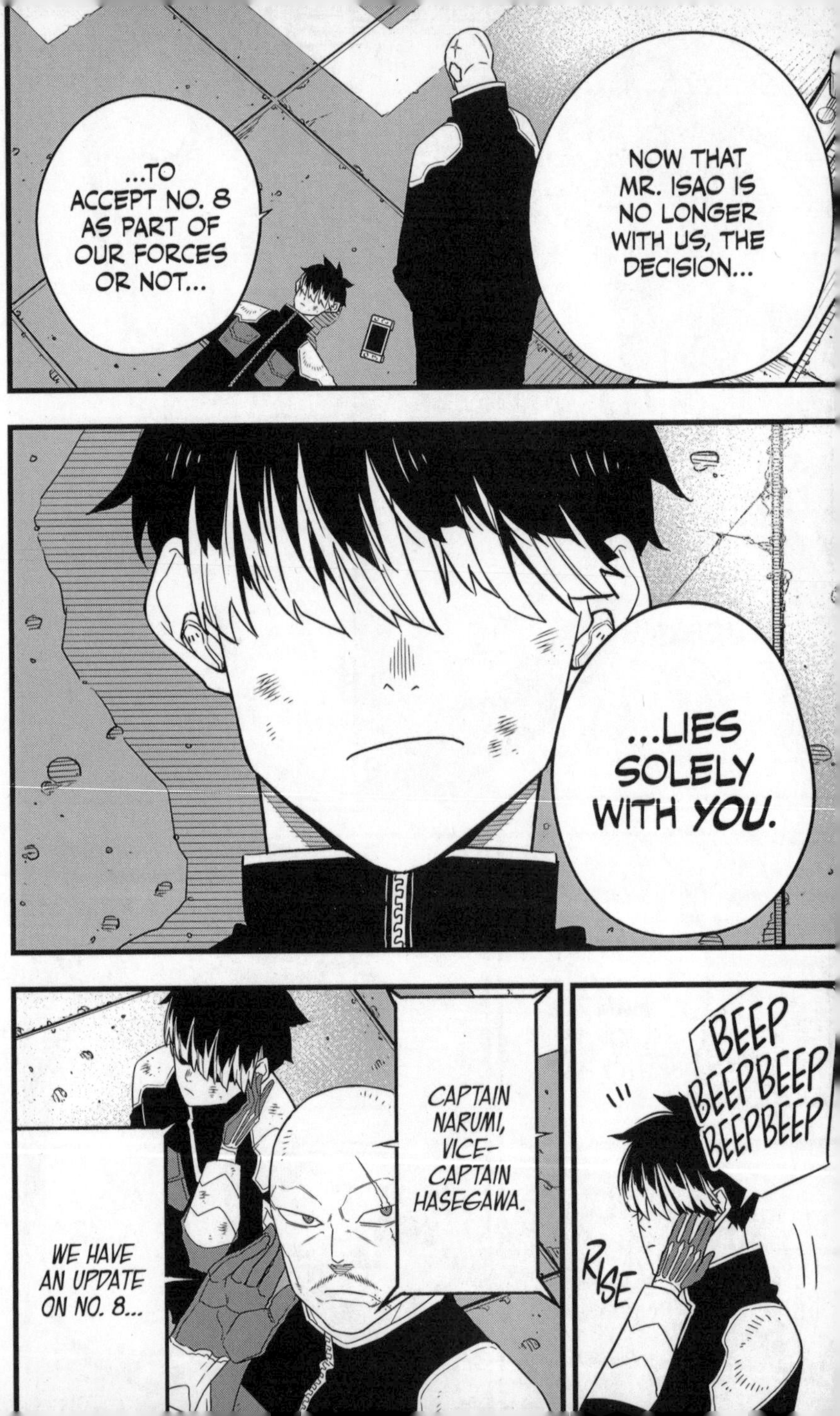
NOW THAT MR. ISAO IS NO LONGER WITH US, THE DECISION...
...TO ACCEPT NO. 8 AS PART OF OUR FORCES OR NOT...
...LIES SOLELY WITH YOU.
BEEP BEEPBEEP BEEPBEEP
RISE
CAPTAIN NARUMI, VICE-CAPTAIN HASEGAWA.
WE HAVE AN UPDATE ON NO. 8...

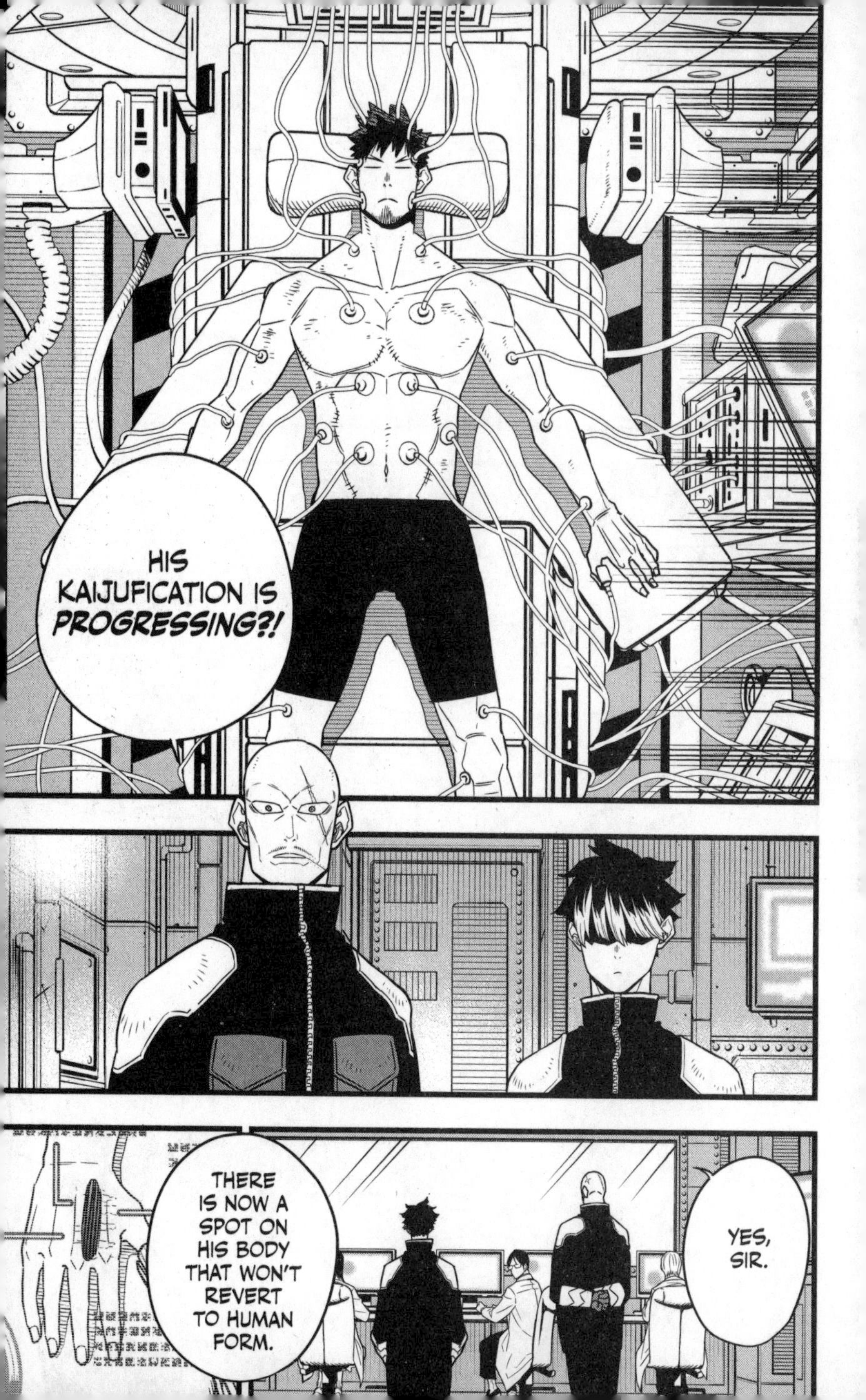
HIS KAIJUFICATION IS PROGRESSING?!
YES, SIR.
THERE IS NOW A SPOT ON HIS BODY THAT WON'T REVERT TO HUMAN FORM.

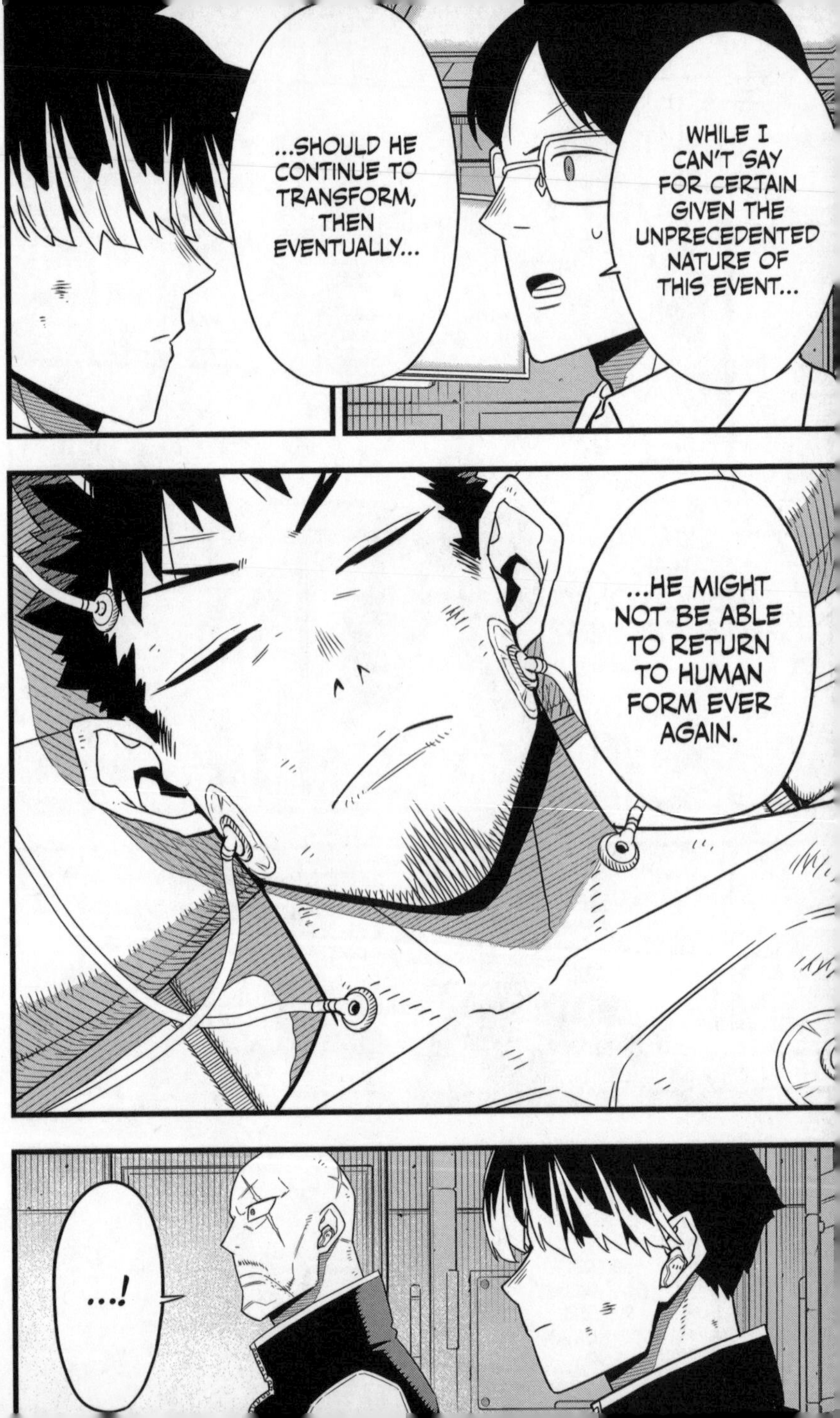
WHILE I CAN'T SAY FOR CERTAIN GIVEN THE UNPRECEDENTED NATURE OF THIS EVENT...
...SHOULD HE CONTINUE TO TRANSFORM, THEN EVENTUALLY...
...HE MIGHT NOT BE ABLE TO RETURN TO HUMAN FORM EVER AGAIN.
...!

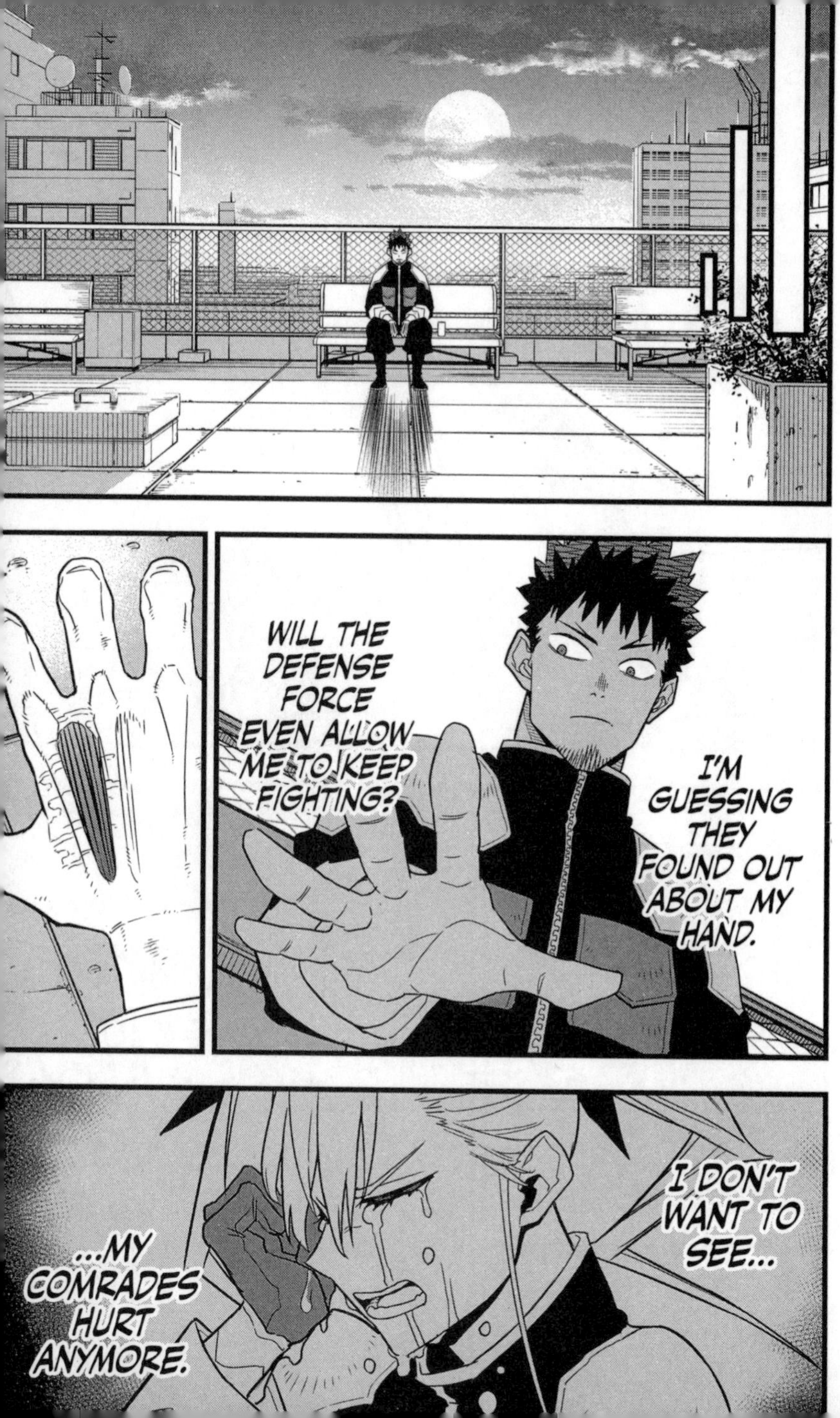
I'M GUESSING THEY FOUND OUT ABOUT MY HAND.
WILL THE DEFENSE FORCE EVEN ALLOW ME TO KEEP FIGHTING?
I DON'T WANT TO SEE...
...MY COMRADES HURT ANYMORE.

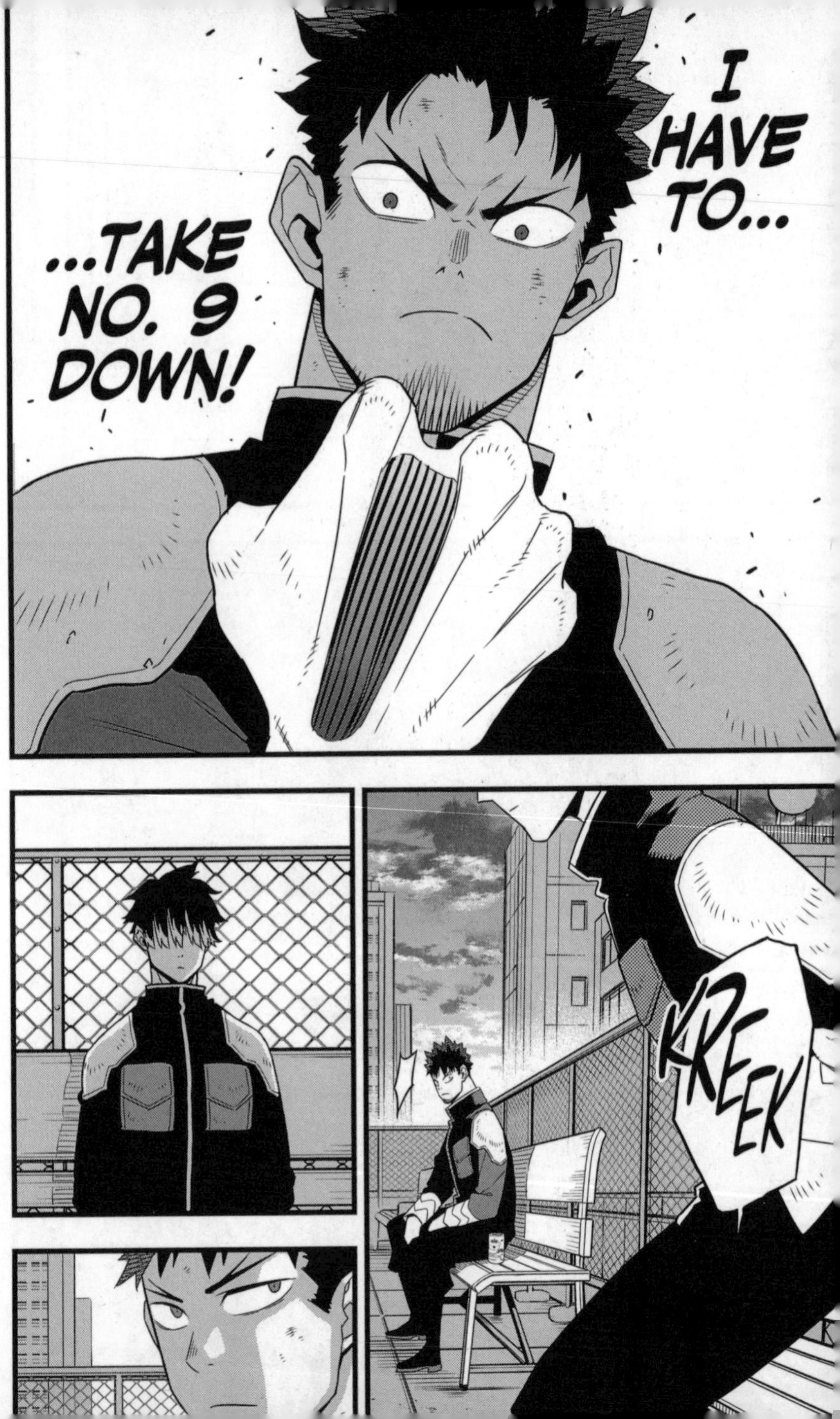
I HAVE TO...
...TAKE NO. 9 DOWN!
KREEK

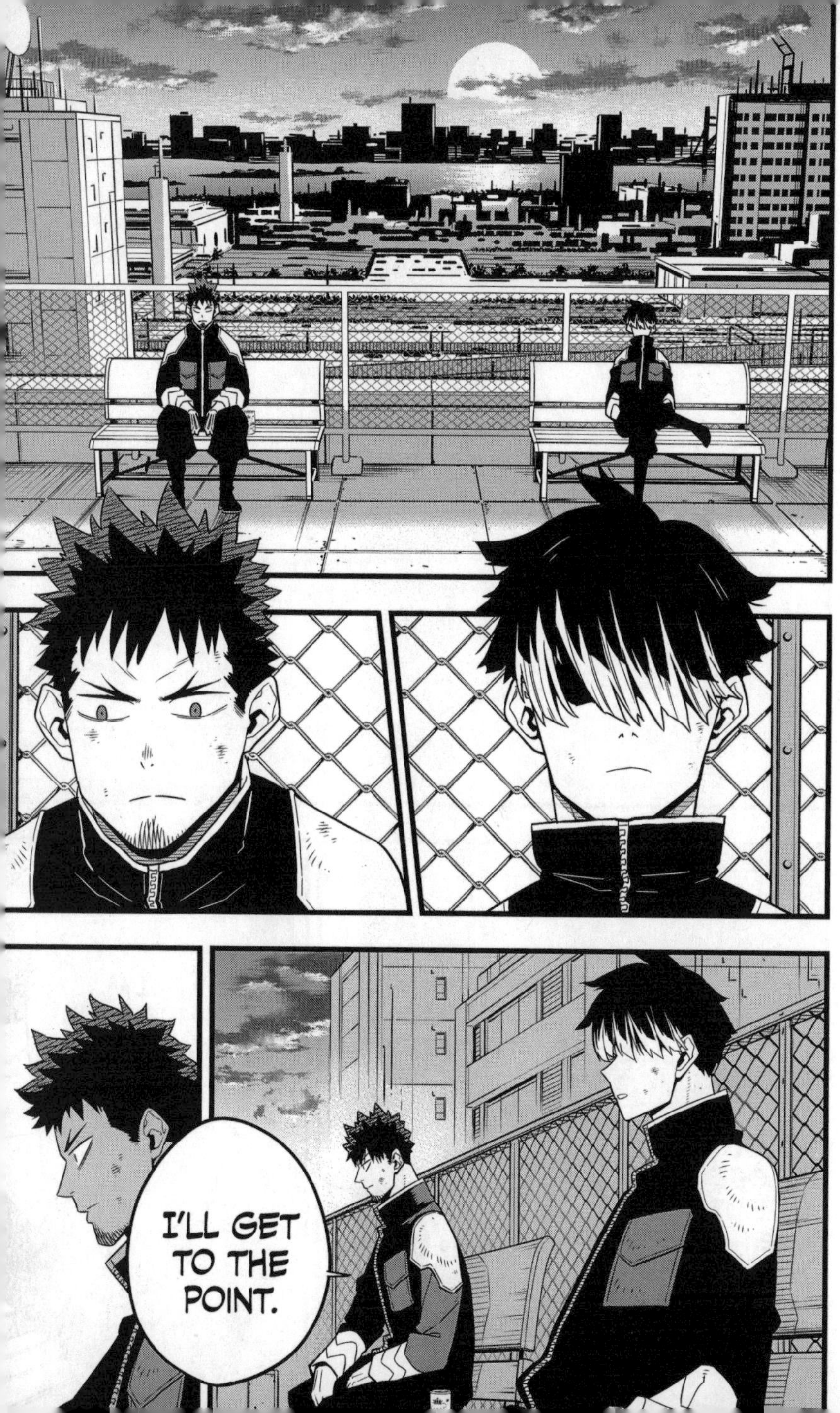
I'LL GET TO THE POINT.

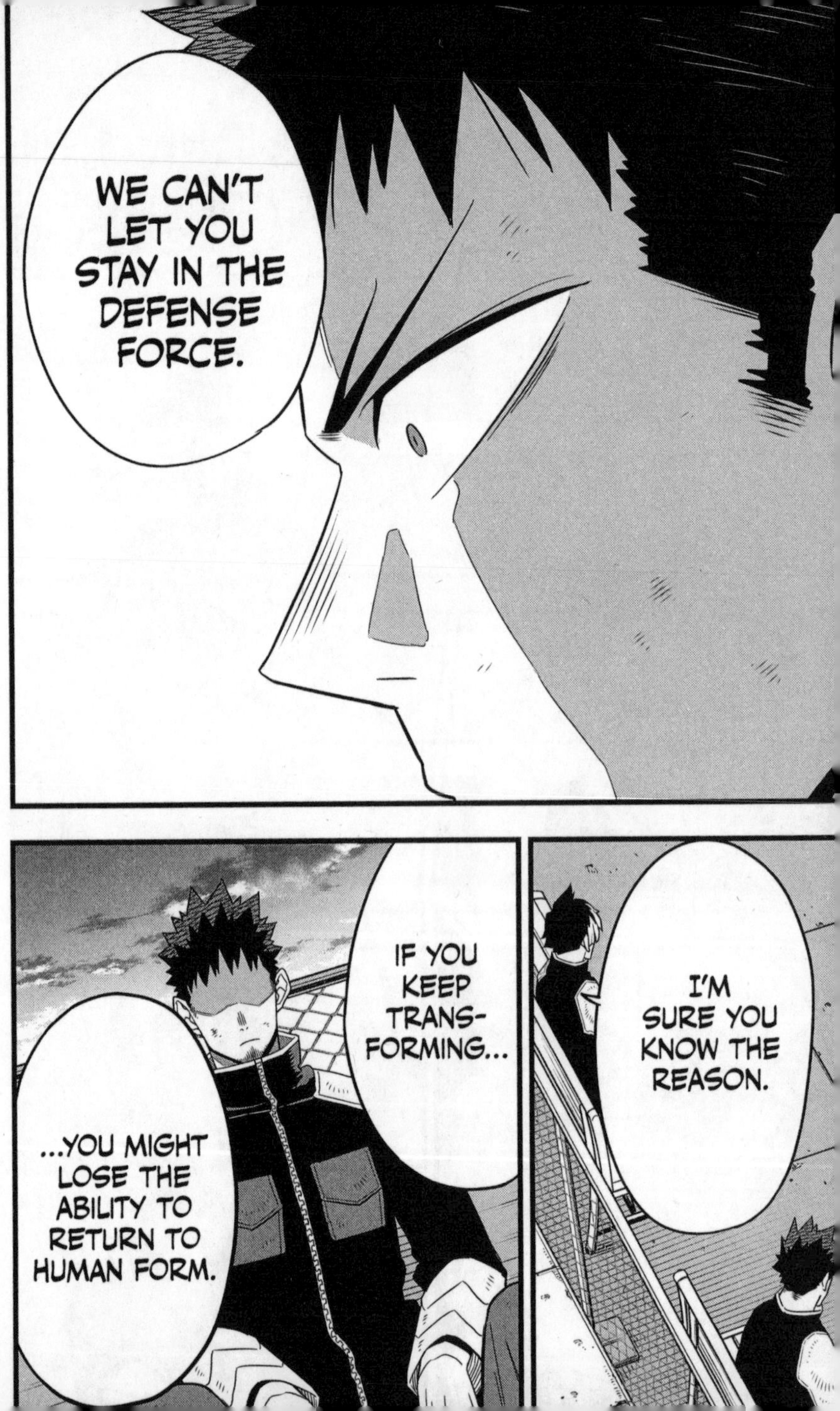
WE CAN'T LET YOU STAY IN THE DEFENSE FORCE.
I'M SURE YOU KNOW THE REASON.
IF YOU KEEP TRANS-FORMING...
...YOU MIGHT LOSE THE ABILITY TO RETURN TO HUMAN FORM.

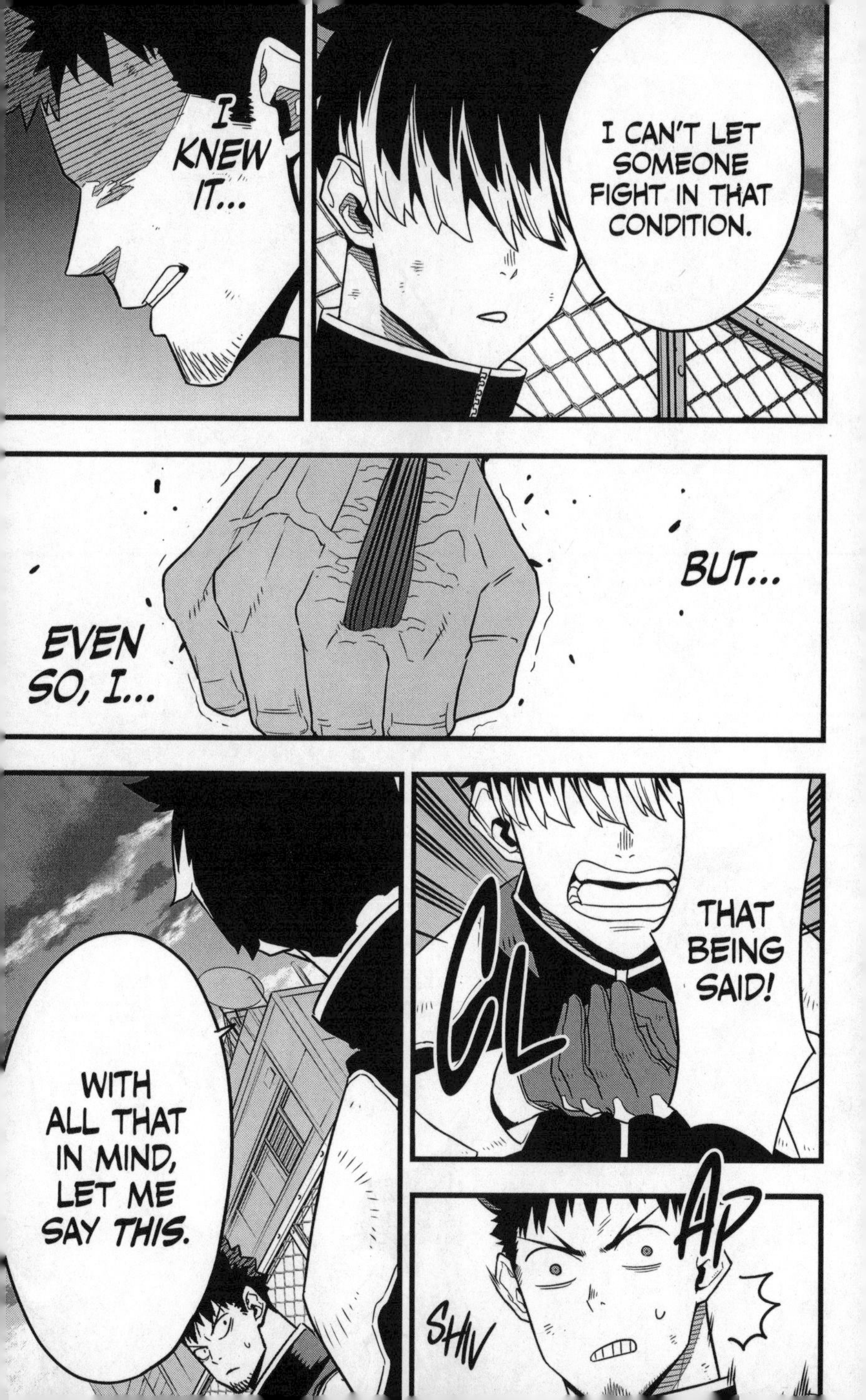
I CAN'T LET SOMEONE FIGHT IN THAT CONDITION.
I KNEW IT...
BUT...
EVEN SO, I...
THAT BEING SAID!
CL
AP
SHIV
WITH ALL THAT IN MIND, LET ME SAY THIS.

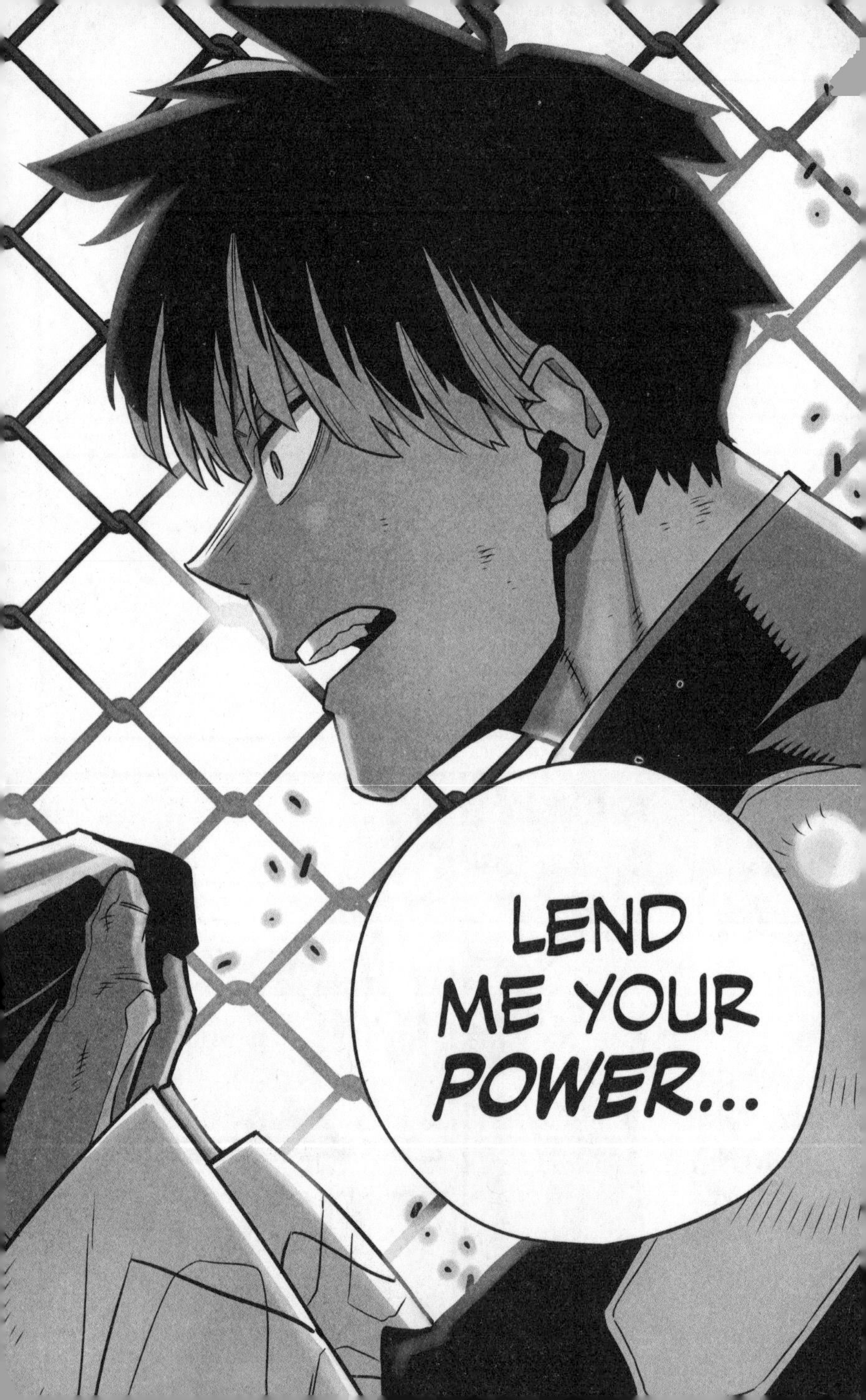
LEND ME YOUR POWER...

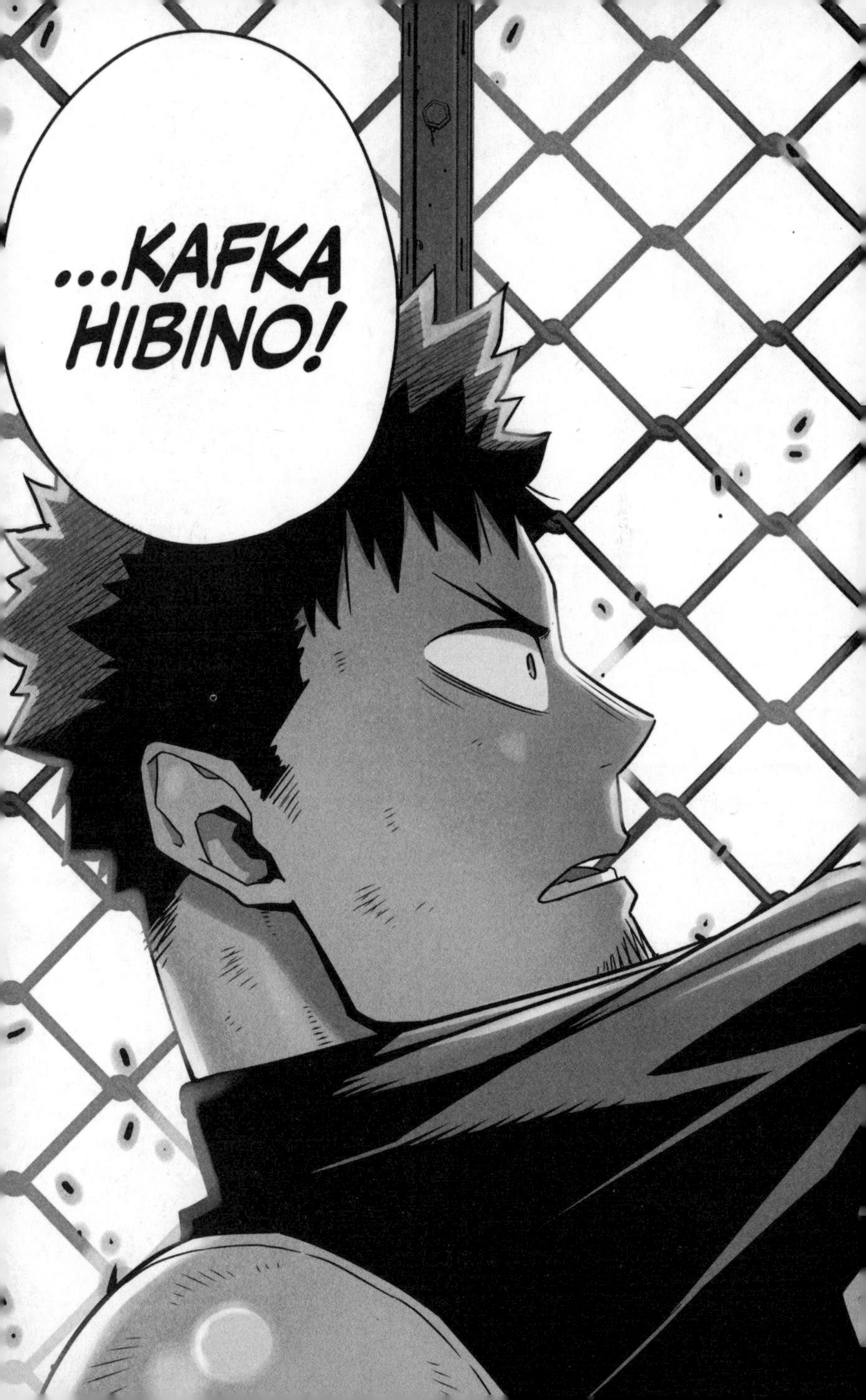
...KAFKA HIBINO!

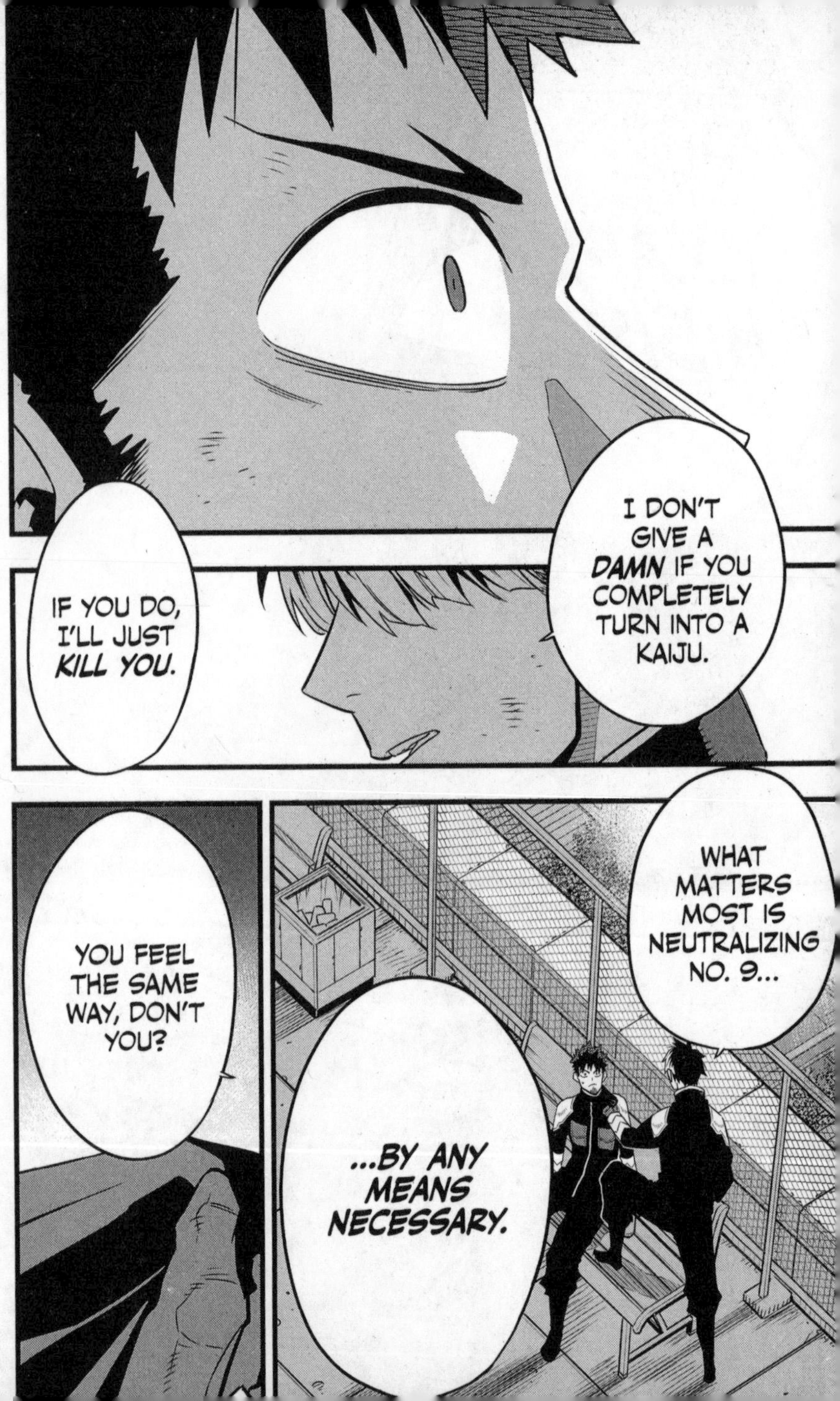
I DON'T GIVE A DAMN IF YOU COMPLETELY TURN INTO A KAIJU.
IF YOU DO, I'LL JUST KILL YOU.
WHAT MATTERS MOST IS NEUTRALIZING NO. 9...
...BY ANY MEANS NECESSARY.
YOU FEEL THE SAME WAY, DON'T YOU?

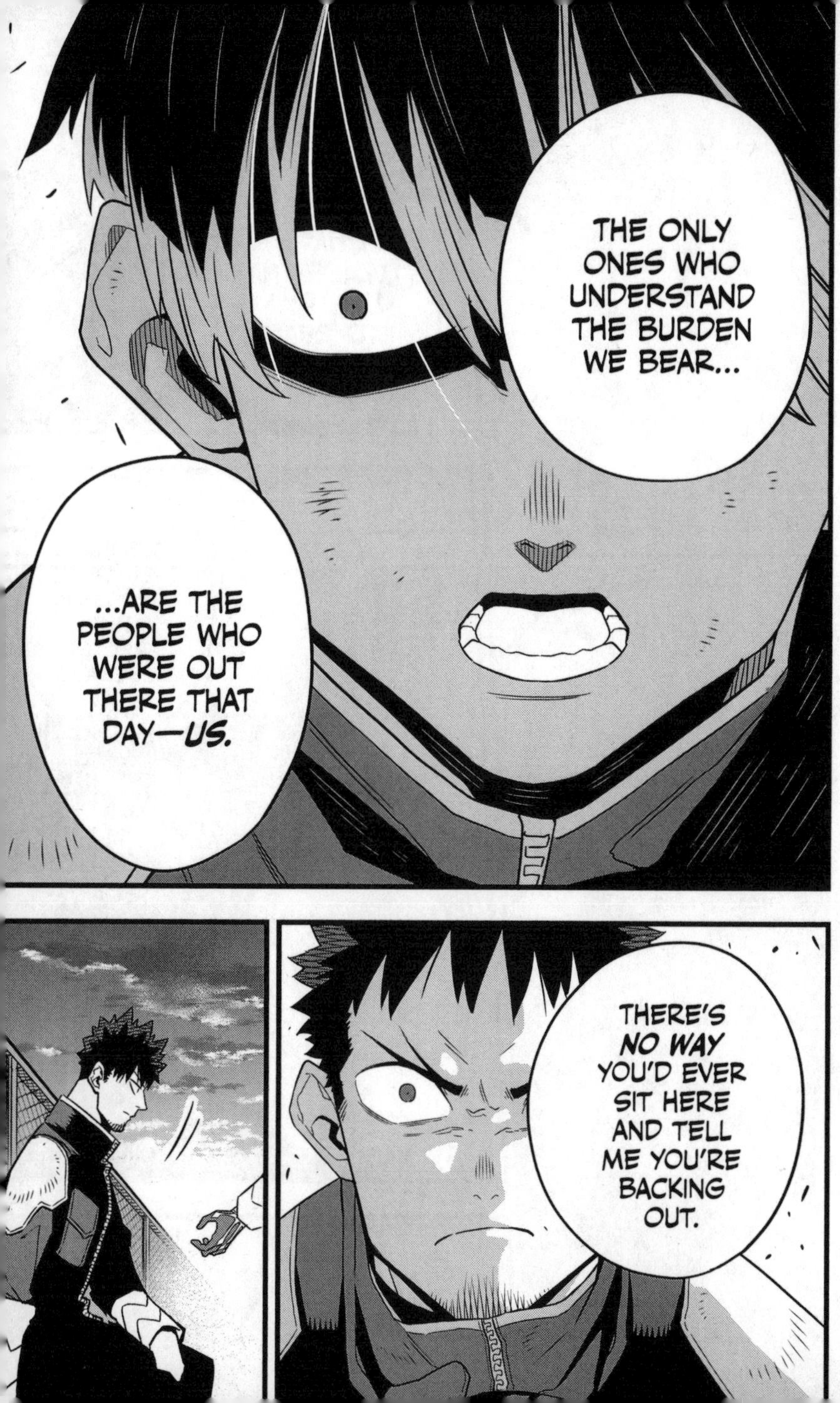
THE ONLY ONES WHO UNDERSTAND THE BURDEN WE BEAR...
...ARE THE PEOPLE WHO WERE OUT THERE THAT DAY—*US.*
THERE'S *NO WAY* YOU'D EVER SIT HERE AND TELL ME YOU'RE BACKING OUT.

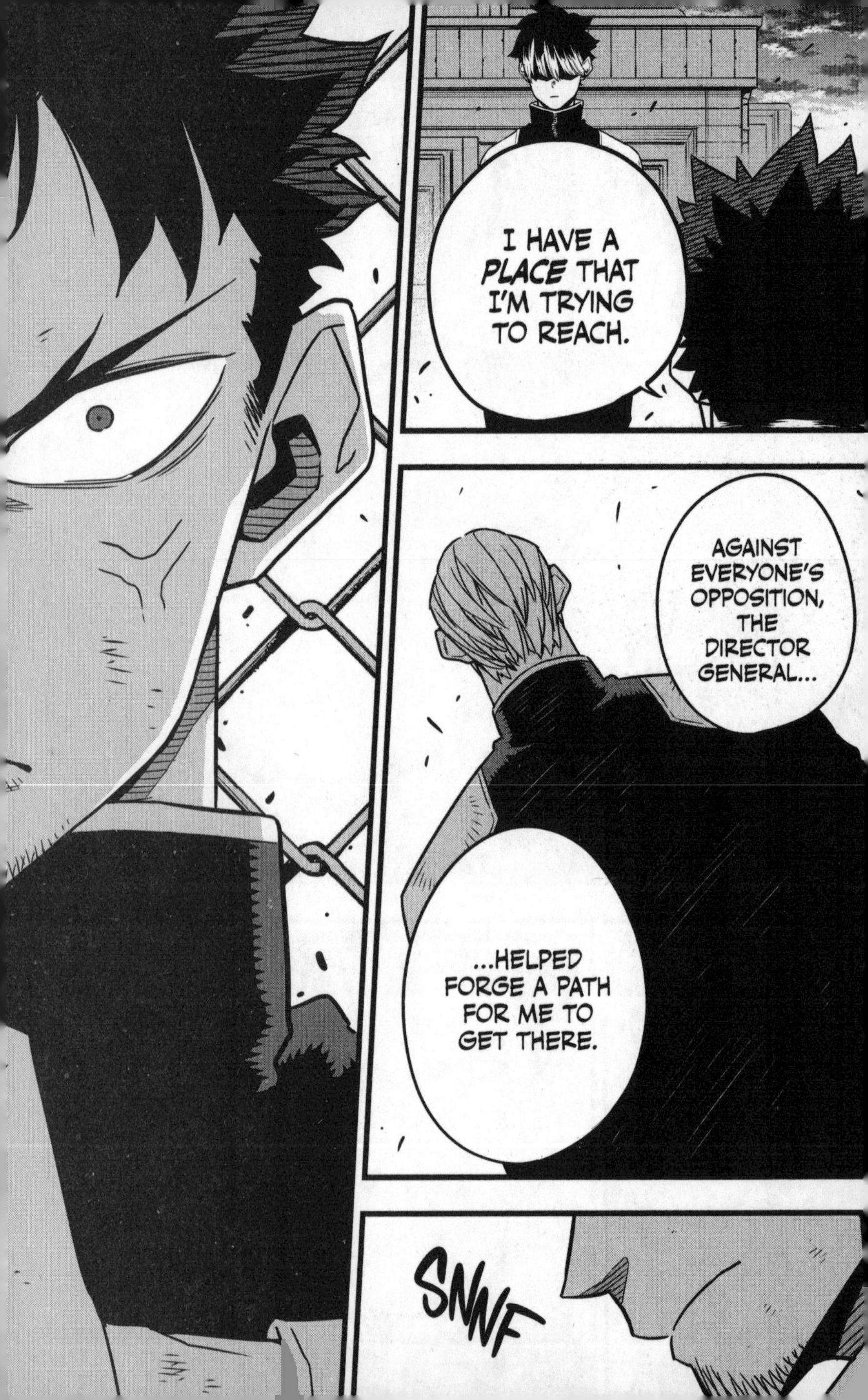
I HAVE A *PLACE* THAT I'M TRYING TO REACH.
AGAINST EVERYONE'S OPPOSITION, THE DIRECTOR GENERAL...
...HELPED FORGE A PATH FOR ME TO GET THERE.
SNNF

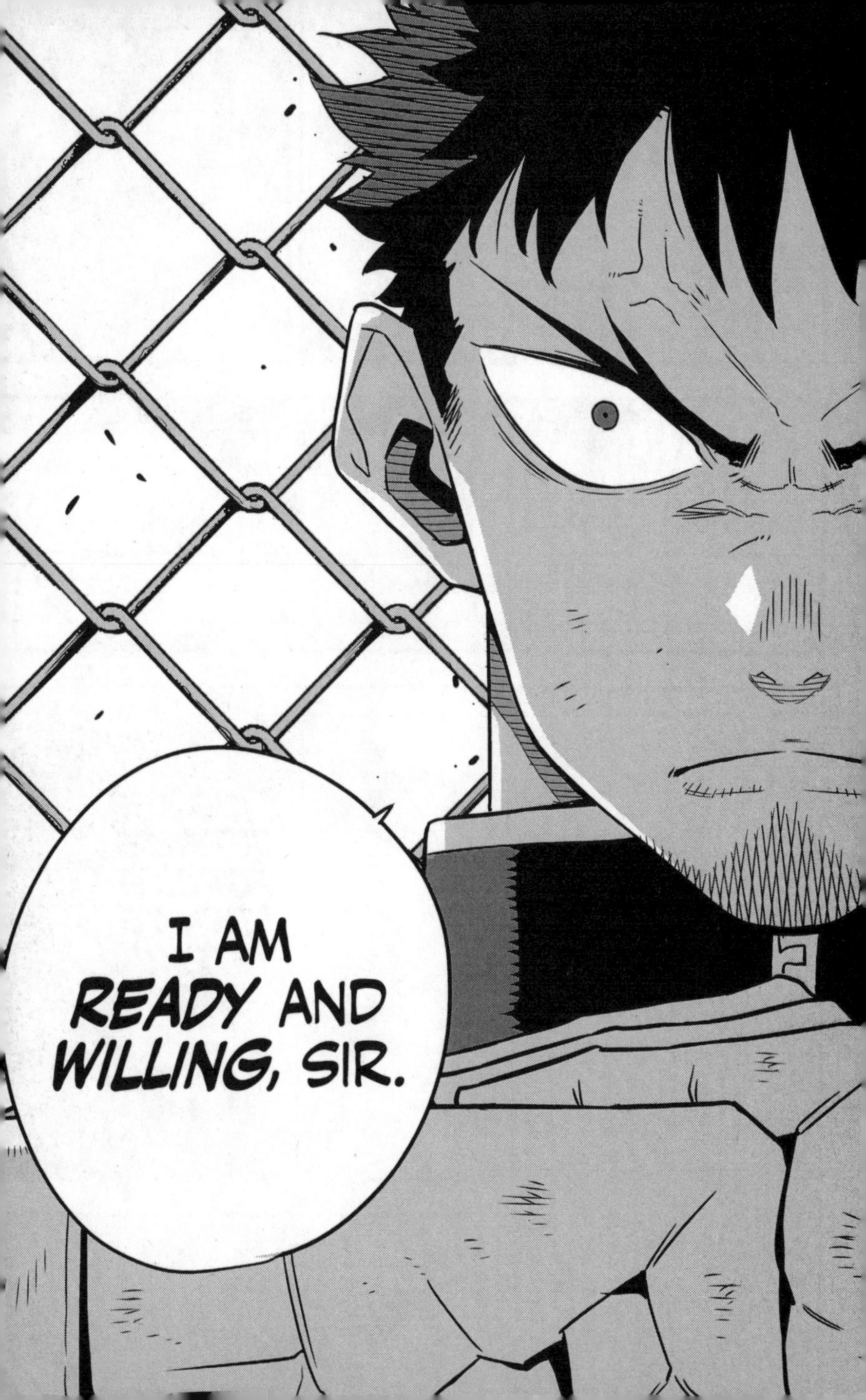
I AM READY AND WILLING, SIR.

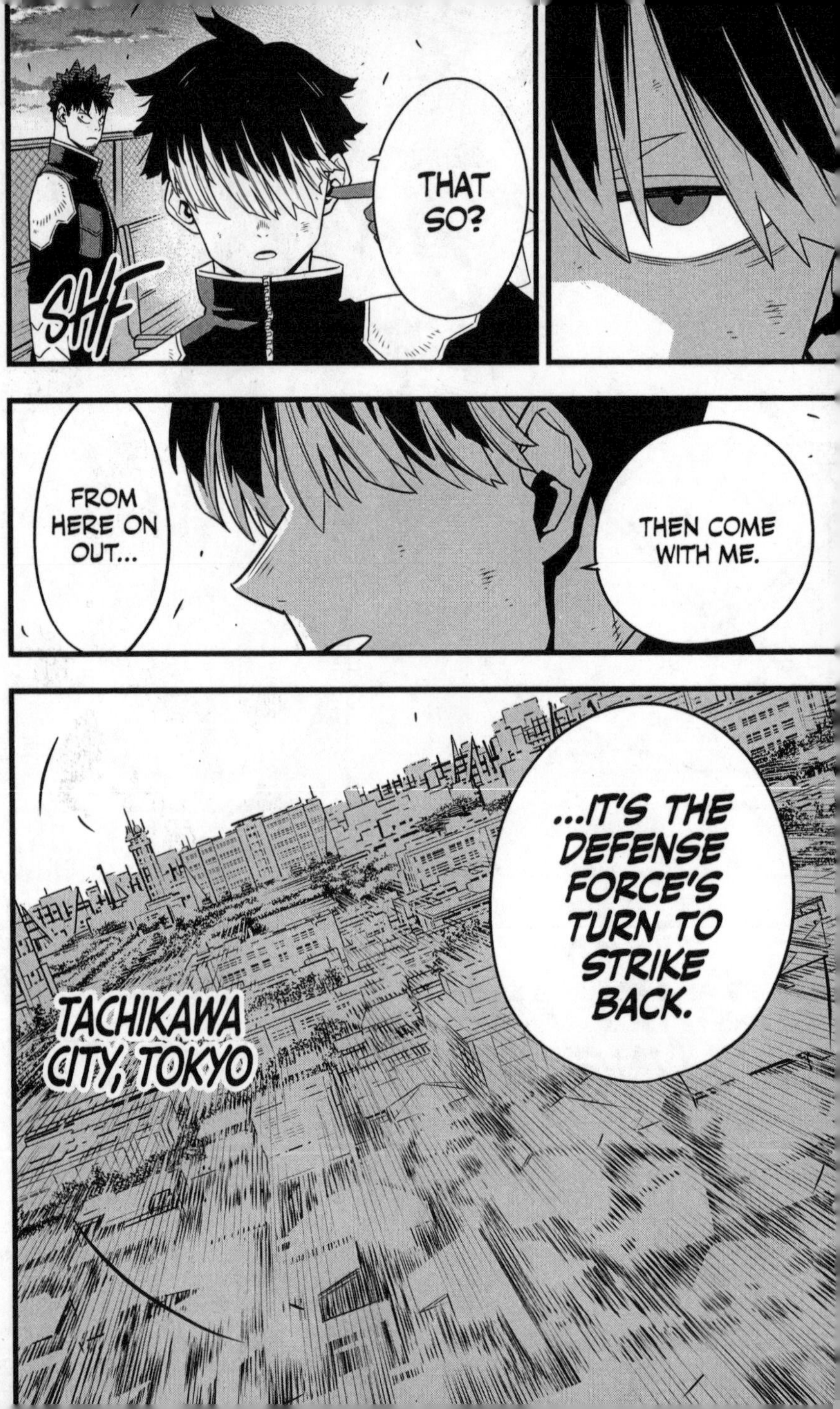
THAT SO?
SHF
THEN COME WITH ME.
FROM HERE ON OUT...
...IT'S THE DEFENSE FORCE'S TURN TO STRIKE BACK.
TACHIKAWA CITY, TOKYO

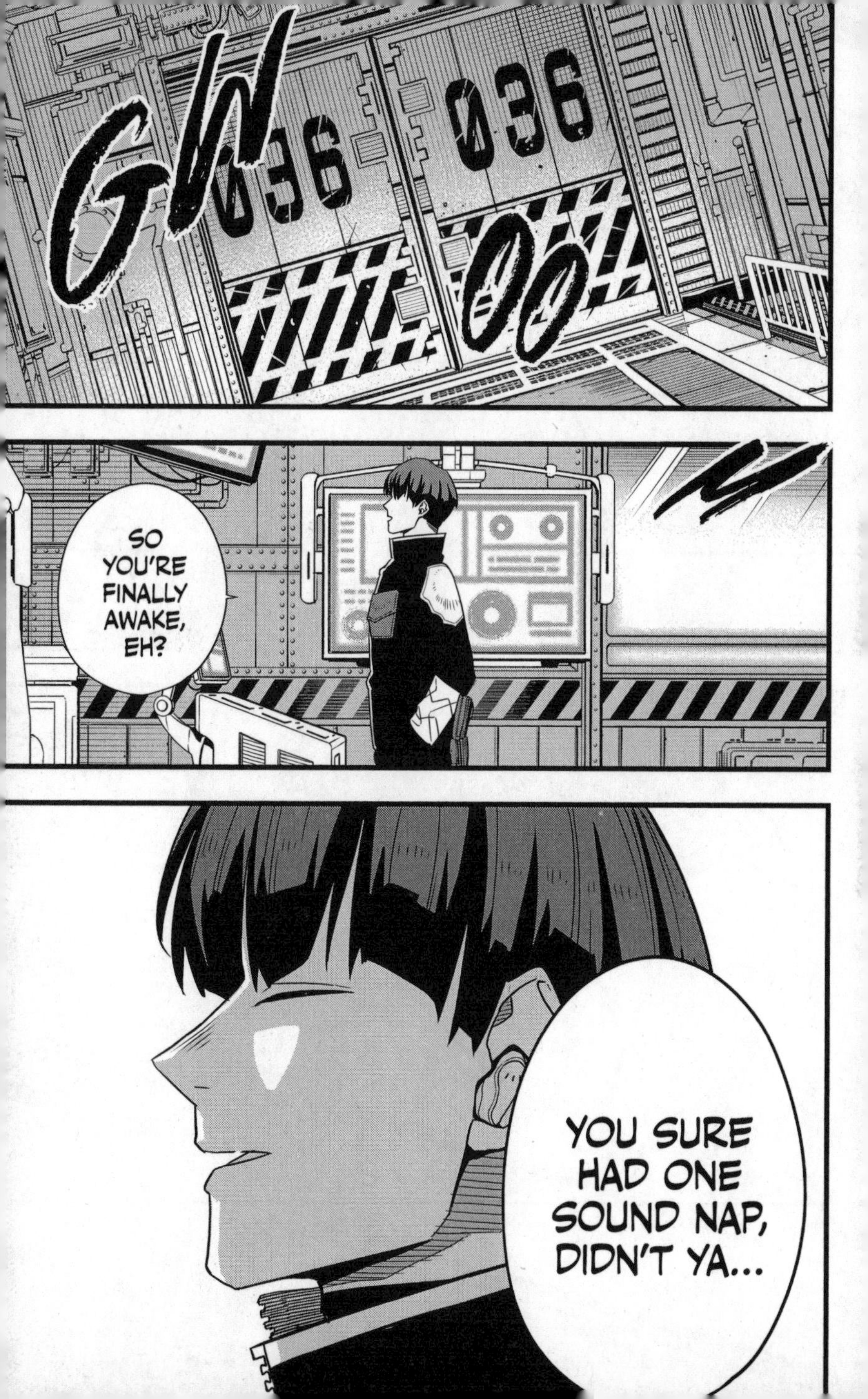
036
036
SO YOU'RE FINALLY AWAKE, EH?
YOU SURE HAD ONE SOUND NAP, DIDN'T YA...

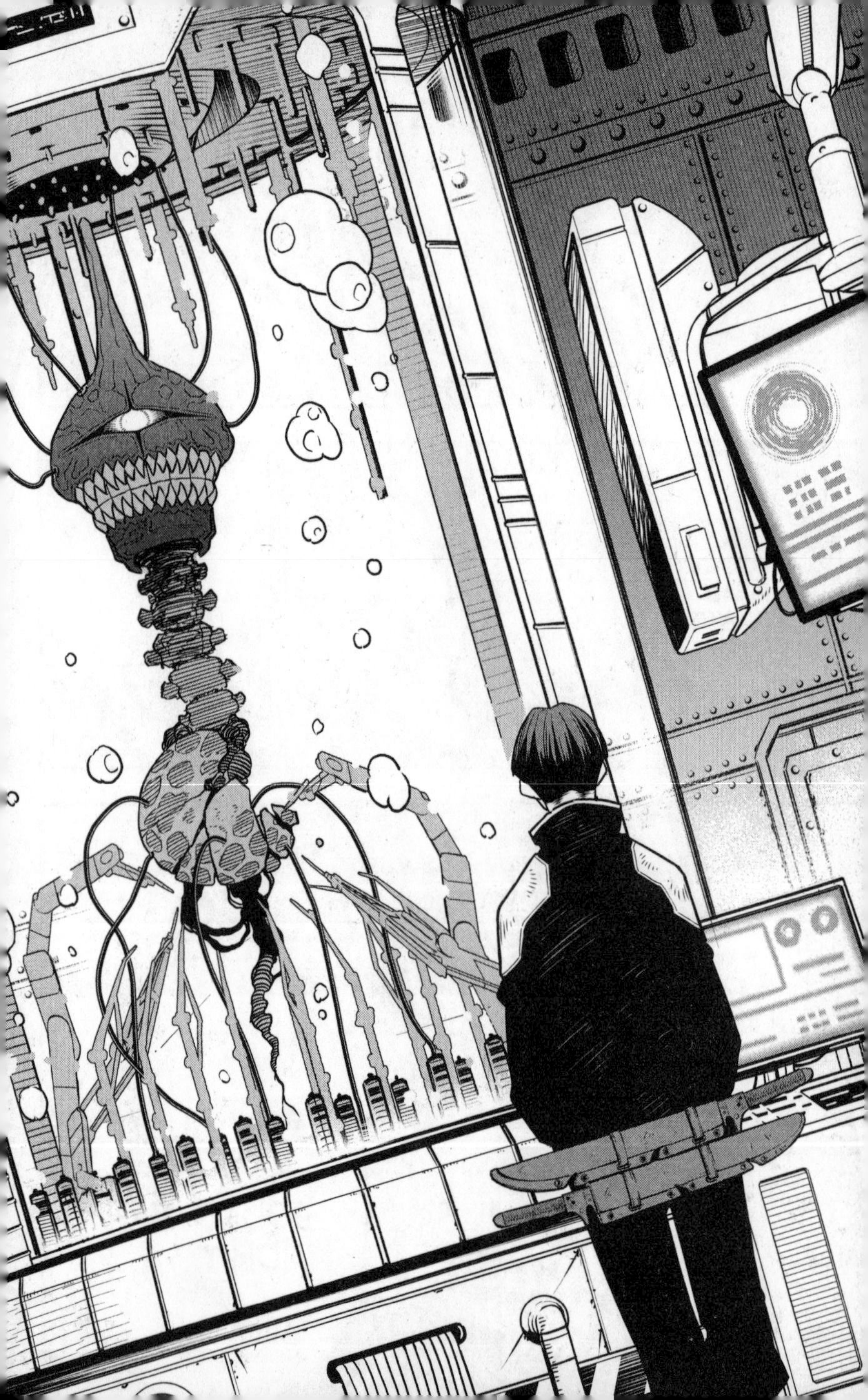

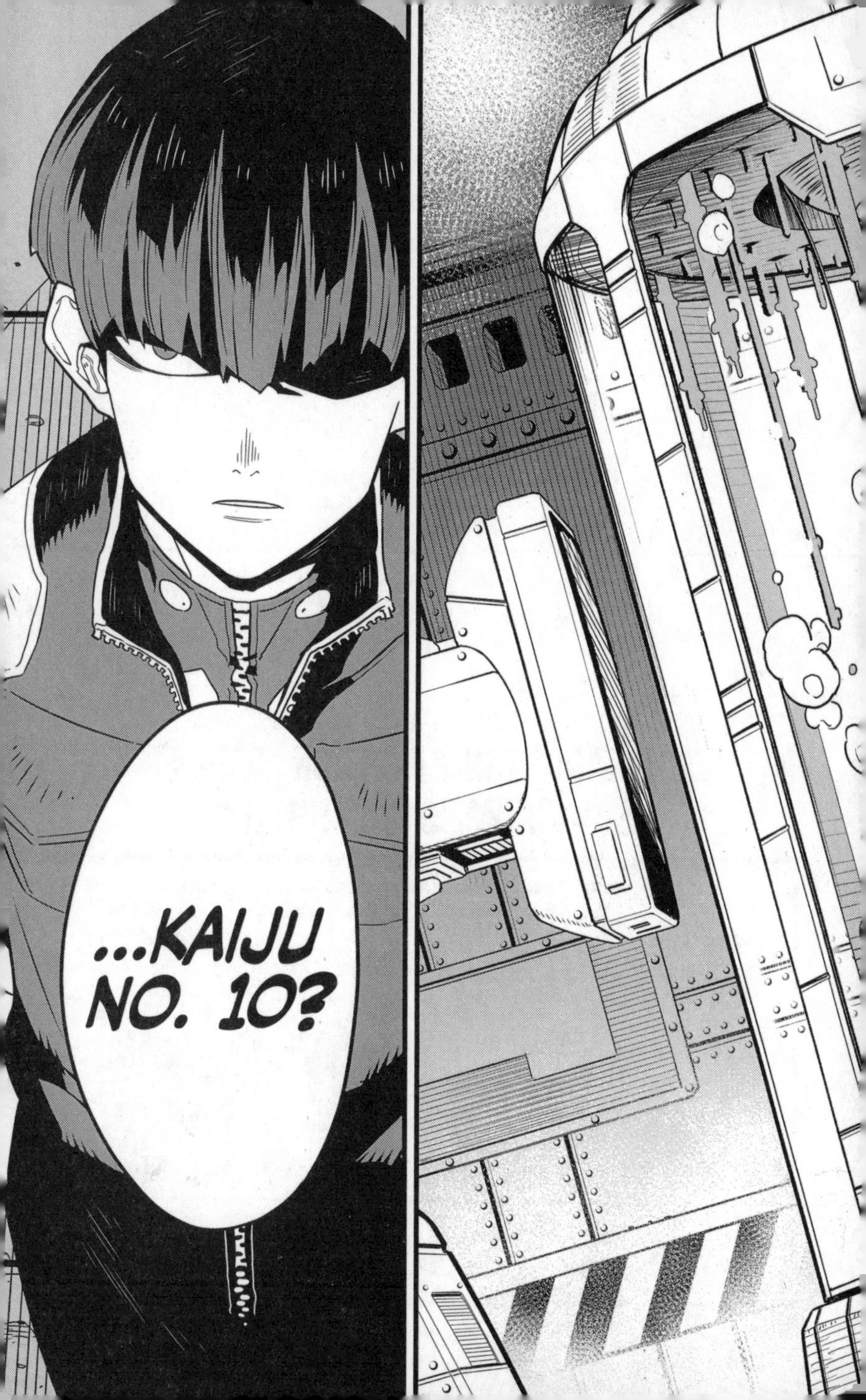
...KAIJU NO. 10?

DISTANCE ISN'T PLATOON LEADER SHINONOME'S ONLY SHTICK

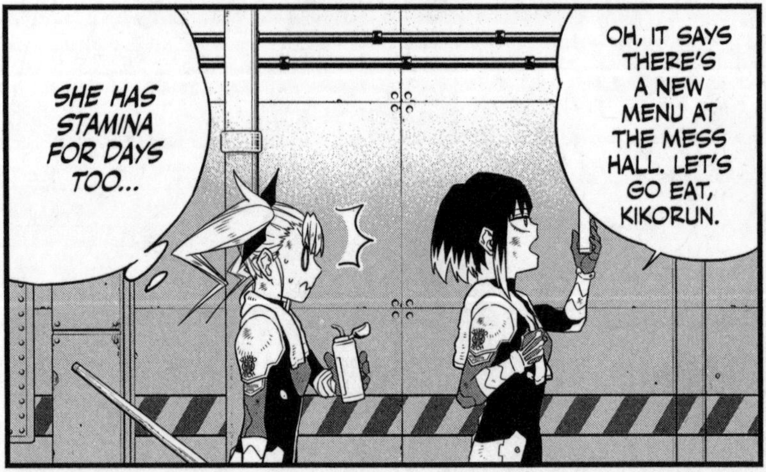
OH, IT SAYS THERE'S A NEW MENU AT THE MESS HALL. LET'S GO EAT, KIKORUN.
SHE HAS STAMINA FOR DAYS TOO...

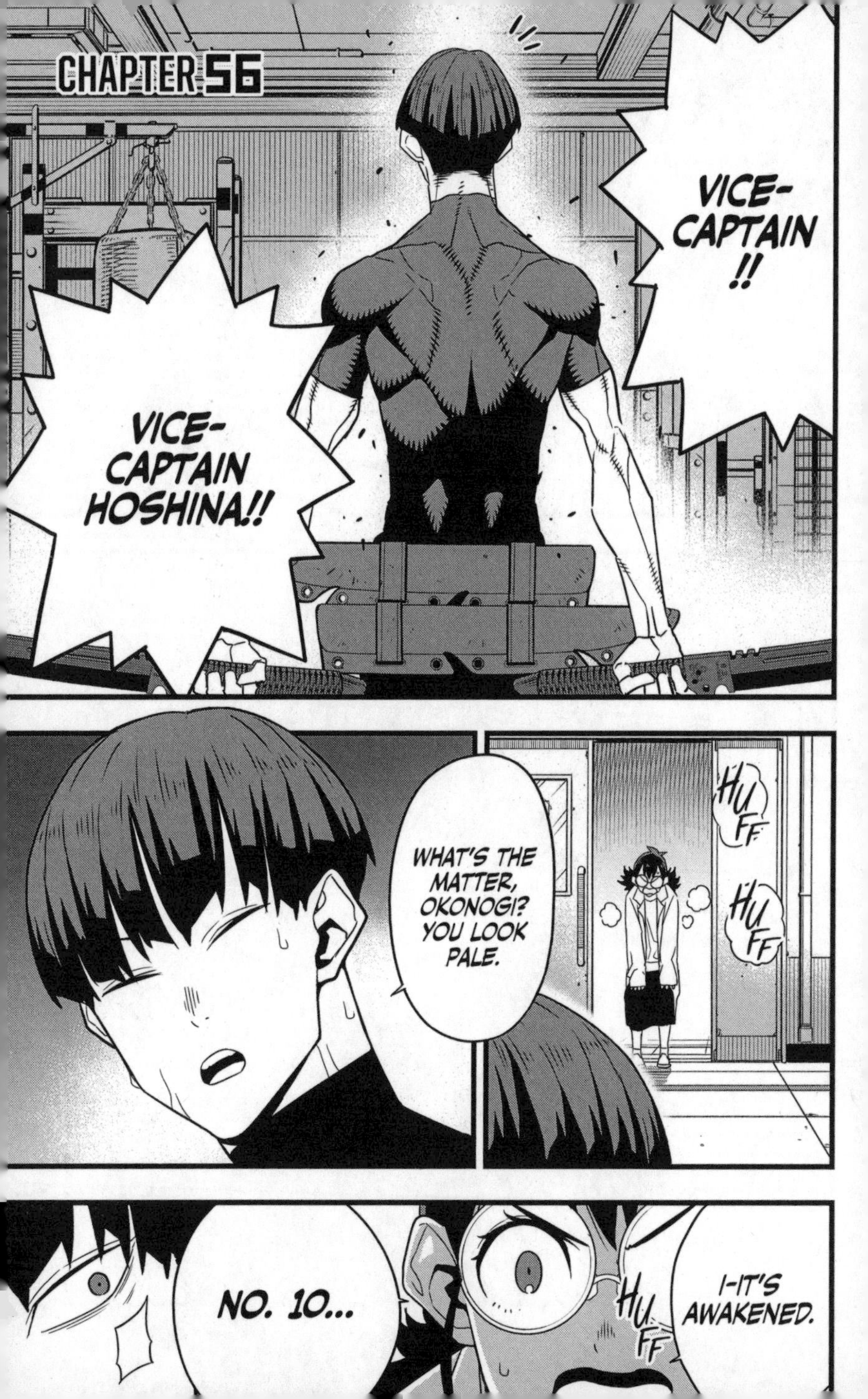
CHAPTER 56
VICE-CAPTAIN!!
VICE-CAPTAIN HOSHINA!!
HUFF
HUFF
WHAT'S THE MATTER, OKONOGI? YOU LOOK PALE.
I-IT'S AWAKENED.
HUFF
NO. 10...

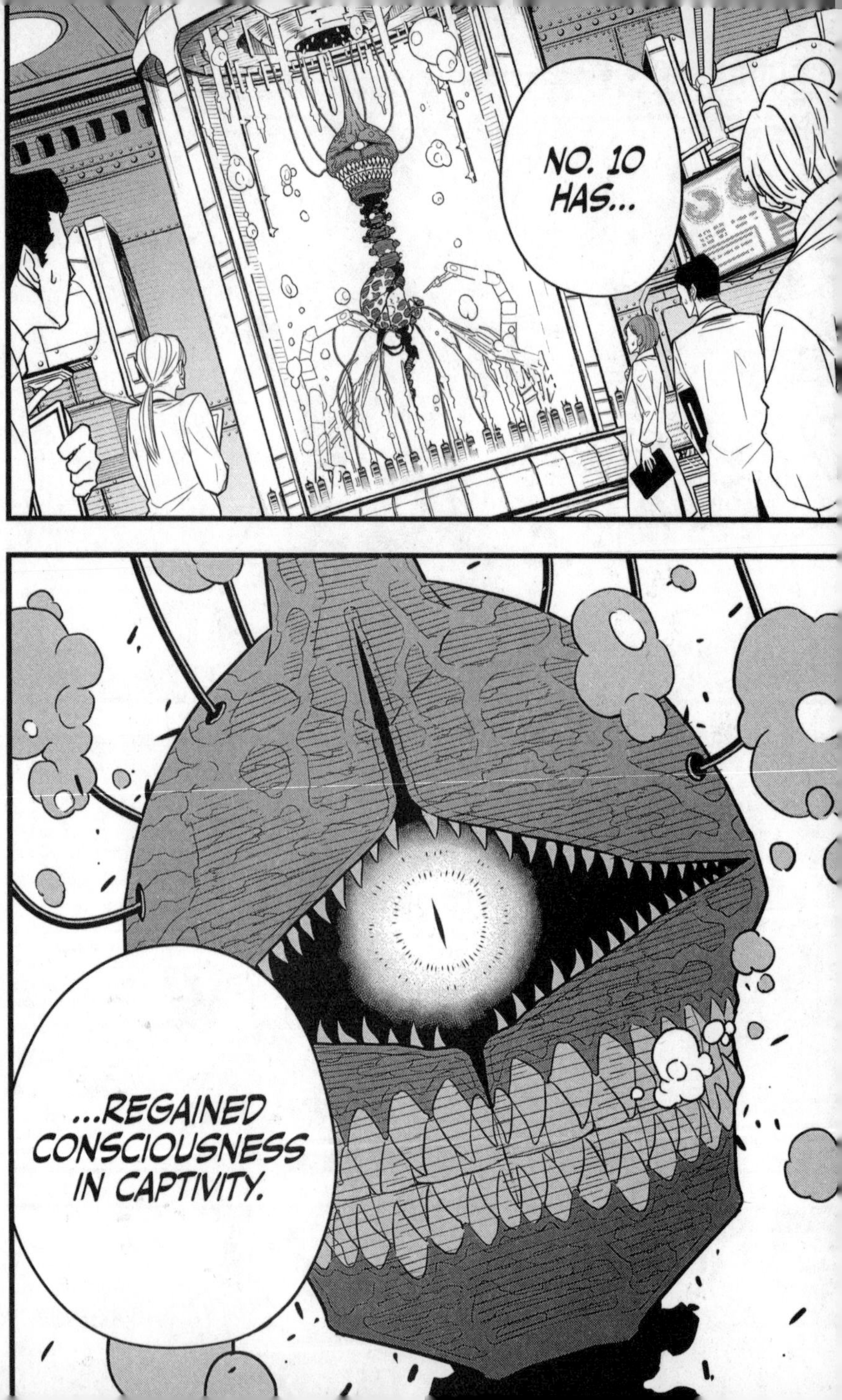
NO. 10 HAS...
...REGAINED CONSCIOUSNESS IN CAPTIVITY.

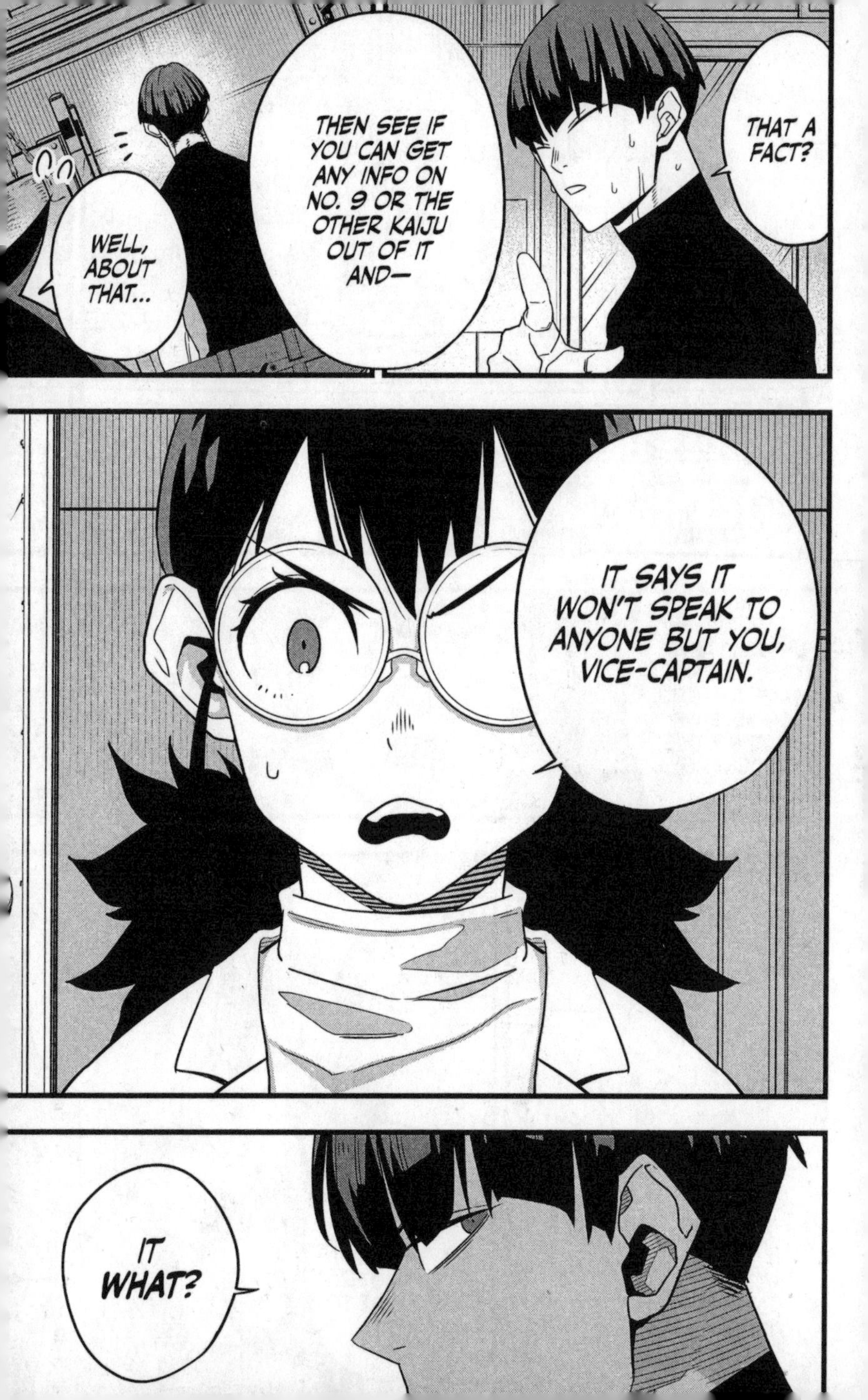
THAT A FACT?
THEN SEE IF YOU CAN GET ANY INFO ON NO. 9 OR THE OTHER KAIJU OUT OF IT AND—
WELL, ABOUT THAT...
IT SAYS IT WON'T SPEAK TO ANYONE BUT YOU, VICE-CAPTAIN.
IT WHAT?

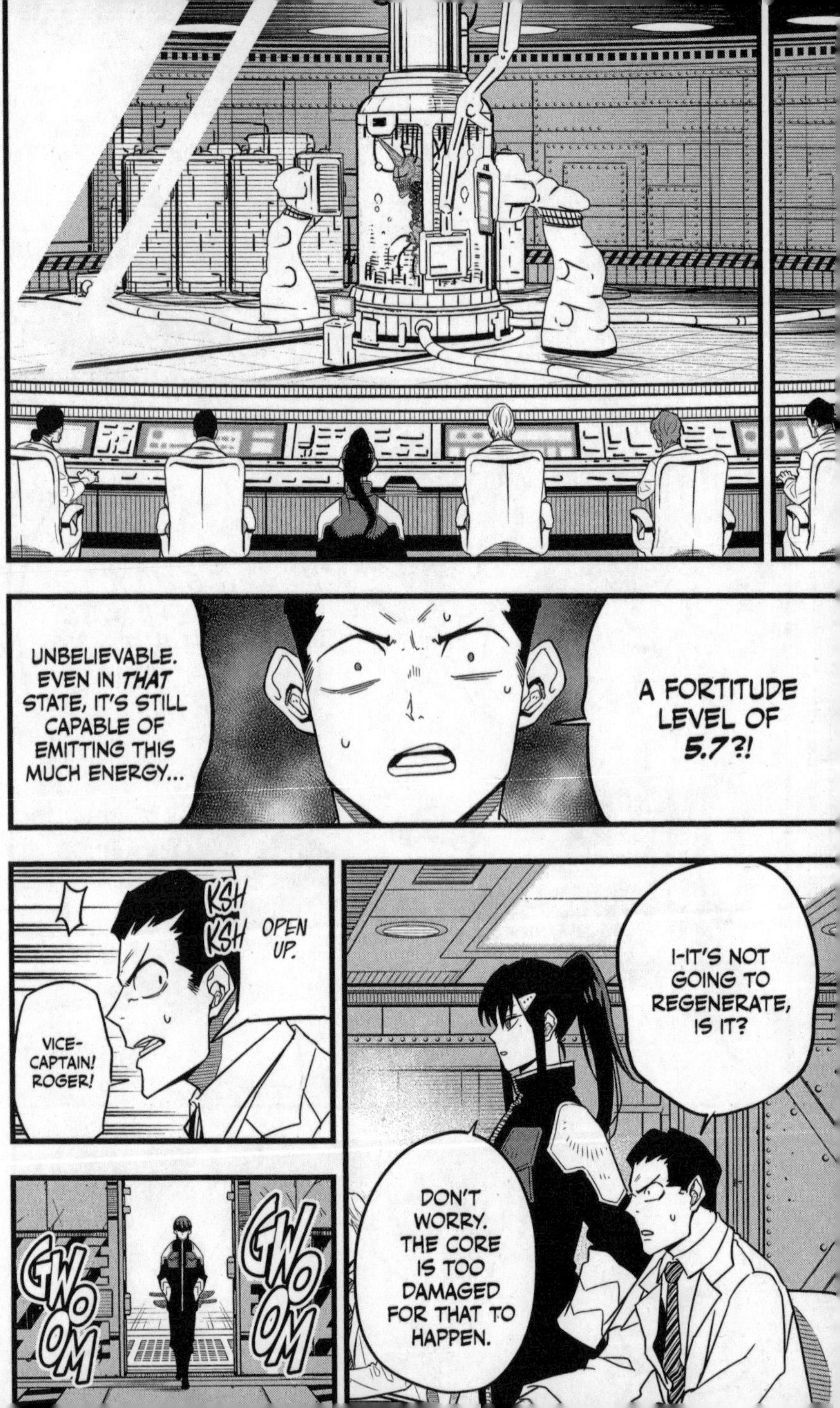
A FORTITUDE LEVEL OF 5.7?!
UNBELIEVABLE. EVEN IN THAT STATE, IT'S STILL CAPABLE OF EMITTING THIS MUCH ENERGY...
I-IT'S NOT GOING TO REGENERATE, IS IT?
DON'T WORRY. THE CORE IS TOO DAMAGED FOR THAT TO HAPPEN.
KSH KSH
OPEN UP.
VICE-CAPTAIN! ROGER!
GWOOM
GWOOM

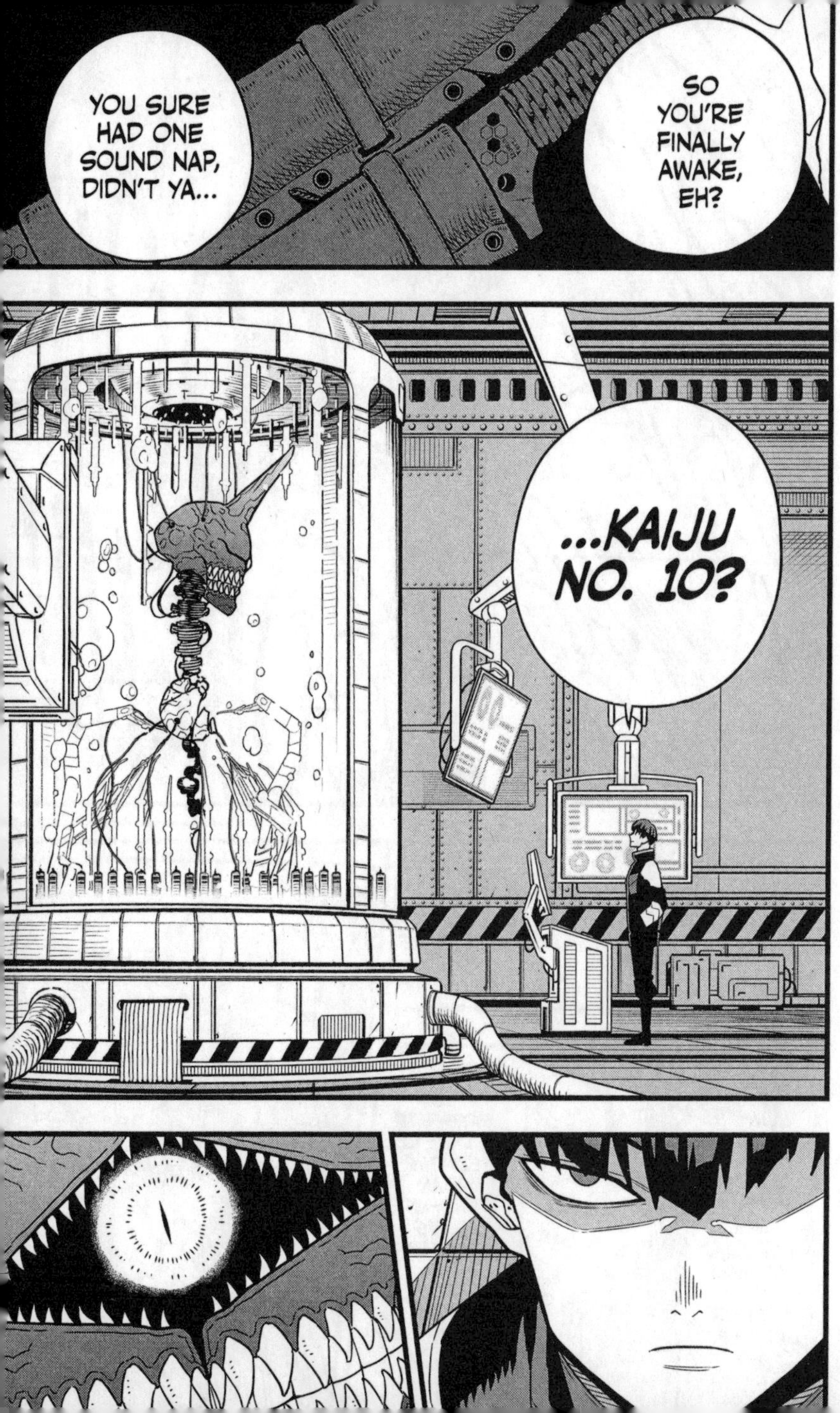
SO YOU'RE FINALLY AWAKE, EH?
YOU SURE HAD ONE SOUND NAP, DIDN'T YA...
...KAIJU NO. 10?

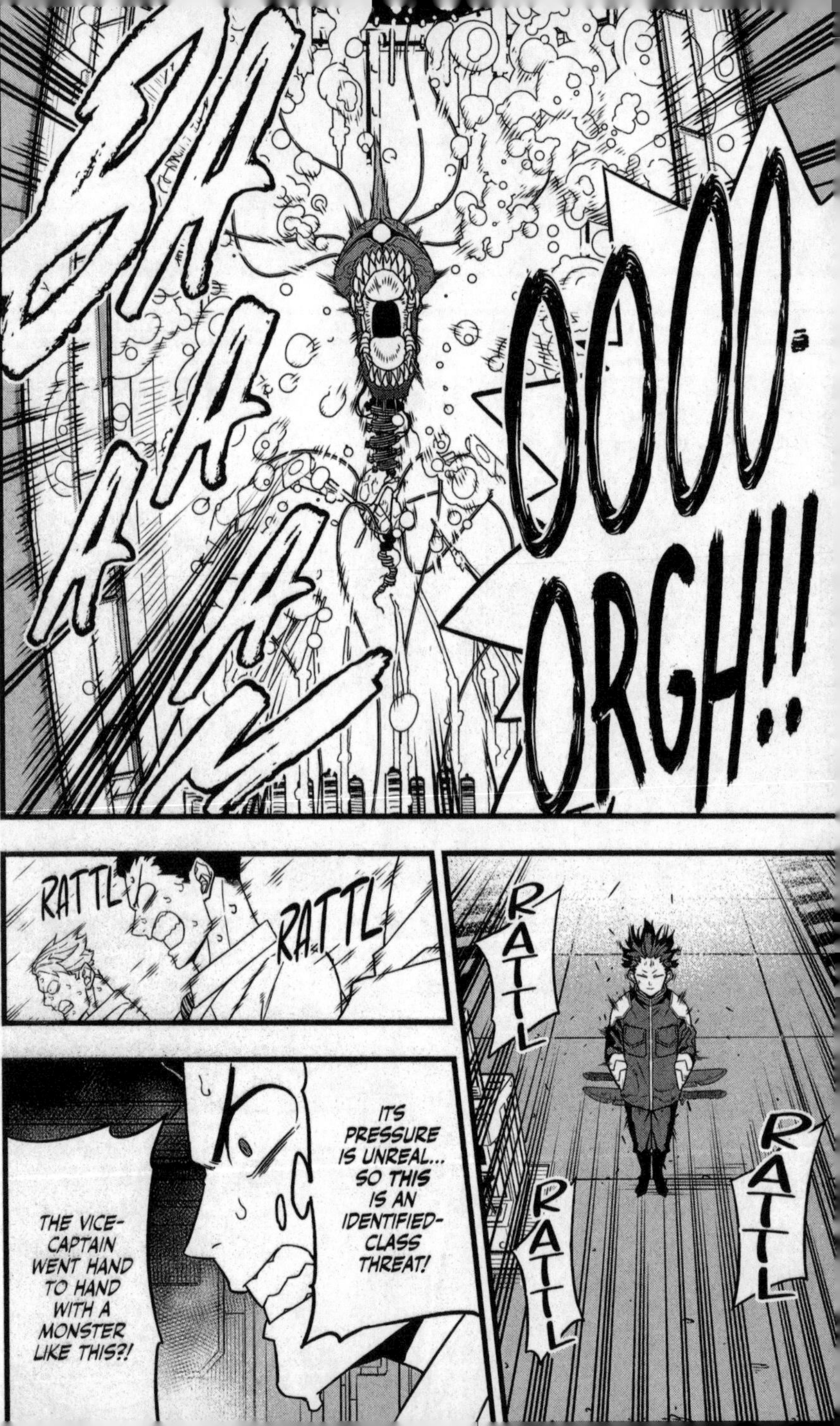
OOOO-
ORGH!!
RATTL
RATTL
RATTL
RATTL
RATTL
ITS PRESSURE IS UNREAL... SO THIS IS AN IDENTIFIED-CLASS THREAT!
THE VICE-CAPTAIN WENT HAND TO HAND WITH A MONSTER LIKE THIS?!

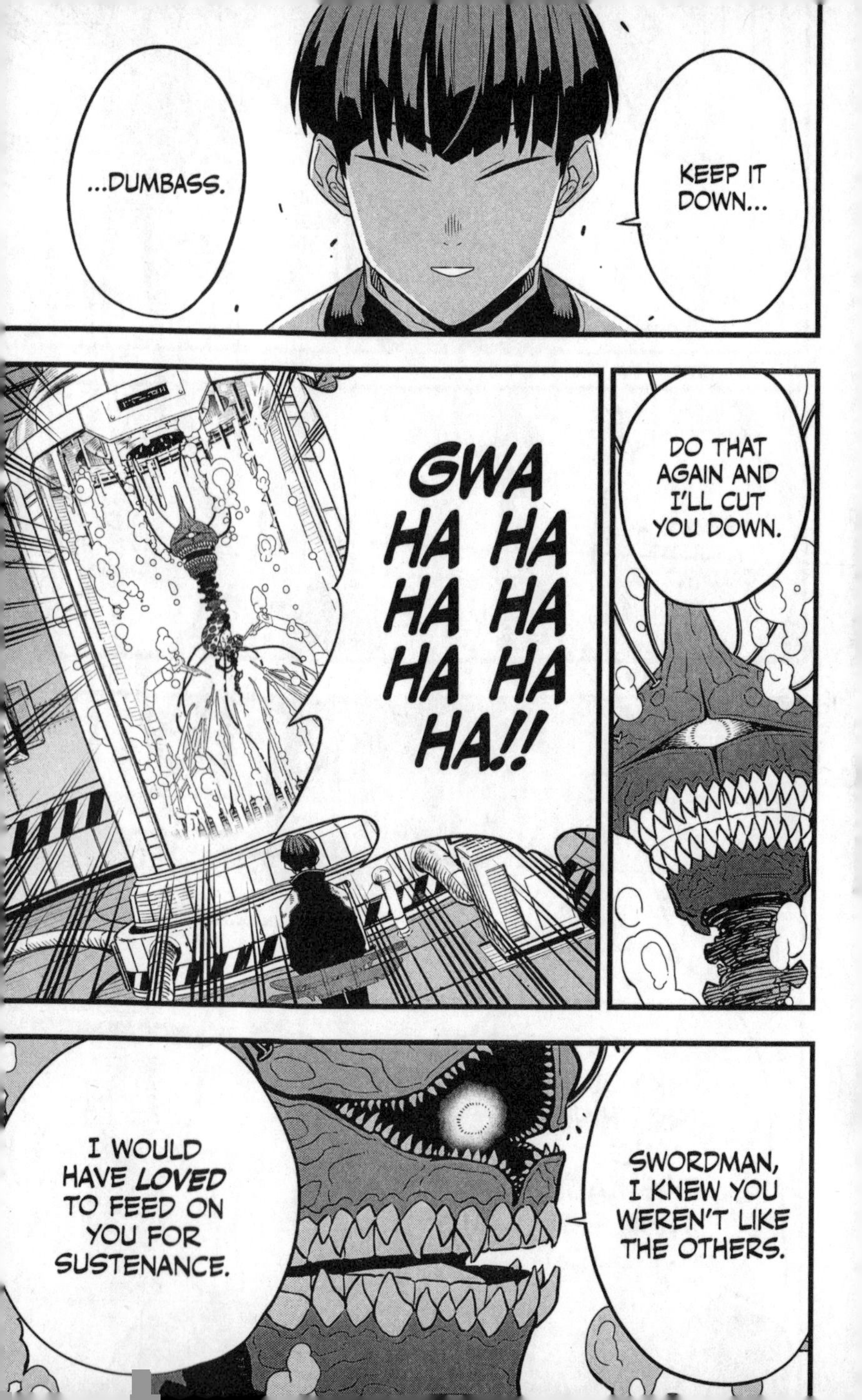
KEEP IT DOWN...
...DUMBASS.
DO THAT AGAIN AND I'LL CUT YOU DOWN.
GWA HA HA HA HA HA HA HA!!
SWORDMAN, I KNEW YOU WEREN'T LIKE THE OTHERS.
I WOULD HAVE *LOVED* TO FEED ON YOU FOR SUSTENANCE.

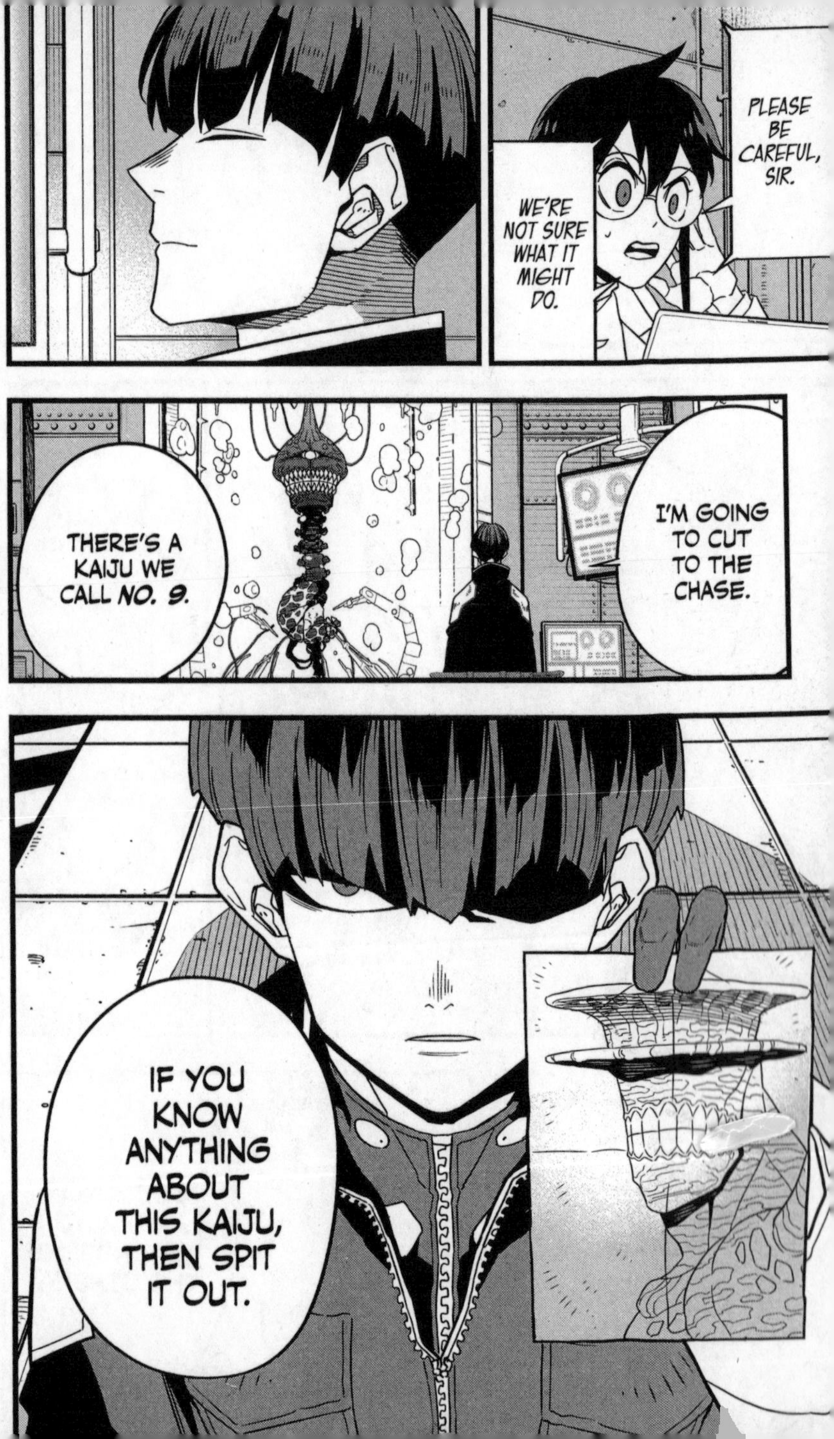
PLEASE BE CAREFUL, SIR.
WE'RE NOT SURE WHAT IT MIGHT DO.
I'M GOING TO CUT TO THE CHASE.
THERE'S A KAIJU WE CALL NO. 9.
IF YOU KNOW ANYTHING ABOUT THIS KAIJU, THEN SPIT IT OUT.

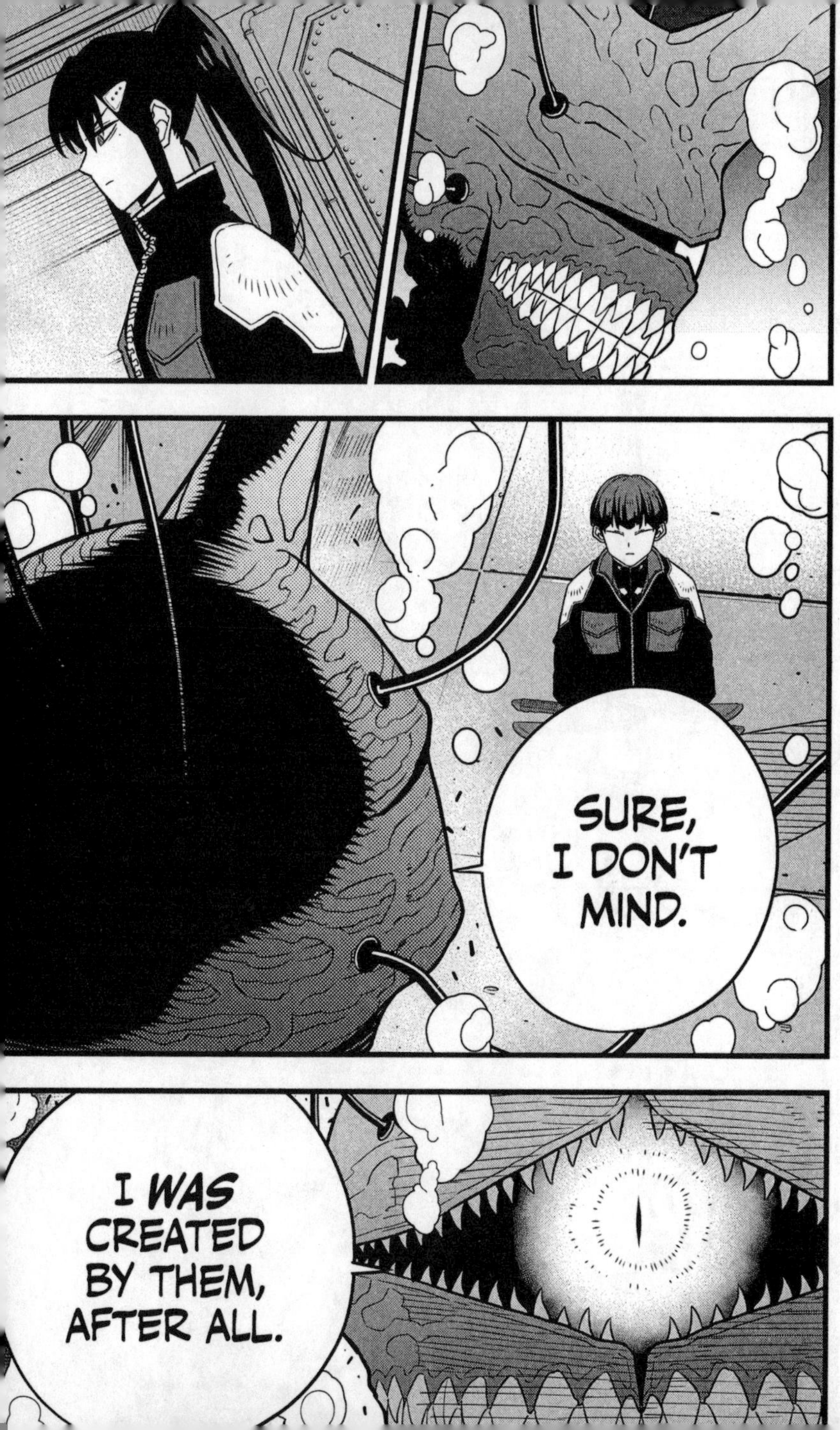
SURE, I DON'T MIND.
I *WAS* CREATED BY THEM, AFTER ALL.

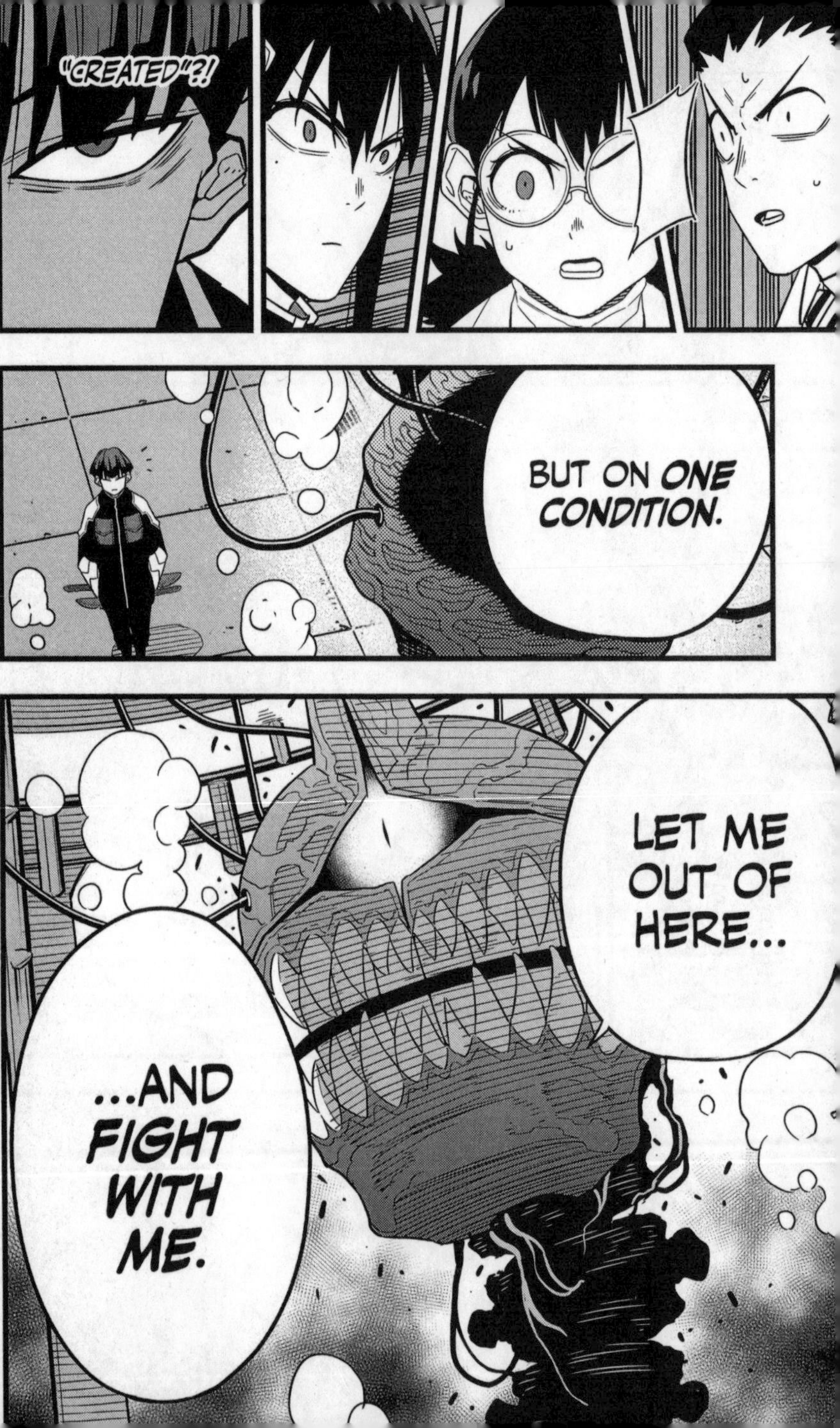
"CREATED"?!
BUT ON ONE CONDITION.
LET ME OUT OF HERE...
...AND FIGHT WITH ME.

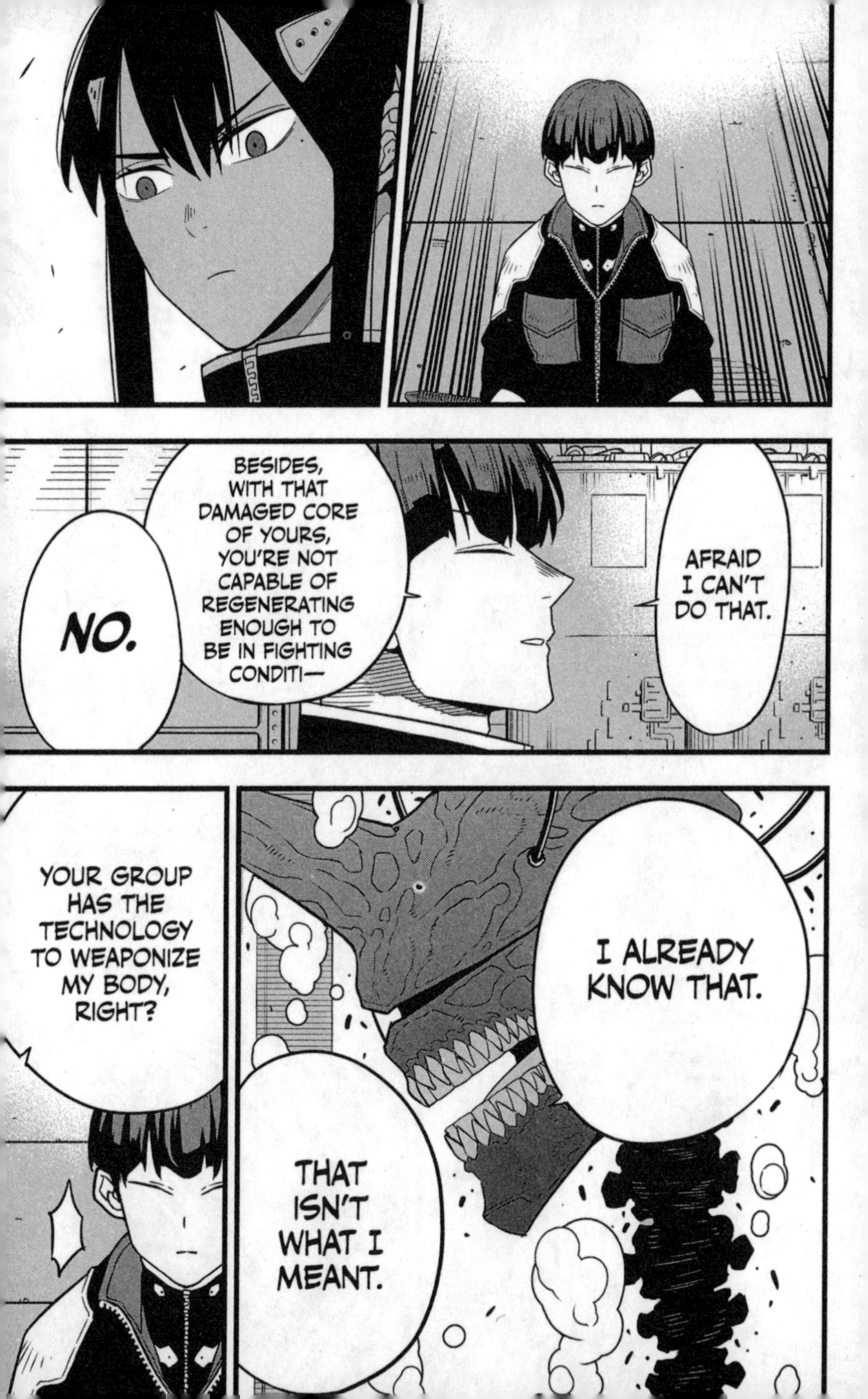
AFRAID I CAN'T DO THAT.
BESIDES, WITH THAT DAMAGED CORE OF YOURS, YOU'RE NOT CAPABLE OF REGENERATING ENOUGH TO BE IN FIGHTING CONDITI—
NO.
I ALREADY KNOW THAT.
THAT ISN'T WHAT I MEANT.
YOUR GROUP HAS THE TECHNOLOGY TO WEAPONIZE MY BODY, RIGHT?

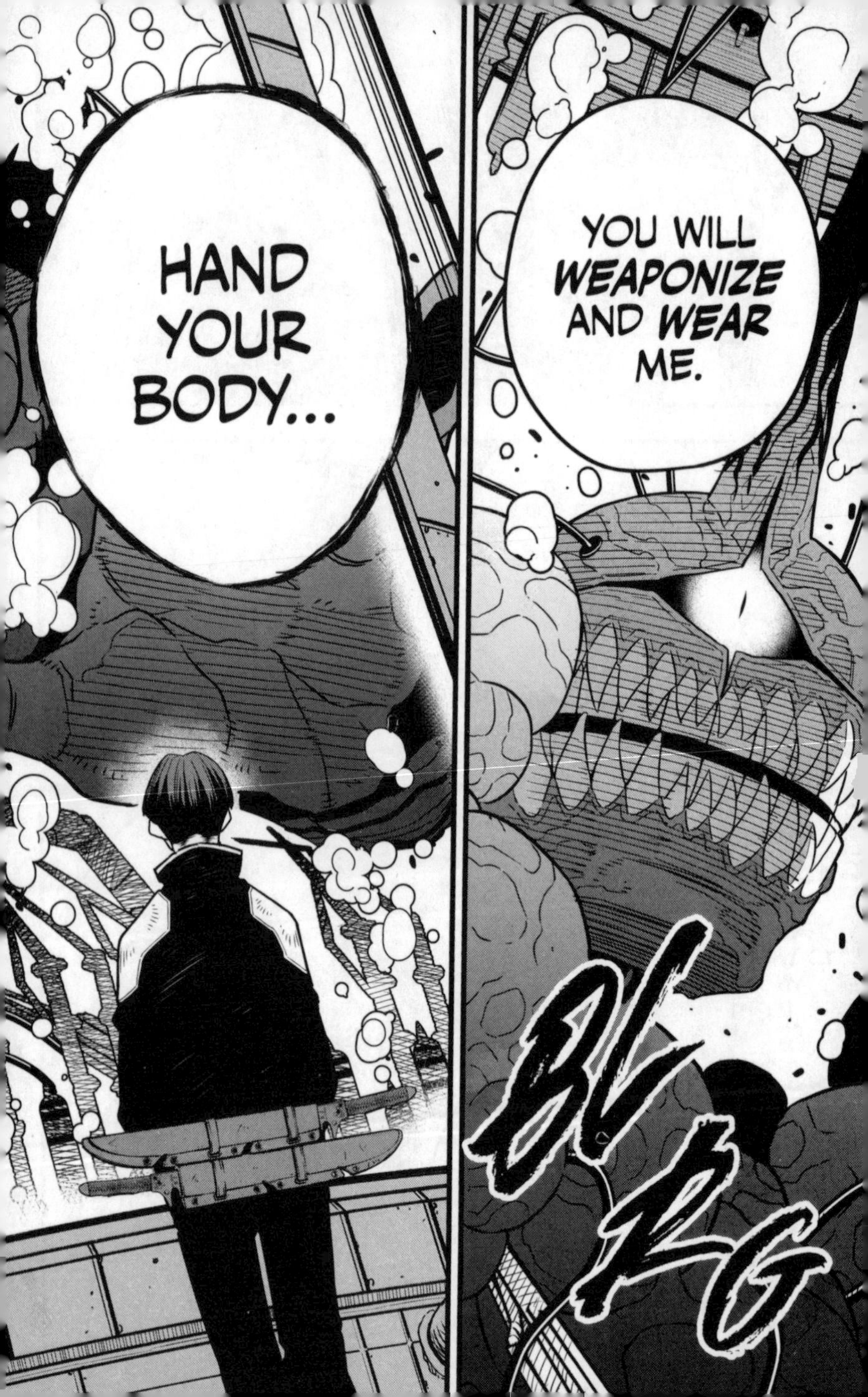
YOU WILL WEAPONIZE AND WEAR ME.
HAND YOUR BODY...

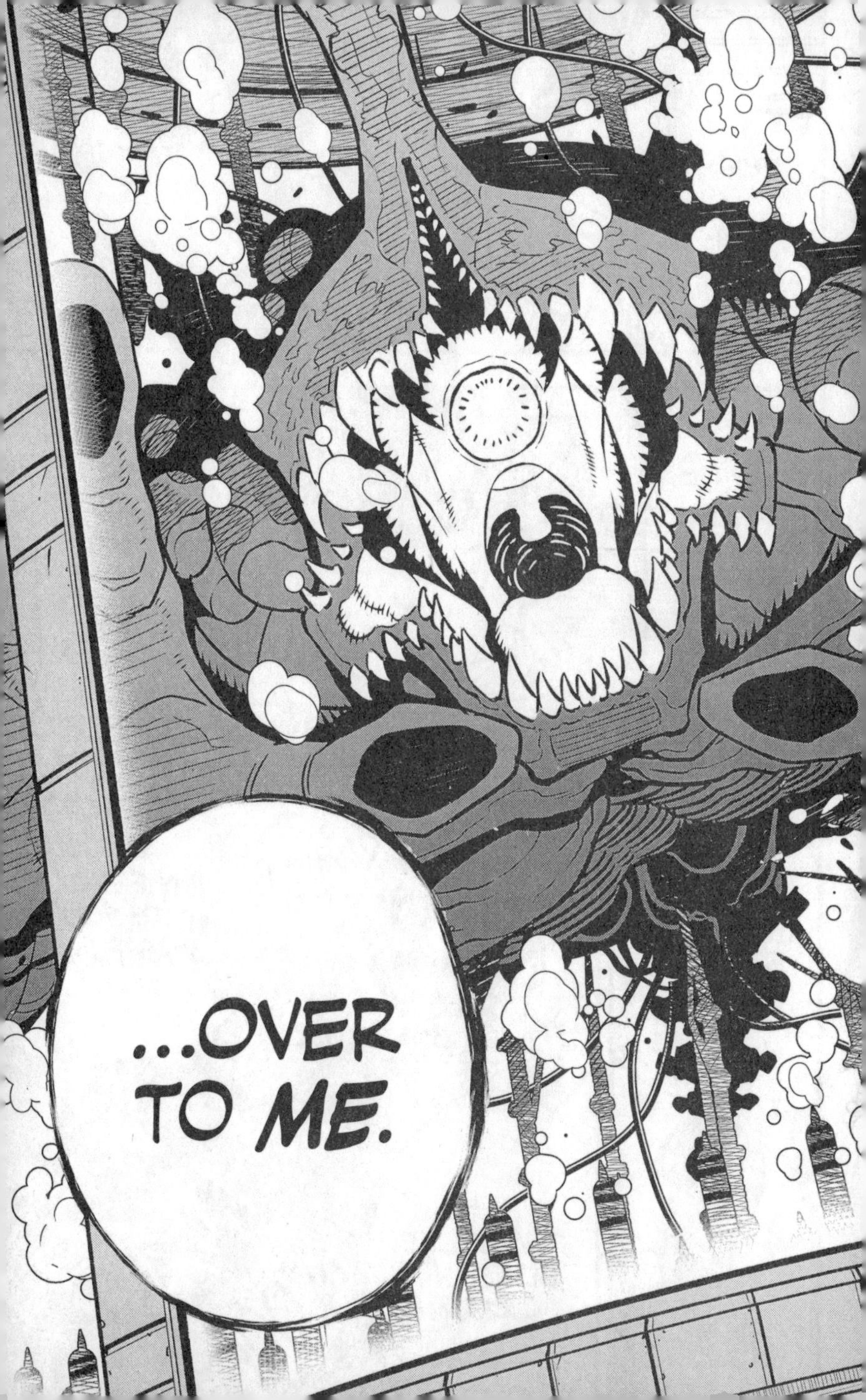
...OVER TO *ME.*

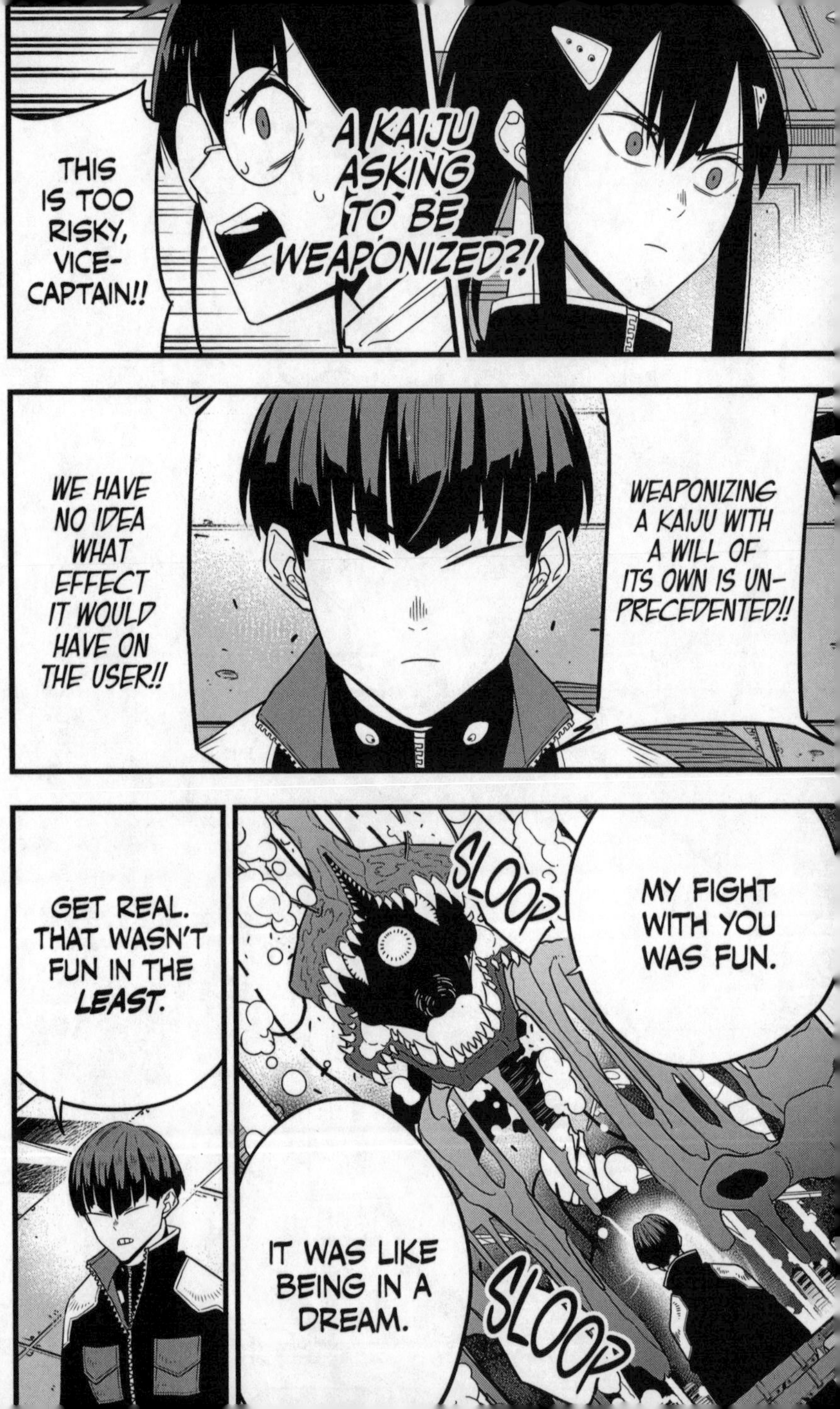
A KAIJU ASKING TO BE WEAPONIZED?!
THIS IS TOO RISKY, VICE-CAPTAIN!!
WEAPONIZING A KAIJU WITH A WILL OF ITS OWN IS UN-PRECEDENTED!!
WE HAVE NO IDEA WHAT EFFECT IT WOULD HAVE ON THE USER!!
MY FIGHT WITH YOU WAS FUN.
SLOOP
IT WAS LIKE BEING IN A DREAM.
SLOOP
GET REAL. THAT WASN'T FUN IN THE *LEAST*.

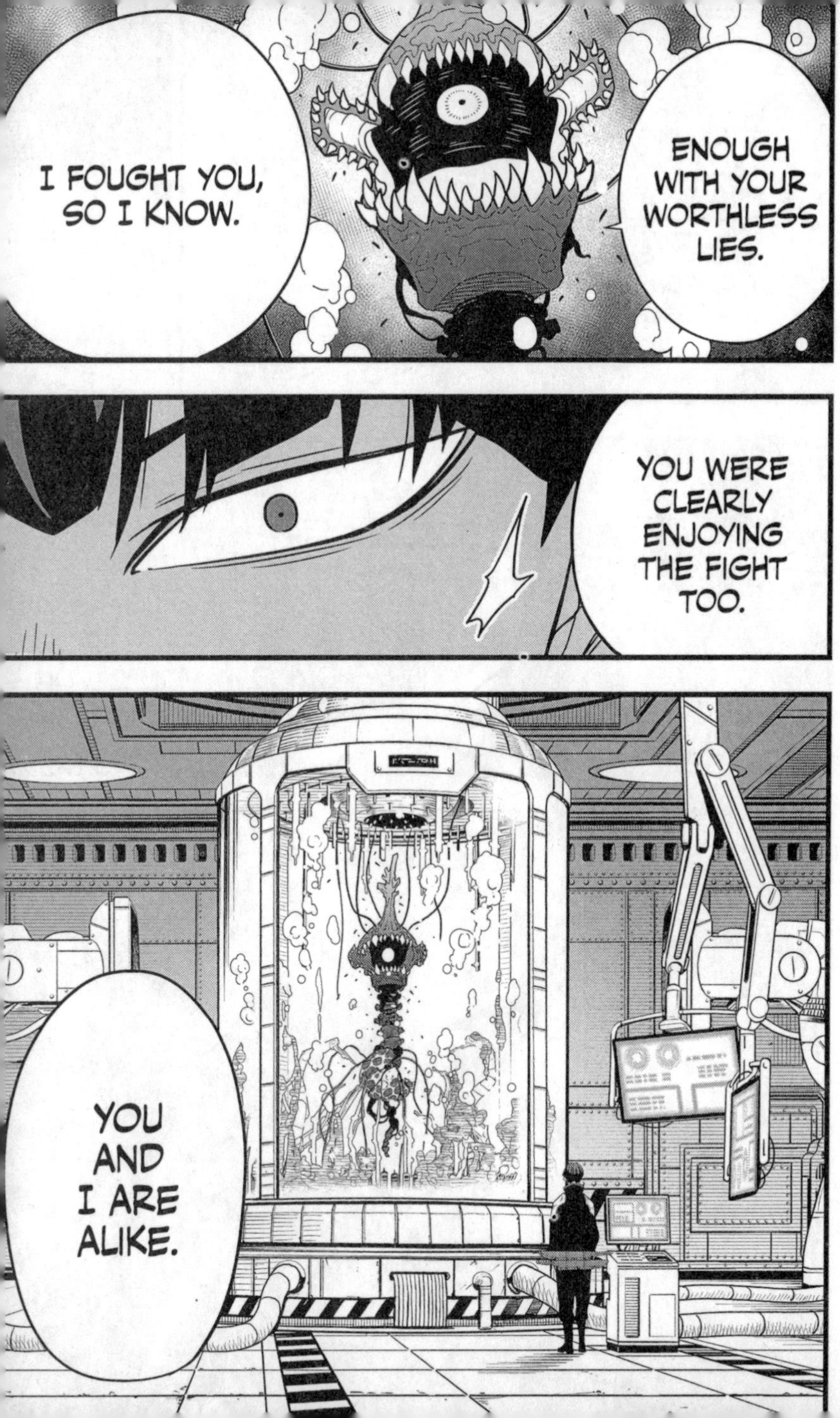
ENOUGH WITH YOUR WORTHLESS LIES.
I FOUGHT YOU, SO I KNOW.
YOU WERE CLEARLY ENJOYING THE FIGHT TOO.
YOU AND I ARE ALIKE.

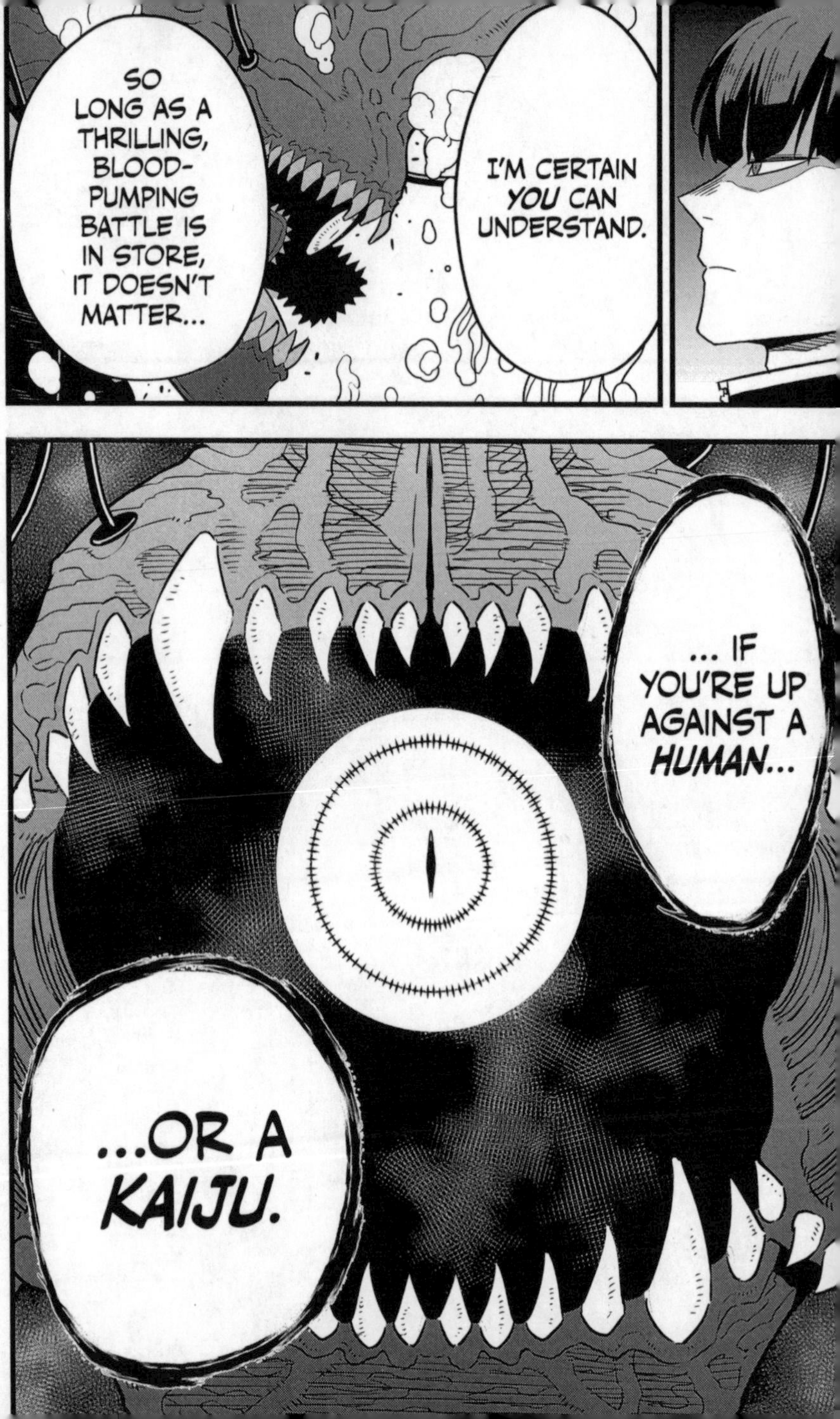
I'M CERTAIN YOU CAN UNDERSTAND.
SO LONG AS A THRILLING, BLOOD-PUMPING BATTLE IS IN STORE, IT DOESN'T MATTER...
... IF YOU'RE UP AGAINST A HUMAN...
...OR A KAIJU.

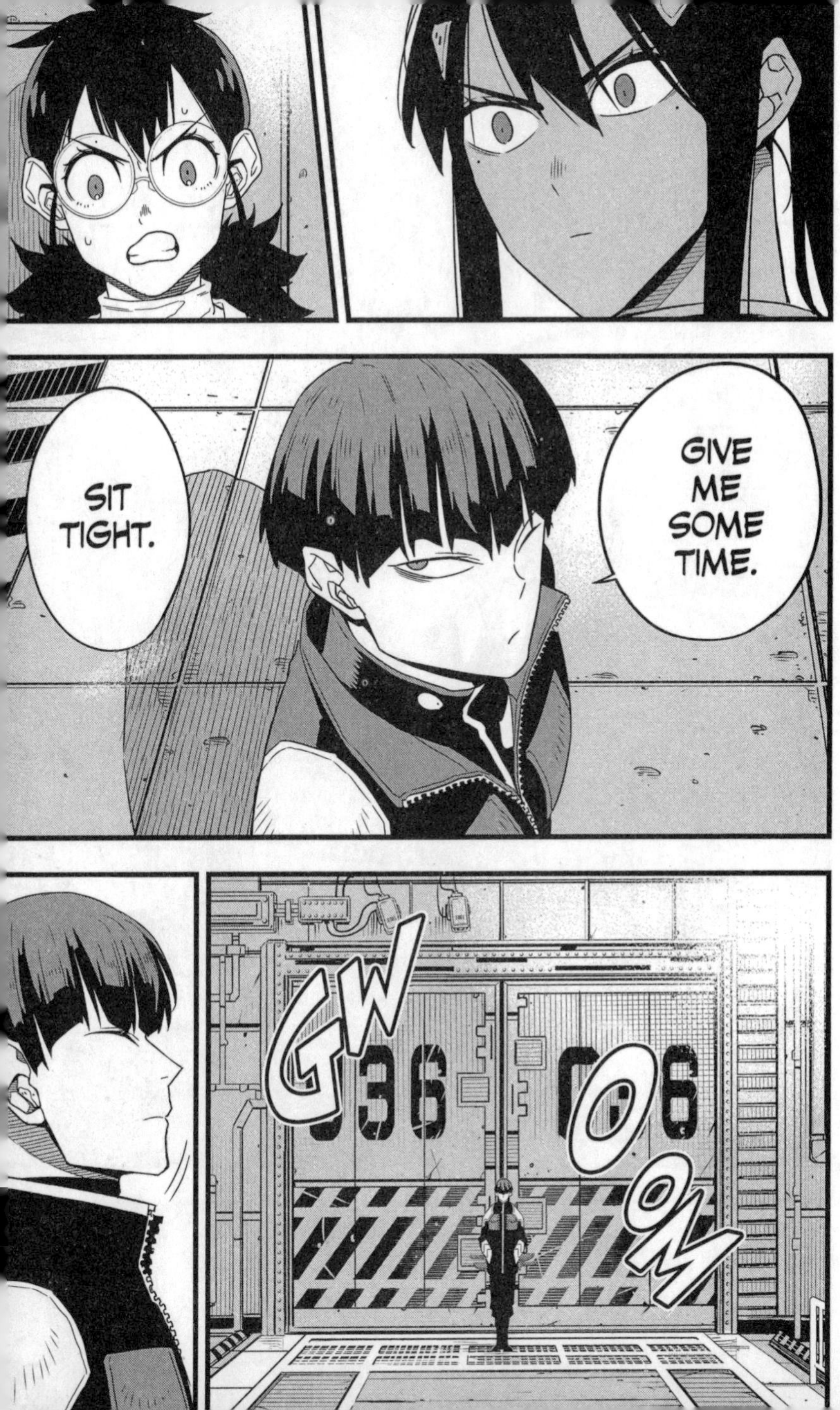
GIVE ME SOME TIME.
SIT TIGHT.
GWOOM

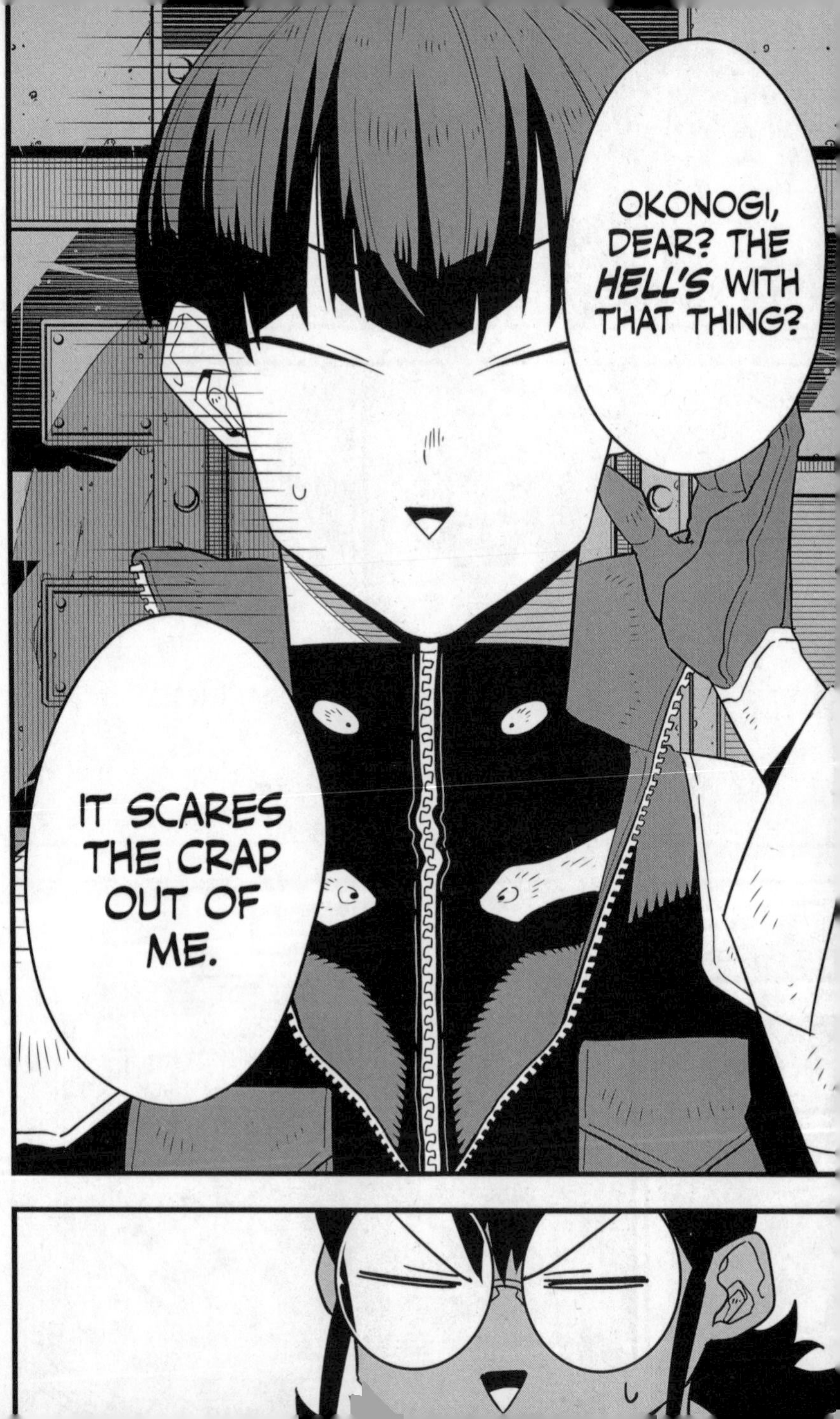
OKONOGI, DEAR? THE *HELL'S* WITH THAT THING?
IT SCARES THE CRAP OUT OF ME.

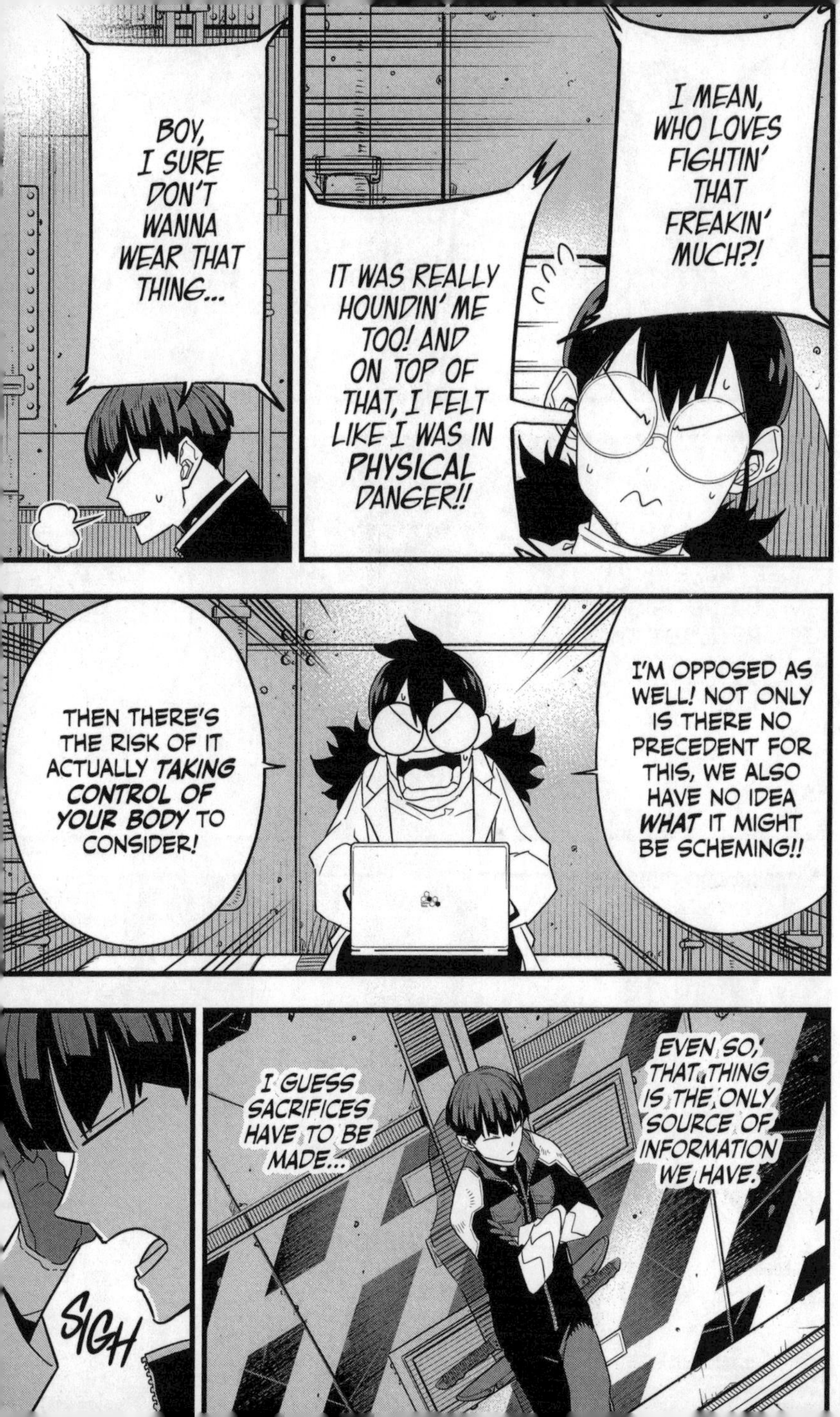
I MEAN, WHO LOVES FIGHTIN' THAT FREAKIN' MUCH?!
IT WAS REALLY HOUNDIN' ME TOO! AND ON TOP OF THAT, I FELT LIKE I WAS IN PHYSICAL DANGER!!
BOY, I SURE DON'T WANNA WEAR THAT THING...
I'M OPPOSED AS WELL! NOT ONLY IS THERE NO PRECEDENT FOR THIS, WE ALSO HAVE NO IDEA *WHAT* IT MIGHT BE SCHEMING!!
THEN THERE'S THE RISK OF IT ACTUALLY *TAKING CONTROL OF YOUR BODY* TO CONSIDER!
EVEN SO, THAT THING IS THE ONLY SOURCE OF INFORMATION WE HAVE.
I GUESS SACRIFICES HAVE TO BE MADE...
SIGH

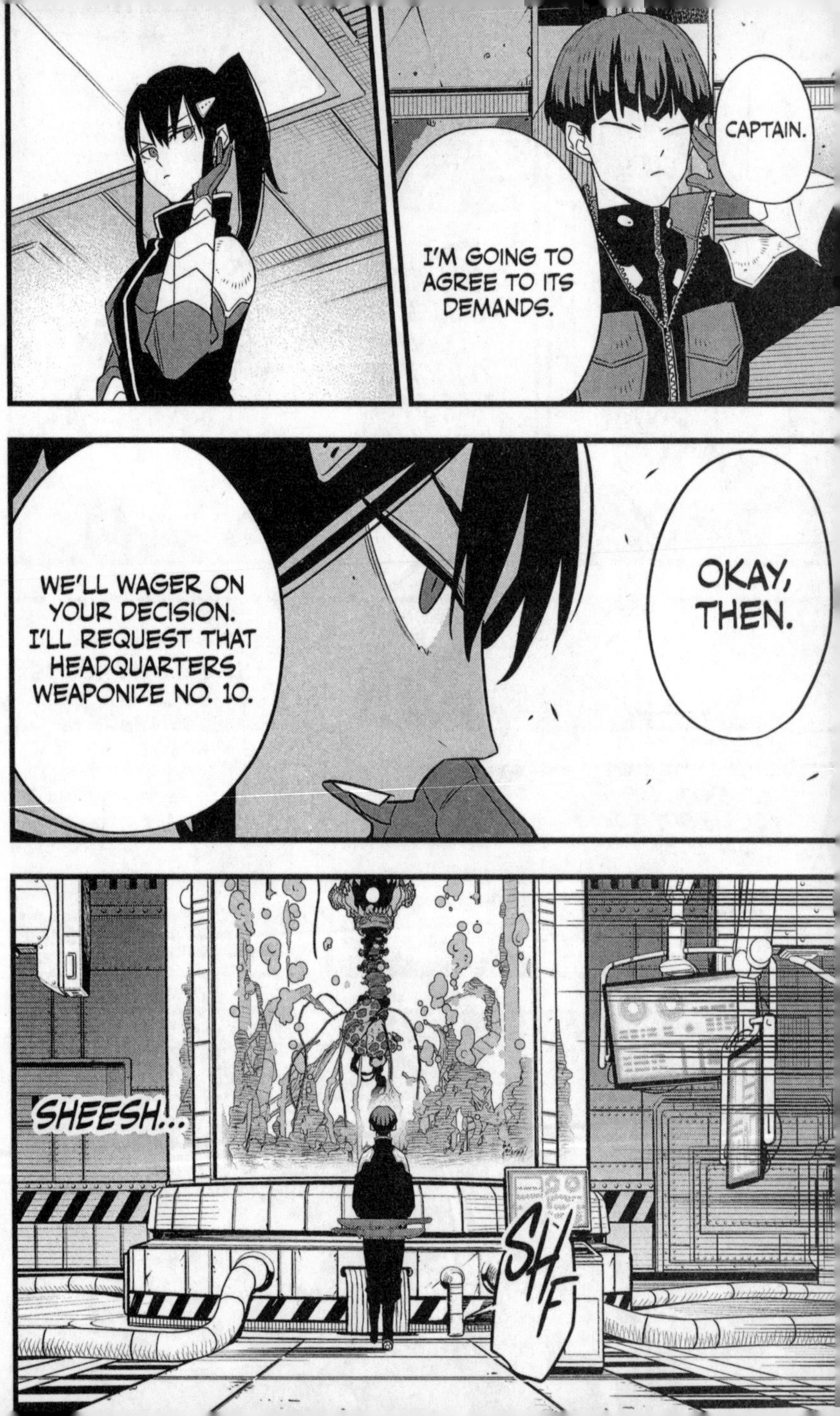
CAPTAIN.
I'M GOING TO AGREE TO ITS DEMANDS.
OKAY, THEN.
WE'LL WAGER ON YOUR DECISION. I'LL REQUEST THAT HEADQUARTERS WEAPONIZE NO. 10.
SHF
SHEESH...

I SURE GOT MYSELF ONE WEIRD ADMIRER.

TALK.

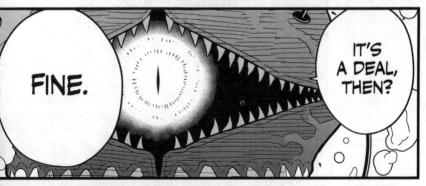

FINE.

IT'S A DEAL, THEN?

BUT LET'S MAKE ONE THING CLEAR.

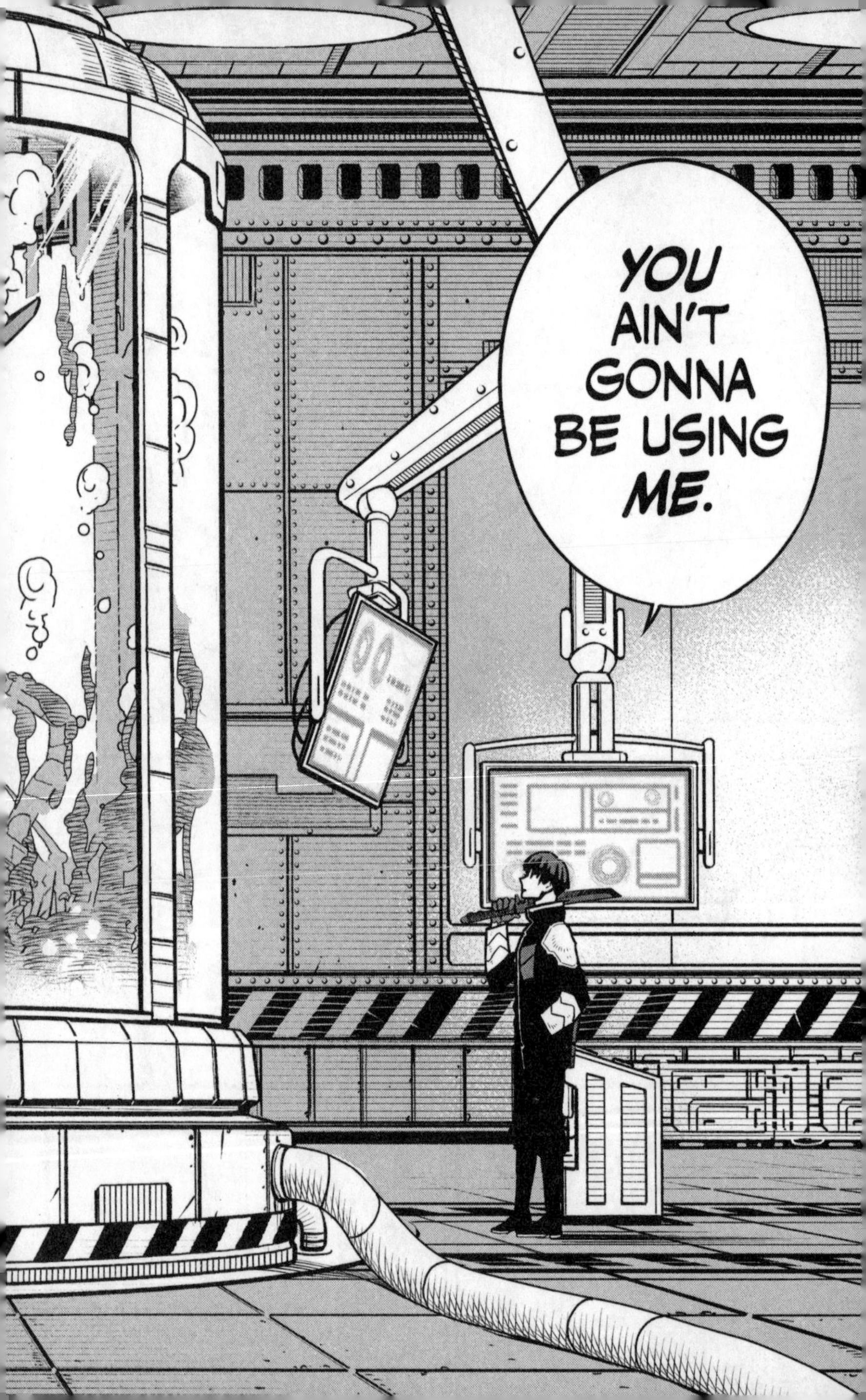
YOU AIN'T GONNA BE USING ME.

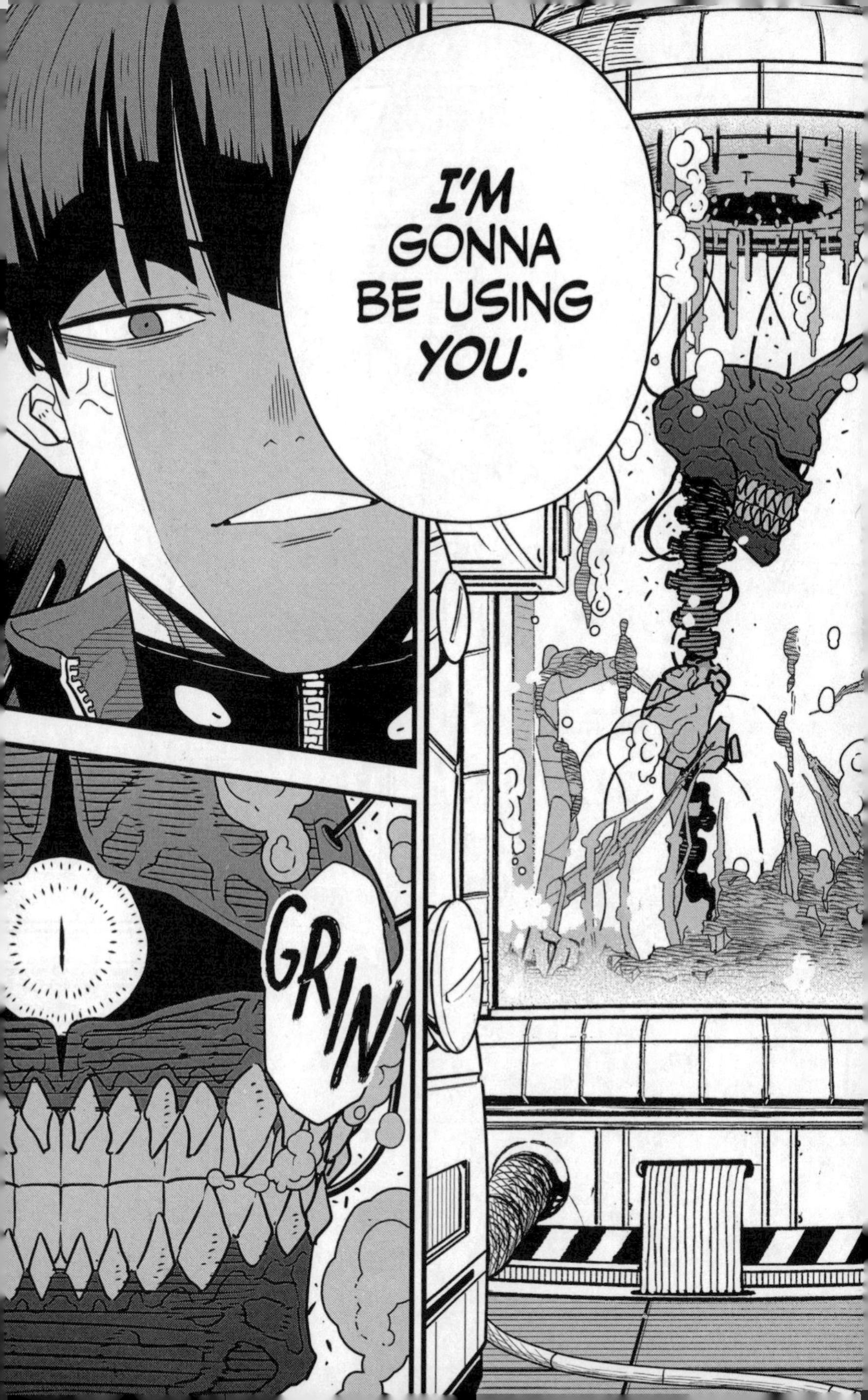
I'M GONNA BE USING YOU.
GRIN

KAIJU NO. 8, EPISODE 6
THE COMPATIBLE USER

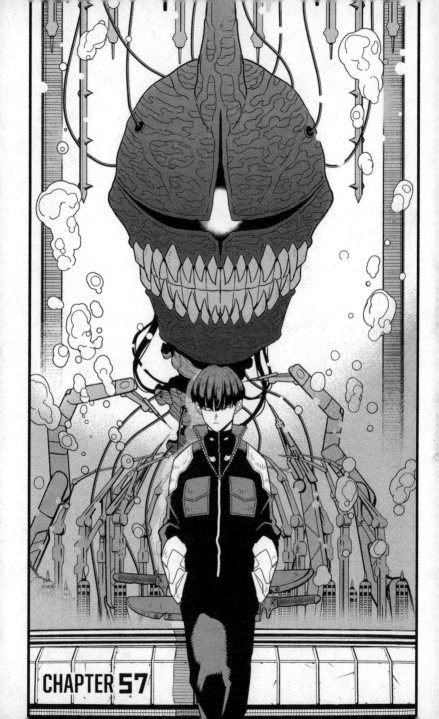

CHAPTER 57

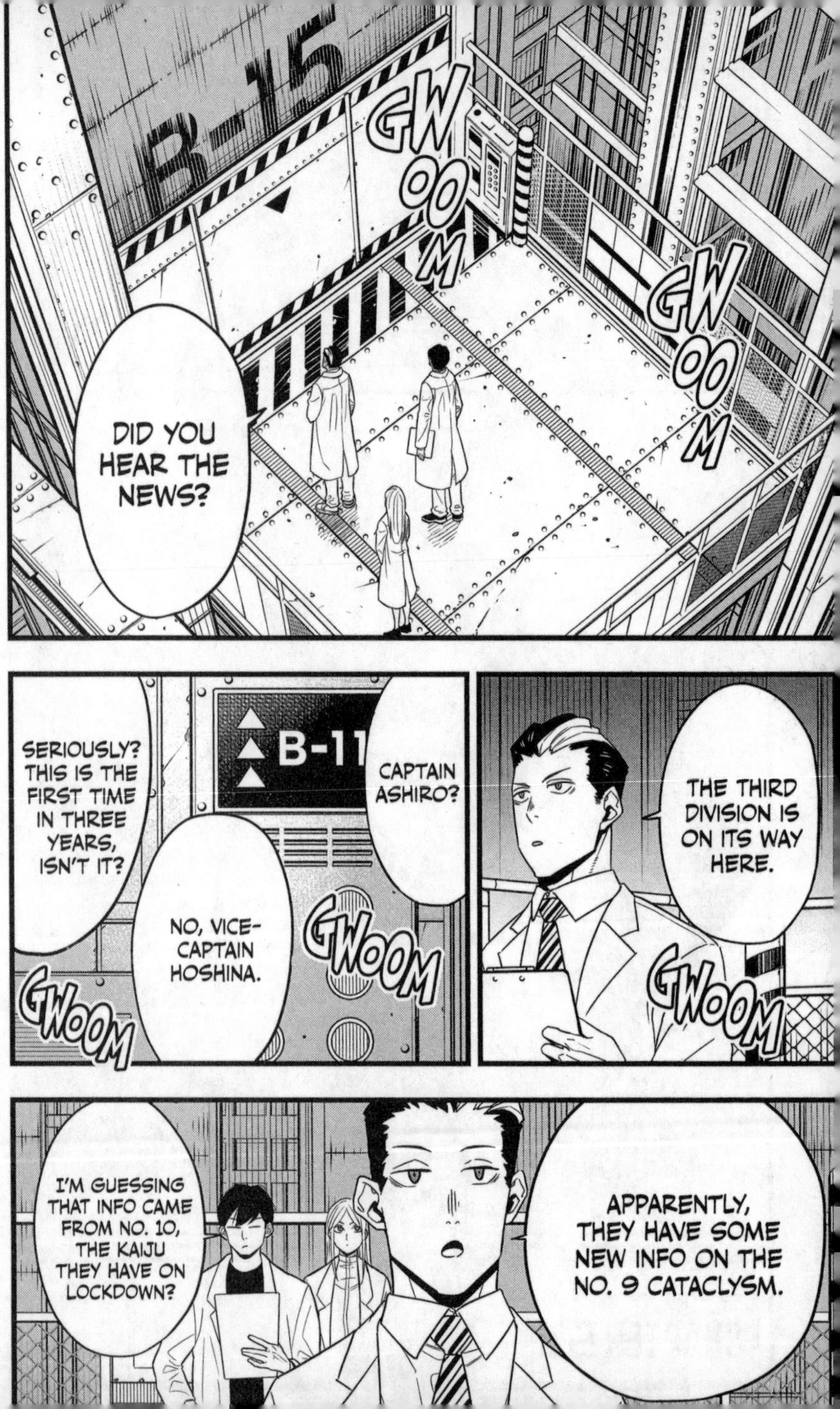
B-15
GWOOOM
GWOOOM
DID YOU HEAR THE NEWS?
THE THIRD DIVISION IS ON ITS WAY HERE.
GWOOM
B-11
CAPTAIN ASHIRO?
SERIOUSLY? THIS IS THE FIRST TIME IN THREE YEARS, ISN'T IT?
NO, VICE-CAPTAIN HOSHINA.
GWOOM
GWOOM
APPARENTLY, THEY HAVE SOME NEW INFO ON THE NO. 9 CATACLYSM.
I'M GUESSING THAT INFO CAME FROM NO. 10, THE KAIJU THEY HAVE ON LOCKDOWN?

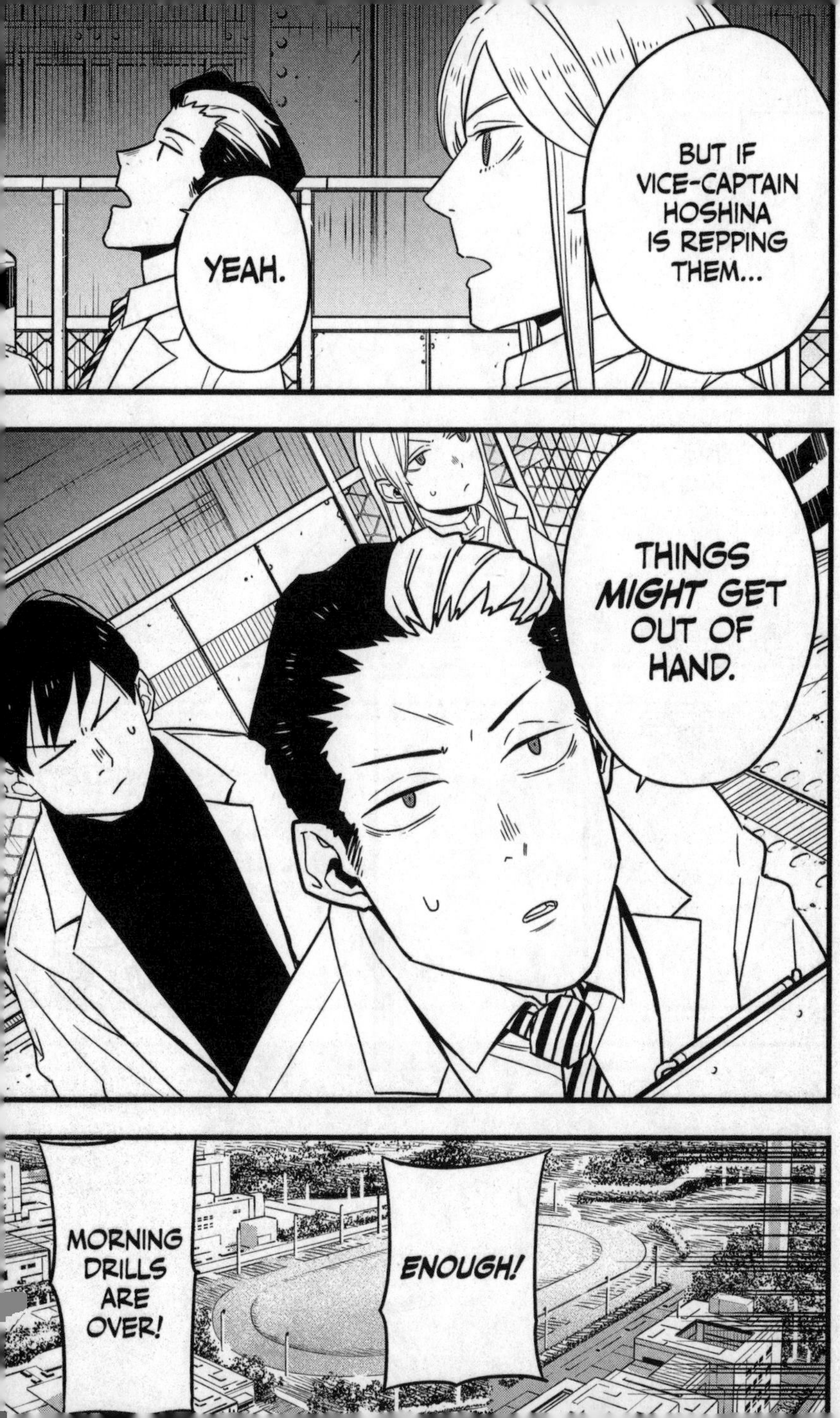
BUT IF VICE-CAPTAIN HOSHINA IS REPPING THEM...
YEAH.
THINGS *MIGHT* GET OUT OF HAND.
ENOUGH!
MORNING DRILLS ARE OVER!

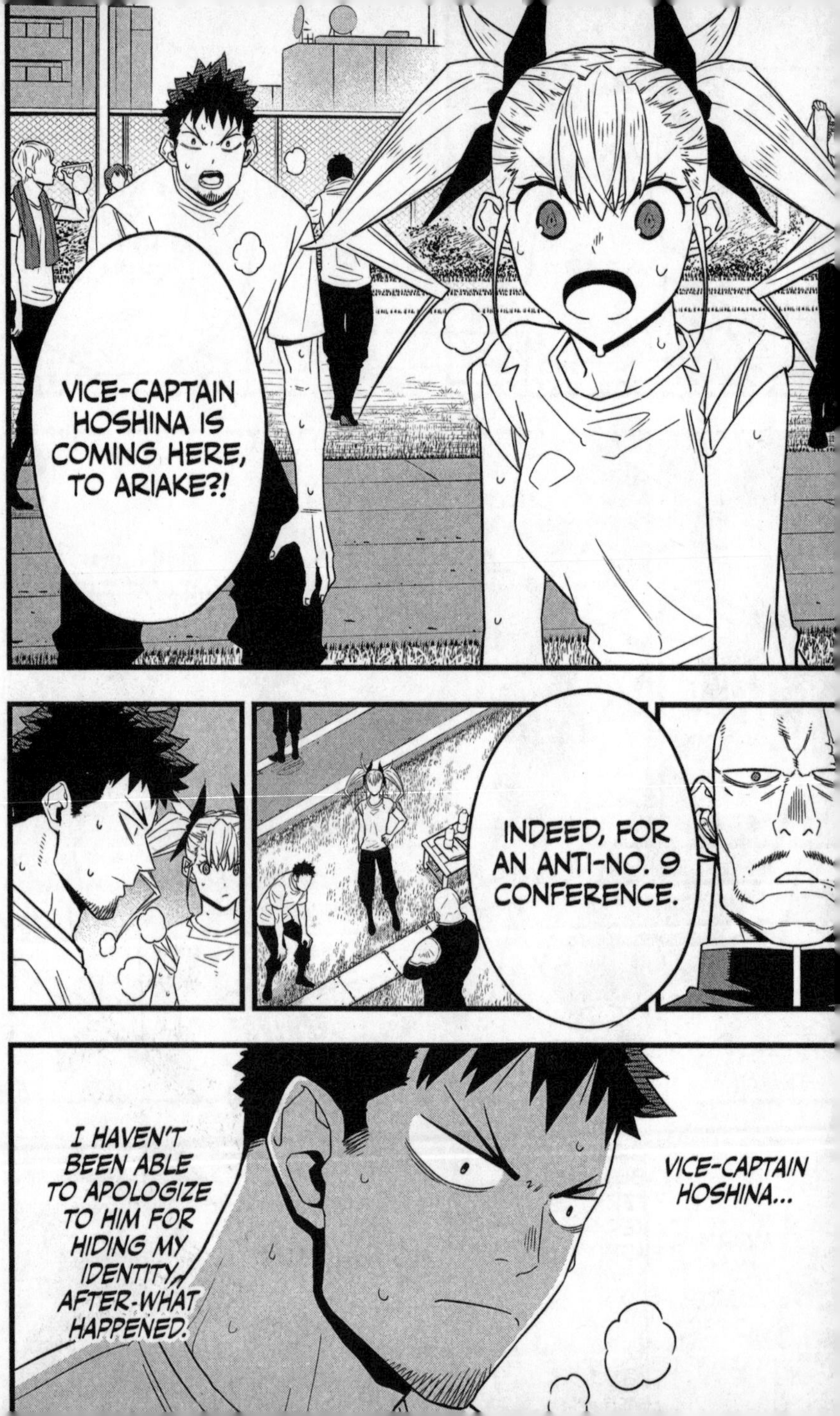
VICE-CAPTAIN HOSHINA IS COMING HERE, TO ARIAKE?!
INDEED, FOR AN ANTI-NO. 9 CONFERENCE.
VICE-CAPTAIN HOSHINA...
I HAVEN'T BEEN ABLE TO APOLOGIZE TO HIM FOR HIDING MY IDENTITY AFTER WHAT HAPPENED.

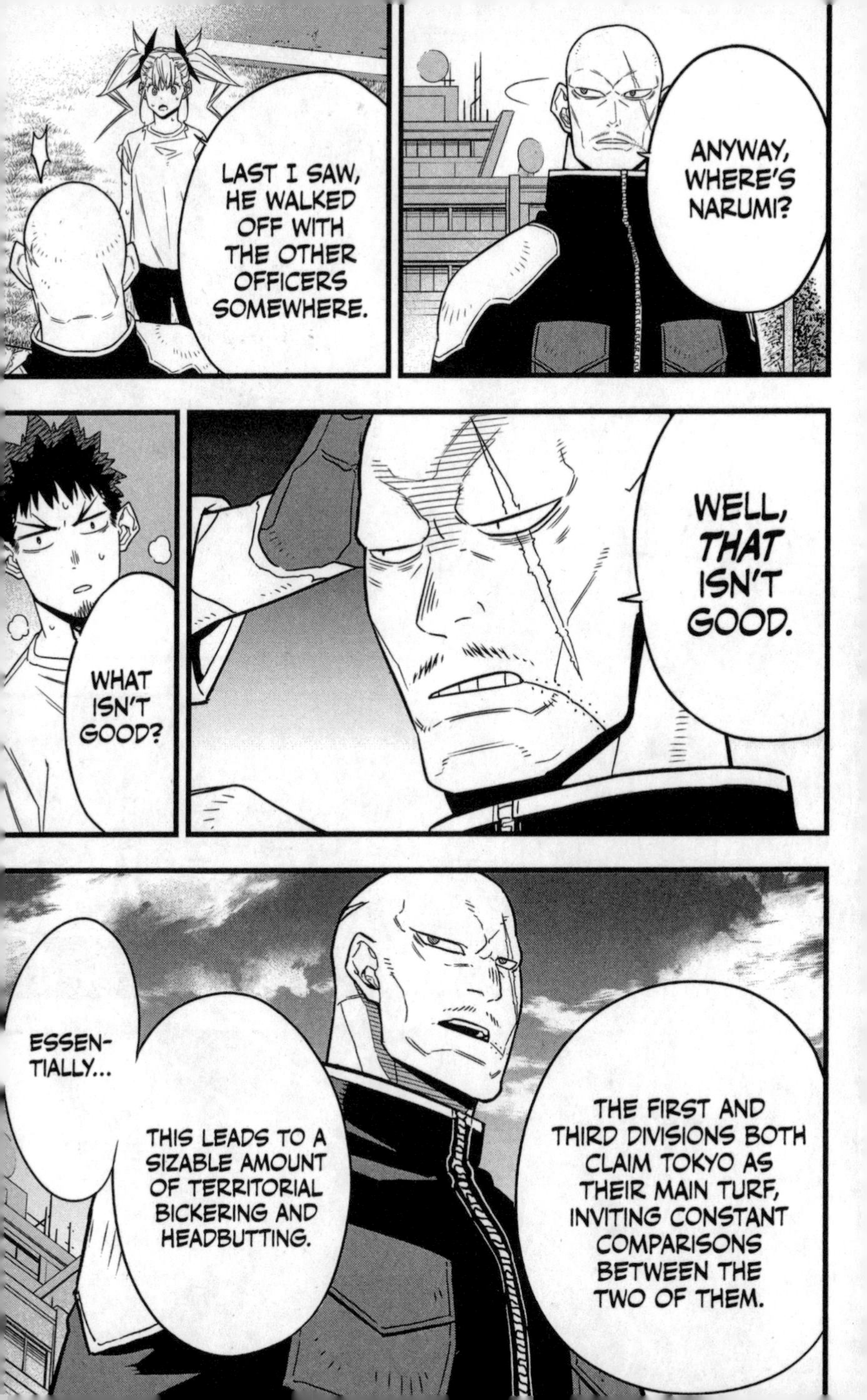
ANYWAY, WHERE'S NARUMI?
LAST I SAW, HE WALKED OFF WITH THE OTHER OFFICERS SOMEWHERE.
WELL, *THAT* ISN'T GOOD.
WHAT ISN'T GOOD?
ESSENTIALLY...
THE FIRST AND THIRD DIVISIONS BOTH CLAIM TOKYO AS THEIR MAIN TURF, INVITING CONSTANT COMPARISONS BETWEEN THE TWO OF THEM.
THIS LEADS TO A SIZABLE AMOUNT OF TERRITORIAL BICKERING AND HEADBUTTING.

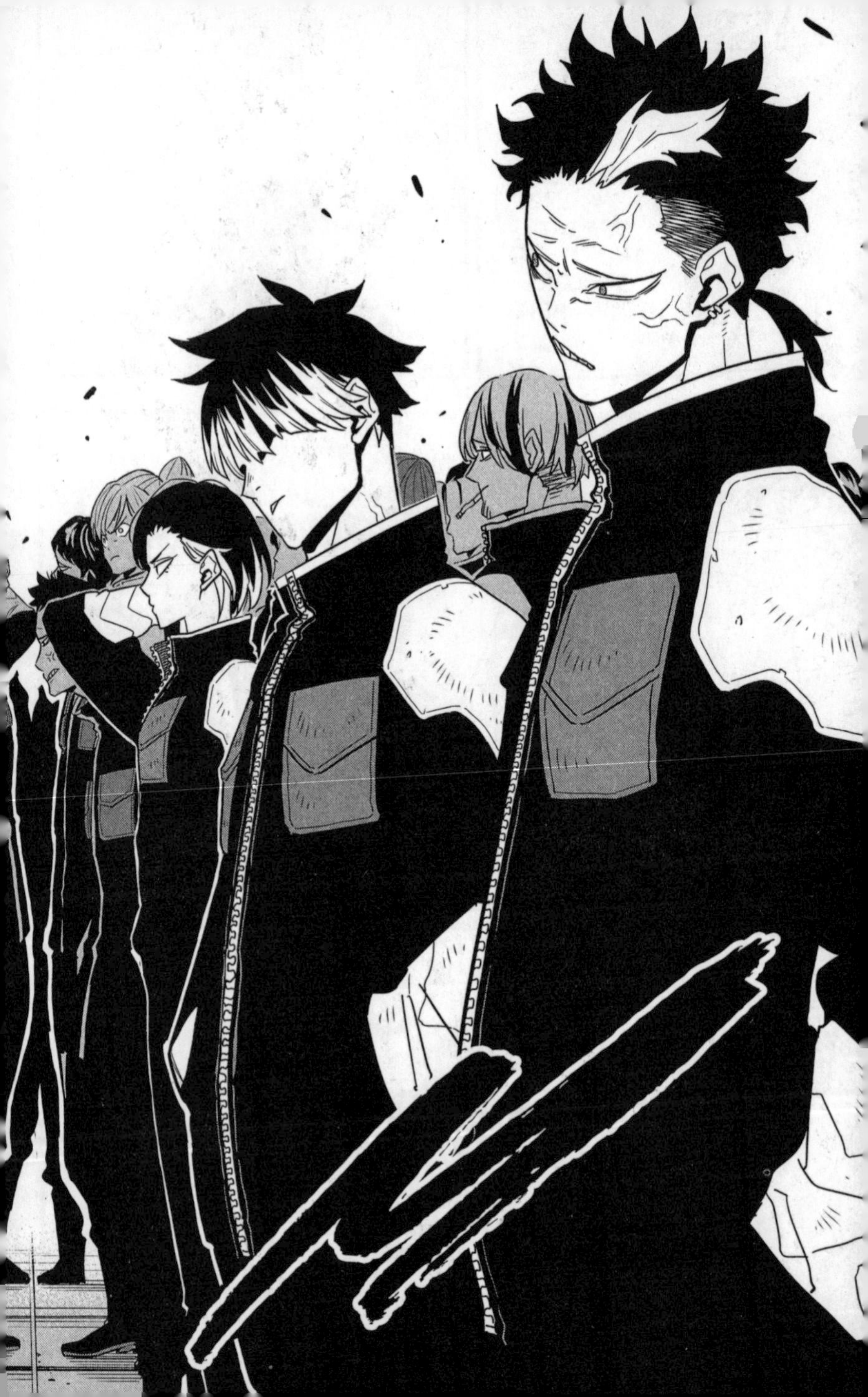

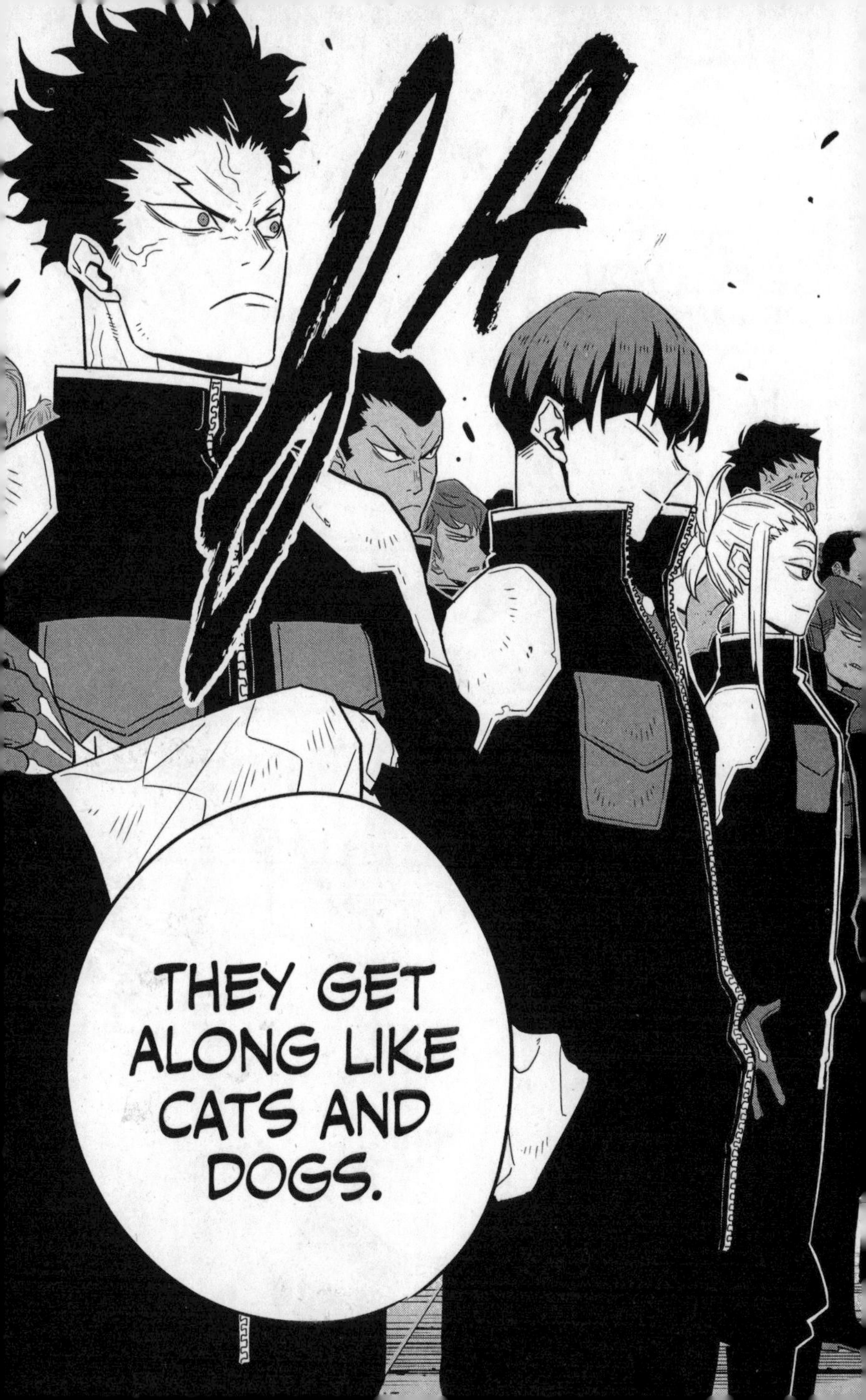
THEY GET ALONG LIKE CATS AND DOGS.

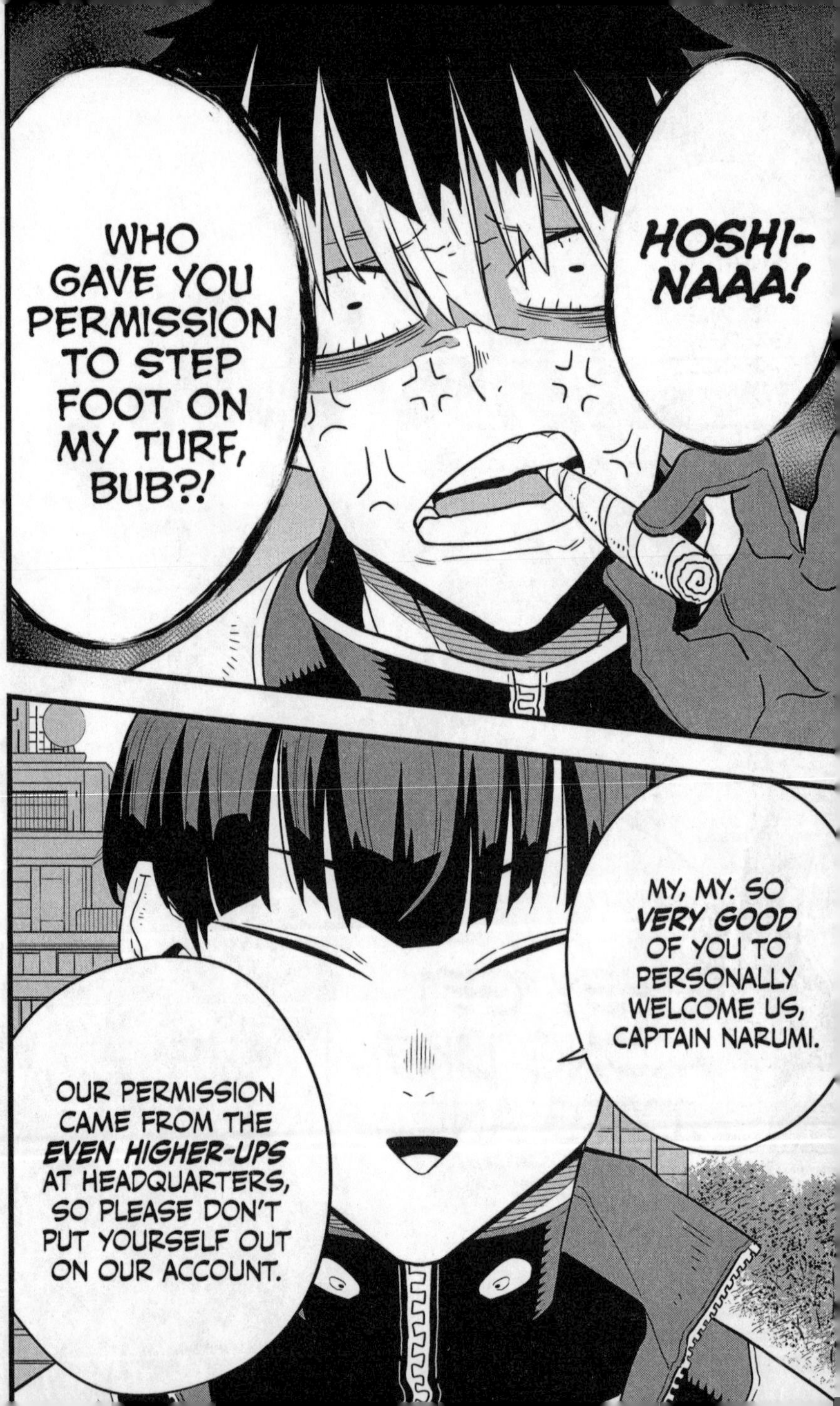
HOSHI-NAAAA!
WHO GAVE YOU PERMISSION TO STEP FOOT ON MY TURF, BUB?!
MY, MY. SO VERY GOOD OF YOU TO PERSONALLY WELCOME US, CAPTAIN NARUMI.
OUR PERMISSION CAME FROM THE EVEN HIGHER-UPS AT HEADQUARTERS, SO PLEASE DON'T PUT YOURSELF OUT ON OUR ACCOUNT.

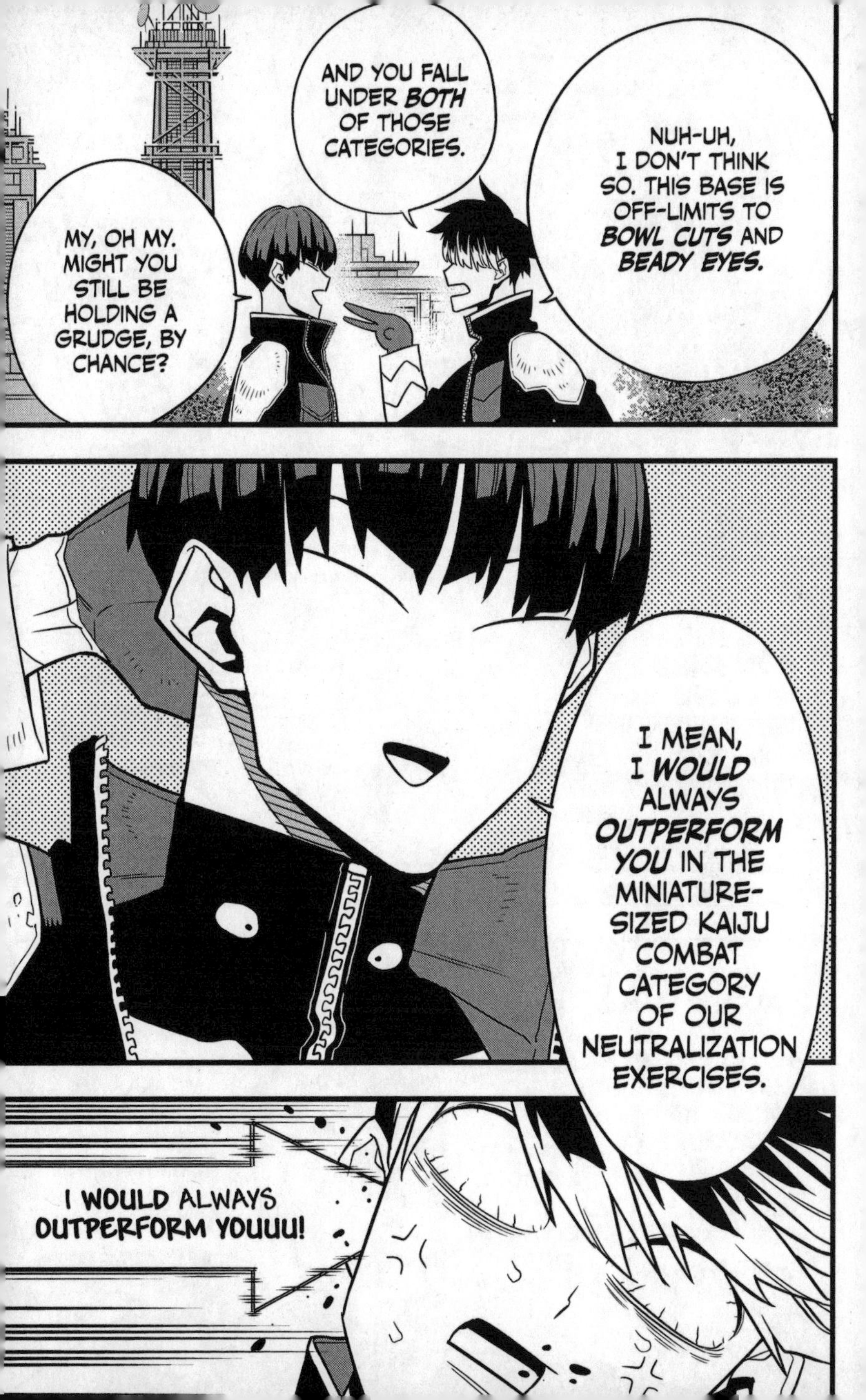

NUH-UH, I DON'T THINK SO. THIS BASE IS OFF-LIMITS TO BOWL CUTS AND BEADY EYES.
AND YOU FALL UNDER BOTH OF THOSE CATEGORIES.
MY, OH MY. MIGHT YOU STILL BE HOLDING A GRUDGE, BY CHANCE?
I MEAN, I WOULD ALWAYS OUTPERFORM YOU IN THE MINIATURE-SIZED KAIJU COMBAT CATEGORY OF OUR NEUTRALIZATION EXERCISES.
I WOULD ALWAYS OUTPERFORM YOUUU!

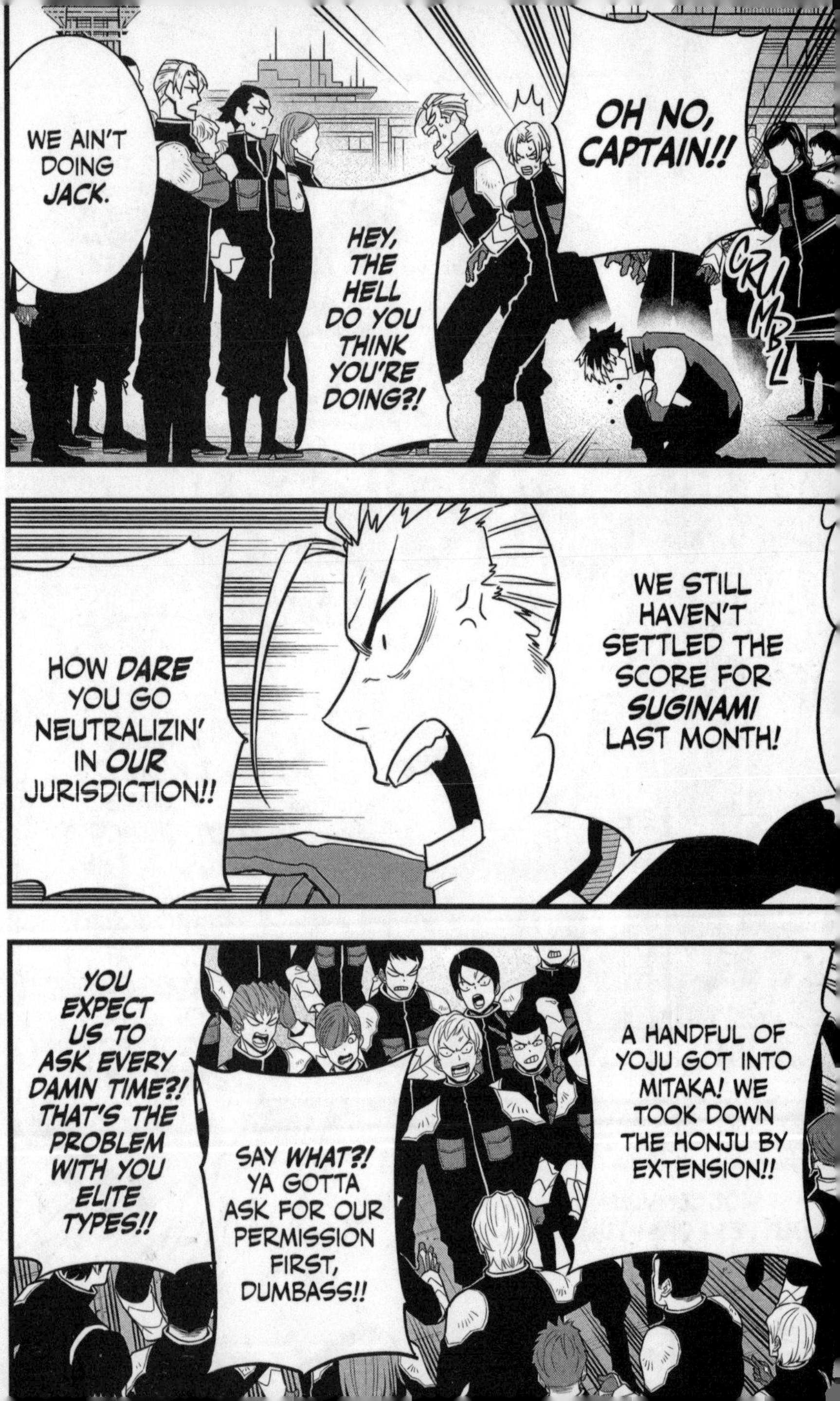
OH NO, CAPTAIN!!
CRUMBL
HEY, THE HELL DO YOU THINK YOU'RE DOING?!
WE AIN'T DOING JACK.
WE STILL HAVEN'T SETTLED THE SCORE FOR SUGINAMI LAST MONTH!
HOW DARE YOU GO NEUTRALIZIN' IN OUR JURISDICTION!!
A HANDFUL OF YOJU GOT INTO MITAKA! WE TOOK DOWN THE HONJU BY EXTENSION!!
SAY WHAT?! YA GOTTA ASK FOR OUR PERMISSION FIRST, DUMBASS!!
YOU EXPECT US TO ASK EVERY DAMN TIME?! THAT'S THE PROBLEM WITH YOU ELITE TYPES!!

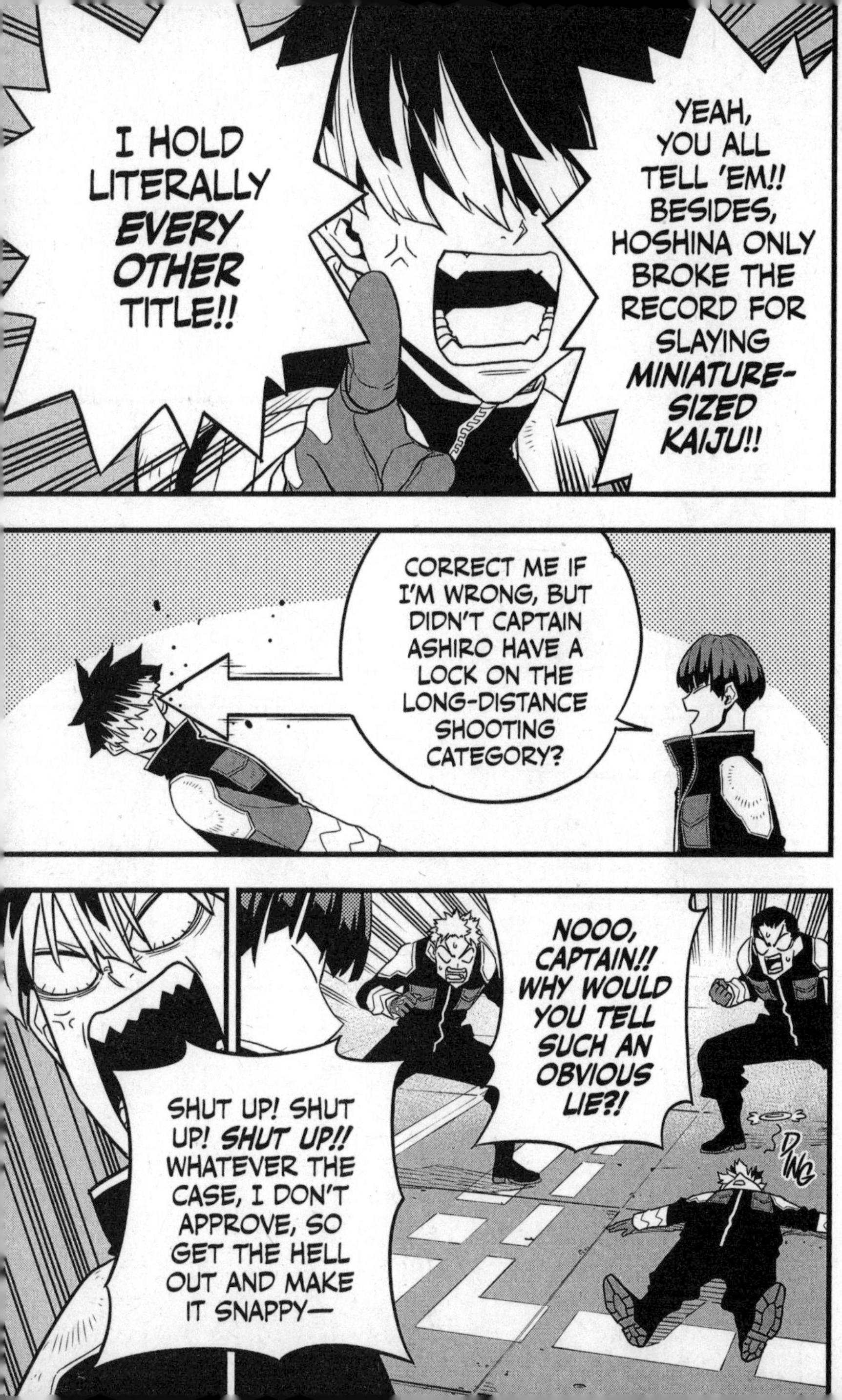
YEAH, YOU ALL TELL 'EM!! BESIDES, HOSHINA ONLY BROKE THE RECORD FOR SLAYING *MINIATURE-SIZED KAIJU!!*
I HOLD LITERALLY *EVERY OTHER* TITLE!!
CORRECT ME IF I'M WRONG, BUT DIDN'T CAPTAIN ASHIRO HAVE A LOCK ON THE LONG-DISTANCE SHOOTING CATEGORY?
NOOO, CAPTAIN!! WHY WOULD YOU TELL SUCH AN OBVIOUS LIE?!
DING
SHUT UP! SHUT UP! *SHUT UP!!* WHATEVER THE CASE, I DON'T APPROVE, SO GET THE HELL OUT AND MAKE IT SNAPPY—

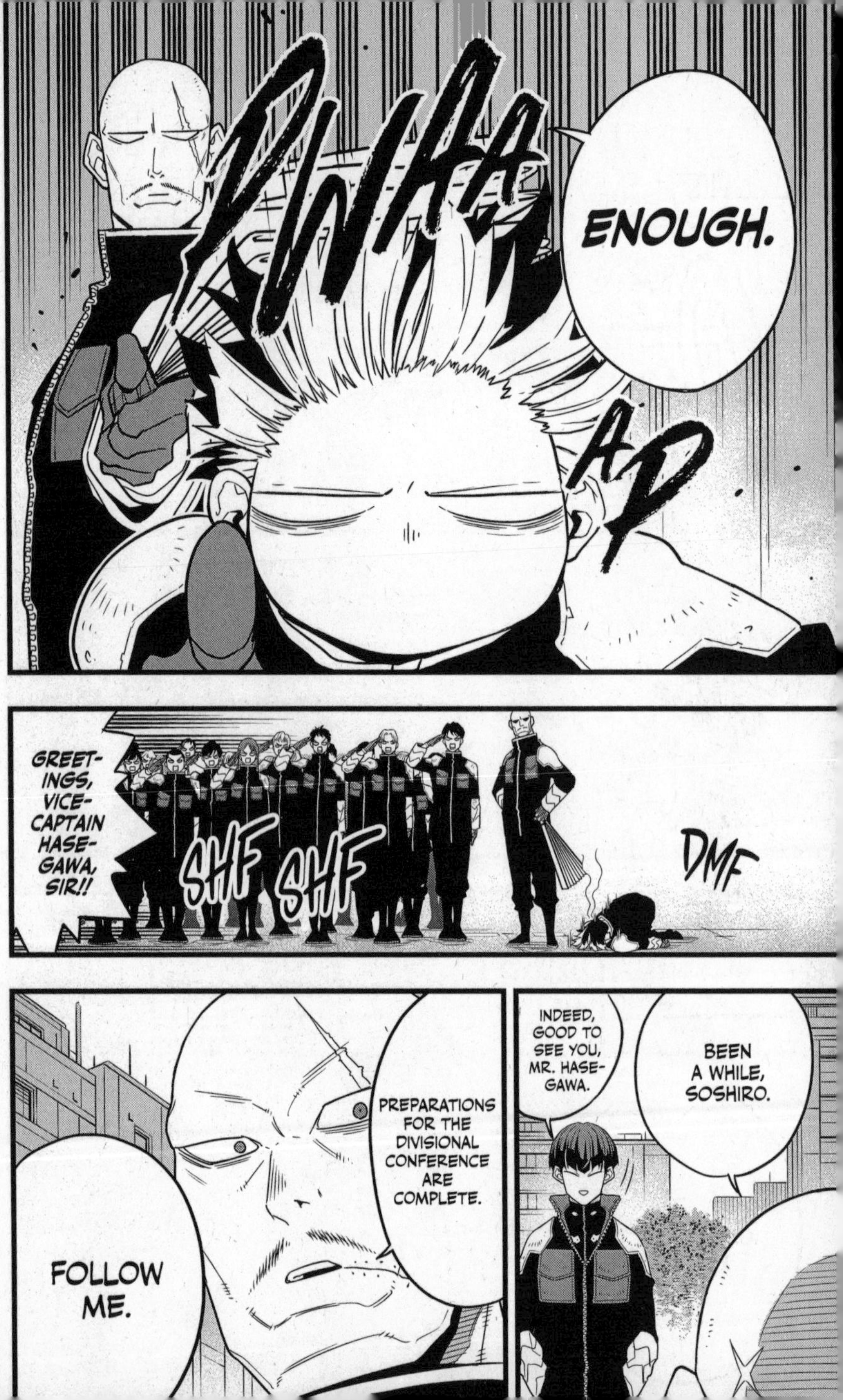
ENOUGH.
DMF
SHF SHF
GREET-INGS, VICE-CAPTAIN HASE-GAWA, SIR!!
BEEN A WHILE, SOSHIRO.
INDEED, GOOD TO SEE YOU, MR. HASE-GAWA.
PREPARATIONS FOR THE DIVISIONAL CONFERENCE ARE COMPLETE.
FOLLOW ME.

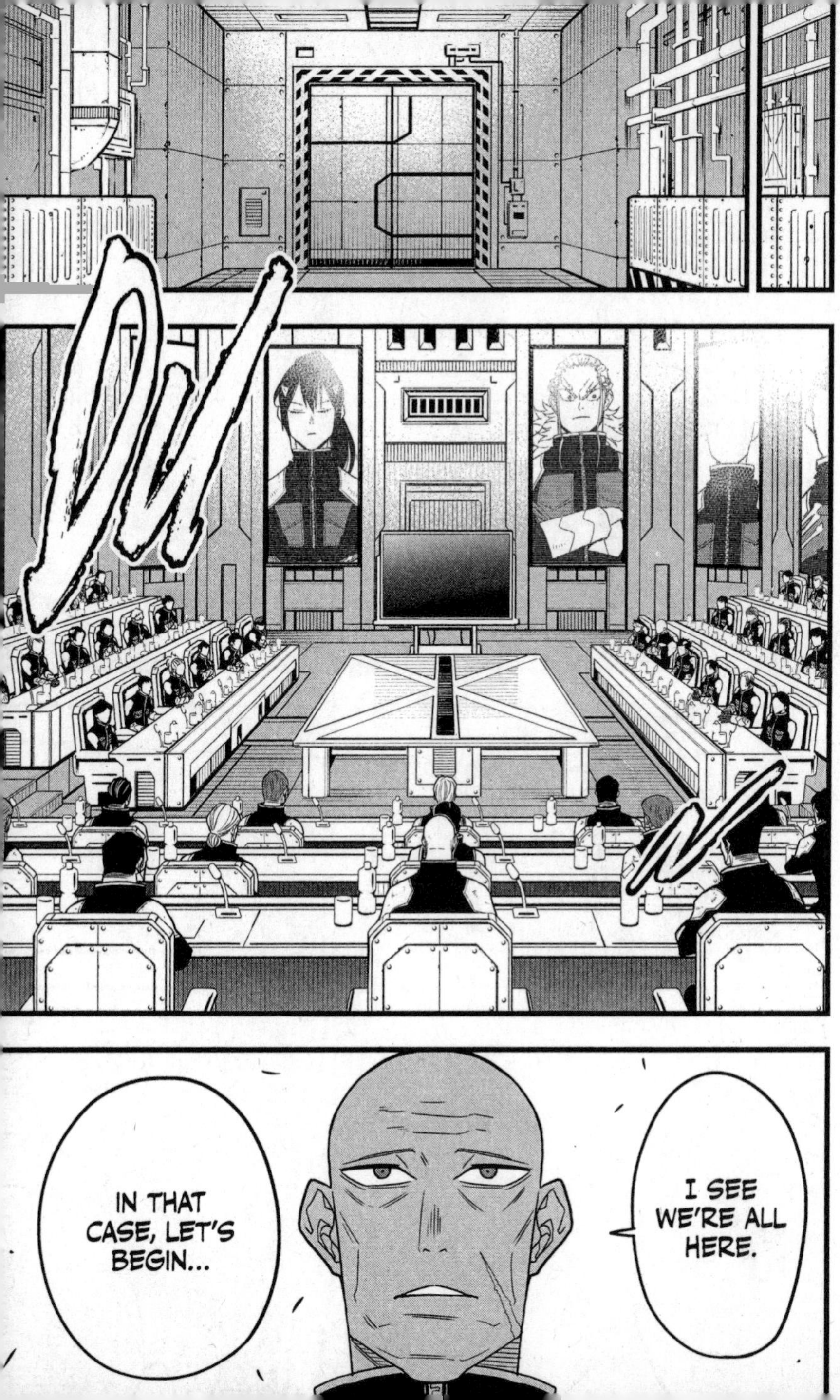
DUN
I SEE WE'RE ALL HERE.
IN THAT CASE, LET'S BEGIN...

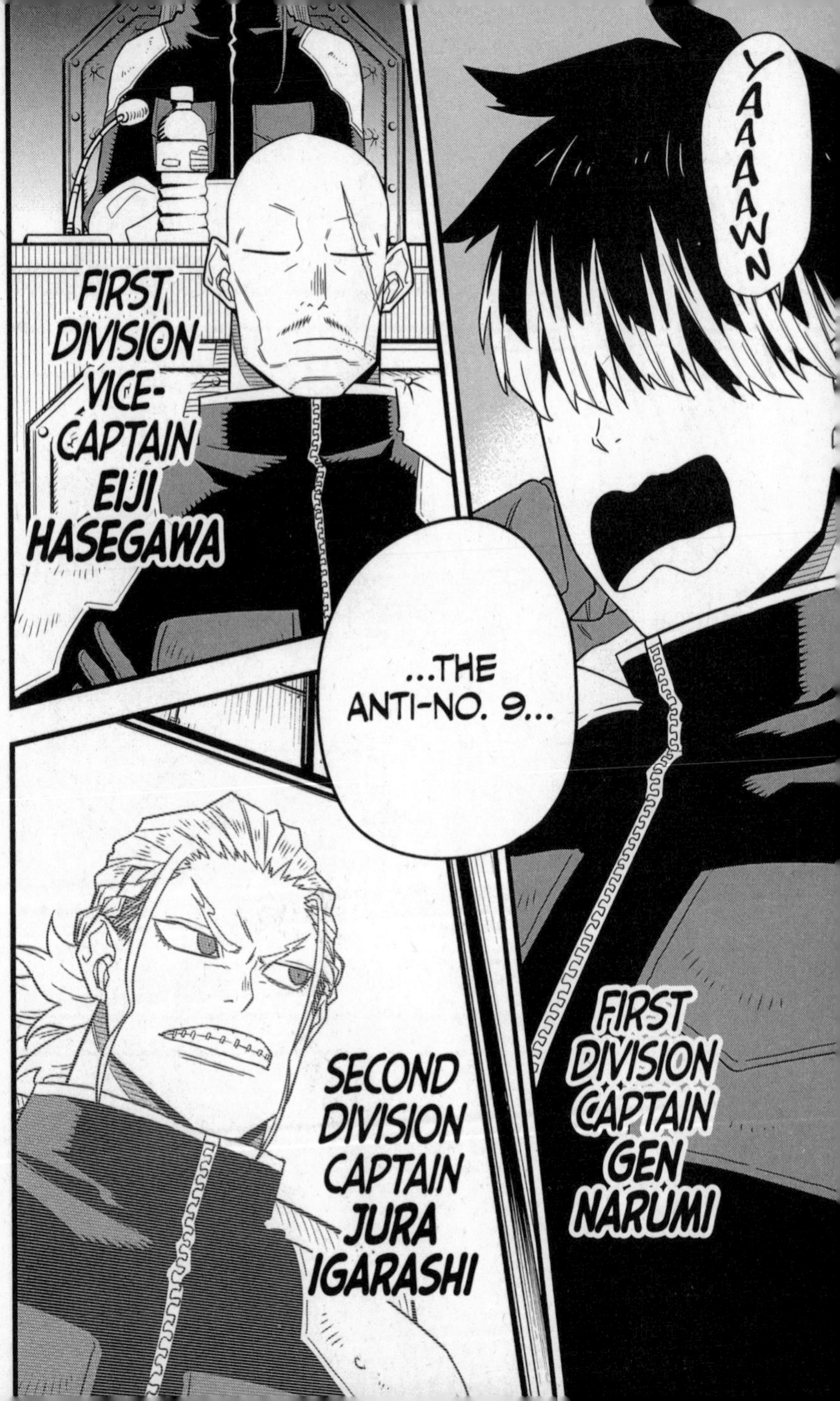
YAAAAWN
...THE ANTI-NO. 9...
FIRST DIVISION CAPTAIN GEN NARUMI
FIRST DIVISION VICE-CAPTAIN EIJI HASEGAWA
SECOND DIVISION CAPTAIN JURA IGARASHI

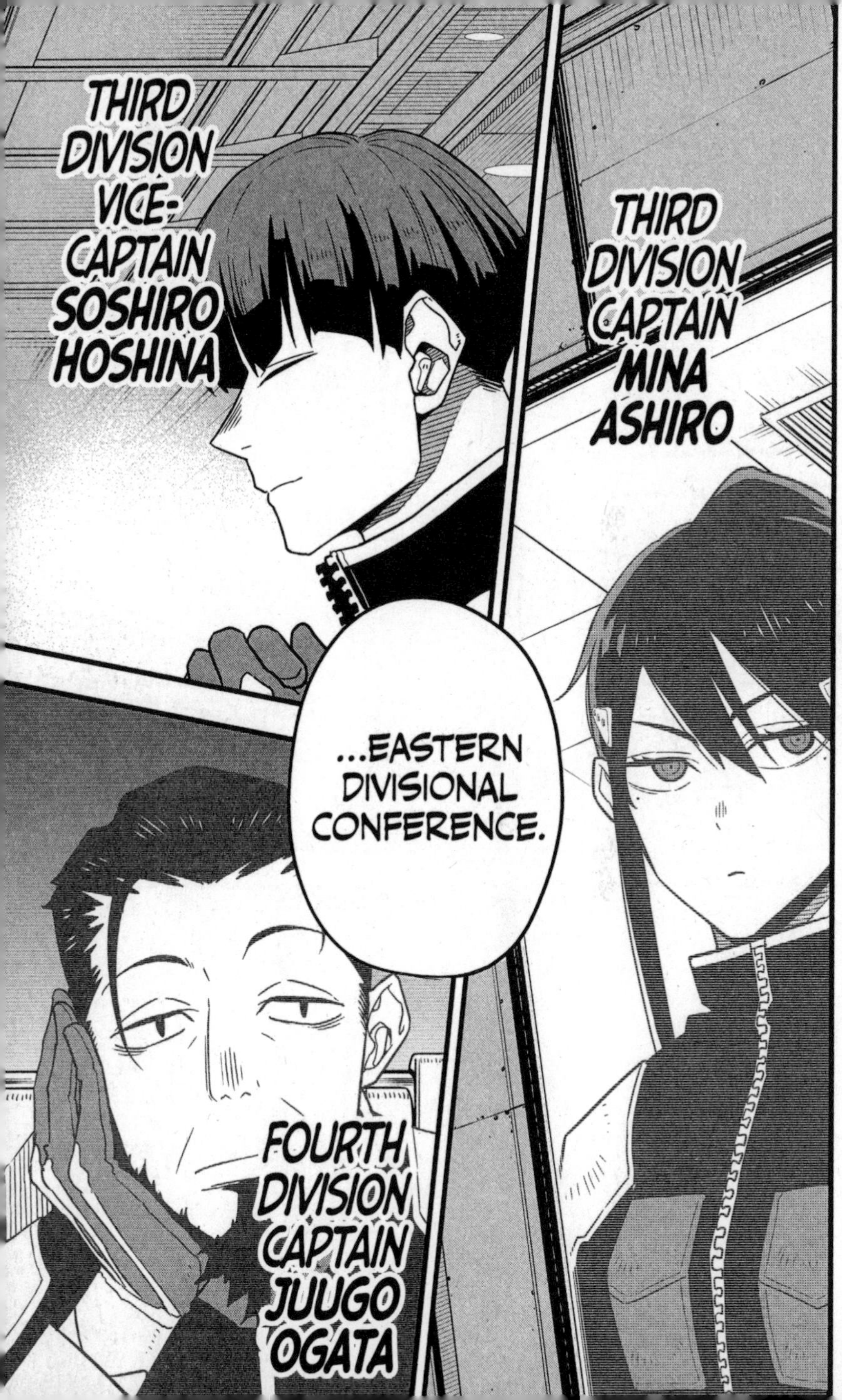
THIRD DIVISION CAPTAIN MINA ASHIRO
...EASTERN DIVISIONAL CONFERENCE.
THIRD DIVISION VICE-CAPTAIN SÓSHIRO HOSHINA
FOURTH DIVISION CAPTAIN JUUGO OGATA

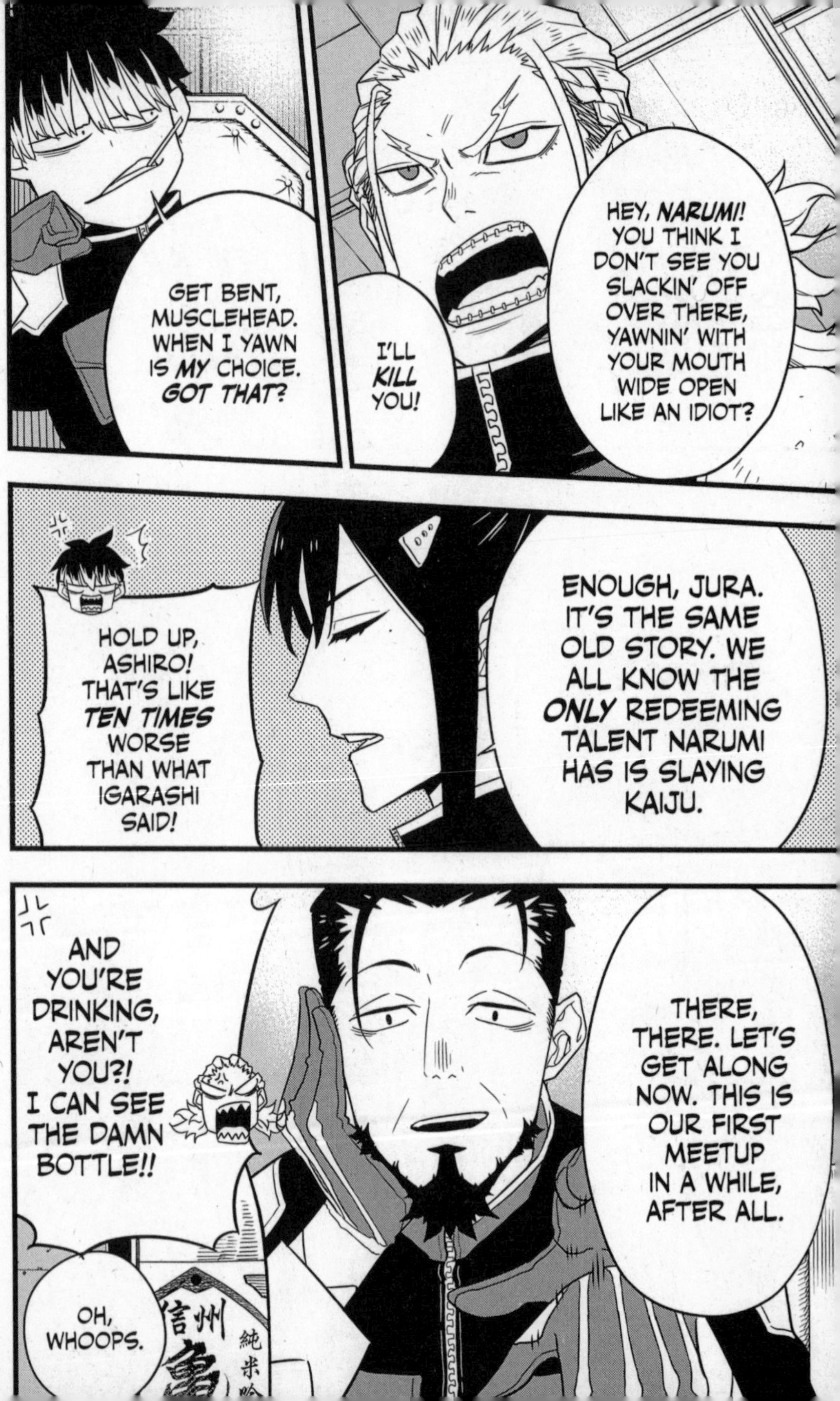
HEY, NARUMI! YOU THINK I DON'T SEE YOU SLACKIN' OFF OVER THERE, YAWNIN' WITH YOUR MOUTH WIDE OPEN LIKE AN IDIOT?
I'LL KILL YOU!
GET BENT, MUSCLEHEAD. WHEN I YAWN IS MY CHOICE. GOT THAT?
ENOUGH, JURA. IT'S THE SAME OLD STORY. WE ALL KNOW THE ONLY REDEEMING TALENT NARUMI HAS IS SLAYING KAIJU.
HOLD UP, ASHIRO! THAT'S LIKE TEN TIMES WORSE THAN WHAT IGARASHI SAID!
THERE, THERE. LET'S GET ALONG NOW. THIS IS OUR FIRST MEETUP IN A WHILE, AFTER ALL.
AND YOU'RE DRINKING, AREN'T YOU?! I CAN SEE THE DAMN BOTTLE!!
OH, WHOOPS.
信州

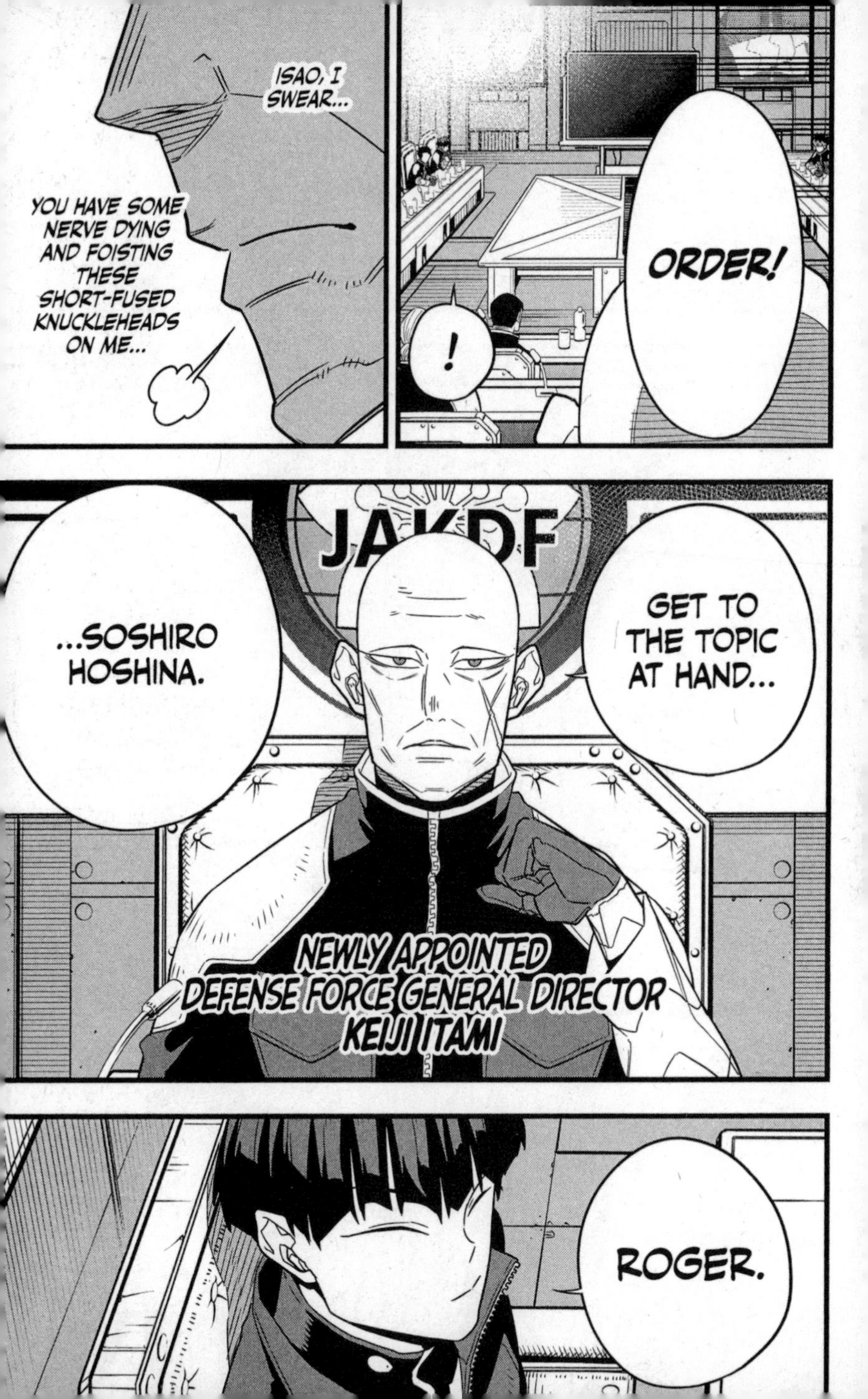
ORDER!
!
ISAO, I SWEAR...
YOU HAVE SOME NERVE DYING AND FOISTING THESE SHORT-FUSED KNUCKLEHEADS ON ME...
JAKDF
GET TO THE TOPIC AT HAND...
...SOSHIRO HOSHINA.
NEWLY APPOINTED DEFENSE FORCE GENERAL DIRECTOR KEIJI ITAMI
ROGER.

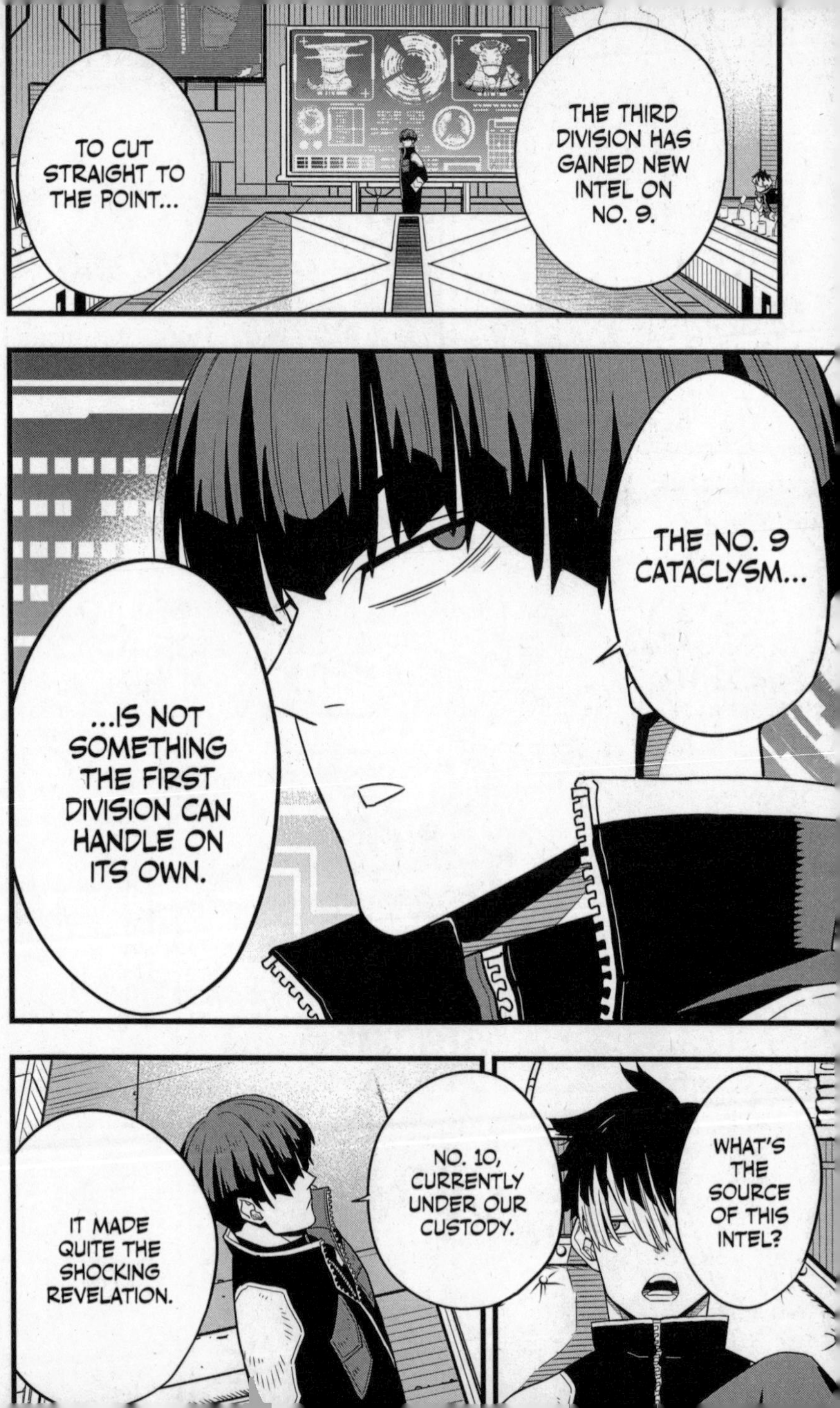
THE THIRD DIVISION HAS GAINED NEW INTEL ON NO. 9.
TO CUT STRAIGHT TO THE POINT...
THE NO. 9 CATACLYSM...
...IS NOT SOMETHING THE FIRST DIVISION CAN HANDLE ON ITS OWN.
WHAT'S THE SOURCE OF THIS INTEL?
NO. 10, CURRENTLY UNDER OUR CUSTODY.
IT MADE QUITE THE SHOCKING REVELATION.

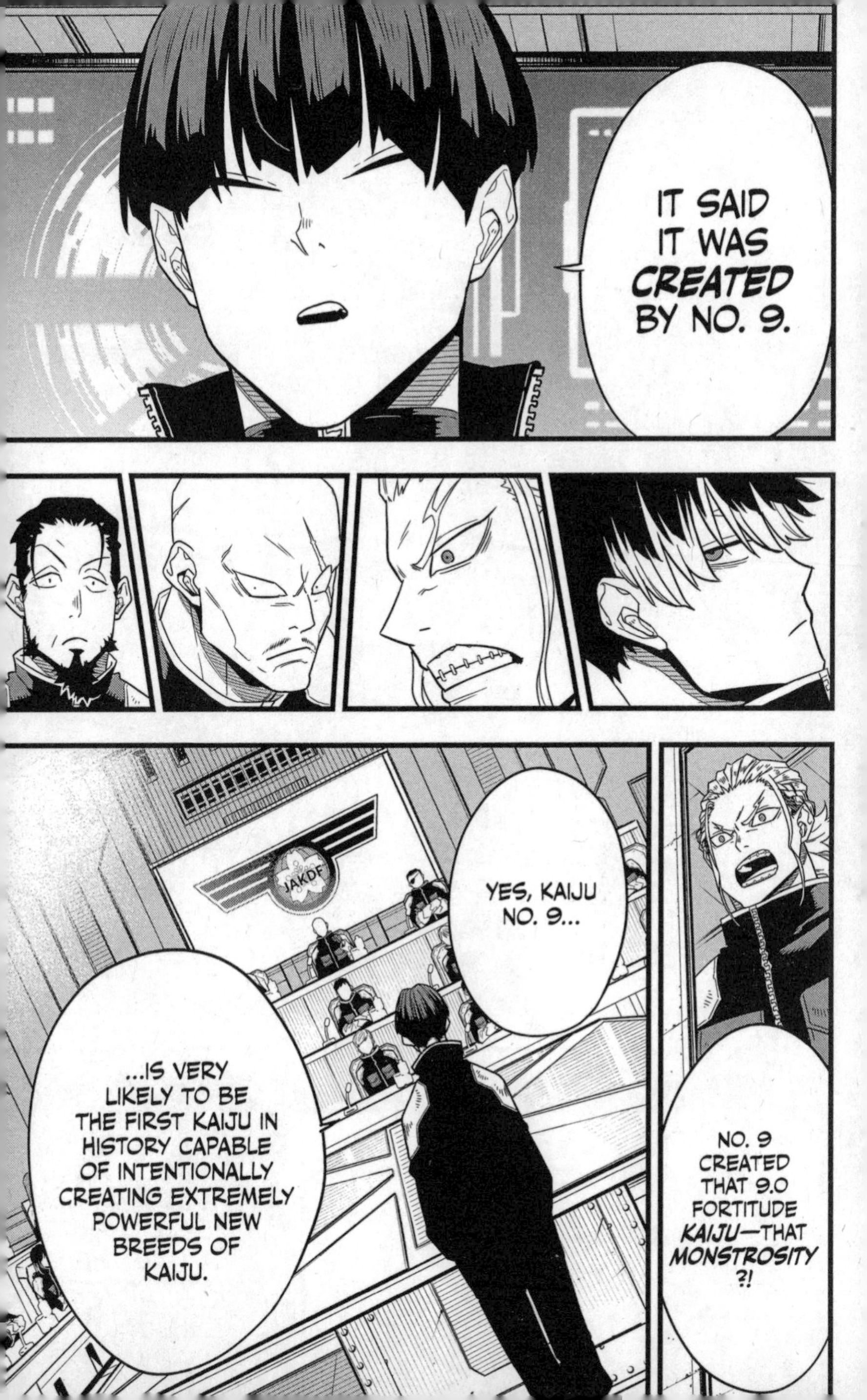

IT SAID IT WAS *CREATED* BY NO. 9.
NO. 9 CREATED THAT 9.0 FORTITUDE *KAIJU*—THAT *MONSTROSITY* ?!
YES, KAIJU NO. 9...
...IS VERY LIKELY TO BE THE FIRST KAIJU IN HISTORY CAPABLE OF INTENTIONALLY CREATING EXTREMELY POWERFUL NEW BREEDS OF KAIJU.
JAKDF

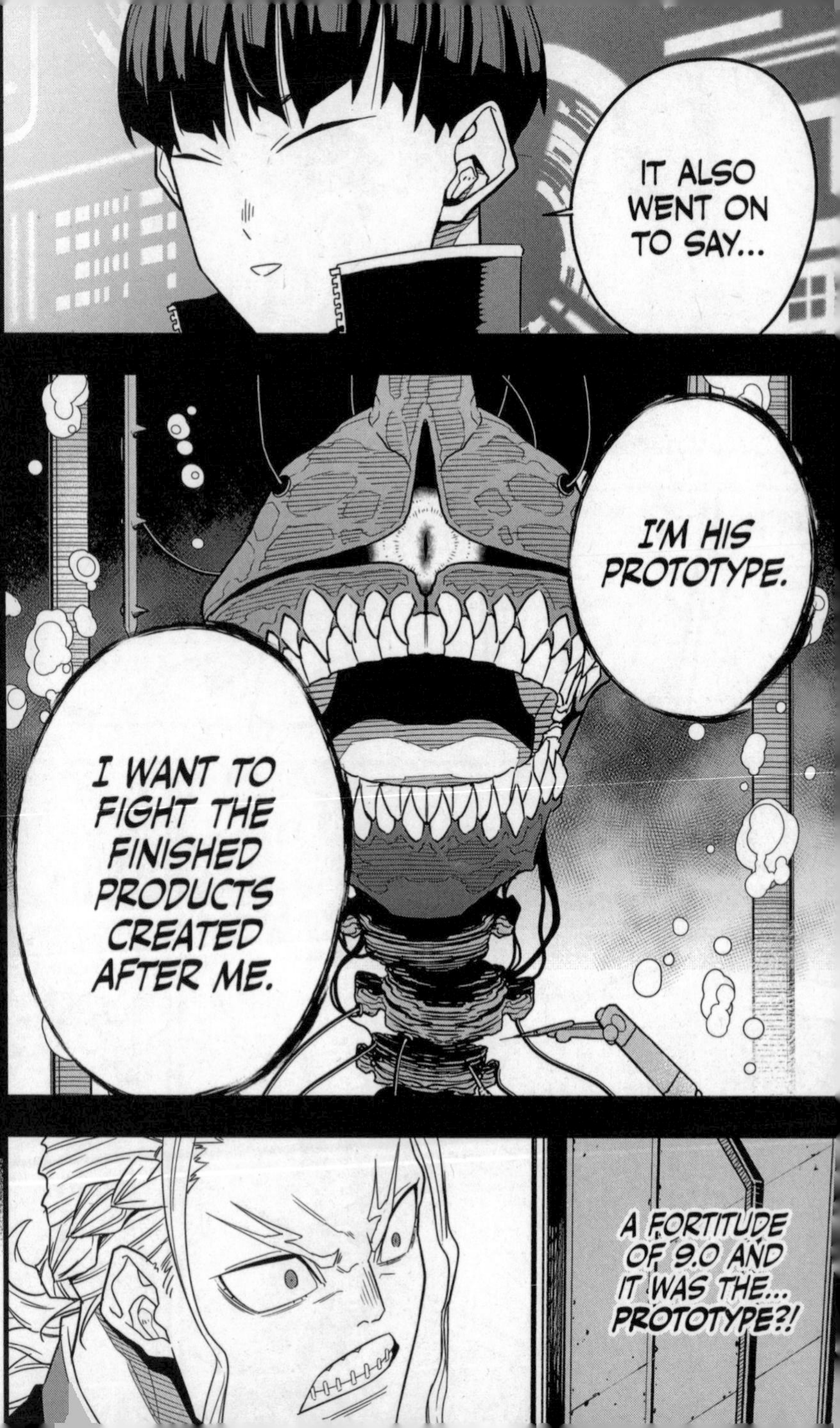
IT ALSO WENT ON TO SAY...
I'M HIS PROTOTYPE.
I WANT TO FIGHT THE FINISHED PRODUCTS CREATED AFTER ME.
A FORTITUDE OF 9.0 AND IT WAS THE... PROTOTYPE?!

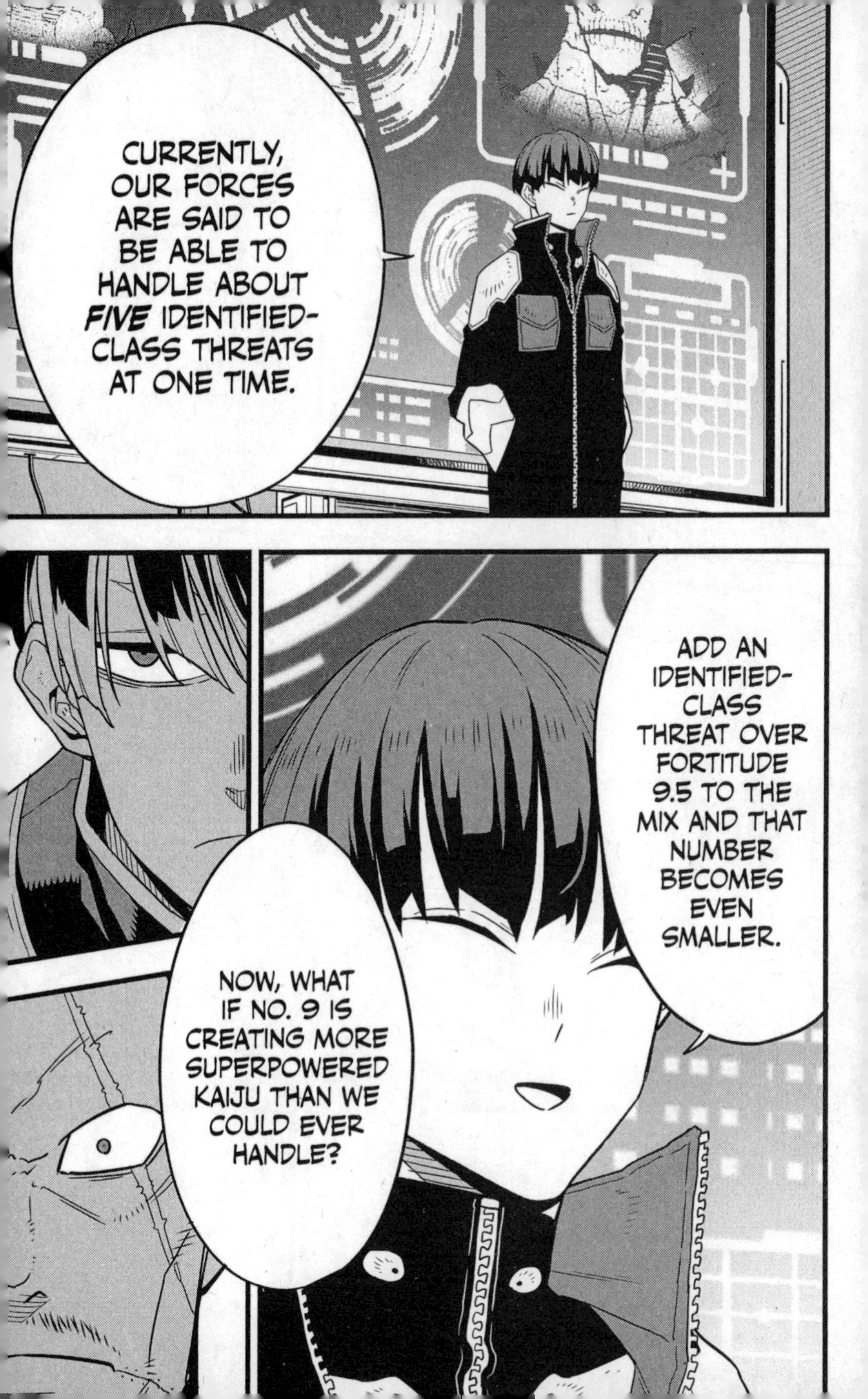
CURRENTLY, OUR FORCES ARE SAID TO BE ABLE TO HANDLE ABOUT *FIVE* IDENTIFIED-CLASS THREATS AT ONE TIME.
ADD AN IDENTIFIED-CLASS THREAT OVER FORTITUDE 9.5 TO THE MIX AND THAT NUMBER BECOMES EVEN SMALLER.
NOW, WHAT IF NO. 9 IS CREATING MORE SUPERPOWERED KAIJU THAN WE COULD EVER HANDLE?

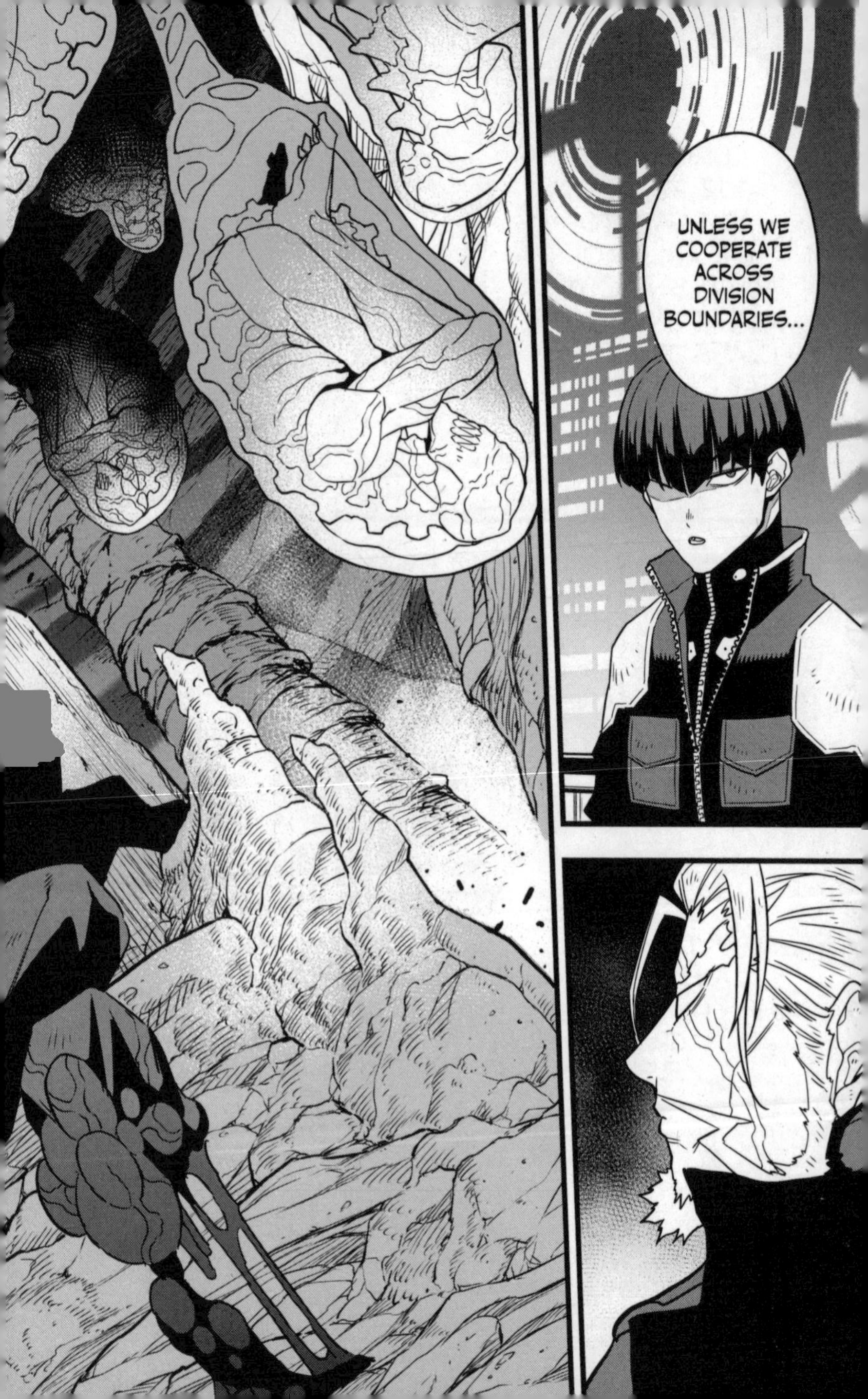
UNLESS WE COOPERATE ACROSS DIVISION BOUNDARIES...

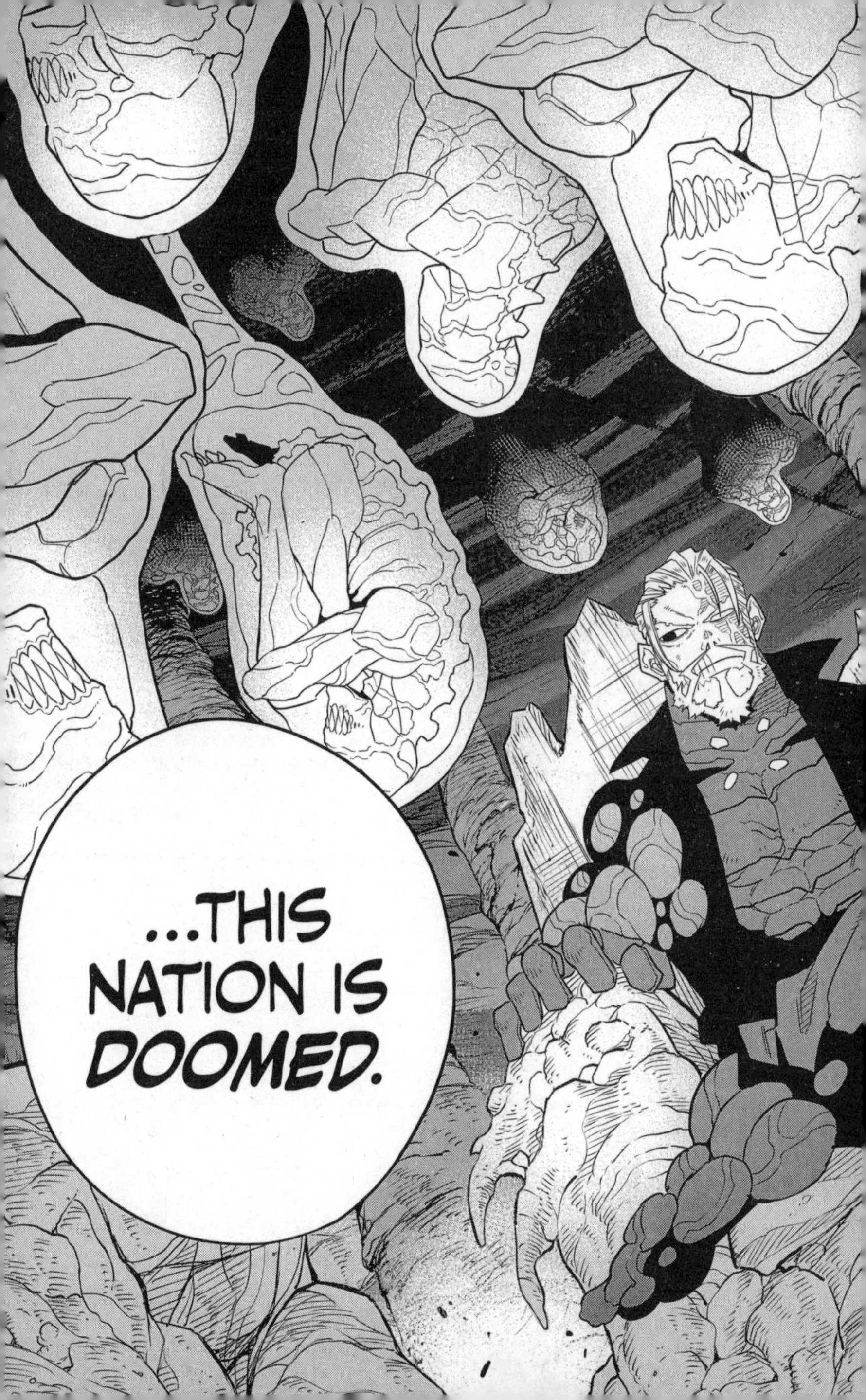
...THIS NATION IS DOOMED.

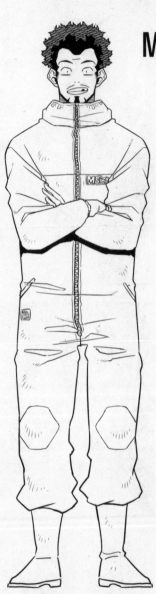

MASAHIDE TOKUDA

Birthday:
December 11

Height:
188 cm

Likes:
Gambling, booze, variety shows, work

Author Comment:
Can be oblivious at times, but that's what gives him the strength to keep moving when other people hesitate. Lovable and physically strong, he's Monster Sweeper's reliable ace.

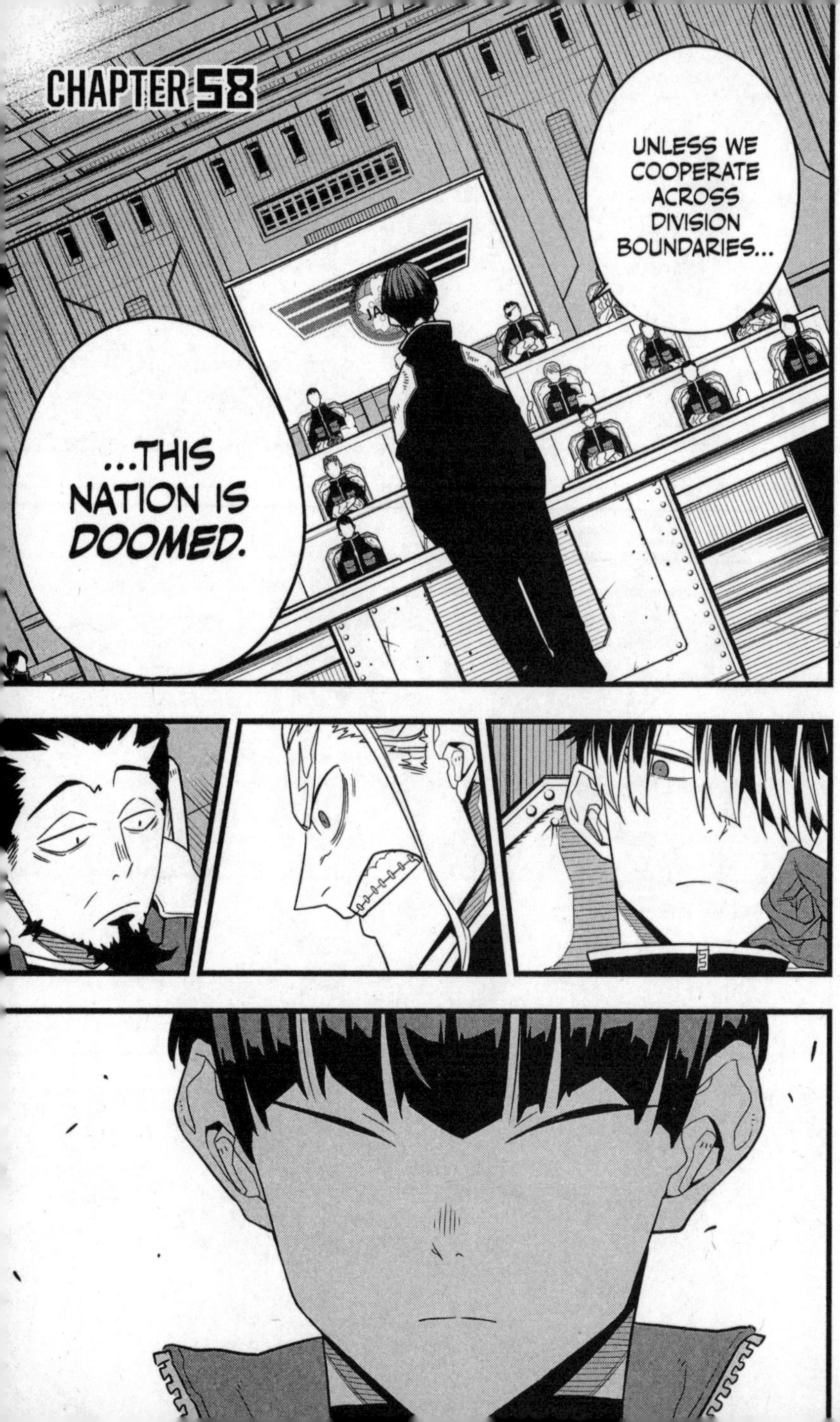
CHAPTER 58
UNLESS WE COOPERATE ACROSS DIVISION BOUNDARIES...
...THIS NATION IS DOOMED.

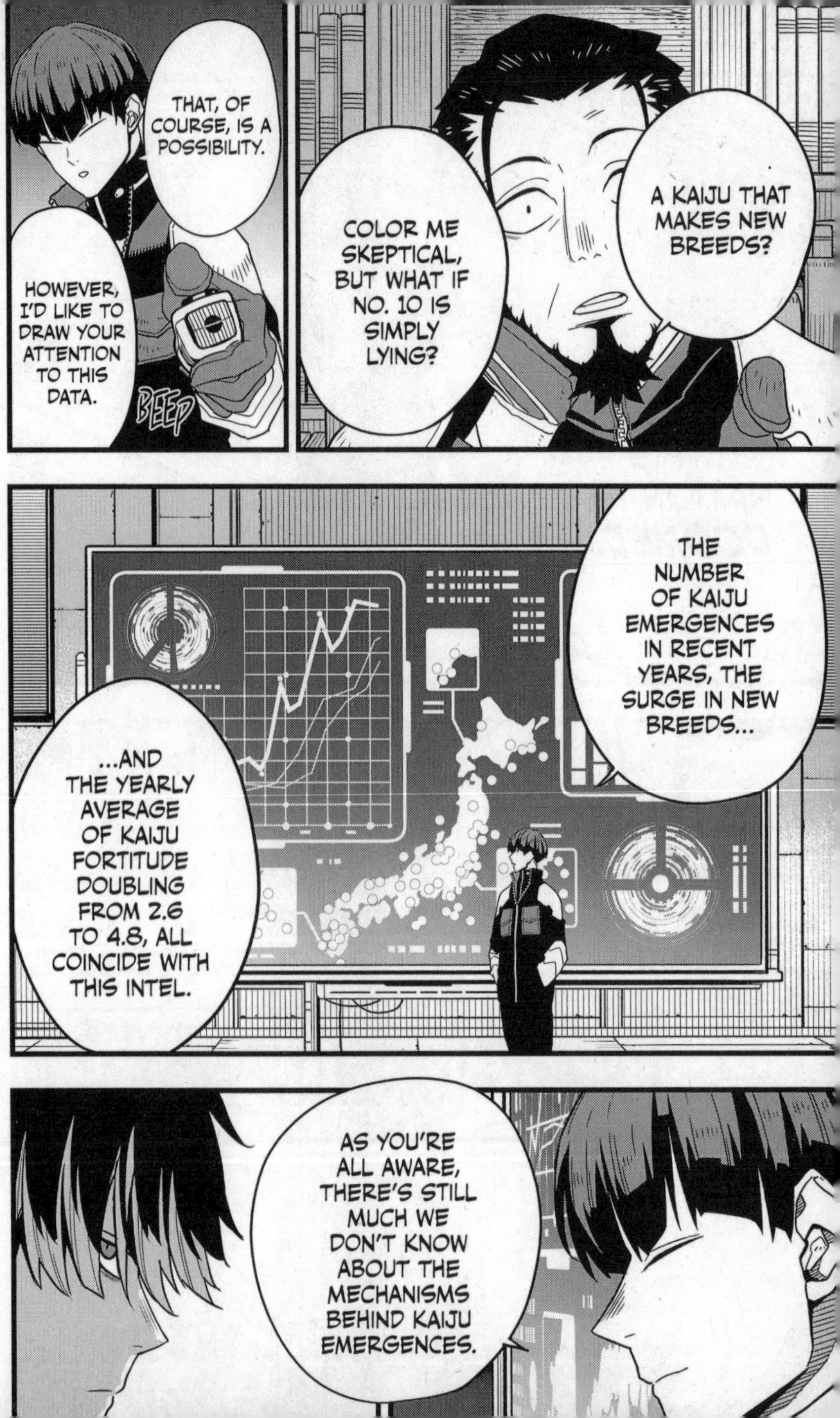
A KAIJU THAT MAKES NEW BREEDS?
COLOR ME SKEPTICAL, BUT WHAT IF NO. 10 IS SIMPLY LYING?
THAT, OF COURSE, IS A POSSIBILITY.
HOWEVER, I'D LIKE TO DRAW YOUR ATTENTION TO THIS DATA.
BEEP
THE NUMBER OF KAIJU EMERGENCES IN RECENT YEARS, THE SURGE IN NEW BREEDS...
...AND THE YEARLY AVERAGE OF KAIJU FORTITUDE DOUBLING FROM 2.6 TO 4.8, ALL COINCIDE WITH THIS INTEL.
AS YOU'RE ALL AWARE, THERE'S STILL MUCH WE DON'T KNOW ABOUT THE MECHANISMS BEHIND KAIJU EMERGENCES.

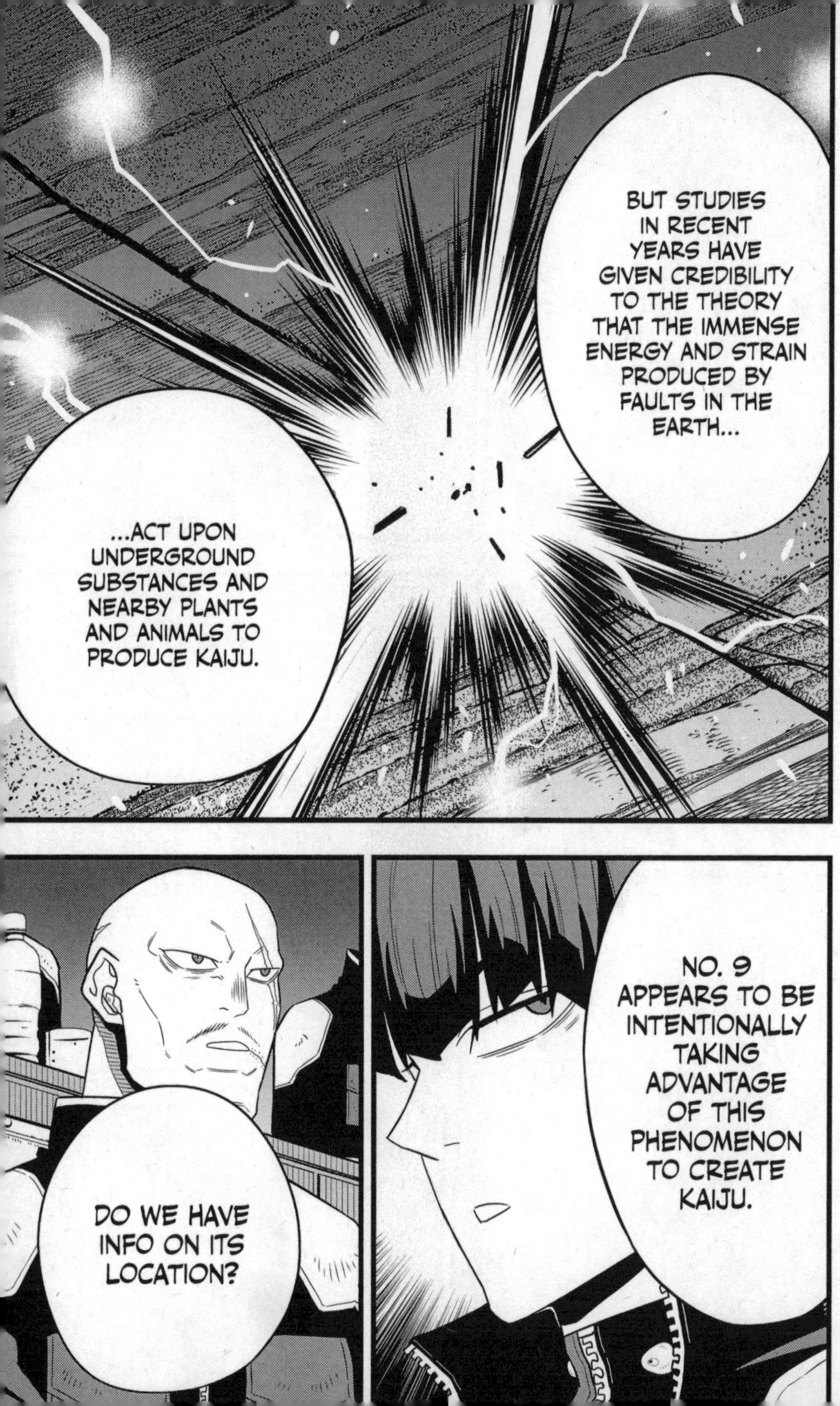
BUT STUDIES IN RECENT YEARS HAVE GIVEN CREDIBILITY TO THE THEORY THAT THE IMMENSE ENERGY AND STRAIN PRODUCED BY FAULTS IN THE EARTH...
...ACT UPON UNDERGROUND SUBSTANCES AND NEARBY PLANTS AND ANIMALS TO PRODUCE KAIJU.
NO. 9 APPEARS TO BE INTENTIONALLY TAKING ADVANTAGE OF THIS PHENOMENON TO CREATE KAIJU.
DO WE HAVE INFO ON ITS LOCATION?

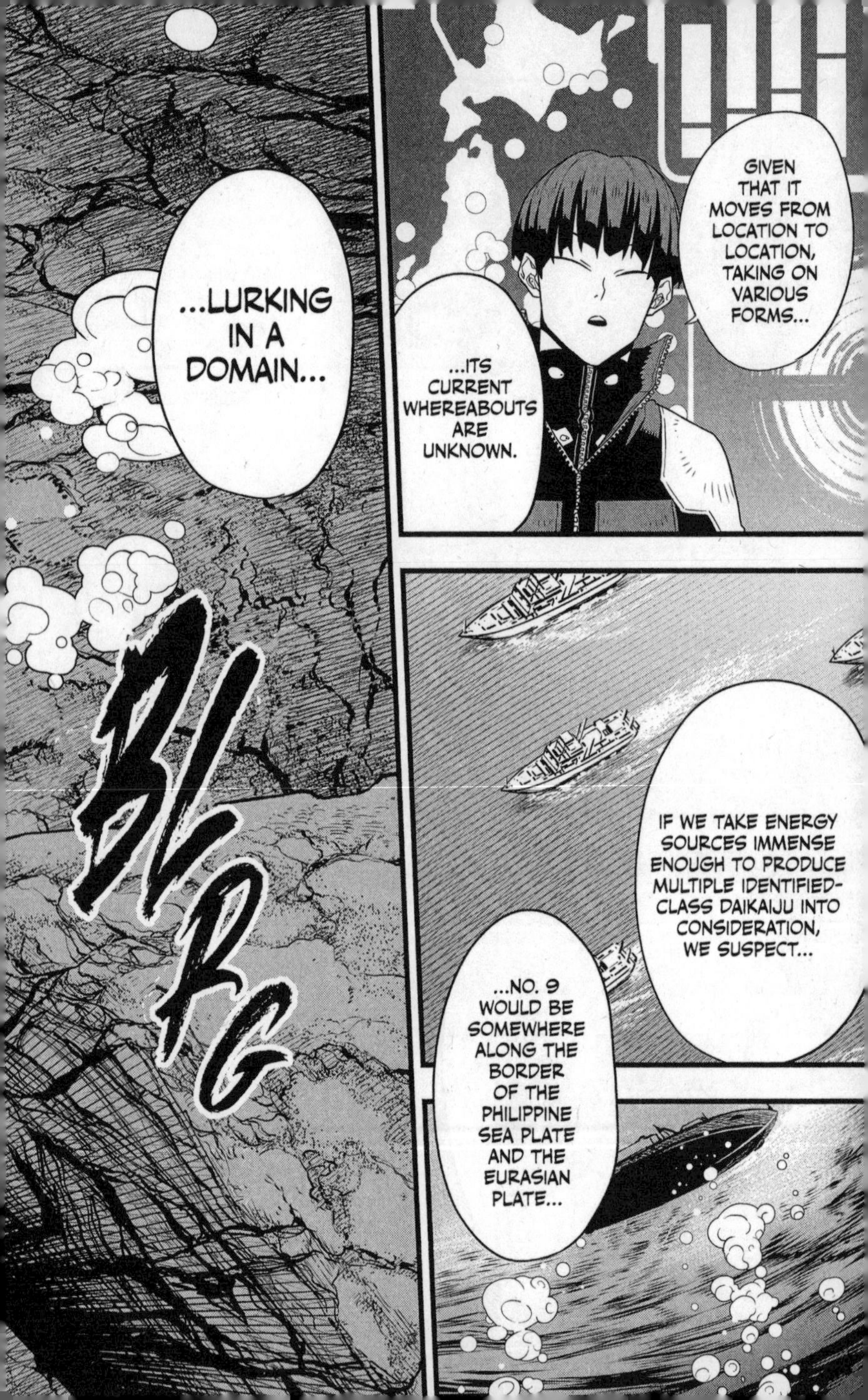
GIVEN THAT IT MOVES FROM LOCATION TO LOCATION, TAKING ON VARIOUS FORMS...
...ITS CURRENT WHEREABOUTS ARE UNKNOWN.
IF WE TAKE ENERGY SOURCES IMMENSE ENOUGH TO PRODUCE MULTIPLE IDENTIFIED-CLASS DAIKAIJU INTO CONSIDERATION, WE SUSPECT...
...NO. 9 WOULD BE SOMEWHERE ALONG THE BORDER OF THE PHILIPPINE SEA PLATE AND THE EURASIAN PLATE...
...LURKING IN A DOMAIN...

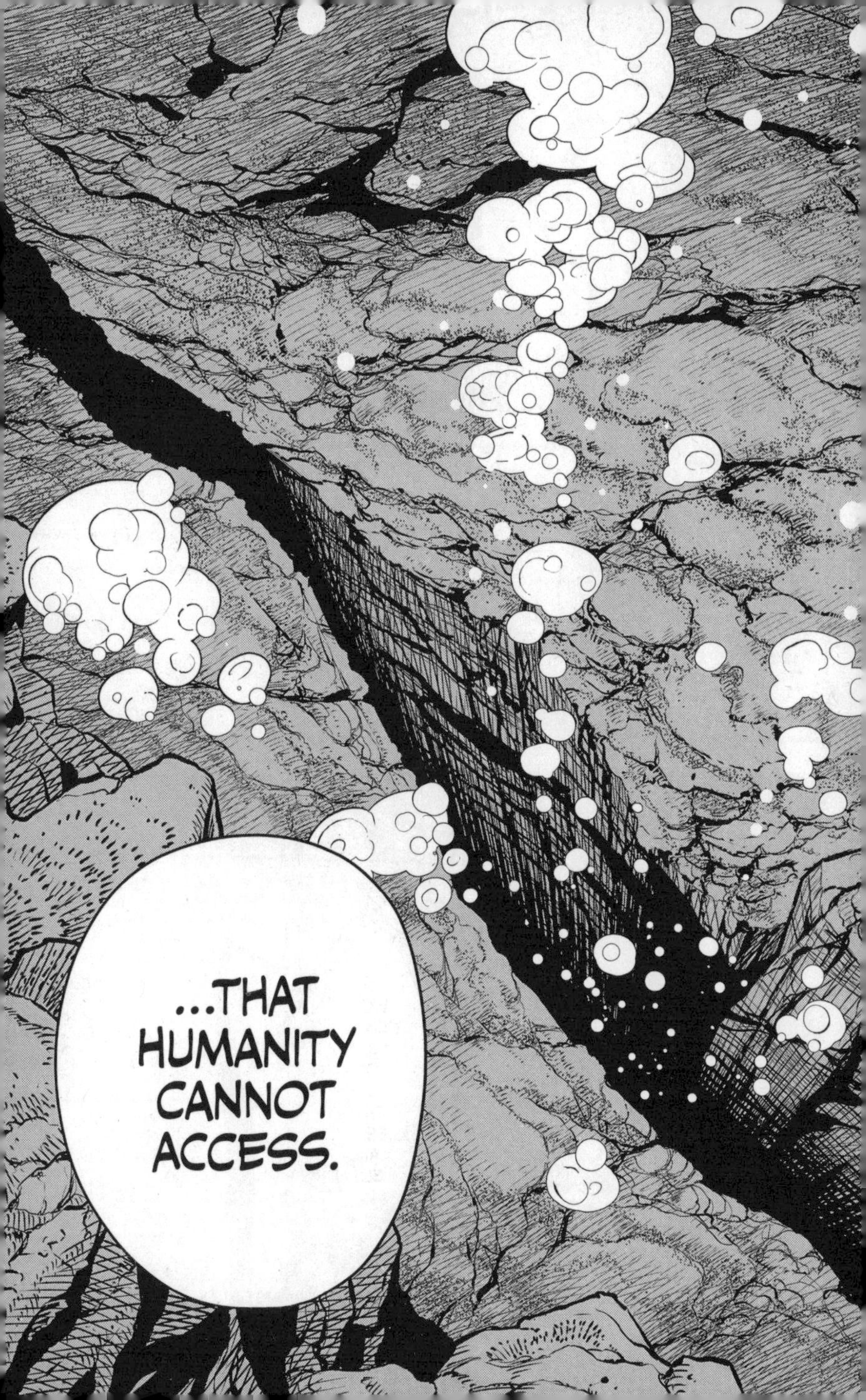
...THAT HUMANITY CANNOT ACCESS.

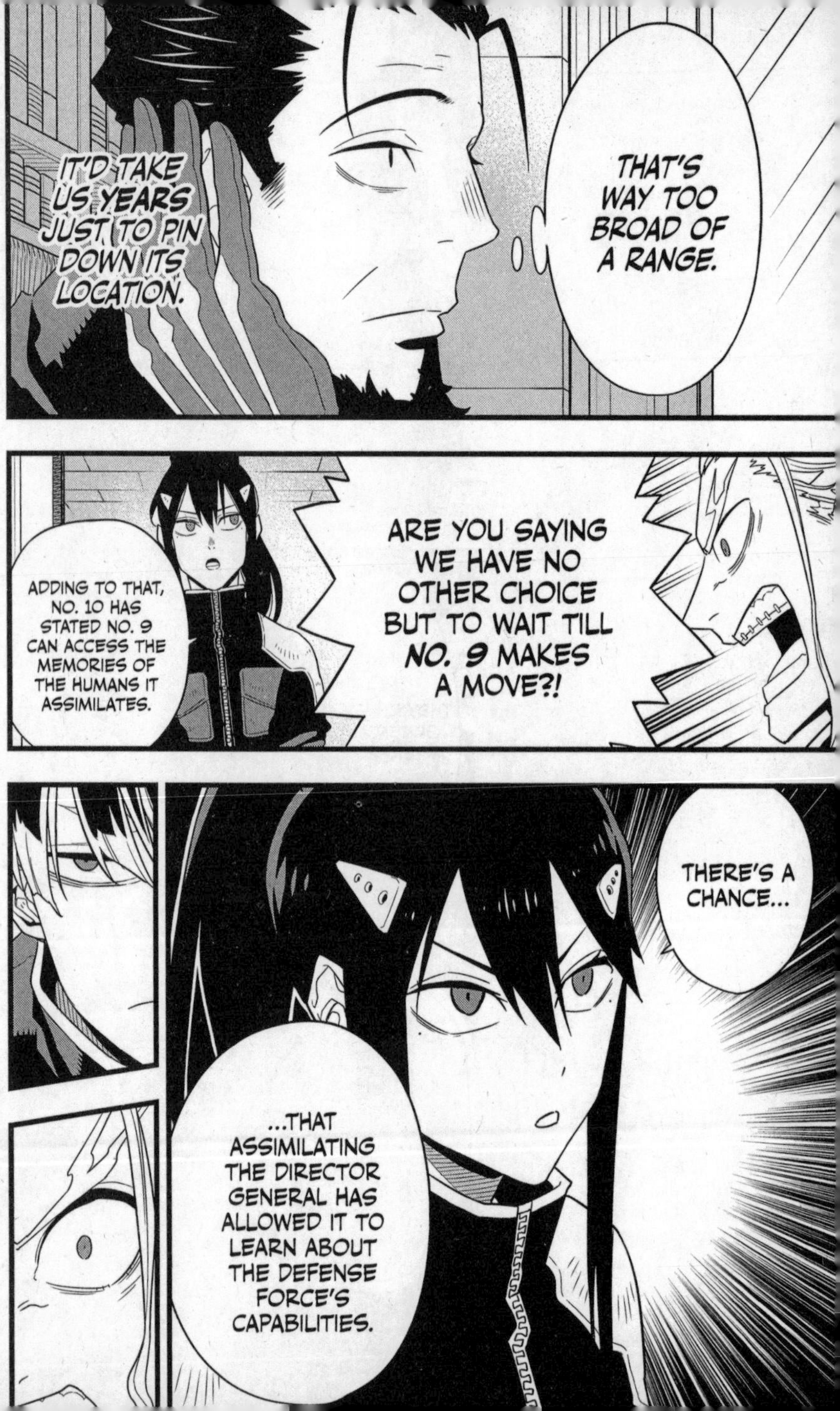
THAT'S WAY TOO BROAD OF A RANGE.
IT'D TAKE US YEARS JUST TO PIN DOWN ITS LOCATION.
ARE YOU SAYING WE HAVE NO OTHER CHOICE BUT TO WAIT TILL NO. 9 MAKES A MOVE?!
ADDING TO THAT, NO. 10 HAS STATED NO. 9 CAN ACCESS THE MEMORIES OF THE HUMANS IT ASSIMILATES.
THERE'S A CHANCE...
...THAT ASSIMILATING THE DIRECTOR GENERAL HAS ALLOWED IT TO LEARN ABOUT THE DEFENSE FORCE'S CAPABILITIES.

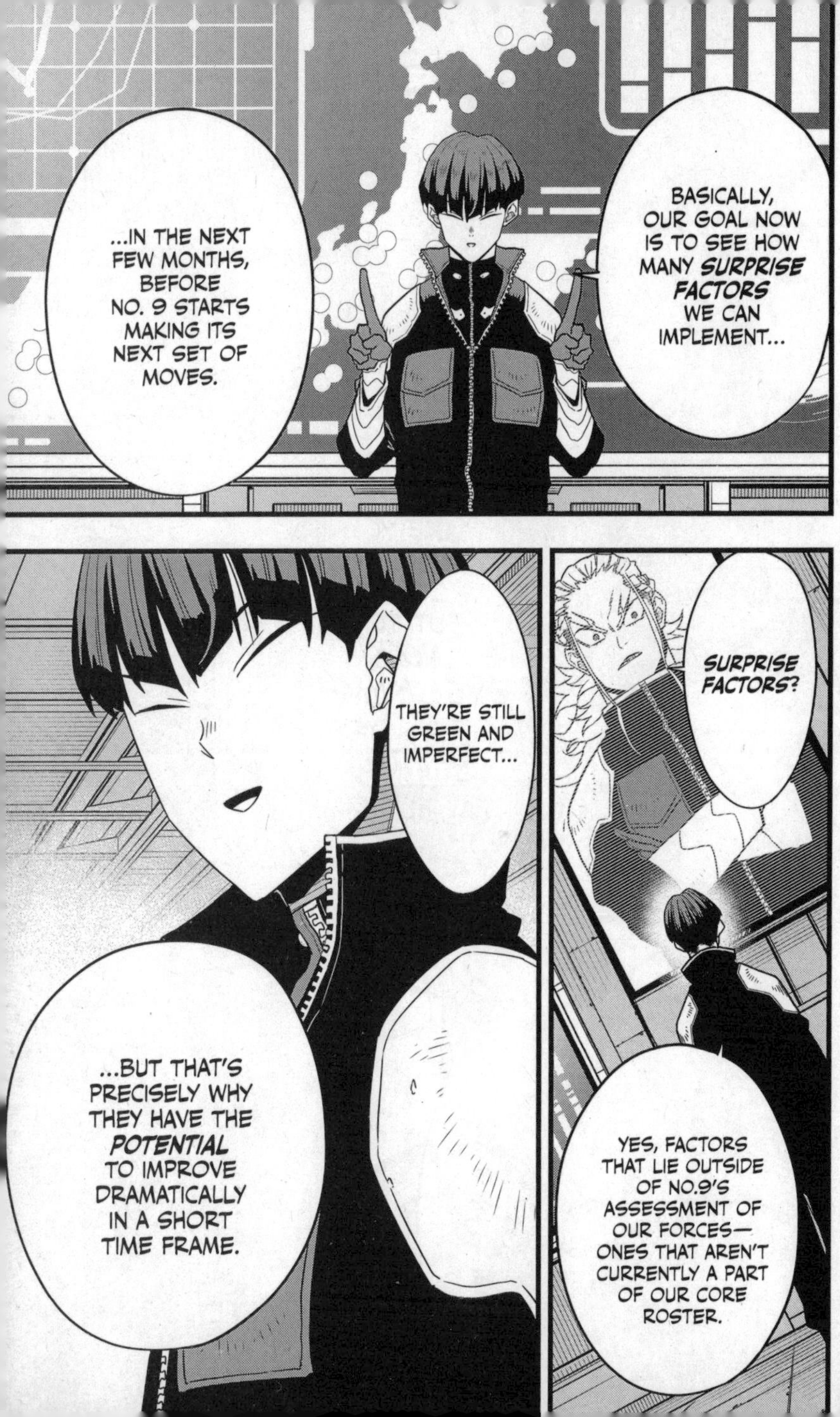
BASICALLY, OUR GOAL NOW IS TO SEE HOW MANY SURPRISE FACTORS WE CAN IMPLEMENT...
...IN THE NEXT FEW MONTHS, BEFORE NO. 9 STARTS MAKING ITS NEXT SET OF MOVES.
SURPRISE FACTORS?
YES, FACTORS THAT LIE OUTSIDE OF NO.9'S ASSESSMENT OF OUR FORCES— ONES THAT AREN'T CURRENTLY A PART OF OUR CORE ROSTER.
THEY'RE STILL GREEN AND IMPERFECT...
...BUT THAT'S PRECISELY WHY THEY HAVE THE POTENTIAL TO IMPROVE DRAMATICALLY IN A SHORT TIME FRAME.

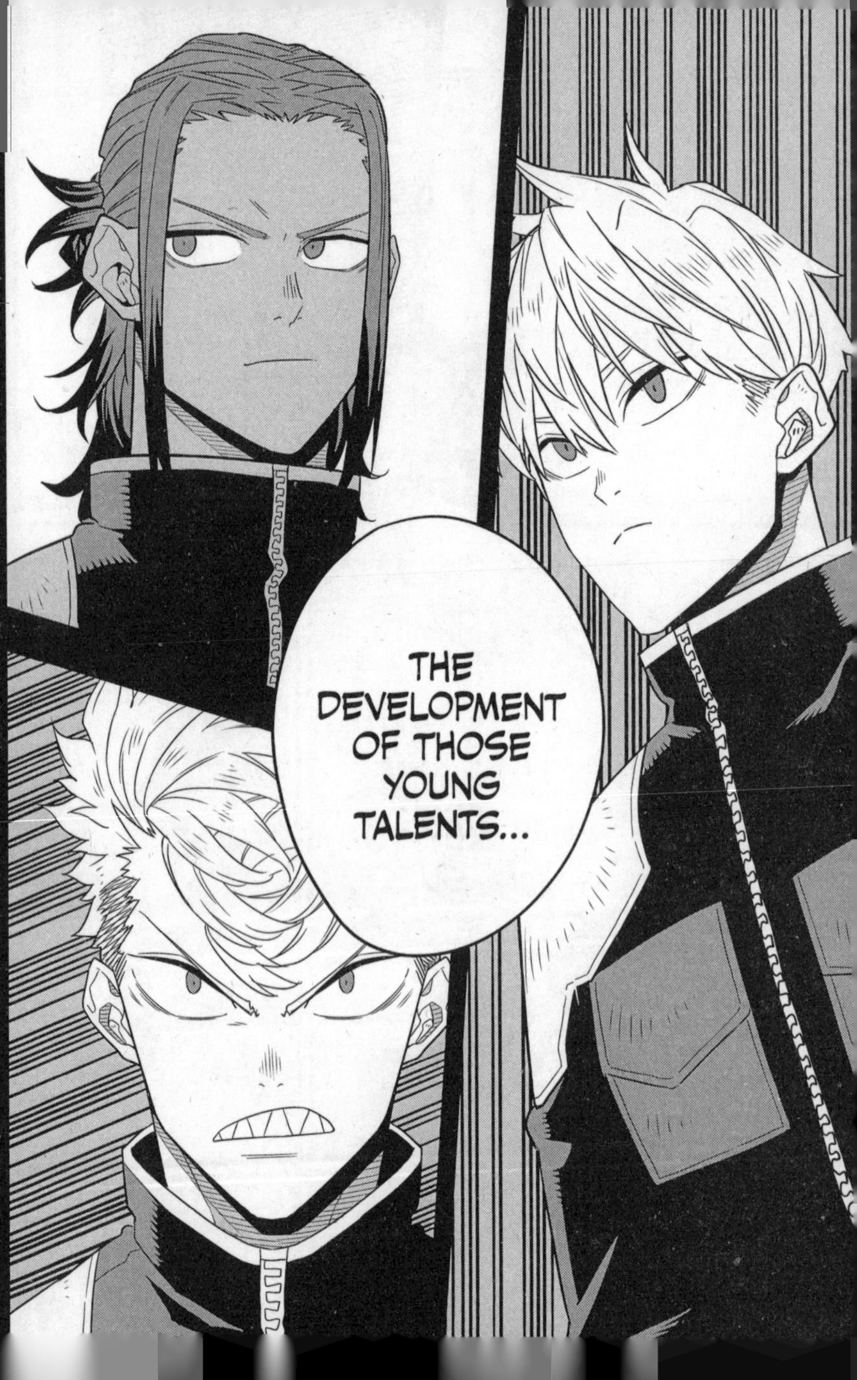
THE DEVELOPMENT OF THOSE YOUNG TALENTS...

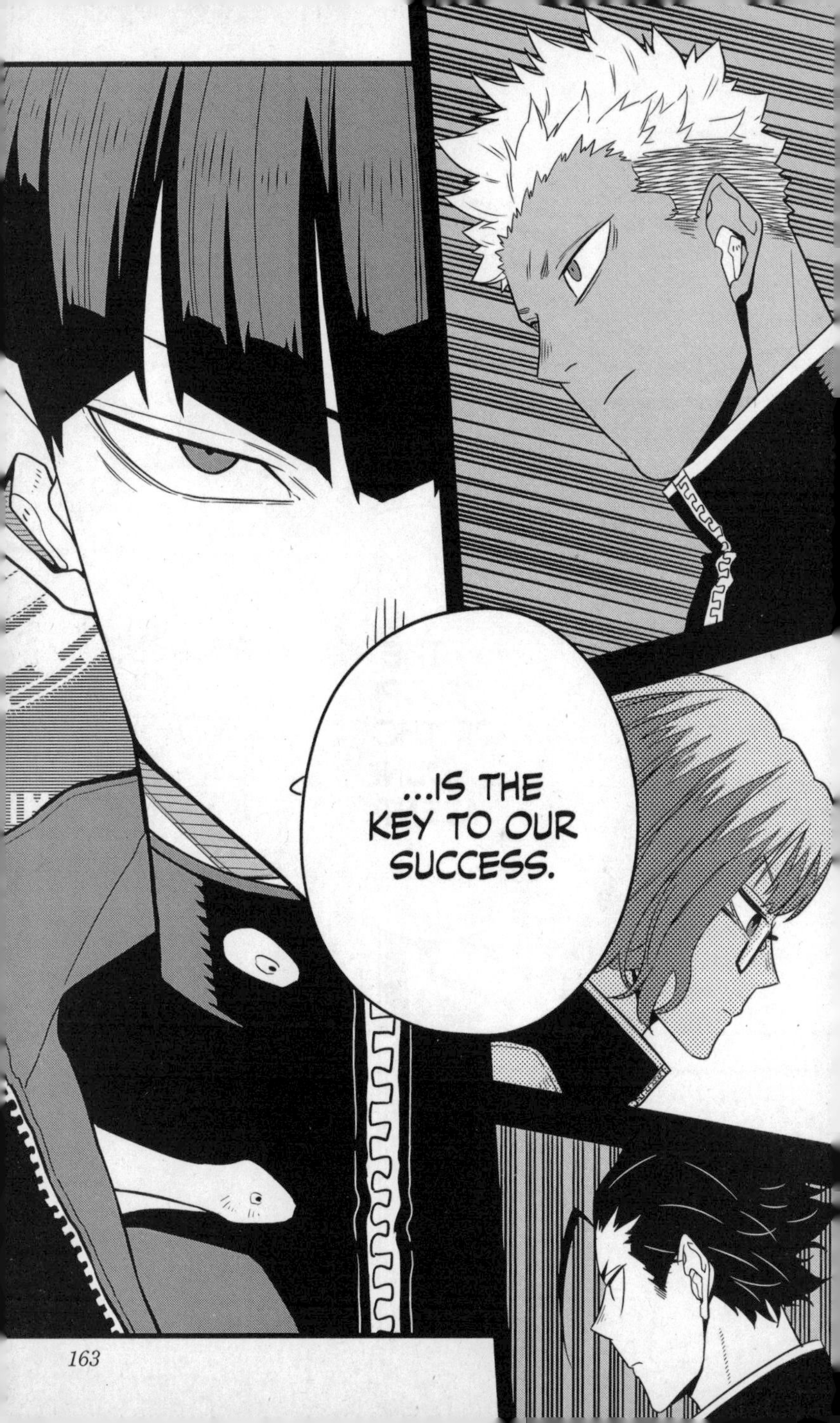
...IS THE KEY TO OUR SUCCESS.

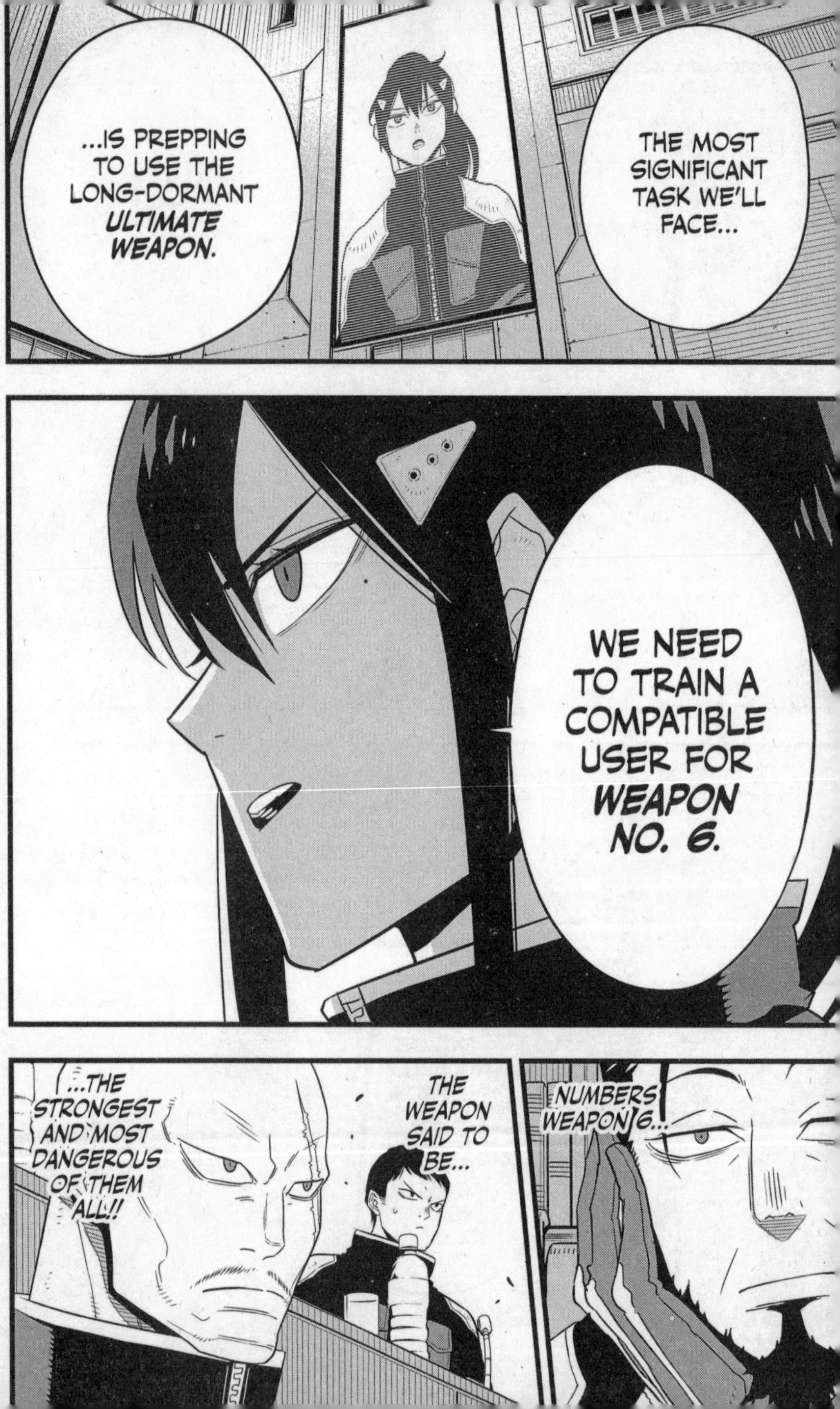
THE MOST SIGNIFICANT TASK WE'LL FACE...
...IS PREPPING TO USE THE LONG-DORMANT ULTIMATE WEAPON.
WE NEED TO TRAIN A COMPATIBLE USER FOR WEAPON NO. 6.
NUMBERS WEAPON 6...
THE WEAPON SAID TO BE...
...THE STRONGEST AND MOST DANGEROUS OF THEM ALL!!

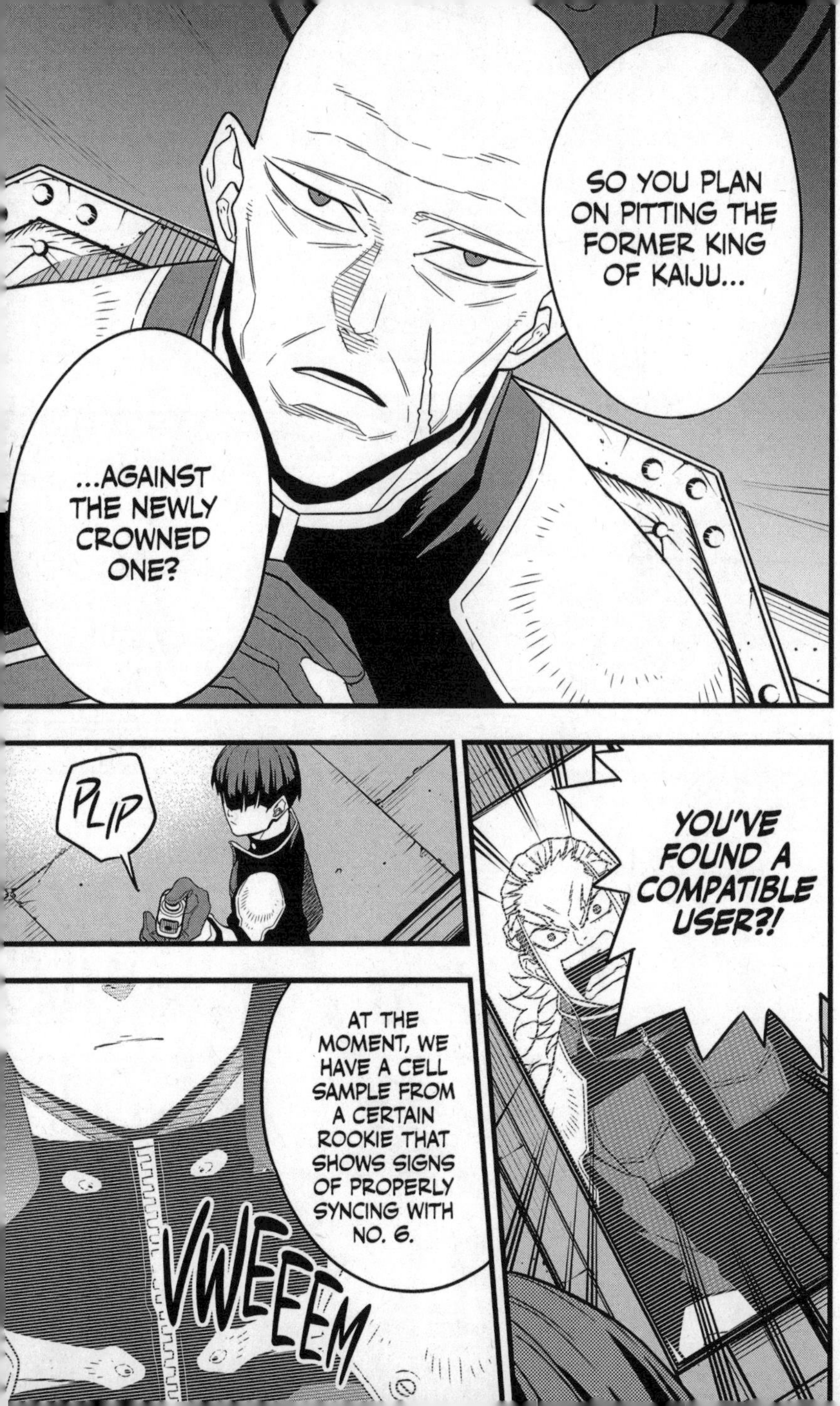
SO YOU PLAN ON PITTING THE FORMER KING OF KAIJU...
...AGAINST THE NEWLY CROWNED ONE?
YOU'VE FOUND A COMPATIBLE USER?!
PLIP
AT THE MOMENT, WE HAVE A CELL SAMPLE FROM A CERTAIN ROOKIE THAT SHOWS SIGNS OF PROPERLY SYNCING WITH NO. 6.
VWEEEM

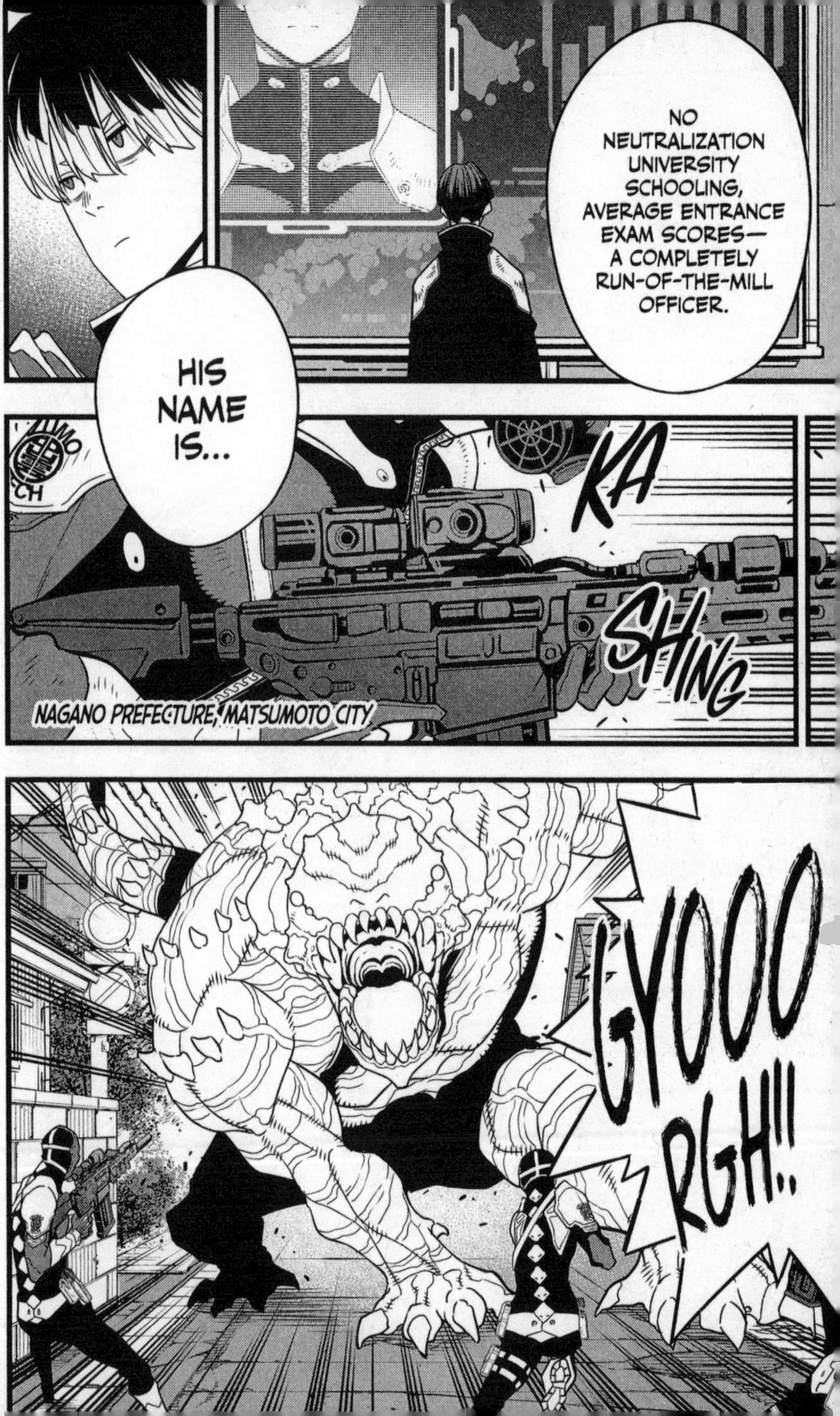
NO NEUTRALIZATION UNIVERSITY SCHOOLING, AVERAGE ENTRANCE EXAM SCORES— A COMPLETELY RUN-OF-THE-MILL OFFICER.
HIS NAME IS...
KA
SHING
NAGANO PREFECTURE, MATSUMOTO CITY
GYOOORGH!!

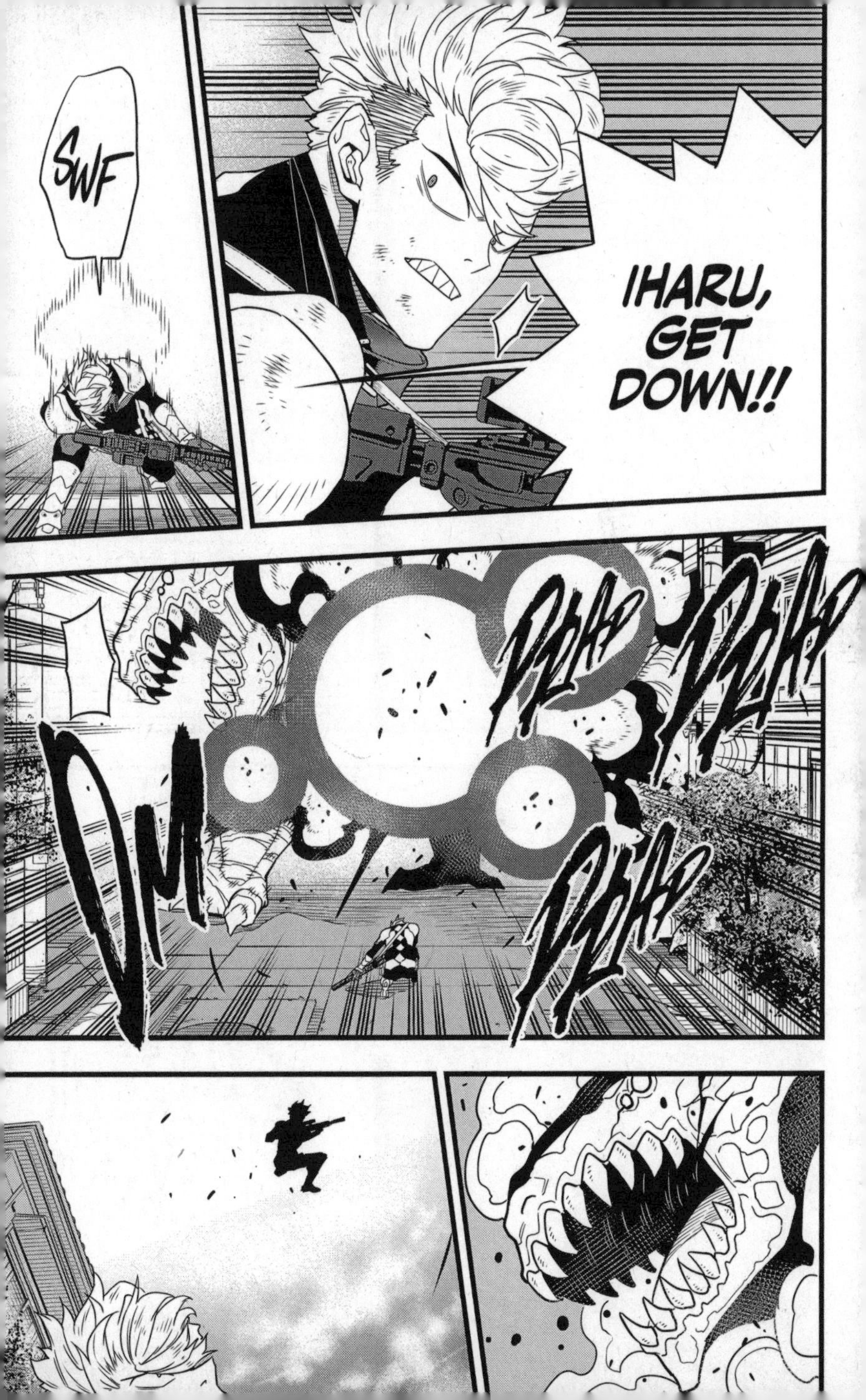
IHARU, GET DOWN!!
SWF

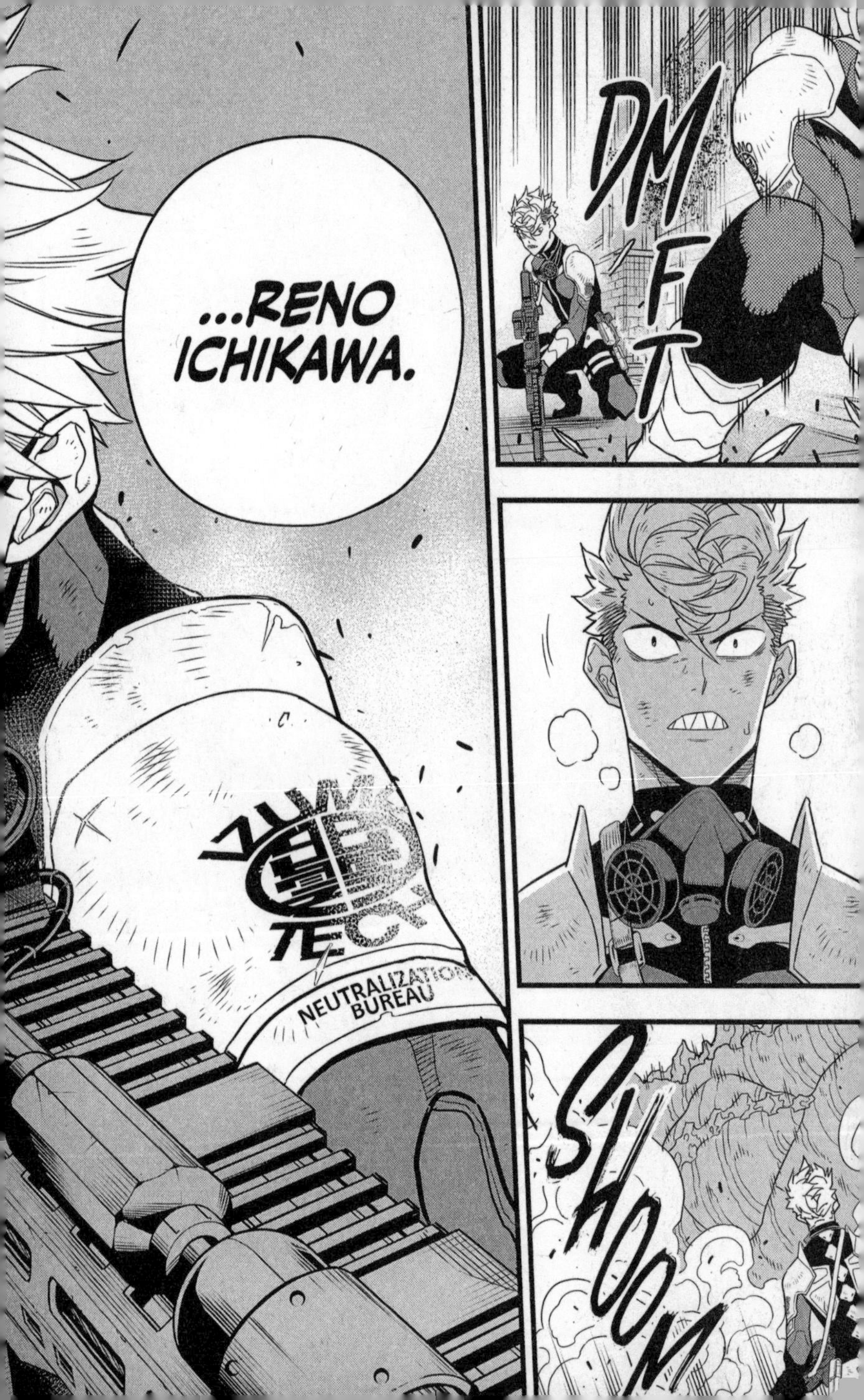
DMFT
SHOOM
...RENO ICHIKAWA.
NEUTRALIZATION BUREAU

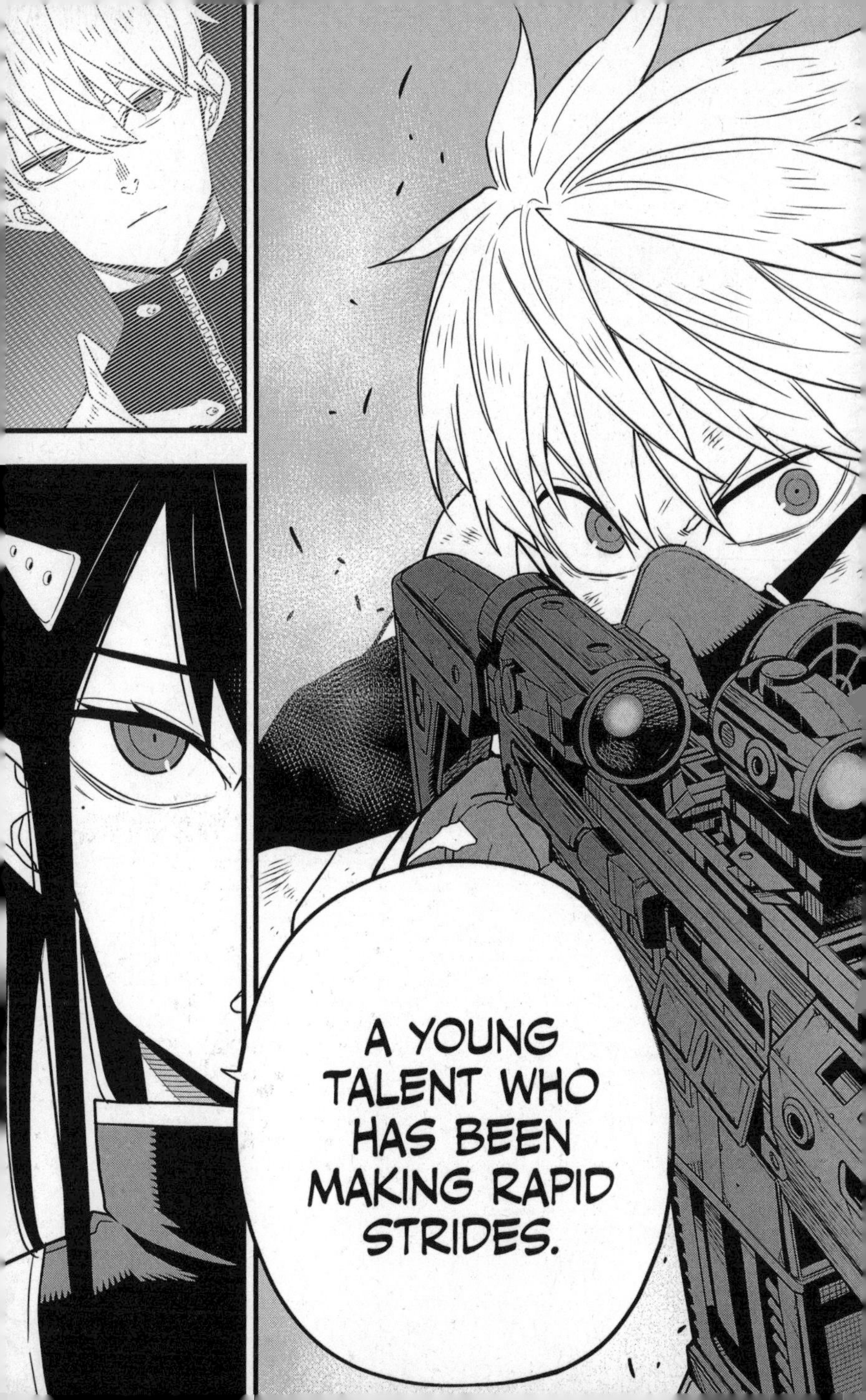
A YOUNG TALENT WHO HAS BEEN MAKING RAPID STRIDES.

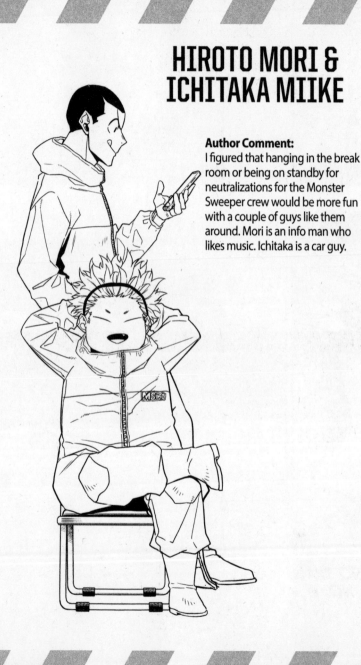

HIROTO MORI & ICHITAKA MIIKE

Author Comment:
I figured that hanging in the break room or being on standby for neutralizations for the Monster Sweeper crew would be more fun with a couple of guys like them around. Mori is an info man who likes music. Ichitaka is a car guy.

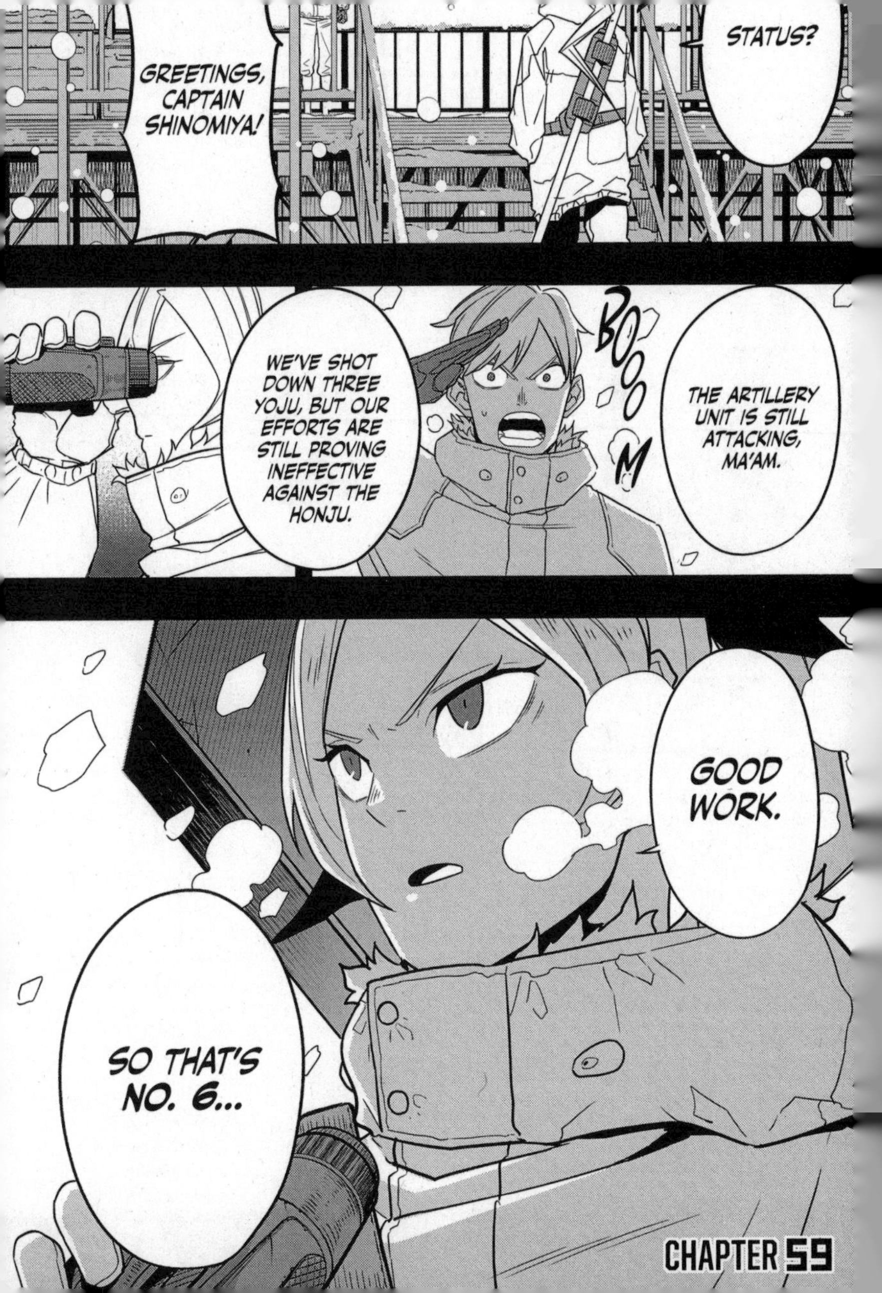
STATUS?
GREETINGS, CAPTAIN SHINOMIYA!
THE ARTILLERY UNIT IS STILL ATTACKING, MA'AM.
BOOOM
WE'VE SHOT DOWN THREE YOJU, BUT OUR EFFORTS ARE STILL PROVING INEFFECTIVE AGAINST THE HONJU.
GOOD WORK.
SO THAT'S NO. 6...
CHAPTER 59

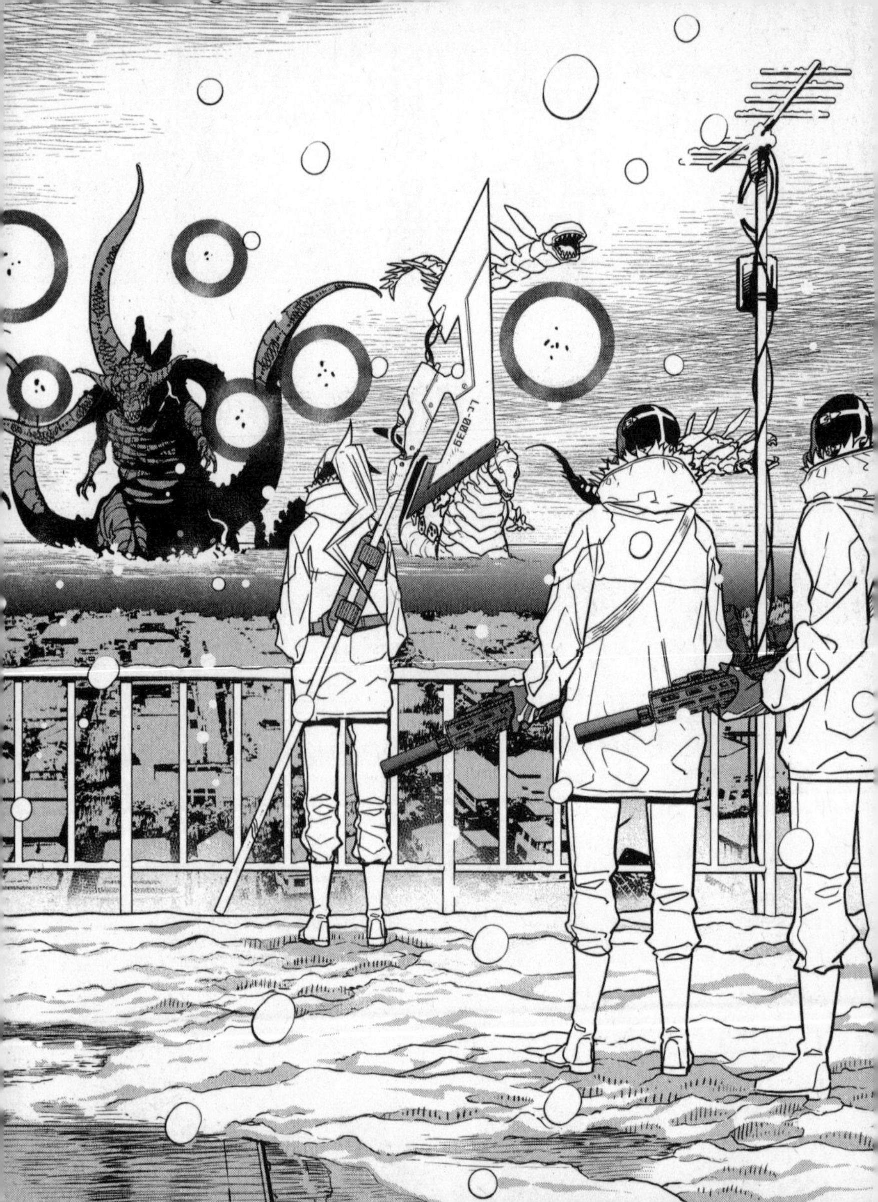
LC-0039

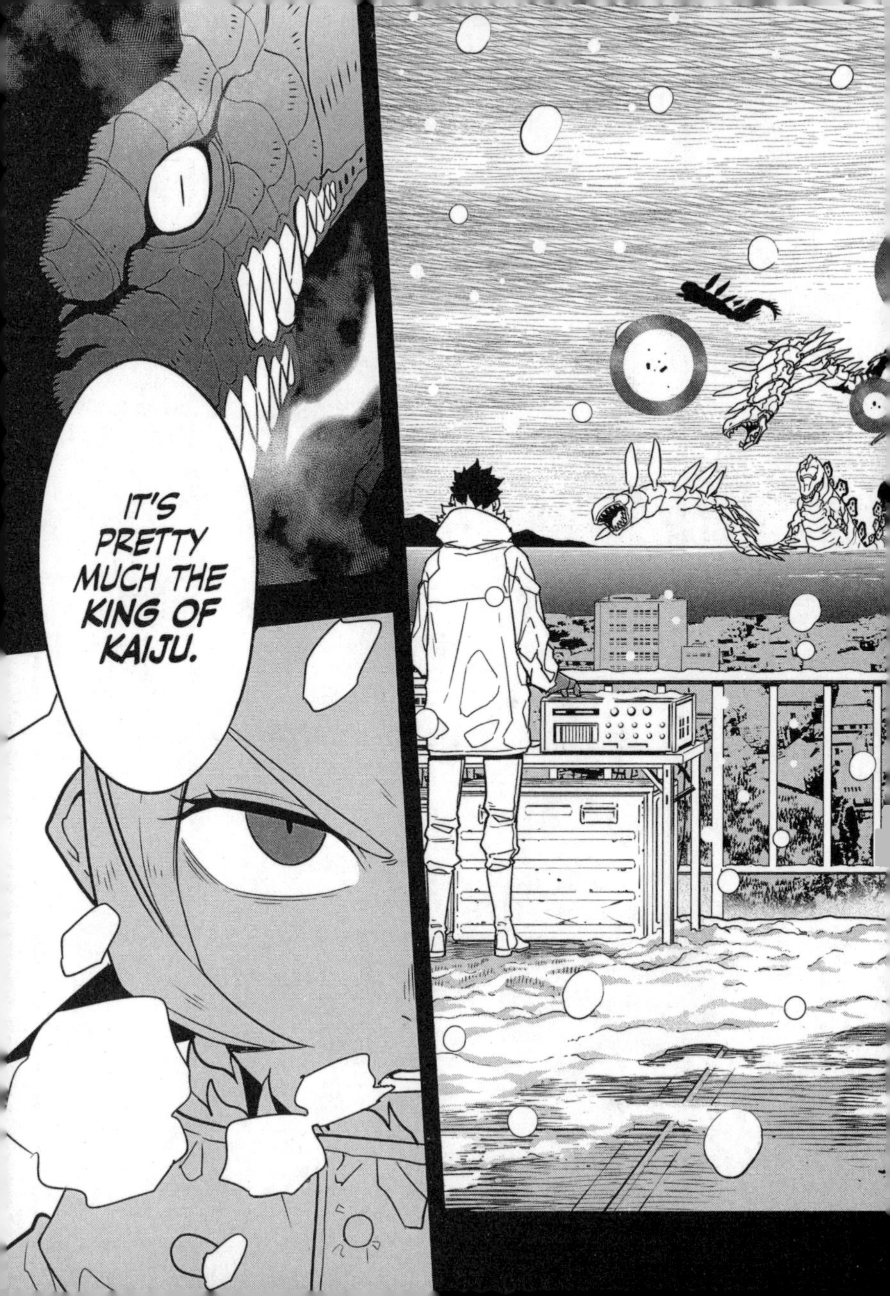
IT'S PRETTY MUCH THE KING OF KAIJU.

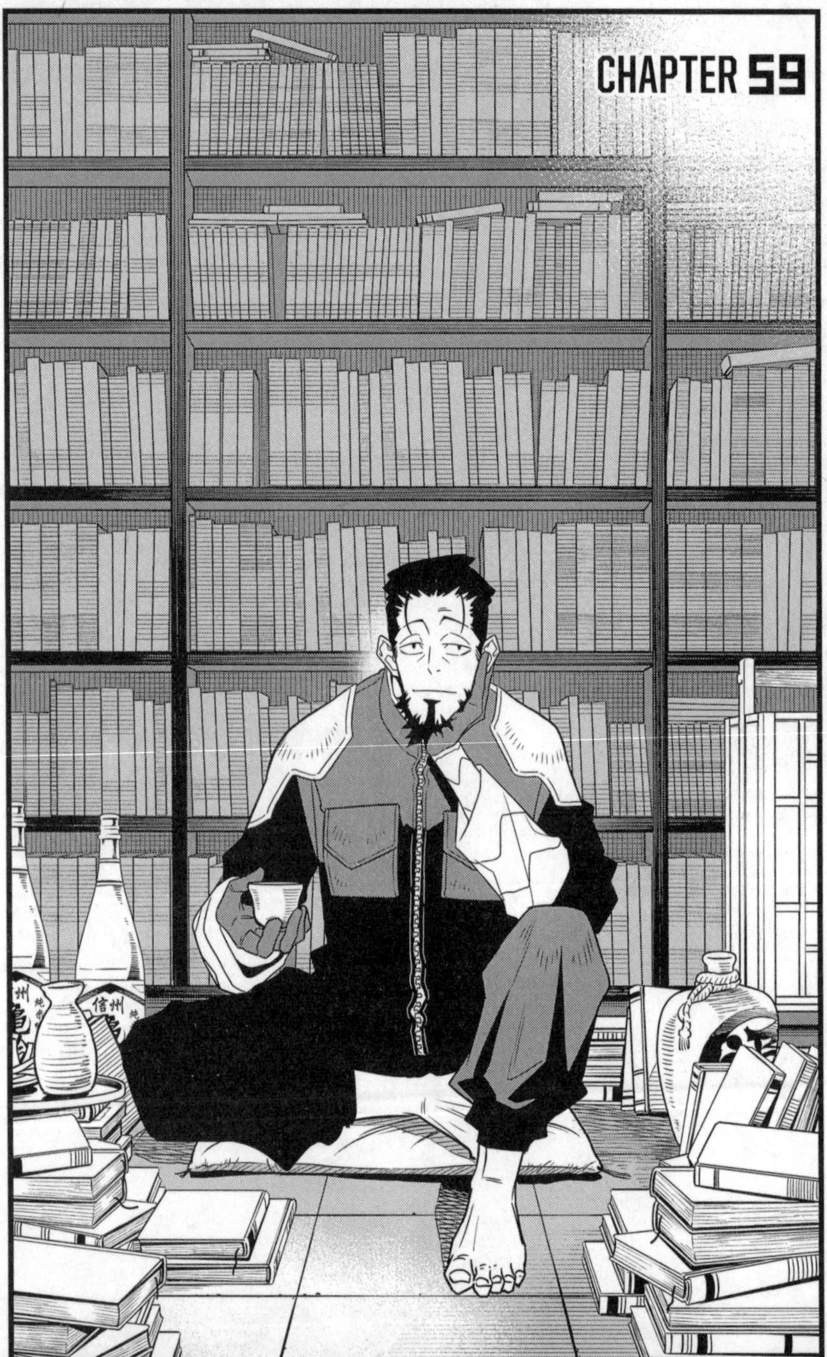
CHAPTER 59
信州

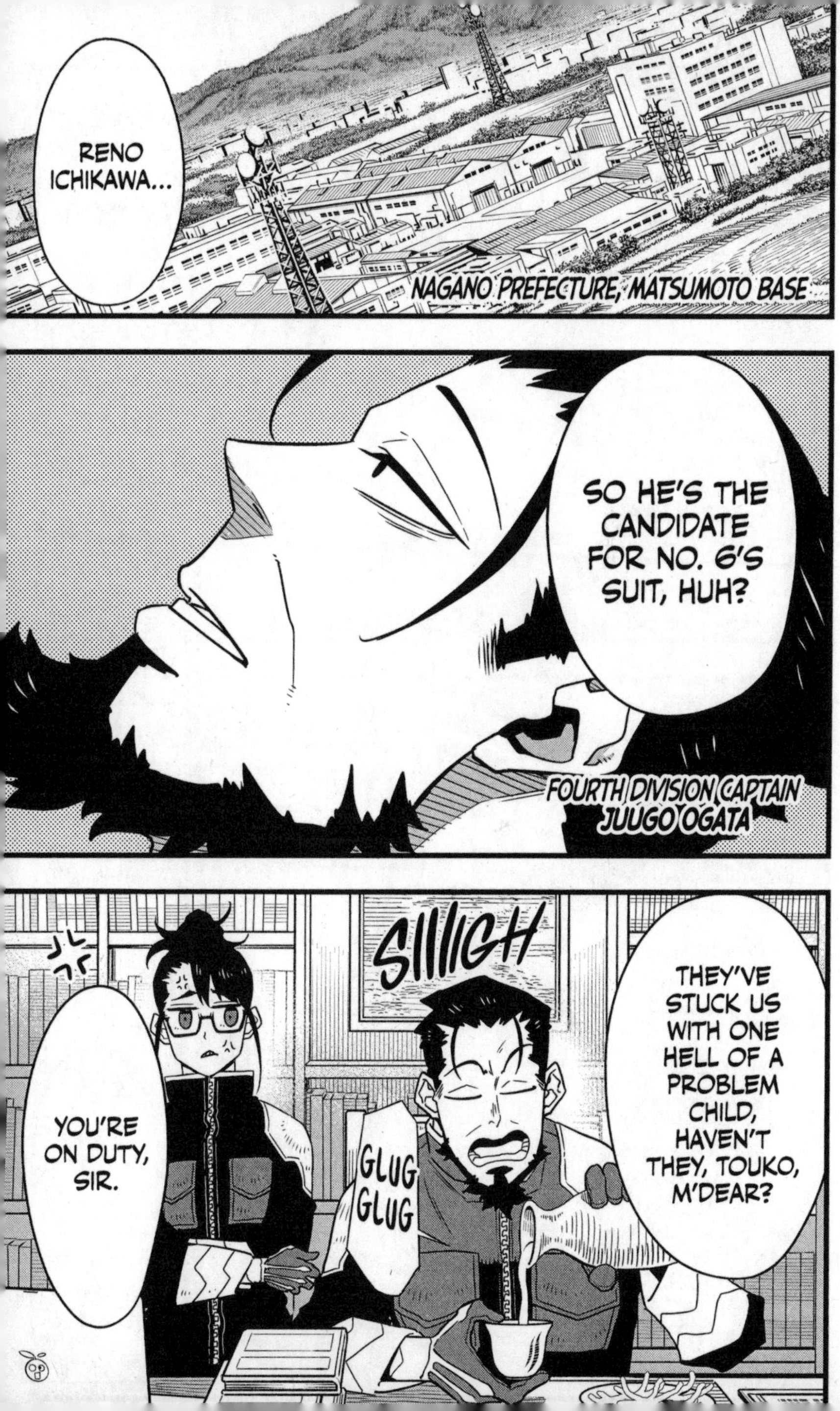
NAGANO PREFECTURE, MATSUMOTO BASE
RENO ICHIKAWA...
SO HE'S THE CANDIDATE FOR NO. 6'S SUIT, HUH?
FOURTH DIVISION CAPTAIN JUUGO OGATA
THEY'VE STUCK US WITH ONE HELL OF A PROBLEM CHILD, HAVEN'T THEY, TOUKO, M'DEAR?
SIIIGH
GLUG GLUG
YOU'RE ON DUTY, SIR.

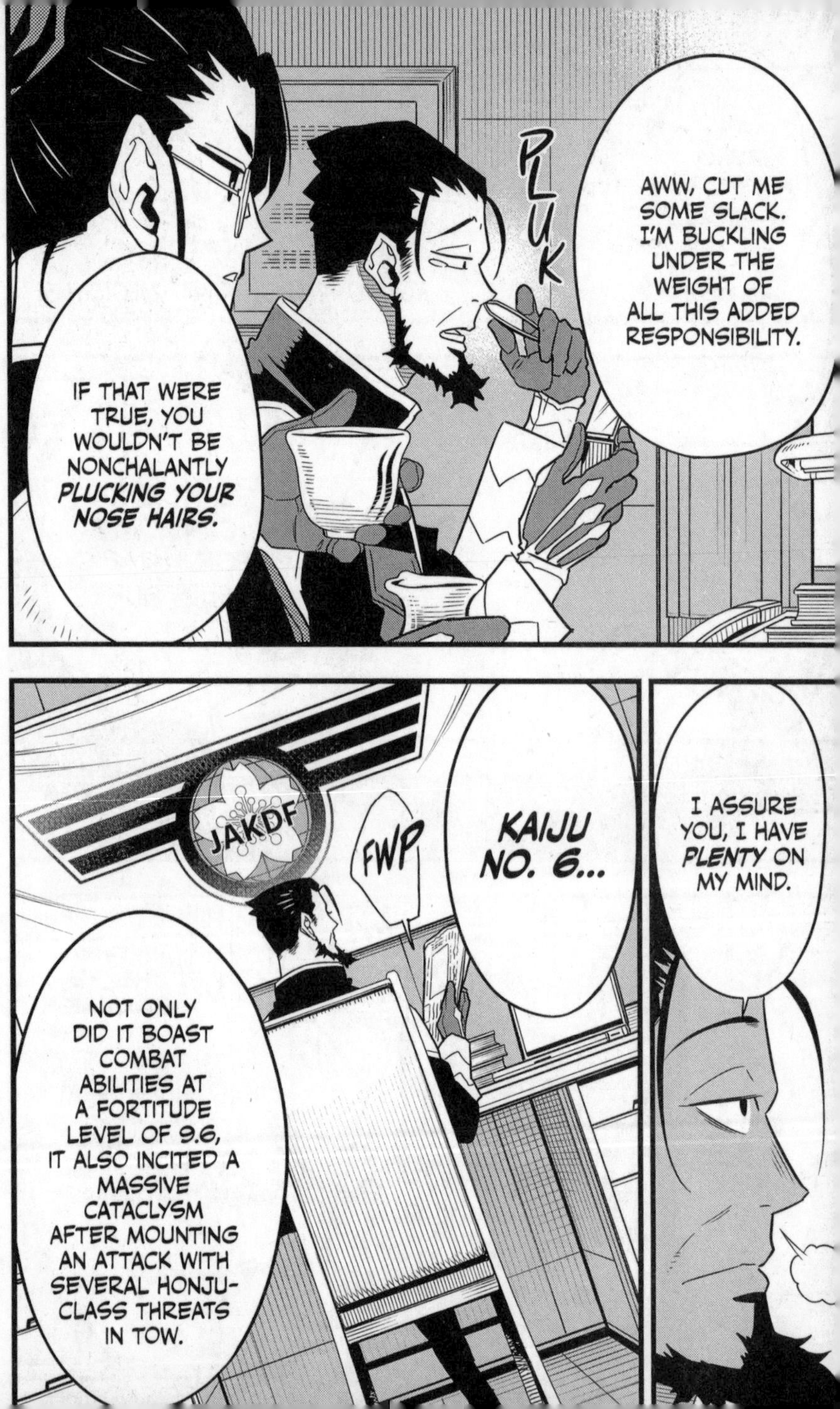
AWW, CUT ME SOME SLACK. I'M BUCKLING UNDER THE WEIGHT OF ALL THIS ADDED RESPONSIBILITY.
PLUK
IF THAT WERE TRUE, YOU WOULDN'T BE NONCHALANTLY PLUCKING YOUR NOSE HAIRS.
I ASSURE YOU, I HAVE PLENTY ON MY MIND.
KAIJU NO. 6...
FWP
JAKDF
NOT ONLY DID IT BOAST COMBAT ABILITIES AT A FORTITUDE LEVEL OF 9.6, IT ALSO INCITED A MASSIVE CATACLYSM AFTER MOUNTING AN ATTACK WITH SEVERAL HONJU-CLASS THREATS IN TOW.

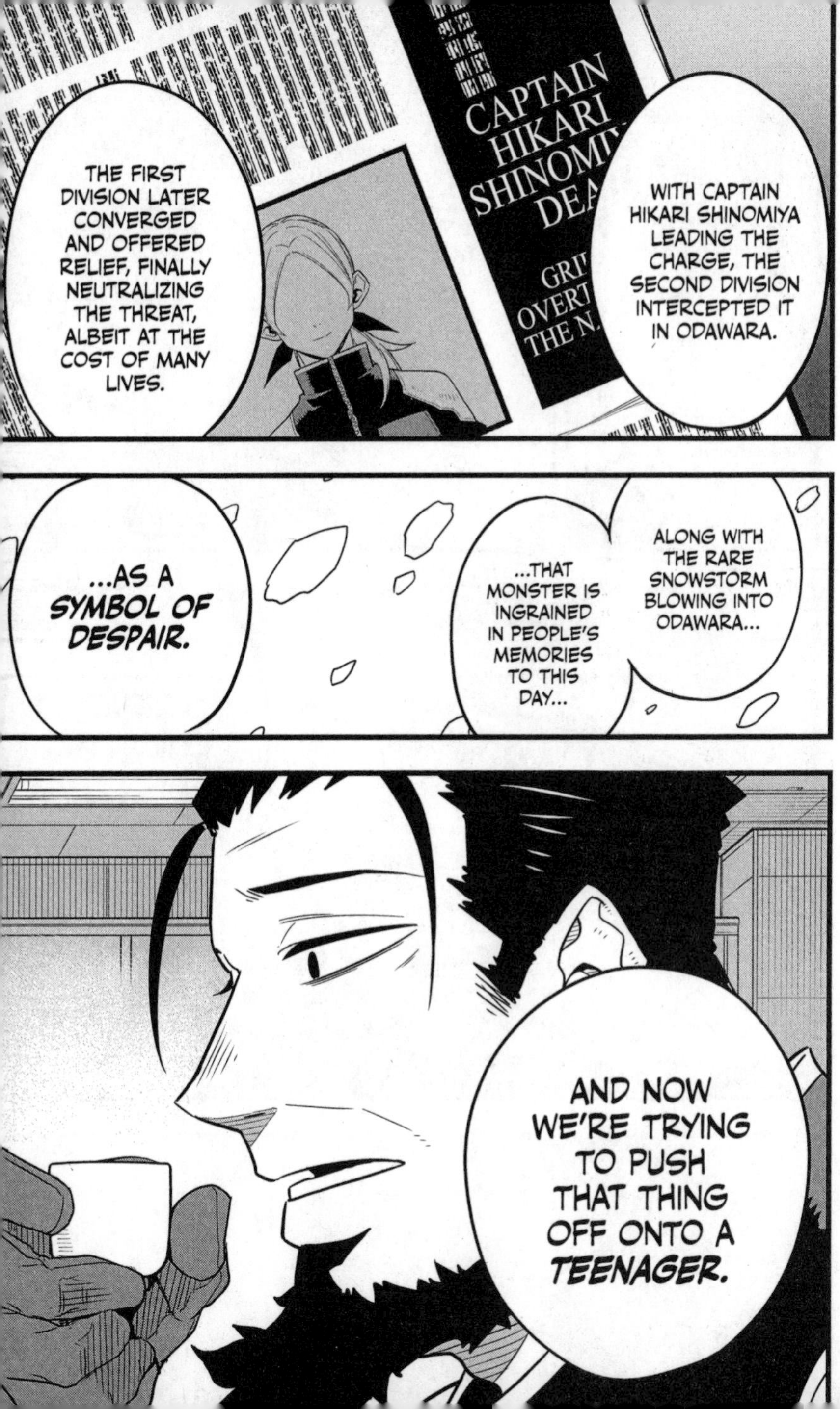
CAPTAIN HIKARI
WITH CAPTAIN HIKARI SHINOMIYA LEADING THE CHARGE, THE SECOND DIVISION INTERCEPTED IT IN ODAWARA.
THE FIRST DIVISION LATER CONVERGED AND OFFERED RELIEF, FINALLY NEUTRALIZING THE THREAT, ALBEIT AT THE COST OF MANY LIVES.
ALONG WITH THE RARE SNOWSTORM BLOWING INTO ODAWARA...
...THAT MONSTER IS INGRAINED IN PEOPLE'S MEMORIES TO THIS DAY...
...AS A *SYMBOL OF DESPAIR.*
AND NOW WE'RE TRYING TO PUSH THAT THING OFF ONTO A *TEENAGER.*

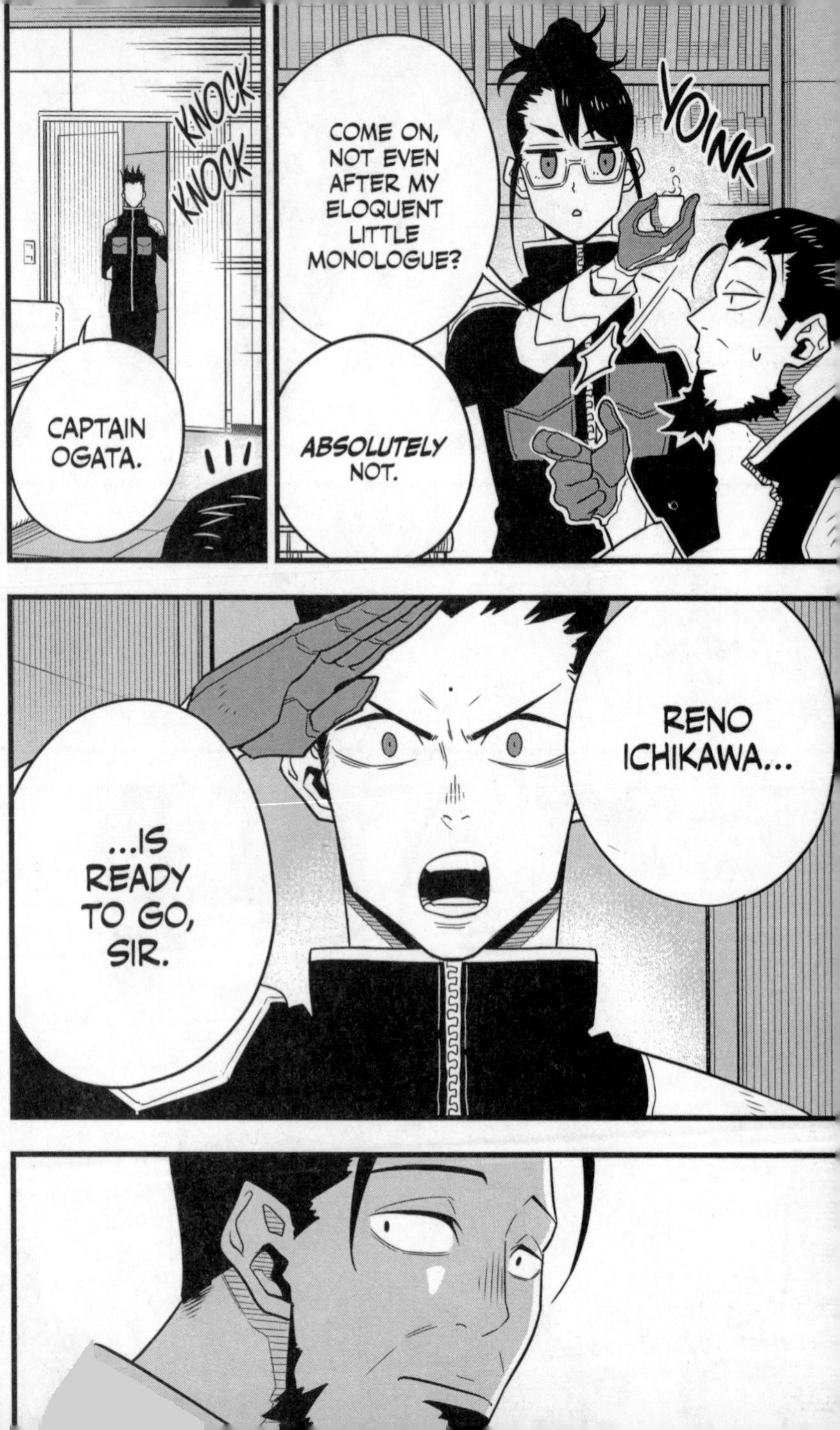
YOINK
COME ON, NOT EVEN AFTER MY ELOQUENT LITTLE MONOLOGUE?
ABSOLUTELY NOT.
KNOCK KNOCK
CAPTAIN OGATA.
RENO ICHIKAWA...
...IS READY TO GO, SIR.

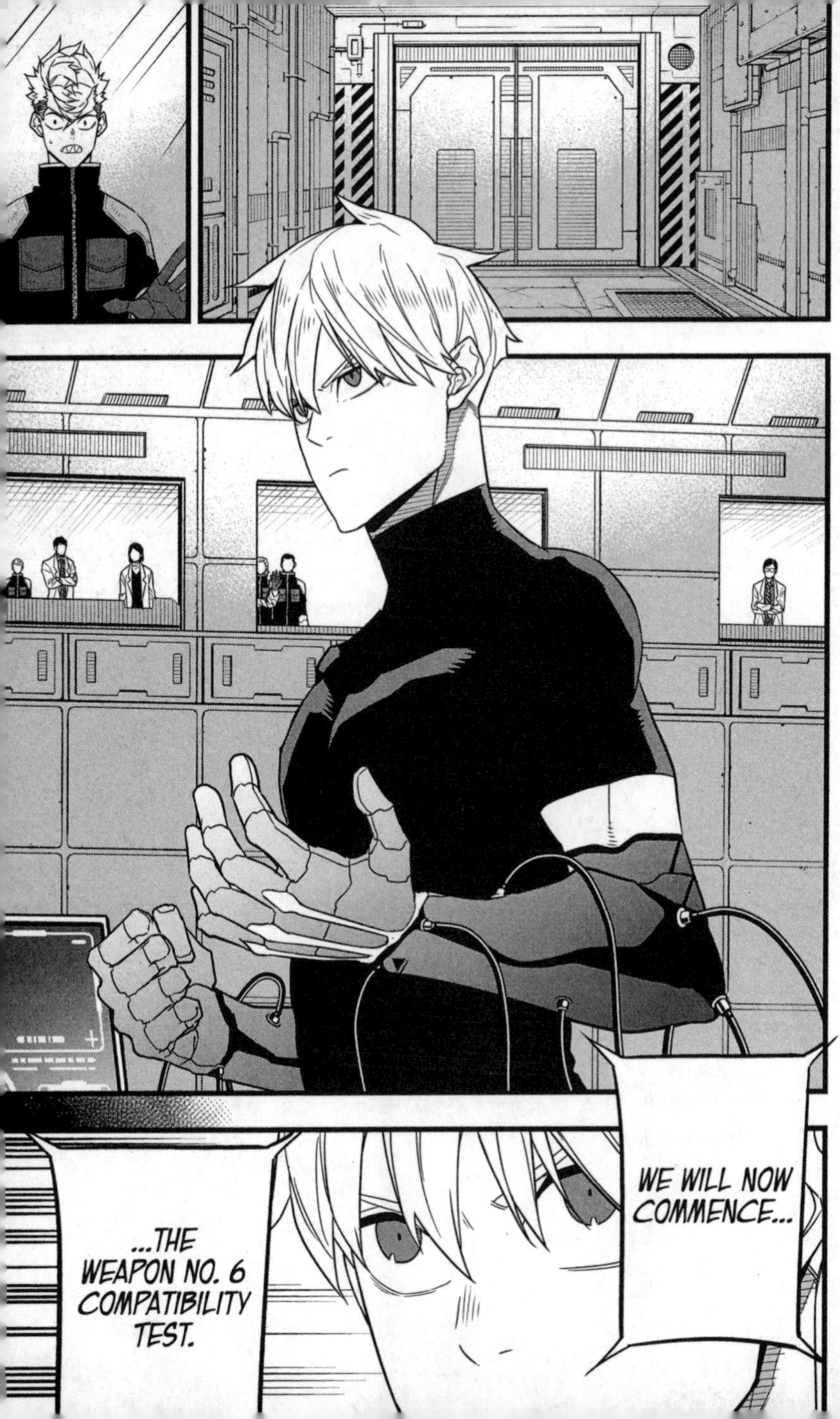
WE WILL NOW COMMENCE...
...THE WEAPON NO. 6 COMPATIBILITY TEST.

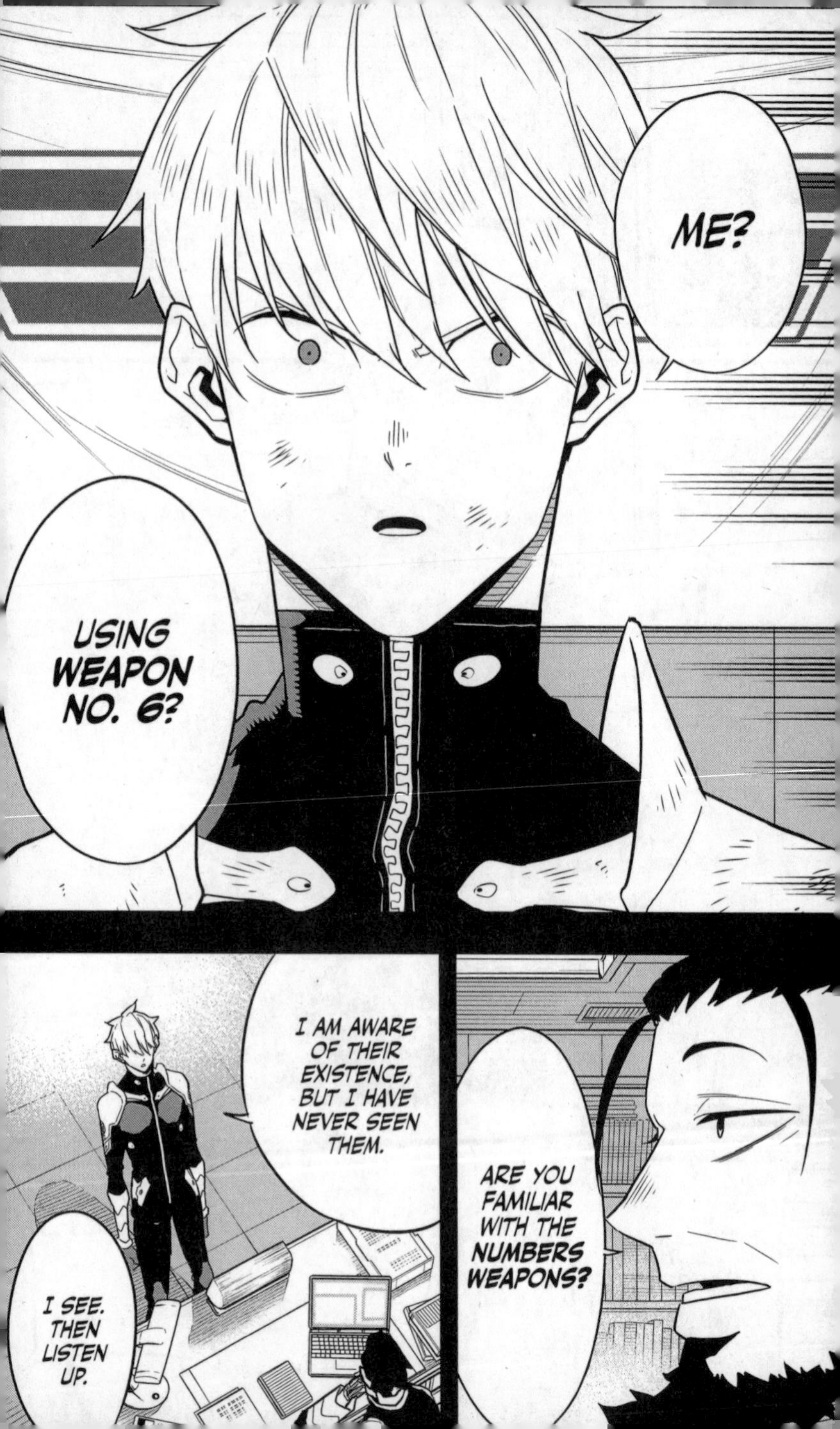
ME?
USING WEAPON NO. 6?
ARE YOU FAMILIAR WITH THE NUMBERS WEAPONS?
I AM AWARE OF THEIR EXISTENCE, BUT I HAVE NEVER SEEN THEM.
I SEE. THEN LISTEN UP.

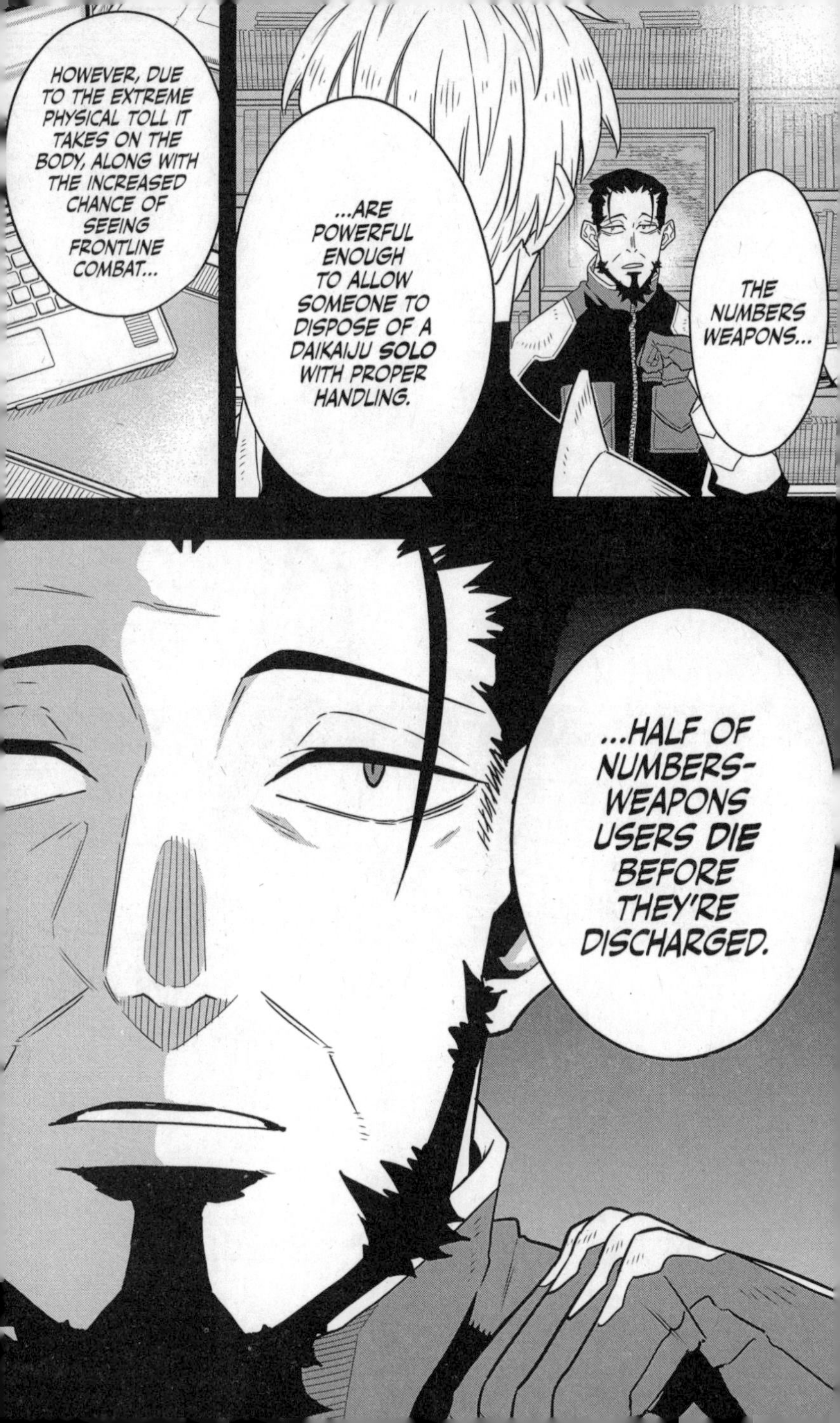
THE NUMBERS WEAPONS...
...ARE POWERFUL ENOUGH TO ALLOW SOMEONE TO DISPOSE OF A DAIKAIJU SOLO WITH PROPER HANDLING.
HOWEVER, DUE TO THE EXTREME PHYSICAL TOLL IT TAKES ON THE BODY, ALONG WITH THE INCREASED CHANCE OF SEEING FRONTLINE COMBAT...
...HALF OF NUMBERS-WEAPONS USERS DIE BEFORE THEY'RE DISCHARGED.

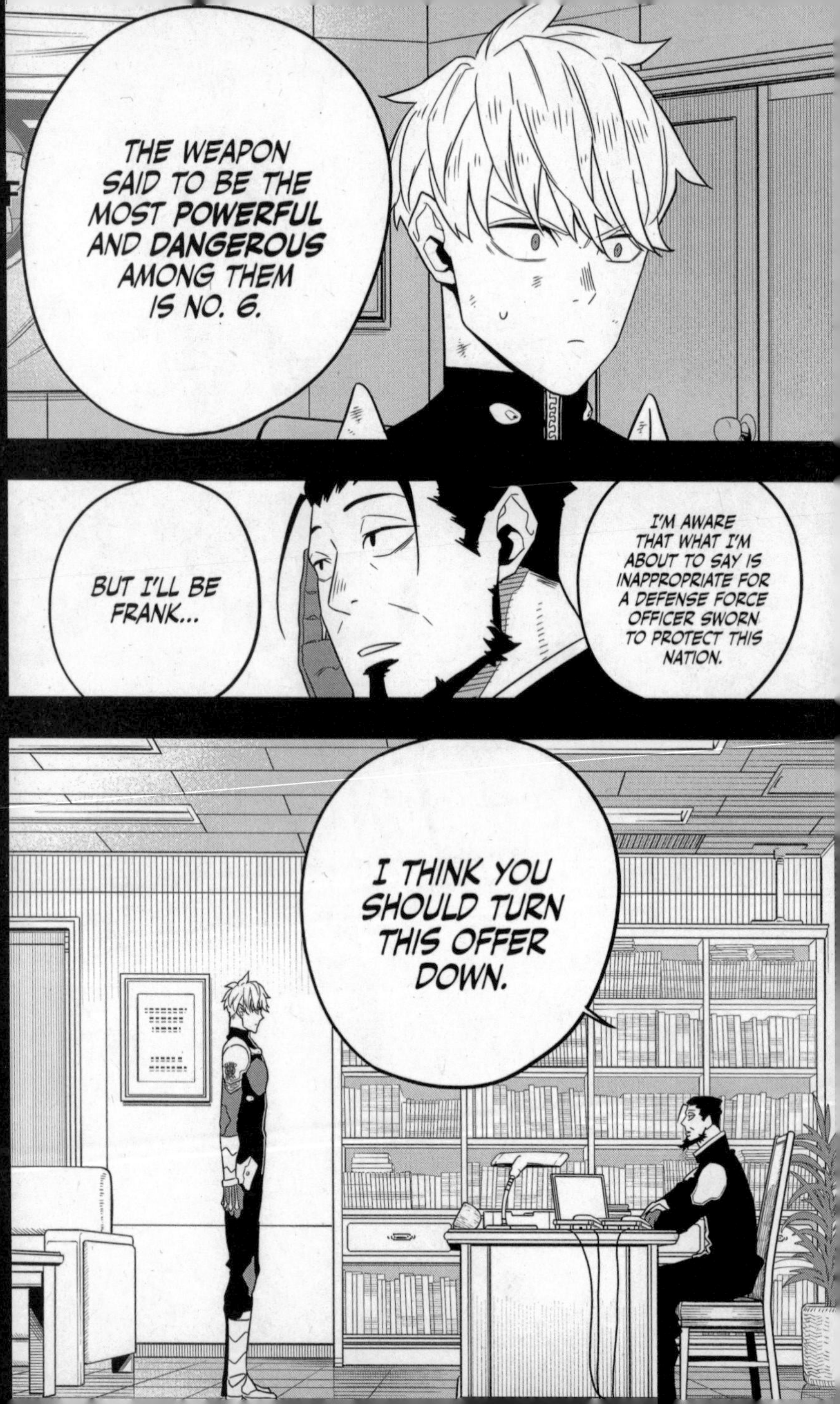
THE WEAPON SAID TO BE THE MOST POWERFUL AND DANGEROUS AMONG THEM IS NO. 6.
I'M AWARE THAT WHAT I'M ABOUT TO SAY IS INAPPROPRIATE FOR A DEFENSE FORCE OFFICER SWORN TO PROTECT THIS NATION.
BUT I'LL BE FRANK...
I THINK YOU SHOULD TURN THIS OFFER DOWN.

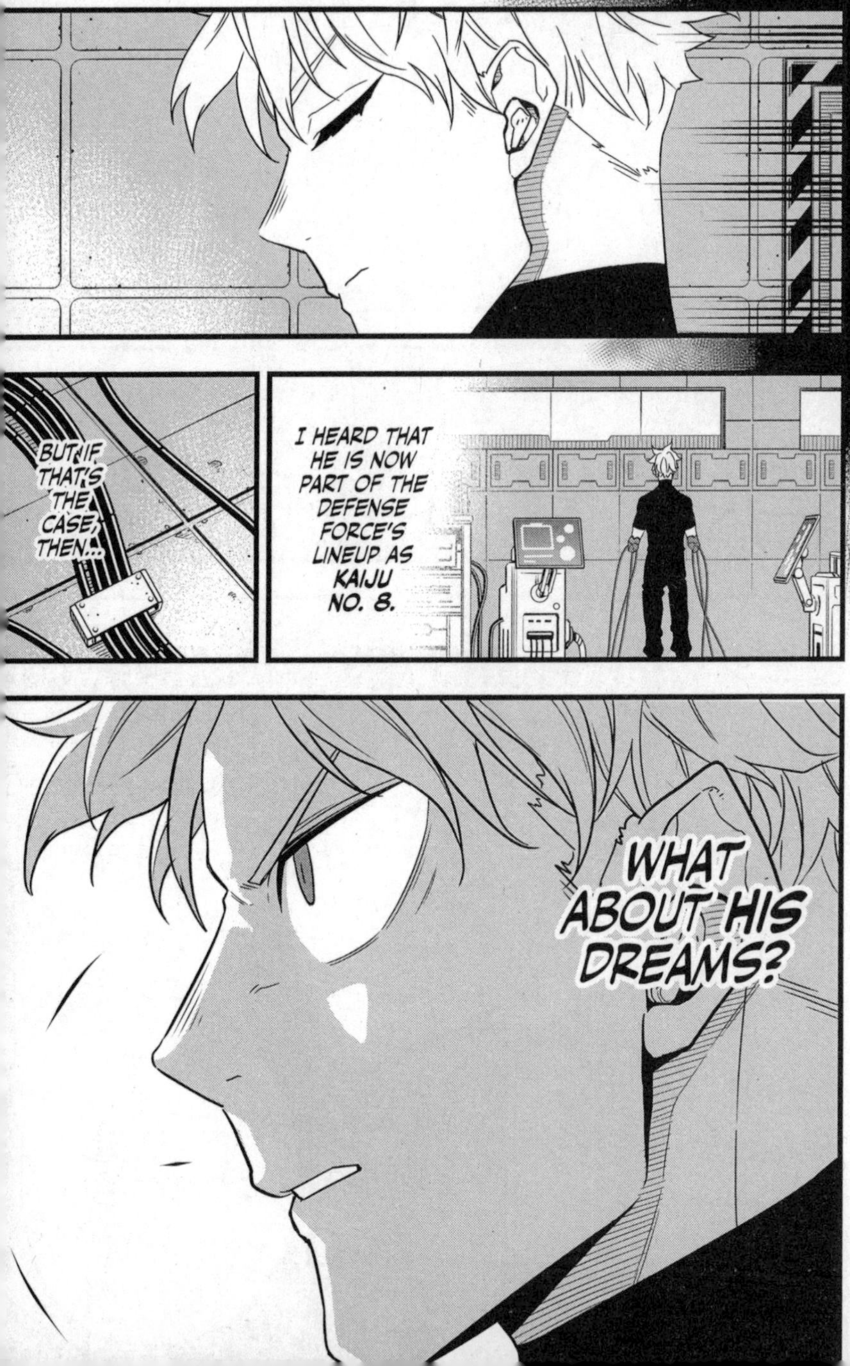
I HEARD THAT HE IS NOW PART OF THE DEFENSE FORCE'S LINEUP AS KAIJU NO. 8.
BUT IF THAT'S THE CASE, THEN...
WHAT ABOUT HIS DREAMS?

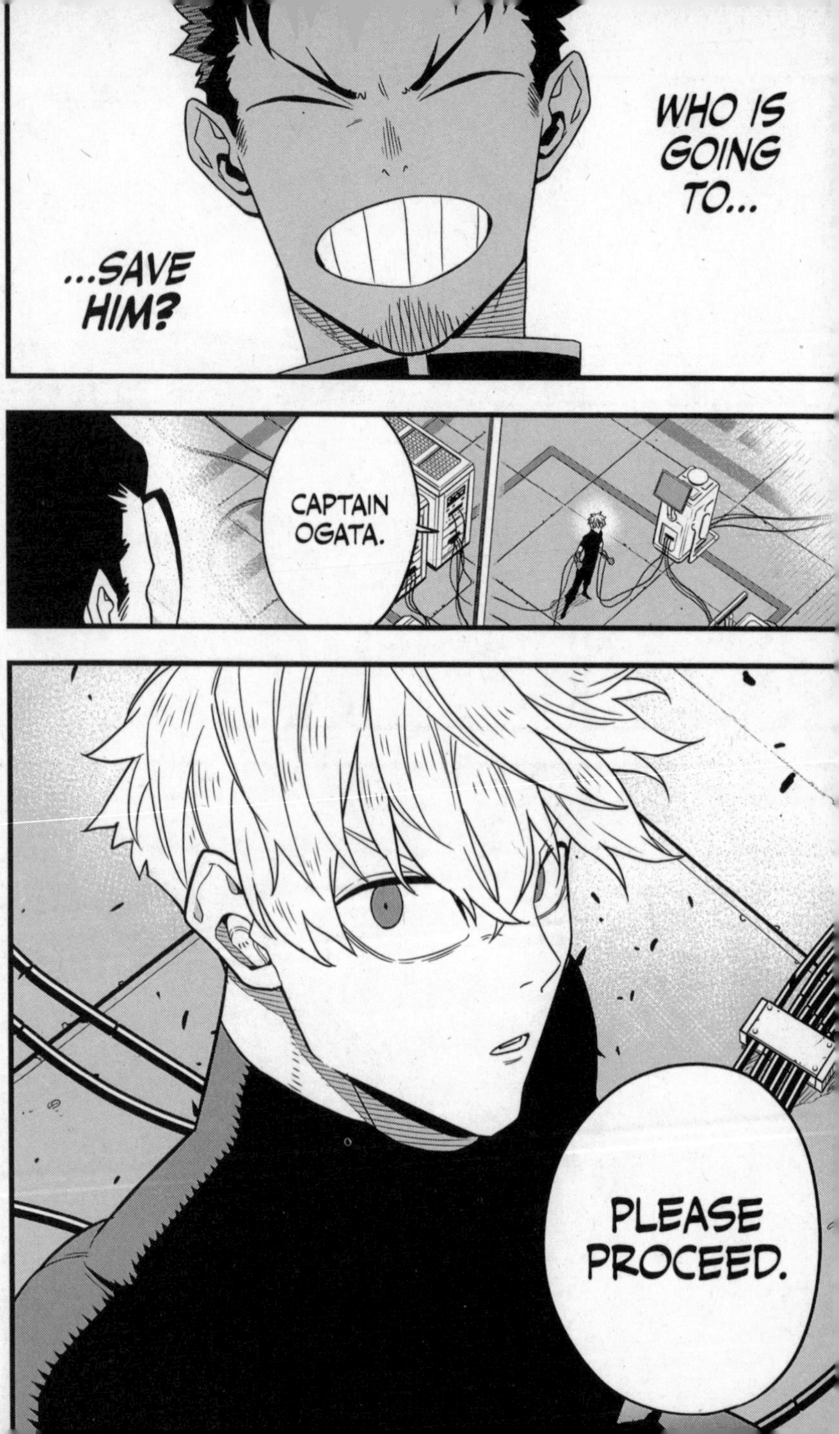
WHO IS GOING TO...
...SAVE HIM?
CAPTAIN OGATA.
PLEASE PROCEED.

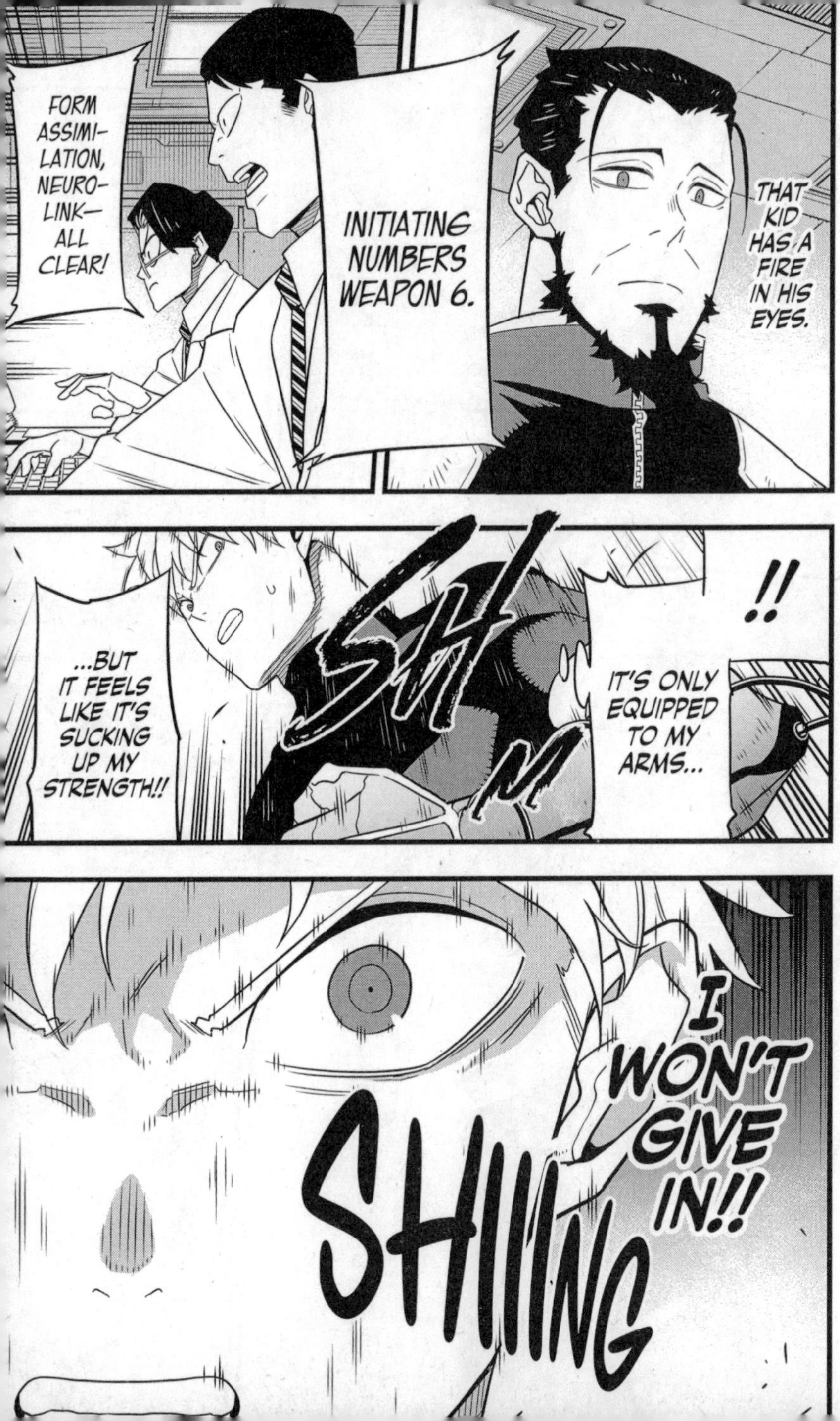

THAT KID HAS A FIRE IN HIS EYES.
INITIATING NUMBERS WEAPON 6.
FORM ASSIMILATION, NEURO-LINK—ALL CLEAR!
!!
IT'S ONLY EQUIPPED TO MY ARMS...
SHM
...BUT IT FEELS LIKE IT'S SUCKING UP MY STRENGTH!!
I WON'T GIVE IN!!
SHIIING

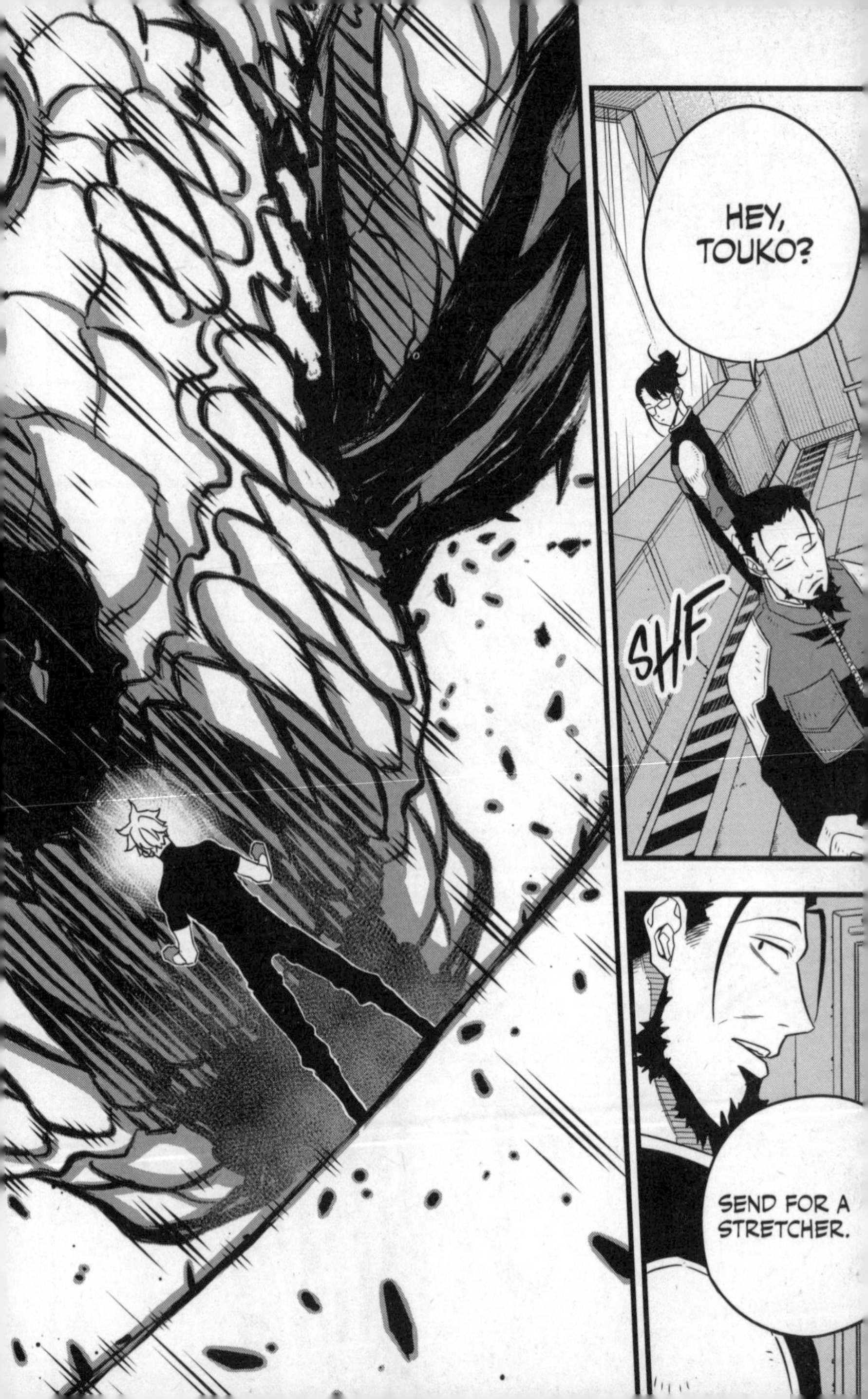
HEY, TOUKO?
SHF
SEND FOR A STRETCHER.

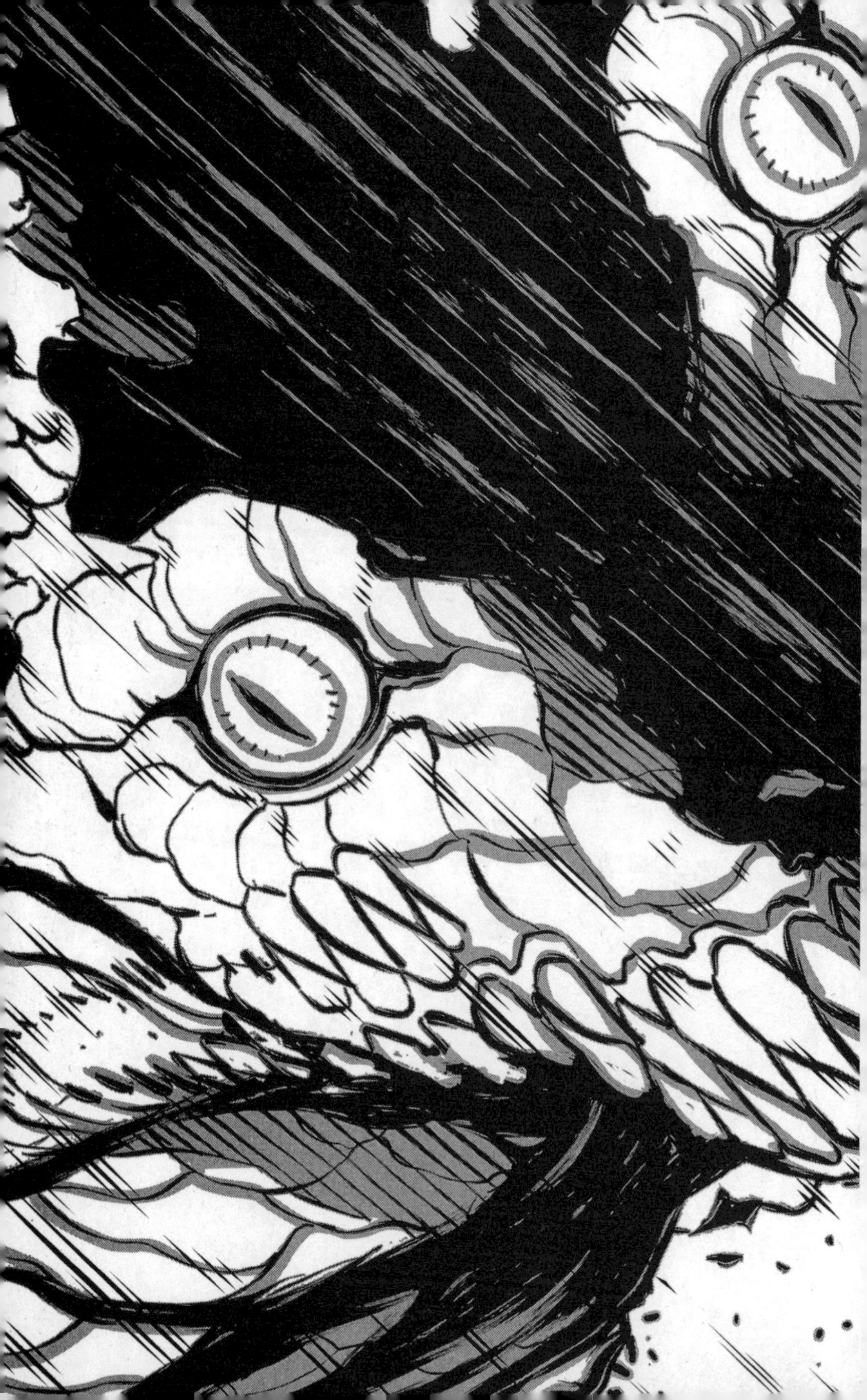

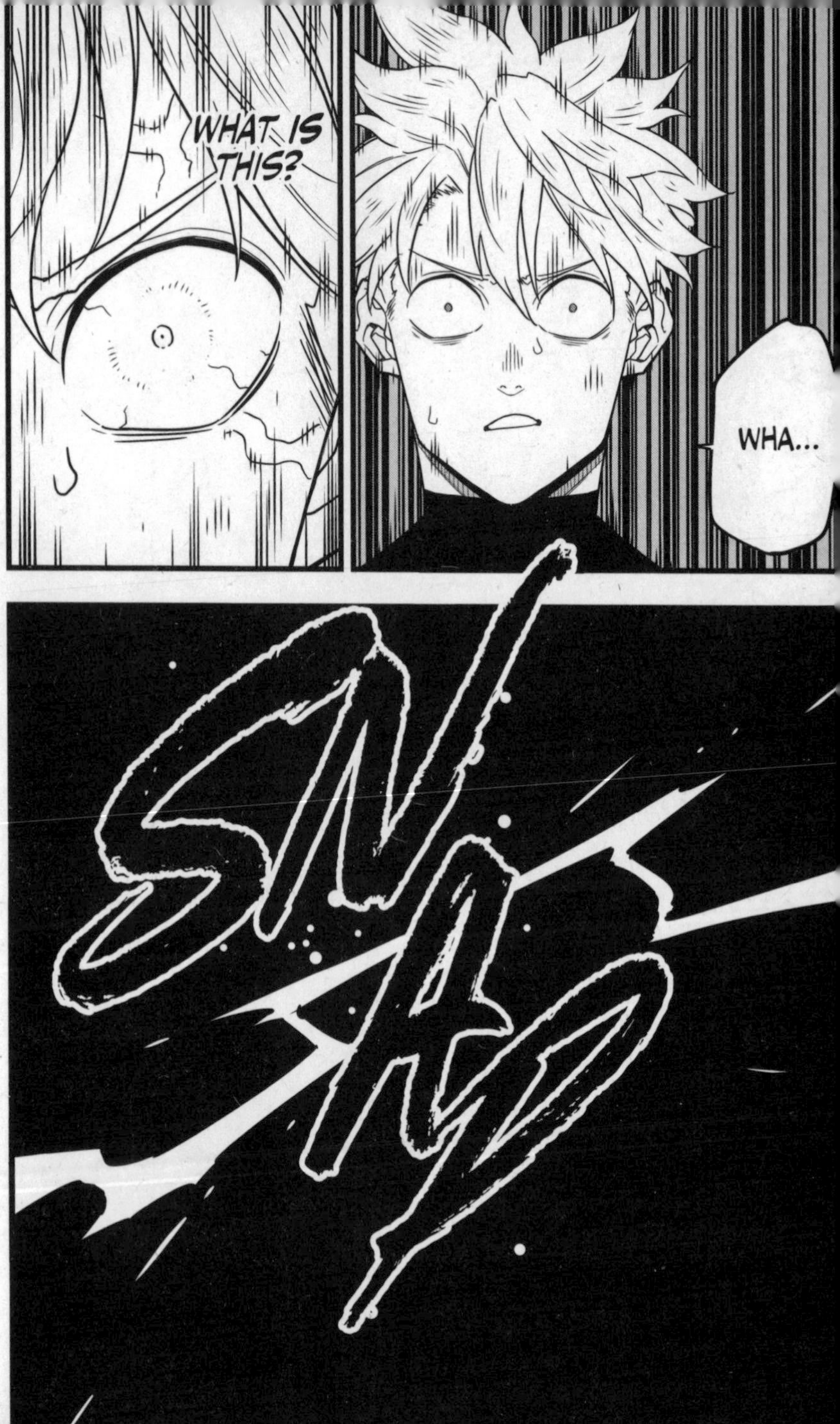
WHA...
WHAT IS THIS?
SNAP

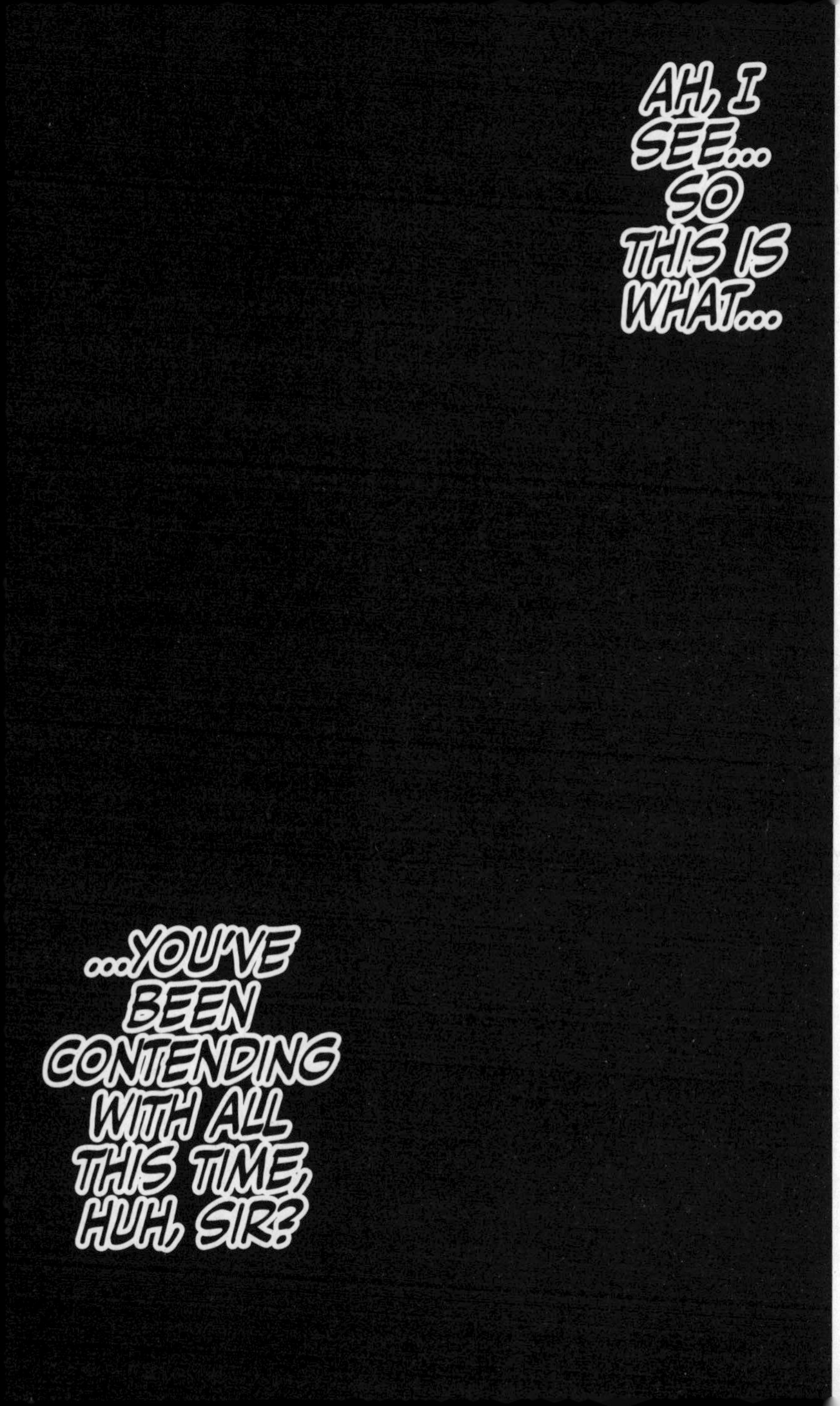
AH, I SEE... SO THIS IS WHAT...
...YOU'VE BEEN CONTENDING WITH ALL THIS TIME, HUH, SIR?

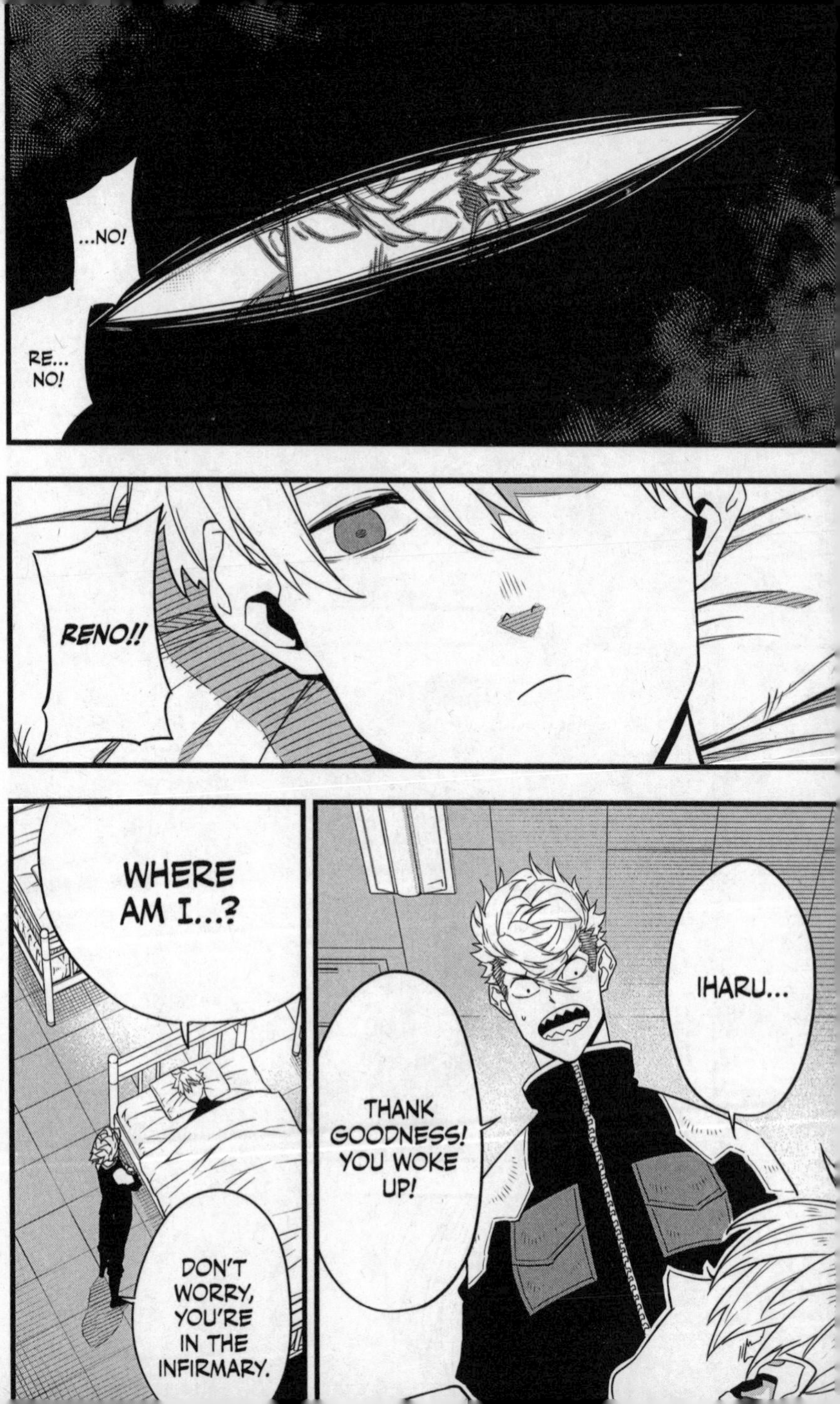
...NO!
RE... NO!
RENO!!
IHARU...
THANK GOODNESS! YOU WOKE UP!
WHERE AM I...?
DON'T WORRY, YOU'RE IN THE INFIRMARY.

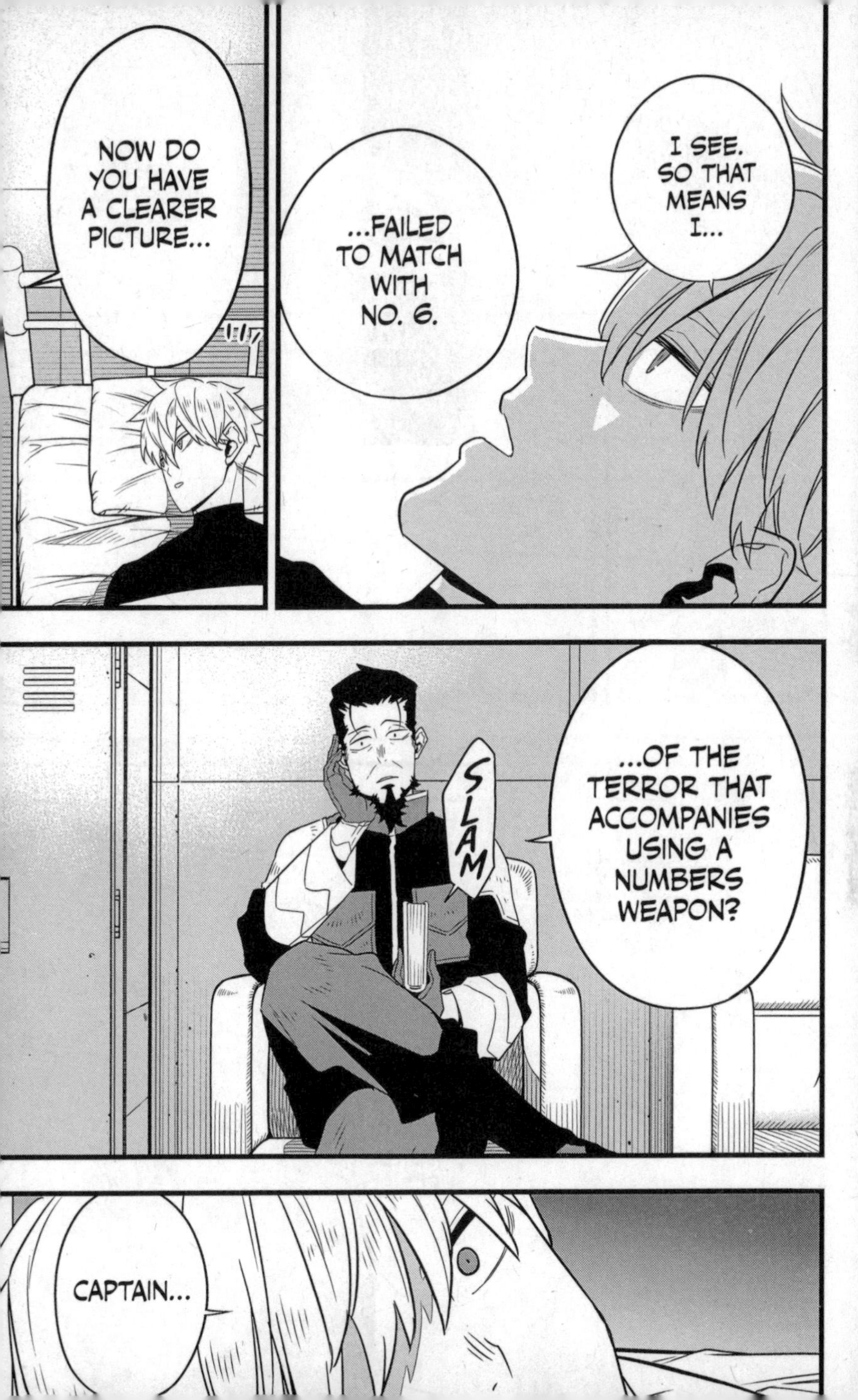
I SEE. SO THAT MEANS I...
...FAILED TO MATCH WITH NO. 6.
NOW DO YOU HAVE A CLEARER PICTURE...
...OF THE TERROR THAT ACCOMPANIES USING A NUMBERS WEAPON?
SLAM
CAPTAIN...

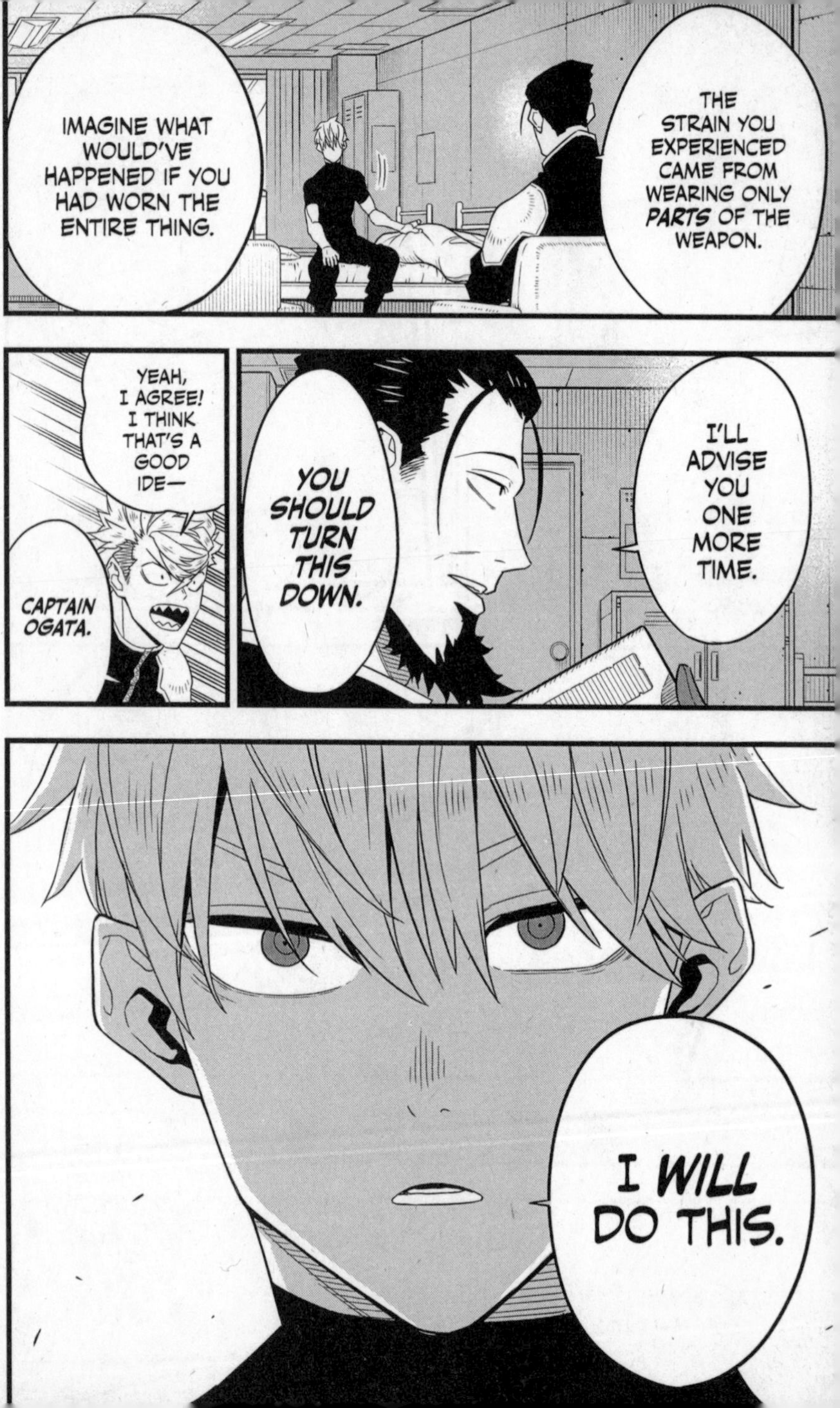
THE STRAIN YOU EXPERIENCED CAME FROM WEARING ONLY *PARTS* OF THE WEAPON.
IMAGINE WHAT WOULD'VE HAPPENED IF YOU HAD WORN THE ENTIRE THING.
I'LL ADVISE YOU ONE MORE TIME.
YOU SHOULD TURN THIS DOWN.
YEAH, I AGREE! I THINK THAT'S A GOOD IDE—
CAPTAIN OGATA.
I *WILL* DO THIS.

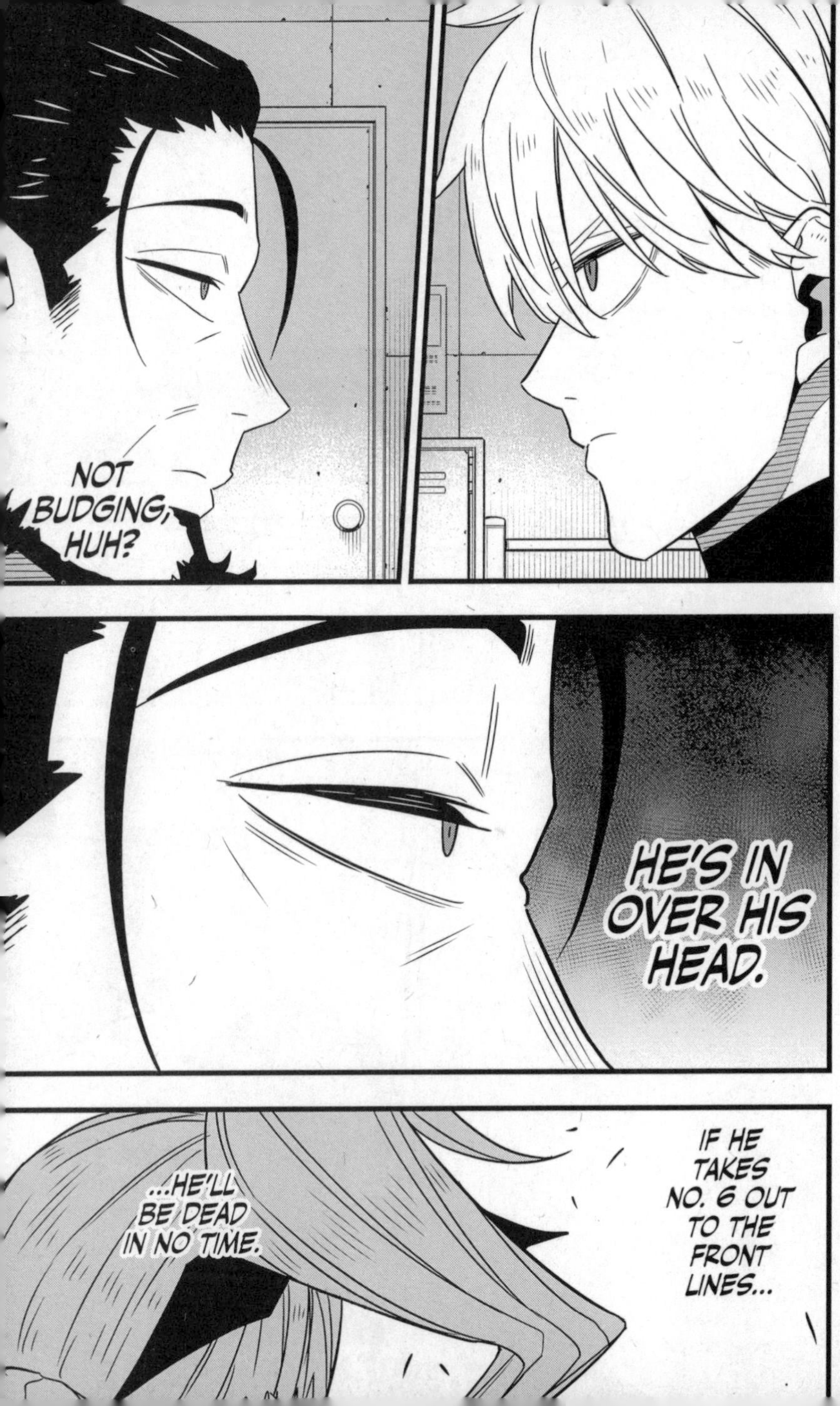
NOT BUDGING, HUH?
HE'S IN OVER HIS HEAD.
IF HE TAKES NO. 6 OUT TO THE FRONT LINES...
...HE'LL BE DEAD IN NO TIME.

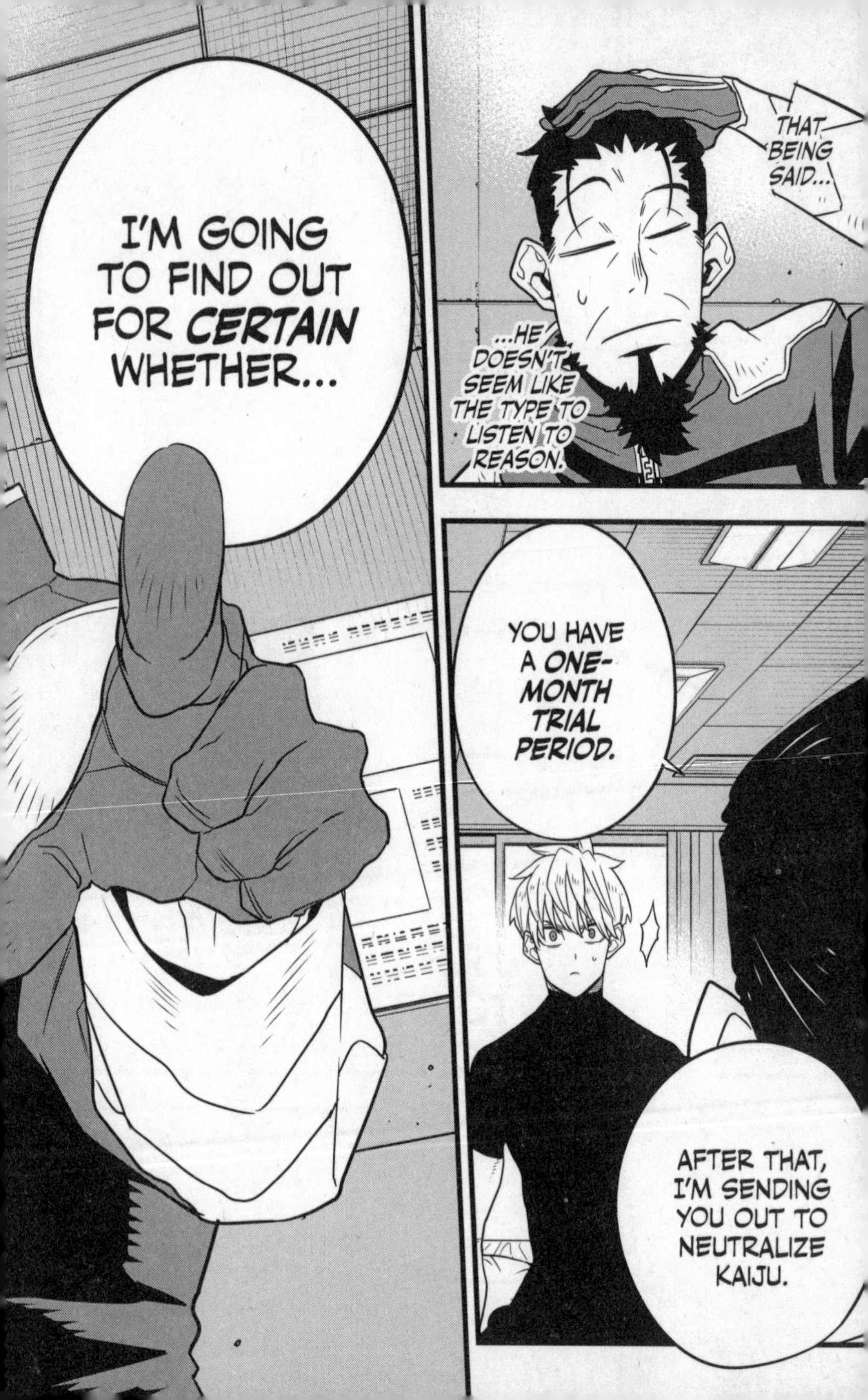
THAT BEING SAID...
...HE DOESN'T SEEM LIKE THE TYPE TO LISTEN TO REASON.
YOU HAVE A *ONE-MONTH TRIAL PERIOD.*
AFTER THAT, I'M SENDING YOU OUT TO NEUTRALIZE KAIJU.
I'M GOING TO FIND OUT FOR *CERTAIN* WHETHER...

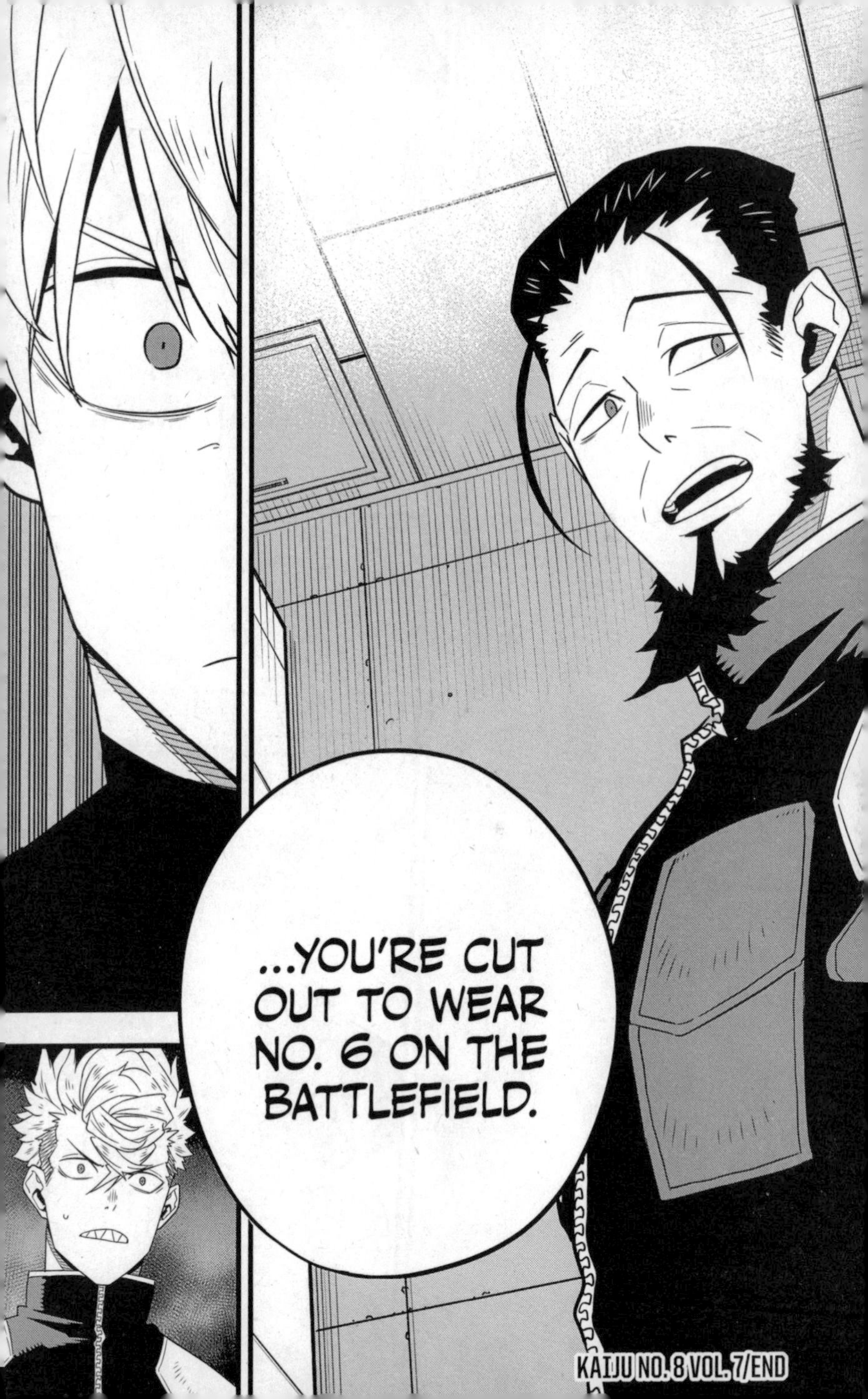
...YOU'RE CUT OUT TO WEAR NO. 6 ON THE BATTLEFIELD.
KAIJU NO. 8 VOL. 7/END

KAIJU NO. 8

7

STORY AND ART BY
NAOYA MATSUMOTO

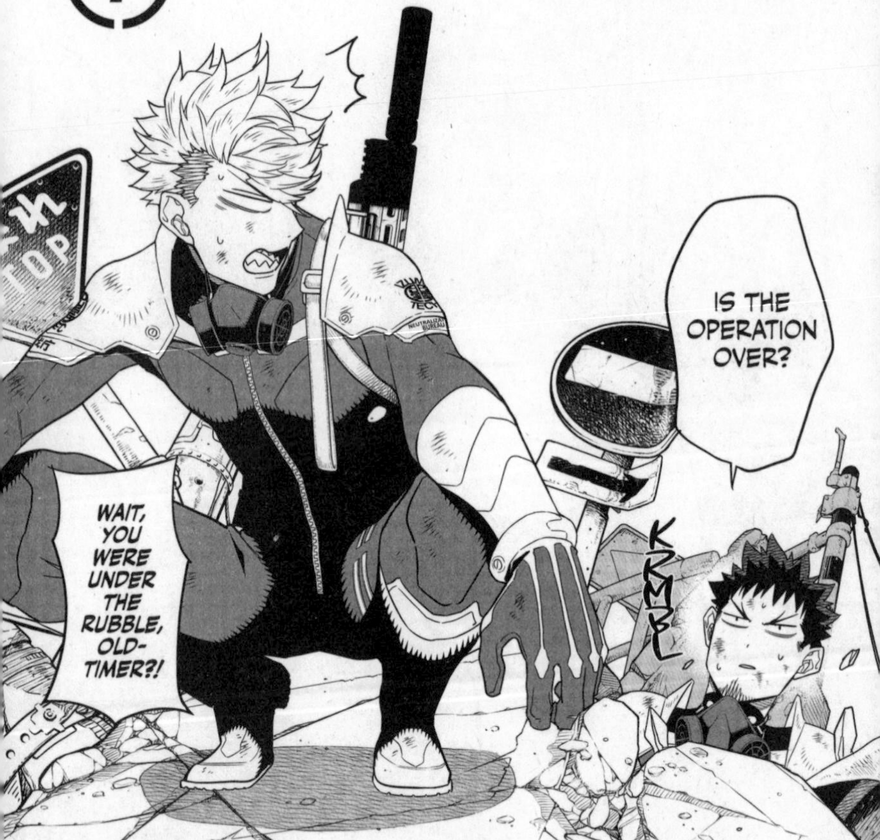

HOSHINA IS PROBABLY A BETTER GAMER TOO

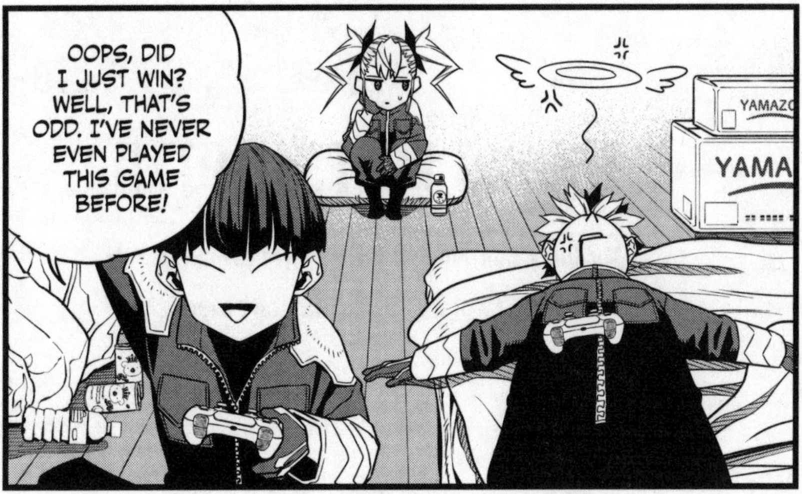
OOPS, DID I JUST WIN? WELL, THAT'S ODD. I'VE NEVER EVEN PLAYED THIS GAME BEFORE!
YAMAZO
YAMA

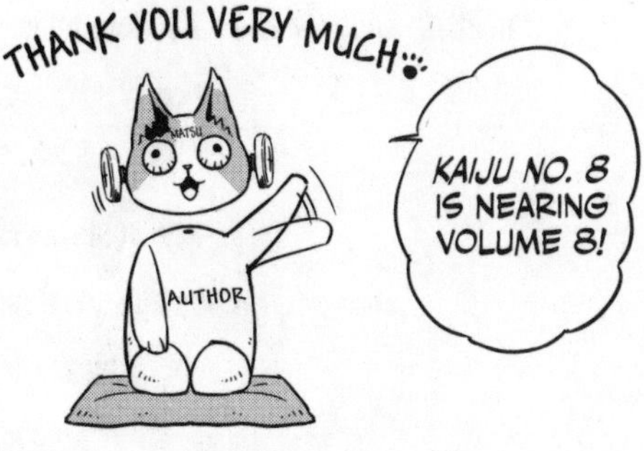
THANK YOU VERY MUCH
MATSU
AUTHOR
KAIJU NO. 8 IS NEARING VOLUME 8!

NAOYA MATSUMOTO

My body has always been stiff, but lately it's gotten even worse. I'll need to start exercising if I want to keep living!

Naoya Matsumoto published his first serialized series, *Neko Wappa!*, in *Weekly Shonen Jump* in 2009. His next series, *Pochi Kuro*, began serialization in *Shonen Jump+* in 2014. *Kaiju No. 8* is his follow-up series.

KAIJU NO. 8 **ASSISTANTS**

BACKGROUND ART **OSAMU KOIWAI (OSA PROD.)**

FINISHING WORK **JIRO SAKURA**

WEAPON DESIGN **MANTOHIHI BINTA**

KAIJU NO. 8 ⑦

SHONEN JUMP EDITION

STORY AND ART BY
NAOYA MATSUMOTO

TRANSLATION
DAVID EVELYN

TOUCH-UP ART & LETTERING
BRANDON BOVIA

DESIGN
JIMMY PRESLER

EDITOR
KARLA CLARK

First published in Japan in 2020 by SHUEISHA Inc., Tokyo.
English translation rights arranged by SHUEISHA Inc.

Printed in the U.S.A.

Published by VIZ Media, LLC
P.O. Box 77010
San Francisco, CA 94107

10 9 8 7 6 5 4 3 2 1
First printing, July 2023

ratings.viz.com RATED T TEEN

PARENTAL ADVISORY
KAIJU NO. 8 is rated T for Teen and is recommended for ages 13 and up. This volume contains crude humor and depictions of violence.

VIZ MEDIA
viz.com

SHONEN JUMP

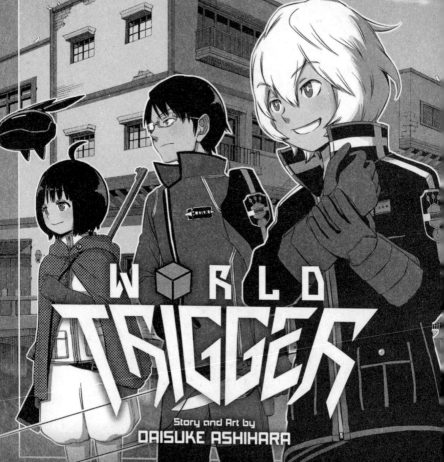

WORLD TRIGGER

Story and Art by
DAISUKE ASHIHARA

DESTROY THY NEIGHBOR!

A gate to another dimension has burst
open, and invincible monsters called
Neighbors invade Earth. Osamu Mikumo
may not be the best among the elite
warriors who co-opt other-dimensional
technology to fight back, but along with his
Neighbor friend Yuma, he'll do whatever it
takes to defend life on Earth as we know it

CAN MUSCLES CRUSH MAGIC?!

MASHLE

MAGIC AND MUSCLES

STORY AND ART BY
HAJIME KOMOTO

In the magic realm, magic is everything—everyone can use it, and one's skill determines their social status. Deep in the forest, oblivious to the ways of the world, lives Mash. Thanks to his daily training, he's become a fitness god. When Mash is discovered, he has no choice but to enroll in magic school where he must beat the competition without revealing his secret—he can't use magic!

MY HERO ACADEMIA
Team-Up Missions

Story and Art by Yoko Akiyama
Original Concept by Kohei Horikoshi

The aspiring heroes of
MY HERO ACADEMIA
team up with pro heroes
for action-packed missions!

VIZ

EXPERIENCE THE INTRODUCTORY ARC OF THE INTERNATIONAL SMASH HIT SERIES *RWBY* IN A WHOLE NEW WAY—MANGA!

RWBY THE OFFICIAL MANGA

Story and Art by BUNTA KINAMI
Based on the Rooster Teeth series created by MONTY OUM

Monsters known as the Grimm are wreaking havoc on the world of Remnant. Ruby Rose seeks to become a Huntress, someone who eliminates the Grimm and protects the land. She enrolls at Beacon Academy and quickly makes friends she'll stand side-by-side with in the battles to come!

ALERT! EMERGENCY ALERT! EMER

YOU'RE READING THE WRONG WAY!

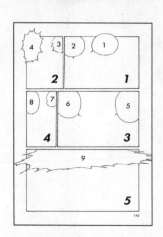

For your own protection, the last page of the book has been sealed off to prevent the ending from being spoiled. To safely consume the contents of *Kaiju No. 8* in their intended order, please flip the book over and start again.

Kaiju No. 8 reads from right to left, starting in the upper-right corner, to preserve the original Japanese orientation of the work. That means that the action, sound effects, and word balloons are completely reversed from English order.

ENTER! DO NOT ENTER! DO NOT